D1196361

SAGE ANNUAL REVIEWS OF
STUDIES IN DEVIANCE
Volume 6

SAGE ANNUAL REVIEWS OF STUDIES IN DEVIANCE ━━━▶

Series Editors: EDWARD SAGARIN
CHARLES WINICK
The City College of the City University of New York

Deviance is one of the most important, exciting and stimulating areas in sociology. It covers the entire spectrum of activities and people who are disvalued, denigrated, punished, ostracized, and in other ways made to feel undesired and undesirable in society— whether this be for something that was done (as the commission of a crime), or for some peculiar stigmatic status. It extends into criminology, social problems, social pathology, and numerous other areas. Despite many texts, readers, and countless journal articles, there has never been a serial publication devoted exclusively to deviance. It is to fill this gap that this annual series is being launched.

Volumes in this series: ━━━━━━━━━━━━━━━━━━━━━━━━━━━━━━▶

Volume 1. Deviance and Social Change (1977)
EDWARD SAGARIN, Editor

Volume 2. Deviance and Mass Media (1978)
CHARLES WINICK, Editor

Volume 3. Deviance and Decency: The Ethics of
Research with Human Subjects (1979)
CARL B. KLOCKARS and
FINBARR W. O'CONNOR, Editors

Volume 4. Crime and Deviance: A Comparative
Perspective (1980)
GRAEME R. NEWMAN, Editor

Volume 5. Law and Deviance (1981)
H. LAURENCE ROSS, Editor

Volume 6. Deviance and Mental Illness (1982)
WALTER R. GOVE, Editor

DEVIANCE
and MENTAL
ILLNESS

Edited by
WALTER R. GOVE

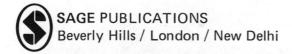

SAGE PUBLICATIONS
Beverly Hills / London / New Delhi

Copyright © 1982 by Sage Publications, Inc.

For information address:

SAGE Publications, Inc.
275 South Beverly Drive
Beverly Hills, California 90212

SAGE Publications India Pvt. Ltd.
C-236 Defence Colony
New Delhi 110 024, India

SAGE Publications Ltd
28 Banner Street
London EC1Y 8QE, England

Printed in the United States of America

Library of Congress Cataloging in Publication Data

Main entry under title:

Deviance and mental illness.

    (Sage annual reviews of studies in deviance ;
v. 6)
    Bibliography: p.
    Contents: The definition and diagnosis of mental
disorder / Robert Spitzer—Learning to label:
the social construction of psychiatrists / Donald
Light—Cultural shaping and mental disorder /
Jane Murphy—[etc.]
    1. Mental illness—Addresses, essays, lectures.
2. Psychiatry—Addresses, essays, lectures.
I. Gove, Walter R. II. Series. [DNLM: 1: Mental
disorders. 2. Behavior—Classification. 3. Psychiatry—Trends. W1 SA125U v.6 / WM 100 D491]
RC458.D46   616.89   82-3386
ISBN 0-8039-1835-6   AACR2
ISBN 0-8039-1836-4 (pbk.)

FIRST PRINTING

Contents

Introduction

WALTER R. GOVE

This volume of the Sage Annual Reviews of Studies in Deviance is devoted exclusively to mental illness. Mental illness, like crime and unlike most other forms of deviance, is extremely common, has a substantial impact on the populace, and involves a large body of personnel whose careers focus on treatment and containment. Mental illness is extremely interesting to social scientists because it has such a profound impact on behavior while, at the same time, it has an ephemeral quality that makes it extremely difficult to define and study. At one extreme, there are those who see mental illness as a myth and view its treatment strictly in terms of social control, whereas others, including most personnel involved in treatment, view it as a relatively distinct phenomenon that is amenable to fairly effective treatment.

For the past two decades the sociology of mental illness has focused primarily on a set of issues linked to labelling theory. These issues include how mental illness is identified and defined, how it is officially and unofficially labelled, the social relativity of mental illness, the role of the mental patient in treatment, the structure and nature of the practice of psychiatry, alternatives to the psychiatric explanation of mental illness, the characteristics of the stereotypes of mental illness in the popular culture, and the social factors affecting the role of the mentally ill. This volume brings together scholars from several disciplines who scrutinize these issues. Although Horwitz (1979) has argued that the debate revolving around the labelling theory of mental illness has not moved forward since the issues were initially outlined, it is clear from the content of the

8 INTRODUCTION

chapters in this volume that many of the issues are well on the way to resolution.

Robert Spitzer and Janet Williams played a critical role in the development of the new *Diagnostic and Statistical Manual of Mental Disorders,* better known as DSM-III. In their chapter they discuss the evolution of psychiatric diagnosis and the definition of mental disorder. They show how the concept of mental disorder has evolved from a rather amorphous one into one that has a fairly clearly defined referent and fairly clearly delineated boundaries. As is obvious from their discussion, the development of definition and categories of mental disorder is a political process, but it is one that appears to be built on a cumulative empirical base. As is clear from their discussion of mental disorders, under the new diagnostic system diagnoses are now quite reliable and there is a growing body of evidence supporting the validity of the diagnostic categories. Pivotal for the sociologist's understanding of mental illness is that, from the psychiatris's position, mental disorders involve a set of fairly distinct entities, and treating them as a unitary phenomenon is something that is anathema to most psychiatrists.

Donald Light is an expert on the socialization of psychiatrists. He begins by noting that sociologists, particularly labelling theorists, have paid very little attention to the socialization of psychiatrists and how this affects their behavior. In his chapter, he focuses on the issue of how psychiatrists learn to apply diagnostic labels to a phenomenon as difficult to measure as mental illness. His chapter reflects the changing state of the field, for virtually all that is known about how psychiatrists go about applying diagnostic labels comes from research conducted prior to the introduction of DSM-III. On the basis of such data, he shows that, given the lack of empirical lab tests and the subjective nature of psychiatric diagnosis, the process of applying psychiatric diagnosis is a very difficult and trying task. He looks at the process of diagnostic training and finds it abysmal. He then looks at how psychiatrists learn to control the uncertainties of diagnosis by modifying their interviewing techniques and at the socialization of psychiatrists as agents of social control. He ends by taking note of the fact that with the development of biopsychiatry the field of psychiatry is becoming reintegrated with the field of medicine.

It is a basic tenet of the social sciences, and particularly of labelling theory, that the culture plays a very active role in shaping the behaviors related to mental illness. Behind this premise is the view that the human personality has a very high level of plasticity. Jane Murphy, an anthropologist who has devoted most of her career to the study of mental illness, begins her chapter by documenting this fact. Using her own research as well as an extensive review of the literature as a base, Dr. Murphy looks across cultures at (1) the general descriptive concepts and labels of mental illness, (2) the specific content of mental illness, (3) inclusion and exclusion of behavior patterns, (4) the social usability of mental illness, (5) the social abuse of the mentally ill, (6) presumed causes of mental illness, (7) treatment of the mentally ill, and (8) outcomes of treatment. Perhaps her most important finding is that while theories of mental illness are culturally patterned, the symptoms of the mentally ill tend to be the same for all societies. This suggests that the causes of insanity, whether genetic or experiential, are ubiquitous in human groups. Furthermore, because psychosis takes a rather similar form in all societies, it seems to be less culturally malleable than some other forms of behavior. She also finds that the role of the mentally ill tends to be relatively similar across cultures and that serious abuses of the mentally ill are rare. Her conclusion thus conflicts directly with labelling theory, which focuses on the tenuous nature of mental illness and on the degree to which the mentally ill are controlled in a deleterious fashion.

Chapter 4, "Labelling Someone Mentally Ill," was written anonymously by two Ph.D. sociologists, a husband and wife, the latter of whom has suffered a serious mental illness. As will be clear to the reader, the wife experienced mental illness as very real and extremely painful, and it was highly disruptive both to her life and to the couple's marriage. This case of mental illness should go far to refute labelling theory's contention that mental illness is caused by the expectations of others and that it lacks a powerful disorder at its core. One of the basic tenets of labelling theory is that once psychiatric symptoms are blatantly manifest, and particularly once psychiatric treatment has been initiated, the person will be labelled as mentally ill. As I have shown elsewhere (Gove, 1980), there is substantial evidence that this tends not to occur, and in the case presented here, mental illness was denied well after the wife became incapacitated by her symptoms and psychiatric treatment had been initiated. This description also conflicts with a narrow psychiatric perspective of mental illness, which tends to focus exclusively on the patient, for it shows that the disorder has a pervasive effect not just on the mentally ill individual but also on others close to that individual, and that it imposes a substantial strain on close social bonds.

One of the basic tenets of labelling theory is that the role of the mental patient in a mental hospital is very debilitating. This, in fact, is a very common theme in various exposés of mental hospitals and is found in such widely read articles as Rosenhan's (1973) "On Being Sane in Insane Places." Raymond Weinstein carefully scrutinizes this proposition. He shows that virtually all of the qualitative reports on the role of the mental patient in a mental hospital present the role as very demeaning. However, he finds a very different pattern among the quantitative studies that look at the experiences of actual mental patients. In the quantitative studies using mental patients, the data consistently show a tendency for the patients to have positive views of their hospitalization, their relationships with the staff, and their treatment. The reason for the difference between the exposés, written by healthy middle-class individuals, and the reports of patients is that the patients enter the hospital from very disturbed environments and are themselves very disturbed. As a consequence, they find the hospital a haven that provides security, order, structure, and help.

In 1955 there was a crucial turning point in the treatment of the mentally ill in that for the first time in a century there was a decline in the resident population in public mental hospitals. This decline proceeded slowly during the next few years, then picked up speed in the sixties and early seventies and now appears to be slowing down. Joseph Morrissey looks at this deinstitutionalization process from 1955 to the present. He pays particular attention to the changes that occurred in New York, California, and Massachusetts, states that have been in the forefront of the deinstitutionalization process. Initially the changes were clearly positive, enabling chronic patients to leave the hospital but leaving the door open for those patients in need of further treatment. Furthermore, the 1960s saw the advent of the community mental health movement and the establishment of community mental health centers, which presumably were going to take over the role, in the community, of public mental hospitals. However, the deinstitutionalization movement has largely come under the control of fiscal conservatives and civil libertarians, and it now is showing the signs of a failing reform. Patients returning to the community are often not well cared for and, with the development of stringent requirements for hospitalization, many patients in need of treatment cannot get into mental hospitals. All in all, it is becoming increasingly evident that there is a substantial population of severely mentally ill persons in need of ongoing treatment, and the deinstitutionalization of public mental hospitals has not been accompanied by the institution of adequate forms of alternative care. Labelling theory played a critical role in the initiation of the deinstitutionalization movement, but it appears that the theory's prediction, that simply leaving the mentally ill alone would solve much of the problem (of the mentally ill), is simply not working. The evidence is continuing to accumulate that a substantial number of mentally ill persons benefit from prolonged treatment and that the premise of labelling theory that they should be left alone does not serve their interests.

Not only has there been a process of deinstitutionalization going on since 1955, but there has been a virtual revolution in psychiatric treatment. Gerald Klerman details the nature of this revolution in his chapter. The revolution has been brought about by the initiation of drug therapy and changes in psychotherapy, and has been put on a firm financial footing by the recent coverage of psychiatric treatment by health insurance. Between 1955 and 1975, the total number of persons receiving some form of institutional psychiatric care rose from 1.7 million to 6.9 million. During this time the rate of inpatient care remained about the same, but there was a major shift in place of treatment, with many more persons being treated in private psychiatric hospitals, on psychiatric wards in general hospitals, and in community mental health centers. However, the major shift has been the increase in the number of persons receiving outpatient care in one of these institutionalized settings. Furthermore, there has been a tremendous increase in the number of persons receiving private psychiatric care. The provision of much of this psychiatric care is increasingly coming from mental health professionals other than psychiatrists. As Klerman shows, the increase in psychiatric care has been accompanied by advances in research, particularly in the areas of genetics, neurobiology, psychopharmacology, and diagnosis, and by a tremendous expansion in the number of forms of psychotherapies. It is now estimated that there is a core group of 30 to 35 million persons with diagnosable psychiatric disorders who could benefit from treatment and that the vast majority of these persons are now receiving some form of psychiatric treatment from a mental health professional or, more typically, from an M.D. Labelling theory has paid little attention to this psychiatric revolution and most sociologists are unaware of its magnitude, particularly the number of persons receiving psychiatric treatment. It is obvious that the vast majority of persons receiving psychiatric treatment now do so voluntarily, with little or no stigma, and that labelling theory is essentially irrelevant to these persons. By ignoring the psychiatric revolution, labelling theory has become a theory that is very much out of date.

As noted above, mental illness has an amorphous quality that makes it very difficult to measure. Around 1960 a movement was started by persons who became known as the antipsychiatrists (some of whom were psychiatrists, some of whom were not). These persons denied the legitimacy of psychiatry and generally agreed with the position of Thomas Szasz that mental illness was a myth. Although not labelling theorists, they took a position very similar to that of labelling theory, and labelling theorists have relied heavily upon them for support. Peter Sedgwick, in his chapter, "Antipsychiatry from the Sixties to the Eighties," looks at the position of four prominent antipsychiatrists, Erving Goffman, R. D. Laing,

Thomas Szasz, and D. L. Rosenhan. Sedgwick finds that Goffman has moved on to other things and that his work on mental illness now seems too dramatic, polemical, and cynical. Laing has now largely recanted his position. Rosenhan has drastically modified his position, so that the issue is no longer the validity of psychiatry as an enterprise but the reliability and validity of psychiatric diagnosis (particularly schizophrenia), an issue that Spitzer and Williams argue has now largely been settled with DSM-III. Only Szasz has maintained his position, which he continues to restate in an essentially unmodified form, and as he does not take into account the psychiatric revolution outlined by Klerman, his arguments seem increasingly dated. Sedgwick, in noting the gradual demise of the antipsychiatric movement, notes that there is a need for criticism of psychiatry due to its hegemony over other systems, but that the new critics need to be responsive to the changes that have occurred and are occurring in psychiatry.

One of the key propositions in Scheff's (1966) labelling theory of mental illness is that persons learn negative and stigmatizing stereotypes of mental illness from the popular culture and that these stereotypes play a critical role in the application of labels of mental illness to particular persons. It is Scheff's position that the popular culture continues to reinforce these very negative stereotypes. Charles Winick, in his chapter, looks at the image of mental illness in the popular culture. He finds that newspapers tend to present a stigmatizing image. In contrast, magazines present a much more diverse picture, one that is largely nonstereotypical and nonstigmatizing, particularly in the more professional magazines aimed at the sophisticated reader. Perhaps surprisingly, he finds that comic books present a fairly accurate image and one that is in accordance with professional thinking. He finds that novels generally represent the mentally ill protagonist in a very sympathetic and understanding fashion. Self-help books are seen as serving an important role in defusing anxiety about mental illness. In recent years there have been numerous accounts of media celebrities who became mentally ill, and these accounts tend to defuse anxiety and give an optimistic outlook. Jokes are generally found to communicate the notion that mental illness is a relatively lighthearted, unimportant condition, and are seen as enabling persons to discuss a difficult subject. Winick finds that, in its early years, television presented a somewhat stigmatizing image of mental illness, but that now it presents a realistic and accurate approach to the subject. He finds that radio also represents current professional thinking. As for movies, in early years they presented a very stigmatizing image, but now they almost invariably present the subject in a sympathetic light. Winick concludes that in recent years the media "may have provided a critical mass context that helped to domesticate the subject of mental illness and made it more acceptable, more a condition that can be dealt with."

Labelling theory argues that the major role of social supports is to help prevent someone from being channeled into the role of the mentally ill. Ronald Kessler looks at social supports and, in contrast to labelling theory, finds that they play a key role in mediating the effects of stressful life events that induce mental illness. His is a highly methodological chapter. He looks at the dimensional representation of life events scales and points to a number of their problems. He then focuses on the issue of causal direction—do life events induce mental illness or vice versa—and poses some methodological solutions to this perplexing problem. Looking at the issue of exposure to stress, he treats triggering effects, chronic stress effects, and modifying effects. He then turns to the issue of who is responsive to stress and focuses on the stress-buffering effects of social support. As he notes, the concept of social support is a complex phenomenon, and he devotes considerable attention to the issues of defining and measuring social support and of estimating its buffering effects. Of all of the chapters in this volume, Kessler's is the least tied to the issues raised by labelling theory, largely because it has moved beyond the bounds of that perspective, and it provides an excellent example of the type of research that increasingly will be at the forefront of the field.

My concluding chapter attempts to summarize the current status of the labelling theory of mental illness, and it draws implicitly and explicitly on a number of the contributions noted above. I begin by documenting the dominance of the labelling theory of mental illness and proceed to give a sketch of labelling theory for those unfamiliar with its details. I then note that the research of the forties and early fifties provided some support for the labelling theory of mental illness, but that the psychiatric revolution has largely undercut the theory as it applies to most persons in psychiatric treatment. An aspect of the psychiatric revolution not discussed in the preceding chapters is the evolving legal rights of mental patients, and this is discussed in detail. Turning to the issue of the relationship between labelling theory and the deinstitutionalization movement, I show that as this movement has come under the influence of fiscal conservatives, civil libertarians, and legislatures, labelling theory has come to be the theoretical buttress supporting the movement, which highlights the continuing importance of the perspective. I then turn to a detailed critique of the empirical predictions of the labelling theory of mental illness. In virtually all cases, the theory is found to be in conflict with the evidence. In light of the overwhelming evidence against the labelling theory of mental illness, I note that the question must arise as to why it continues in an essentially unmodified form. In an attempt to answer this question, I examine the metasociological assumptions upon which sociology is based, and show that they incline the discipline to treat labelling theory in a positive fashion.

This book is, in part, an attempt to bring an end to the dominance of the labelling theory of mental illness in sociology. Because in the past the theory has been supported by research, and thus is known to point to real processes, it should not be simply buried. However, it has been so unresponsive to changes in the field of psychiatry that it is now not only dated, but largely in conflict with present facts. What is needed is a new attempt at integration. Labelling theory has not been without value. Psychiatry has been insufficiently aware of the social processes surrounding the mentally ill, focusing instead on biological and intrapsychic concerns. The debate between the labelling theorists and psychiatry, therefore, has been profitable, for it has clarified a number of issues that without the debate would have gone unresolved. Furthermore, the practice of psychiatry has benefited from the debate. However, it is now time to put the old debate behind us and go forward. As we do, we should acknowledge that mental illness exists as a pathological phenomenon with which we must deal.

REFERENCES

GOVE, W. R. (1980) "Labelling and mental illness: a critique," pp. 53-99 in W. R. Gove (ed.) Labelling Deviant Behavior. Beverly Hills, CA: Sage.

HORWITZ, A. (1979) "Models, muddles and mental illness labeling." Journal of Health and Social Behavior 20: 296-300.

ROSENHAN, D. L. (1973) "On being sane in insane places." Science 179: 250-258.

SCHEFF, T. J. (1966) Being Mentally Ill: A Sociological Theory. Chicago: Aldine.

THE DEFINITION AND DIAGNOSIS OF MENTAL DISORDER

ROBERT L. SPITZER
JANET B.W. WILLIAMS

In 1980, the American Psychiatric Association published the third edition of its *Diagnostic and Statistical Manual of Mental Disorders,* better known as DSM-III. This crystallized renewed interest on the part of American psychiatrists in diagnosis and classification. DSM-III, now the official classification of mental disorders used by mental health professionals throughout the United States, differs from its predecessor, DSM-II (American Psychiatric Association, 1968), in a number of significant ways. Not only is the classification organized differently (for example, the concept of neurosis is no longer used as a classifying principle), but also each specific category is defined by specified diagnostic criteria. In addition, a multiaxial system is provided that contains axes for describing psychological (mental disorders), biological (physical disorders and conditions), and social factors (severity of psychosocial stressors and highest level of adaptive functioning). Thus a more comprehensive and systematic approach to evaluation is encouraged (Williams, 1981). Finally, DSM-III, in its introduction and glossary of technical terms, provides a definition of "mental disorder" that represents the culmination of a great deal of thought about the boundaries of mental disorder and that expresses many basic concepts that guided the development of the DSM-III classification. This chapter will trace the history of efforts to define mental disorder that eventually resulted in the definition presented in DSM-III. The explicit and implicit assumptions of this definition and its specific expression in the descriptions of the various disorders will be discussed. Finally, we will discuss the process of making a psychiatric diagnosis and recent efforts to improve its reliability and validity. (The reader interested in greater detail about the development of classification systems in psychiatry is referred to Spitzer and Williams, 1980.)

HISTORY OF ATTEMPTS
TO DEFINE MENTAL DISORDER

As Kendell (1975) has noted, physicians rarely concern themselves with defining what a medical disorder is and instead spend their time, as best they can, diagnosing and treating individual patients. Psychiatrists as well, until fairly recently, ignored the issue of what a mental disorder is and left the problem to sociologists, psychologists, philosophers of science, and members of the legal profession (Ausubel, 1971; Moore, 1977; Parsons, 1951; Sedgwick, 1973). In the early 1970s, however, gay activists forced American psychiatry to reassess its attitude toward the nosologic status of homosexuality (Bayer, 1981). Arguing that homosexuality by itself was not evidence of illness, gay activists insisted that homosexuality be removed from the official classification (then DSM-II). In 1973, the senior author (Robert L. Spitzer, M.D.), at that time a junior member of the American Psychiatric Association's Task Force on Nomenclature and Statistics, was given the task of reviewing the controversy and proposing a solution. In reviewing the characteristics of the various mental disorders included in DSM-II, Spitzer concluded that, with the exception of homosexuality, and perhaps some of the other "sexual deviations," they all regularly caused subjective distress or were associated with generalized impairment in social effectiveness or functioning. It was argued that the *consequences* of a condition, and not its *etiology*, determined whether the condition should be considered a disorder. Therefore, it was irrelevant whether a condition, such as homosexuality, was the result of childhood conflicts and intrapsychic anxieties, since many desirable conditions that no one would suggest are disorders, such as ambition and self-discipline, may also result from such conflict. Therefore, it was proposed that the criterion for a mental disorder was either subjective distress or generalized impairment in social effectiveness. Based on these criteria, homosexuality (and many other conditions generally associated with heterosexuality, such as inhibited sexual desire and inhibited sexual excitement) did not qualify as a mental disorder. According to this view, it was inconsistent for homosexuality (and not any of these other conditions) to be singled out as a mental disorder merely because of negative societal attitudes.

This view was formulated in a position paper, presented to the Board of Trustees of the American Psychiatric Association, that called for the removal of homosexuality per se from the classification and, in its place, the insertion of a category called Sexual Orientation Disturbance, that was for "individuals whose sexual interests are directed primarily toward people of the same sex and who are either disturbed by, in conflict with, or wish to change their sexual orientation." After much bitter debate within the Association, the Board of Trustees endorsed the proposal, and this action led to a revision in the seventh and subsequent printings of DSM-II. In retrospect, this controversy, which also included an unsuccessful attempt by a portion of the membership to overturn the decision by means of a referendum, had more to do with the issue of the boundaries of mental disorder than facts about homosexuality. For the time being, then, the profession implicitly endorsed the very rudimentary notion that mental disorder requires either subjective distress or generalized impairment in social effectiveness, without examining the full implications of this approach.

In 1975 a new Task Force on Nomenclature and Statistics, chaired by the senior author, was formed to begin work on DSM-III. It became necessary to reconsider the appropriate boundaries of mental disorder for several reasons. First of all, if the concepts used to resolve the homosexuality controversy were applied to such conditions as necrophilia (sexual attraction to dead bodies) and fetishism (sexual attraction to inanimate objects), conditions commonly accepted as mental disorders, there would be startlingly problematic results: Necrophilia and fetishism would be considered disorders only if the individuals with the conditions were distressed by them! Otherwise, such conditions would merely be considered normal variations of sexuality. Second, with greater attention given to defining each diagnostic category with precision, it was not at all clear what criteria should be used to differentiate personality traits from personality disorders. Finally, it was not at all clear why normal bereavement, which often has the same clinical picture as a mild depressive disorder, should not be classified as a mental disorder, although traditionally it never has been.

With the help of other colleagues on the APA Task Force, Spitzer evolved a complicated definition of medical and mental disorder, replete with specified criteria; in abbreviated form, mental disorder was defined as

a relatively distinct condition resulting from an organismic dysfunction which in its fully developed or extreme form is directly and
intrinsically associated with distress, disability, or certain other types
of disadvantage. The disadvantage may be of a physical, perceptual,
sexual or interpersonal nature [Spitzer and Endicott, 1978].

The underlying assumptions of this definition are the following: The
concept of disorder is human-made. Over the course of time, all cultures
have evolved concepts of illness or disease in order to identify certain
conditions that, because of their negative consequences, implicitly have a
call to action to a special group of caretakers (in our society, the health
professions to provide treatment), to the person with the condition (to
assume the sick or patient role), and to society (to provide a means for
delivery of health care, and in some instances to exempt the sick individual
from certain responsibilities). Finally, there are the assumptions that
something has gone wrong with the human organism and that a mental
disorder is merely a medical disorder, the manifestations of which are
primarily signs or symptoms of a psychological (behavioral) nature, or, if
physical, can only be understood using psychological concepts.

The reaction of the profession to this attempt to define not only
mental disorder, but medical disorder as well, was less than enthusiastic.[1]
In particular, the other members of the Task Force believed that such a
precise definition was not helpful and, in fact, was merely a symptom of
Spitzer's compulsive personality. However, the Task Force was generally
sympathetic to the notion that mental disorders could be conceptualized
as a subset of medical disorders. In fact, in a 1977 article discussing the
early development of DSM-III, it was stated that the Task Force planned
to include in the Introduction to DSM-III a statement that mental disorders were a subset of medical disorders (Spitzer et al., 1977). As might
be expected, this announcement alarmed many psychologists (Schacht and
Nathan, 1977; Zubin, 1977). It became clear that the inclusion of such a
statement would only fan the fires of professional rivalry and might be a
real obstacle to the use of DSM-III by nonmedical health professionals
who had used DSM-I and DSM-II in their clinical and research work. After
an agonizing reappraisal, the Task Force concluded that the purpose of
DSM-III was to describe and classify mental disorders, not to clarify the
relationship of psychiatry to the rest of medicine. Therefore, DSM-III
contains no explicit reference to mental disorders being a subset of
medical disorders, although it is noted that the DSM-III categories are all

included in the official classification of medical disorders used in this country, ICD-9-CM (*The International Classification of Diseases*, Ninth Revision, Clinical Modification).

No further attempt to define the concept of mental disorder was made during the next several years of development of DSM-III, although that issue was faced in defining many of the controversial categories, such as the sexual deviations, referred to as "Paraphilias" in DSM-III. Eventually, in the last few months of work on DSM-III another attempt was made to define mental disorder incorporating certain key concepts that had been helpful in providing a rationale for decisions as to which conditions should be included or excluded from the DSM-III classification of mental disorders and as guides in defining the boundaries of the various mental disorders.

THE DSM-III DEFINITION
OF MENTAL DISORDER

The following definition of mental disorder was developed by the authors of this chapter and presented to members of the Task Force. They helped refine it so that it was finally acceptable to the many components of the APA that reviewed DSM-III prior to its approval:

In DSM-III each of the mental disorders is conceptualized as a clinically significant behavioral or psychological syndrome or pattern that occurs in an individual and that is typically associated with either a painful symptom (distress) or impairment in one or more important areas of functioning (disability). In addition, there is an inference that there is a behavioral, psychological, or biological dysfunction, and that the disturbance is not only in the relationship between the individual and society. (When the disturbance is *limited* to a conflict between an individual and society, this may represent social deviance, which may or may not be commendable, but is not by itself a mental disorder.)

The following is an explanation of the key components of this definition. The phrase "clinically significant" acknowledges that there are many behavioral or psychological conditions that can be considered "pathological" but the clinical manifestations of which are so mild that clinical attention is not indicated. For this reason, such conditions are not included in a classification of mental disorders. Some examples illustrate the distinction between conditions that are clinically significant and those that are not. Television viewers may be familiar with the advertisement for a certain brand of decaffeinated coffee, which vividly portrays how such symptoms as irritability and insomnia can be due to excessive caffeine use. This condition, called Caffeinism, does occasionally account for anxiety symptoms severe enough to cause individuals to seek professional help. For this reason, although the condition is relatively mild and rare, it is included in the DSM-III classification as Caffeine Intoxication. On the other hand, as many heavy coffee drinkers know, abrupt cessation of caffeine intake often leads to a very uncomfortable withdrawal syndrome, with such symptoms as headache and lethargy. However, this syndrome of caffeine withdrawal never leads to seeking professional help. Therefore, it is not included in DSM-III as a mental disorder, although, in a scientific sense, it is as "real" a condition as is Caffeine Intoxication.

Early in the development of DSM-III consideration was given to including a classification of sleep disorders. A group of investigators in that area proposed a classification, although it eventually became clear that many of its categories, such as "Jet Lag Syndrome" and "Insomnia Due to Environmental Noise," could not be justified as syndromes that were clinically significant to mental health professionals. For that reason, only two relatively severe sleep disorders usually first occurring in childhood, Sleep Terror Disorder and Sleepwalking Disorder, are included in DSM-III.

The specification in the above definition that a mental disorder "occurs in an individual" acknowledges that the DSM-III classification is limited to disorders that occur in individuals, rather than in interpersonal systems, such as family units or friendship dyads. Clinicians using DSM-III who treat pairs or groups of individuals, as family or marital therapists, must therefore assess the diagnostic status of each individual member. This approach, of course, does not preclude assessment of the functioning of a family system as a whole for understanding possible causes of an individual's mental disorder and for treatment planning. (Several efforts are now under way to develop a classification of disturbed family units. Perhaps such a classification will be included in DSM-IV.)

Almost all of the disorders in DSM-III are associated with subjective distress or some impairment in functioning. However, some disorders, such as the Paraphilias, are not always; hence the statement in the definition that mental disorders are "*typically* associated with either a painful symptom (distress) or impairment in one or more important areas of functioning (disability)." This statement is also important for clarifying the boundary between personality traits and Personality Disorders. DSM-III describes personality *traits,* which we all have, as "enduring patterns of perceiving, relating to, and thinking about the environment and oneself . . . exhibited in a wide range of important social and personal contexts."

Personality *Disorders,* on the other hand, are diagnosed only when personality traits become "inflexible and maladaptive and cause either significant impairment in social or occupational functioning or subjective distress."

The assumption that something has gone wrong with the organism, referred to in Spitzer's and Klein's previous definitions, is in DSM-III expressed in the phrase, "there is an inference that there is a behavioral, psychological, or biological dysfunction." This central concept was useful in justifying the inclusion in the DSM-III classification of the Paraphilias, whether or not they were accompanied by distress. The key feature of a Paraphilia, that is, the need for either implicit or explicit coercion (for example, exhibitionism) or inanimate objects (for example, fetishism or necrophilia) for sexual arousal, reflects a dysfunction in the process of normal psychosexual development. (The issue of homosexuality, which used to be classified as a sexual deviation, will be discussed below.)

The concept of an inferred dysfunction also clarifies the nosologic status of normal bereavement. Bereavement, that is, a depressive reaction to the loss of a loved one, is accepted as a normal, and even healthy, response. Bereavement is a price we pay for being social animals. In fact, a psychological dysfunction can be inferred when an individual does not have the capacity to mourn such a loss.

The next statement, that "the disturbance is not only in the relationship between the individual and society," attempts to clarify the relationship between mental disorder and social deviance. An individual whose behavior brings him or her into conflict with society should not be regarded as having a mental disorder unless there is strong evidence supporting the inference of a behavioral, psychological, or biological dysfunction. For example, antisocial behavior that is sanctioned by subcultural norms, as in group delinquency, does not by itself warrant a diagnosis of a mental disorder. However, when it is part of a pervasive pattern that includes inability to function at work or at school, the mental disorder Conduct Disorder or Antisocial Personality Disorder is diagnosed because a psychological dysfunction can then reasonably be inferred.

The last statement, "(When the disturbance is *limited* to a conflict between an individual and society, this may represent social deviance, which may or may not be commendable, but is not by itself a mental disorder.)," was added to express indignation at the abuse of psychiatry, as when, in the Soviet Union, political dissidents without signs of mental illness are labelled as having mental disorders and under that guise incarcerated in mental hospitals.

Homosexuality. The application of the DSM-III definition of mental disorder to homosexuality is problematic (Spitzer, 1981). It is now clear that homosexuality often is not associated with distress. Does homosexuality represent "impairment in one or more important areas of functioning"? Gay activists and their supporters argue that the answer is clearly "no," since they refuse to accept *hetero*sexuality as the norm. Furthermore, they argue that if some homosexuals cannot function heterosexually, far more heterosexuals cannot function homosexually. Yet no one in authority suggests classifying exclusive heterosexuality as a mental disorder. In our judgment, the question of whether or not heterosexual functioning should be used as the norm, so that inability to function heterosexually constitutes impairment in a major area of functioning, is a value judgment and not a factual matter. It is true that there is always a value judgment involved in deciding that a particular area of functioning is "important." However, no one would argue that the ability to function socially and occupationally is unimportant. Although mental health professionals agree that sexuality is an important area of functioning, there is no consensus on whether or not heterosexual functioning should be the norm.

DSM-III takes the position that the mental health profession cannot now arrive at a consensus as to whether or not homosexuality represents a sexual dysfunction. However, if an individual patient asserts that his or her problem is a sustained homosexual arousal pattern and absent or inadequate heterosexuality, the absent heterosexual functioning is accepted as a legitimate focus of professional attention. Therefore, DSM-III includes a category called Ego-dystonic Homosexuality for such cases, and in so doing acknowledges that an appropriate therapeutic activity may include helping a homosexual to develop a heterosexual arousal pattern and not merely to become more comfortable with his or her homosexuality.

Assumptions not made. The DSM-III definition of mental disorder makes no assumption that each mental disorder is a discrete entity with sharp boundaries betweeen it and other mental disorders or between it and no mental disorder. This statement becomes clear when one tries to apply the principles included in the definition of mental disorder to the following clinical case.

A sophomore college student majoring in pre-law came to the counseling service two weeks after being jilted by his girl friend. For reasons that he did not understand, he felt much more upset than he thought he should be. In the past two weeks he had been unable to concentrate or do his schoolwork, had difficulty sleeping, and was preoccupied with the unfair way he had been treated by her. No other symptoms of psychopathology were present.

Applying the definition, we first consider whether this student's distress is "clinically significant." Certainly the student thought so, since he came to the counseling center for help. On the other hand, had there not been a counseling service available, would this young man have sought outside professional help? In this case, there is clear distress as well as impairment in his ability to function in his school role. However, can we infer a dysfunction in this man's normal coping mechanism? The answer to this is not clear, since one would expect some transient distress and perhaps some difficulty functioning after breakup with a romantic partner. Some clinicians might regard this as the mildest form of mental disorder, Adjustment Disorder in DSM-III, whereas others might consider his reaction as a life problem, but not a mental disorder. DSM-III even has a limited classification of conditions that are not attributable to a mental disorder but that are, nevertheless, an appropriate focus of professional attention or treatment. The DSM-III classification thereby acknowledges that not all problems in living are symptoms of mental disorder.

DSM-III makes no assumption that a biological abnormality accounts for each of the mental disorders. There is only one class of mental disorders for which a specific biological etiology is established, the Organic Mental Disorders. In some of the other categories, such as the psychotic disorders and the severe forms of Affective Disorder, a biological abnormality is assumed by many, although not included in the DSM-III description. It is also widely assumed that whatever biological abnormality may eventually be discovered for these disorders, it is only one component of a multifactorial etiology that almost certainly involves environmental and psychological factors.

DSM-III mental disorder and its relationship to other kinds of individual variation. The complex relationship of the DSM-III concept of mental disorder to other kinds of individual variation is illustrated in Figure 1.1. The boundary of the DSM-III concept of mental disorder is represented by a dotted line, to indicate the lack of a clear boundary between it and no mental disorder. The overlap of mental disorder and physical disorder constitutes the DSM-III category of Organic Mental Disorders. These are the only mental disorders that, strictly speaking, are diseases—that is, with a known etiology or pathophysiological process. Examples of Organic Mental Disorders include the Dementias (behavioral manifestations associated with aging), while the underlying physical diseases are classified as neurological disorders.

Figure 1.1 shows that recreational drug use is on the border of the Substance Use Disorders, which in DSM-III are the maladaptive behavioral syndromes associated with obtaining and taking various substances (such as Alcohol Abuse and Opioid Dependence). Several other conditions also border classes of mental disorder. Examples include normal variations in the development of certain biological functions and the Specific Develop-

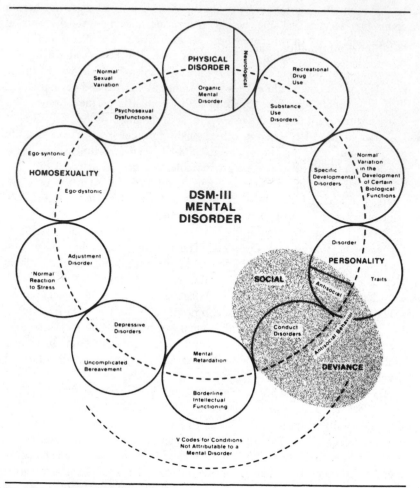

Figure 1.1 DSM-III Mental Disorder and Its Relationship to Other Kinds of Individual Variation

mental Disorders (such as Developmental Reading Disorder and Developmental Language Disorder) and personality traits and Personality Disorders. Other examples are included in Figure 1.1.

DIAGNOSING MENTAL DISORDER

The process of making a psychiatric diagnosis generally consists of a mental health professional interviewing a patient, on one or more occasions, and inquiring about the development and course of the disturbance. Frequently family members or friends are included as valuable sources of additional information, particularly when the patient may be reluctant to acknowledge certain disturbing symptoms. Although laboratory and neuropsychological testing may be necessary in the diagnosis of an Organic Mental Disorder, for the other categories the diagnosis is based entirely on the evaluation of the patient's current and past behavior—including mood, cognitions, speech, appearance, and motor behavior. In research settings, a variety of structured interviews have been developed to ensure that assessment is standardized and comprehensive (Endicott and Spitzer, 1978; Robins et al., 1981).

There is a vast literature that critiques the reliability and validity of the process of psychiatric diagnosis because of the absence of laboratory tests and a lack of agreement on the rules for summarizing clinical observations into a diagnosis. This literature includes the notions that the very concept of mental illness is a myth (Szasz, 1961), that psychiatrists are unable to distinguish the "sane" from the "insane" in psychiatric hospitals, and that the traditional psychiatric classification of mental disorders is unreliable, invalid, and harmful to the welfare of patients (Rosenhan, 1973). Elsewhere in this book, the positions of Szasz and other "antipsychiatrists" are critiqued. For an exhausting and exhaustive critique of Rosenhan's (1973) famous study, "On Being Sane in Insane Places," the reader is referred to an article by the senior author (Spitzer, 1976). That article demonstrates that certain invalid research designs can make psychiatrists appear foolish, but that a correct interpretation of Rosenhan's own data contradicts his conclusion that psychiatric diagnoses are, in his words, "in the minds of the observers," and do not reflect any characteristics inherent in patients.

In developing DSM-III it was recognized that recent methodological developments could greatly improve the reliability and validity of psychiatric diagnoses. The major strategy for improving diagnostic reliability was the use of specified diagnostic criteria for virtually all of the mental disorders. Rather than diagnosing a patient's illness with the brief and very general descriptions found in DSM-II, in DSM-III a lengthy description of the important features of each mental disorder is followed by a set of descriptive criteria that must be present before the diagnosis can be made. Table 1.1 contrasts the DSM-II definition of Schizophrenia with the DSM-III diagnostic criteria for that category.

Another important innovative feature of DSM-III that has contributed to improved diagnostic reliability is the provision of a multiaxial system for evaluation. In this system, five axes are included on which each patient is to be evaluated. The first two axes include all of the mental disorders,

TABLE 1.1 Comparison of DSM-II and DSM-III Definitions of Schizophrenia

DSM-II Description of Schizophrenia[a]	DSM-III Diagnostic Criteria for Schizophrenia[b]
This large category includes a group of disorders manifested by characteristic disturbances of thinking, mood and behavior. Disturbances in thinking are marked by alterations of concept formation which may lead to misinterpretation of reality and sometimes to delusions and hallucinations, which frequently appear psychologically self-protective. Corollary mood changes include ambivalent, constricted and inappropriate emotional responsiveness and loss of empathy with others. Behavior may be withdrawn, regressive and bizarre. The schizophrenias, in which the mental status is attributable primarily to a *thought* disorder, are to be distinguished from the *Major affective illnesses* (q.v.) which are dominated by a *mood* disorder. The *Paranoid states* (q.v.) are distinguished from schizophrenia by the narrowness of their distortions of reality and by the absence of other psychotic symptoms.	A. At least one of the following during a phase of the illness: (1) Bizarre delusions (content is patently absurd and has *no* possible basis in fact), such as delusions of being controlled, thought broadcasting, thought insertion, or thought withdrawal. (2) Somatic, grandiose, religious, nihilistic or other delusions without persecutory or jealous content. (3) Delusions with persecutory or jealous content, if accompanied by hallucinations of any type. (4) Auditory hallucinations in which either a voice keeps up a running commentary on the individual's behavior or thoughts, or two or more voices converse with each other. (5) Auditory hallucinations on several occasions with content of more than one or two words having no apparent relation to depression or elation. (6) Incoherence, marked loosening of associations, markedly illogical thinking or marked poverty of content of speech, if associated with at least one of the following: (a) blunted, flat or inappropriate affect (b) delusions or hallucinations (c) catatonic or other grossly disorganized behavior B. Deterioration from a previous level of functioning in such areas as work, social relations, and self-care.

C. *Duration*: Continuous signs of the illness for at least six months at some time during the person's life with some signs of the illness at present. The six-month period must include an active phase during which there were symptoms from A, with or without a prodromal or residual phase, as defined below:

Prodromal phase: A clear deterioration in functioning before the active phase of the illness not due to a disturbance in mood or to a Substance Use Disorder, and involving at least *two* of the symptoms noted below.

Residual phase: Persistence following the active phase of the illness, of at least *two* of the symptoms noted below, not due to a disturbance in mood or to a Substance Use Disorder.

Prodromal or Residual Symptoms

(a) social isolation or withdrawal

(b) marked impairment in role functioning as wage-earner, student, or homemaker

(c) markedly peculiar behavior (e.g., collecting garbage, talking to self in public, hoarding food)

(d) marked impairment in personal hygiene and grooming

(e) blunted, flat, or inappropriate affect

(f) digressive, vague, overelaborate, circumstantial, or metaphorical speech

(g) odd or bizarre ideation, or magical thinking, e.g., superstitiousness, clairvoyance, telepathy, "sixth sense," "others can feel my feelings," overvalued ideas, ideas of reference

(h) unusual perceptual experiences, e.g., recurrent illusions, sensing the presence of a force or person not actually present

(continued)

TABLE 1.1 Continued

DSM-II Description of Schizophrenia[a]	DSM-III Diagnostic Criteria for Schizophrenia[b]
	Examples: Six months of prodromal symptoms with one week of symptoms from A; no prodromal symptoms with six months of symptoms from A; no prodromal symptoms with two weeks of symptoms from A and six months of residual symptoms; six months of symptoms from A, apparently followed by several years of complete remission, with one week of symptoms in A in current episode.
	D. The full depressive or manic syndrome (criteria A and B of major depressive or manic episode), if present, developed after any psychotic symptoms, or was brief in duration relative to the duration of the psychotic symptoms in A.
	E. Onset of prodromal or active phase of the illness before age 45.
	F. Not due to any Organic Mental Disorder or Mental Retardation.

a. Adapted from American Psychiatric Association (1968).
b. Adapted from American Psychiatric Association (1980); used with permission.

TABLE 1.2   A Multiaxial Evaluation

Axis I:	296.34 Major Depression, Recurrent, with Psychotic Features
Axis II:	301.83 Borderline Personality Disorder
Axis III:	No physical disorder
Axis IV:	Psychosocial Stressors: Argument with neighbor Severity: 3—Mild
Axis V:	Highest level of adaptive functioning past year: 4—Fair

with Axis II reserved for Personality Disorders (usually diagnosed in adults) and Specific Developmental Disorders (usually diagnosed in children and adolescents and previously referred to as "learning disabilities"). This separation ensures that these Axis II disorders, which tend to be relatively mild, chronic, and stable, will not be overlooked when attention is paid to the usually more florid Axis I condition. Axis III is for noting physical disorders and conditions that are relevant to the management or treatment of the individual. Axis IV provides a rating scale for severity of psychosocial stressors, and Axis V a rating scale for indicating the highest level of adaptive functioning that the individual was able to sustain for at least a few months during the past year. This multiaxial system results in a comprehensive "psycho-bio-social" evaluation (Williams, 1981). An example of the results of a complete multiaxial evaluation is presented in Table 1.2.

The reliability of the DSM-III classification and its multiaxial system was examined during a formal 2-year field trial sponsored by the National Institute of Mental Health (Spitzer et al., 1979; Spitzer and Forman, 1979). This field trial was conducted during the final phase of development of DSM-III in order to assess its clinical usefulness prior to its final adoption by the American Psychiatric Association. Approximately 300 clinicians, mostly psychiatrists, evaluated a total of 670 adult patients (18 years and older). Approximately 84 clinicians evaluated a total of 126 child and adolescent patients, approximately half of whom were below the age of 11. The reliability results, presented elsewhere (Williams and Spitzer, 1980), demonstrate that for most of the major diagnostic categories the reliability is quite acceptable and much higher than had been obtained with previous classifications (see Spitzer and Fleiss, 1974, for a survey of the generally sorry state of diagnostic reliability in psychiatry prior to DSM-III). There is also evidence that Axes IV and V can be fairly reliably judged (Williams and Spitzer, 1980).

The validity of a diagnostic classification is the extent to which there is a demonstrated relationship between the diagnostic categories and variables, such as treatment response, prognosis, and familial association, that are external to the definitions of the categories (Feighner et al., 1972).

The degree of demonstrated validity for the different DSM-III categories varies greatly. For some of the categories, such as Schizophrenia and Bipolar Disorder (previously referred to as Manic-Depressive Illness) there are countless research studies that provide the kinds of validity evidence noted above. For most of the other categories the validity data are far less, and for a few of the categories there is little more than agreement among some clinicians about the clinical features defining the disorder. It should be recognized that clinicians and researchers need a language to communicate about the conditions for which they assume professional responsibility. They cannot wait until a category is fully validated before it is included in the official nomenclature that defines the conditions for which their help is sought. Therefore, as noted in the Introduction to DSM-III, the DSM-III classification represents "only one still frame in the ongoing process of attempting to better understand mental disorders."

NOTE

1. Donald Klein, another member of the Task Force, at the same time proposed another definition that stressed the issues of evolution and hierarchical organization of functions (Klein, 1978). Like Spitzer's definition, it was largely ignored.

REFERENCES

American Psychiatric Association (1980) Diagnostic and Statistical Manual of Mental Disorders. 3rd ed. Washington, DC: Author.
––– (1968) Diagnostic and Statistical Manual of Mental Disorders. 2nd ed. Washington, DC: Author.
AUSUBEL, D. P. (1971) "Personality disorder is disease." American Psychologist 16: 59-74.
BAYER, R. (1981) Homosexuality and American Psychiatry: The Politics of Diagnosis. New York: Basic Books.
ENDICOTT, J. and R. L. SPITZER (1978) "A diagnostic interview: the schedule for affective disorders and schizophrenia." Archives of General Psychiatry 35, 7: 837-844.
FEIGHNER, J. P., E. ROBINS, S. B. GUZE, R. A. WOODRUFF, G. WINOKUR, and R. MUNOZ (1972) "Diagnostic criteria for use in psychiatry research." Archives of General Psychiatry 26, 1: 57-63.
KENDELL, R. E. (1975) "The concept of disease and its implications for psychiatry." British Journal of Psychiatry 127: 305-315.
KLEIN, D. F. (1978) "A proposed definition of mental illness," in R. L. Spitzer and D. F. Klein (eds.) Critical Issues in Psychiatric Diagnosis. New York: Raven.
MOORE, M. (1977) "Legal conceptions of mental illness," in Philosophy and Medicine, Vol. 5. The Netherlands: Reidel.
PARSONS, T. (1951) The Social System. New York: Macmillan.

ROBINS, L. N., J. E. HELZER, J. CROUGHAN, and K. S. RATCLIFF (1981) "National Institute of Mental Health diagnostic interview schedule." Archives of General Psychiatry 38, 4: 381-389.

ROSENHAN, D. L. (1973) "On being sane in insane places." Science 179: 250-258.

SCHACHT, T. and P. E. NATHAN (1977) "But is it good for the psychologist? Appraisal and status of DSM-III." American Psychologist 32: 1017-1025.

SEDGWICK, P. (1973) "Illness—mental and otherwise." Hastings Center Studies 3: 19-58.

SPITZER, R. L. (1981) "The diagnostic status of homosexuality in DSM-III: a reformulation of the issues." American Journal of Psychiatry 138, 2: 210-215.

——— (1976) "More on pseudoscience in science and the case for psychiatric diagnosis." Archives of General Psychiatry 33, 4: 459-470.

——— (1975) "On pseudoscience in science, logic in remission, and psychiatric diagnosis: a critique of Rosenhan's 'On being sane in insane places.' " Journal of Abnormal Psychology 84: 442-452.

——— and J. ENDICOTT (1978) "Medical and mental disorder: proposed definition and criteria," pp. 15-39 in R. L. Spitzer and D. F. Klein (eds.) Critical Issues in Psychiatric Diagnosis. New York: Raven.

SPITZER, R. L. and J. L. FLEISS (1974) "A re-analysis of the reliability of psychiatric diagnosis." British Journal of Psychiatry 125, 10: 341-347.

SPITZER, R. L. and J. B. FORMAN (1979) "DSM-III field trials: II. Initial experience with the multiaxial system." American Journal of Psychiatry 136, 6: 818-820.

SPITZER, R. L. and J. B. WILLIAMS (1980) "Classification of mental disorders and DSM-III," pp. 1035-1072 in H. Kaplan et al. (eds.) Comprehensive Textbook of Psychiatry, Vol. 1. 3rd ed. Baltimore: Williams & Wilkins.

SPITZER, R. L., J. B. FORMAN, and J. NEE (1979) "DSM-III field trials: I. Initial interrater diagnostic reliability." American Journal of Psychiatry 136, 6: 815-817.

SPITZER, R. L., M. SHEEHY, and J. ENDICOTT (1977) "DSM-III: guiding principles," pp. 1-24 in V. M. Rakoff et al. (eds.) Psychiatric Diagnosis. New York: Brunner/Mazel.

SZASZ, T. S. (1961) The Myth of Mental Illness. New York: Harper & Row.

WILLIAMS, J.B.W. (1981) "DSM-III: a comprehensive approach to diagnosis." Social Work 26, 3: 101-106.

——— and R. L. SPITZER (1980) "Appendix F: DSM-III field trials: interrater reliability and list of project staff and participants," pp. 467-481 in American Psychiatric Association, Diagnostic and Statistical Manual of Mental Disorders, 3rd ed. Washington, DC: American Psychiatric Association.

ZUBIN, J. (1977) "But is it good for science?" Clinical Psychologist 31 (January): 5-7.

2

LEARNING TO LABEL
The Social Construction of Psychiatrists

DONALD W. LIGHT

AUTHOR'S NOTE: I am indebted to Robert Scott, William Binder, and Edmund Erde for their good advice, to Nancy Velez for her assistance, and to Benjamin Cohen and Richard Leedy, without whose support this chapter would not have been completed.

One irony in the study of mental health as a form of deviance is that those who define it and act on those definitions have not been taken seriously as a subject of investigation. Yet they provide the language for describing mental disorders, shape laws that affect this form of deviance, direct or strongly influence major institutions dealing with mental illness as a form of deviance, and construct the social reality of mental disorders. Even the Scheff-Gove debate about the extent to which the "mentally ill" are distinguished by having been singled out through the labelling process or by being mentally disturbed ignores the silent master builder, psychiatry, which constructs the house of language, metaphor, and culture in which the drama of parents, spouses, friends, and other social control agents coping with emotionally troubled individuals takes place.

The debate and the literature employed by Scheff and Gove provide little ethnographic information about how the language and influence of psychiatry shape those interactions that determine how "emotionally disturbed" persons will be handled (Scheff, 1966, 1974, 1975, 1979; Gove, 1970, 1975, 1979). Concerning Gove's argument, the crucial questions of which social linguistic categories those close to a "mentally ill" person employ and what happens when such people finally decide that the person is "mentally ill" have yet to be well researched. For Scheff, the psychiatric construction of reality is of crucial concern, but the problematic nature of that reality and the reasons for its prevalence are only partially explored. Rather, his emphasis is on the power of that reality and on descriptions of it in operation. It was not until Horwitz (1979) emphasized that we should study the behavior and categorizations of those doing the labelling (be they intimates or official agents) and that the behavior of the actor being labelled mentally ill must be distinguished from the behavior of the person doing the labelling that the central issue was identified.

The sociology of psychiatry and of psychiatrists is central to any analysis of "mental illness" as a social construct, and, from a historical and cross-cultural perspective, psychiatry has become increasingly powerful. Many observers, including Horwitz (1982), have observed that as village and family life have weakened, the power of psychiatric reality has increased. The less intimate the observer is with the person whose behavior is in question, the more likely is a psychiatric label to be employed. This tendency increases as affluence and level of education grow. Informal systems of social control progressively weaken, and formal systems of control in which professional psychiatry has great influence grow. People become increasingly inclined to exclude and label deviants as the cohesiveness of their own social groups weakens (Horwitz, 1982: chs. 3-5). In fact, one might say that a distinguishing characteristic of modern societies is the influence of professional psychiatry in defining social and interpersonal deviance.

The recent decline of physicians entering psychiatry and funds for psychiatry should not be interpreted as a sign of waning influence. On the contrary, the psychiatric domain has been steadily growing (Light, 1980: ch. 1). The phenomenal growth of psychotherapeutic activities and of psychotherapists outside the medical profession during the last twenty years has been significantly affected by the psychiatric construction of reality, even among those practitioners who claim to be using different techniques. The current retrenchment in psychiatry appears to be a period of stock-taking during which the profession has responded to its critics by incorporating many of their ideas (Braceland, 1981; Biegel, 1979; Langsley, 1981), emphasizing the integration of mind and body that characterizes holistic medicine, biofeedback, and other mind-body approaches (Stroebel, 1981; Gordon, 1981), putting Freud in proper historical and theoretical perspective, and abandoning the public mental health sector so as to minimize its role as incarcerators of the innocent and deprivers of individual freedom (Szasz, 1977). Most impressive of all, research psychiatrists have profoundly altered the *Diagnostic and Statistical Manual* (American Psychiatric Association, 1980) and thereby defined the nature and categories of "mental illness" for another generation of police, social workers, judges, lawyers, counselors of all kinds, and laypersons. The widespread and rapid acceptance of DSM-III, despite swirling controversies in inner-professional circles, is a sociological phenomenon worth investigating. For the psychiatric profession, even in its period of retrenchment and bad press, has issued without any contenders a new bible of mental illness that significantly expands the number of human behaviors that are considered "mentally ill" and explains them in far more concrete detail than ever before.

A central issue in the sociology of mental health is how the gatekeepers are trained so that novices at recognizing forms of deviance and labelling them become quite comfortable and "competent" at it. This is especially relevant given the phenomenological character of psychiatric diagnosis. As a distinguished professor of physiology at Oxford recently wrote, almost all the signs and symptoms of mental disorders are referred or indirect, rather than being direct measures of pathology (Blakemore, 1981). This leads to a preoccupation with symptoms and a false leap of inference: "While it is accepted that illnesses result from pathological states, mental illnesses are tacitly or explicitly attributed to non-corporeal systems to which the disease has been assigned" (Blakemore, 1981: 32). Thus the diagnosis rests almost entirely on the judgment of the clinician, which in turn is profoundly influenced by his or her theoretical background, training, social setting, and organizational pressures. Blakemore (1981: 35) reports an experiment in which a colleague asked 100 Oxford undergraduates whether they had ever experienced any of 98 disturbances generally regarded as signs of schizophrenia. Almost half of the Oxford students had experienced 30 percent or more of the disturbances at least once.

American psychiatrists in particular are inclined to declare patients psychotic. In a comparative study using matched cases, there was "the pronounced tendency of American psychiatrists to diagnose schizophrenia in patients who had been specifically picked to represent non-psychotic disorders (e.g., neurosis, character disorder)" (Townsend, 1980: 269). Among such patients, British psychiatrists identified 2-7 percent as psychotic while American psychiatrists diagnosed 69-85 percent as psychotic (Kendell et al., 1971). This professional bias has powerful consequences, because nonpsychotics diagnosed as psychotic by agents of social control trained in the American psychatric tradition are more likely to be treated involuntarily, hospitalized, given phenothiazines or electroshock therapy, and declared mentally or legally incompetent. Besides having a heavy bias toward diagnosing people as schizophrenic, American psychiatrists tend to affirm the psychiatric judgment of relatives and other social control agents rather than to act as independent arbiters using autonomous professional criteria (Townsend, 1980; Horwitz, 1982).

For these reasons, one needs to know how psychiatrists are trained so that they comfortably carry out their tendencies. How do they cope with the fact that psychiatric diagnoses repeatedly show themselves to predict outcome or treatment response poorly? How are they socialized so that they ignore social factors that often predict patient behavior better than psychological ones? What is the nature of the training received about psychopharmacology such that many of them prescribe large doses of neuroleptics with little regard to the harmful and irreversible effects they have? These are research questions that even the best sociological studies today have only begun to address.

The experience of learning how to diagnose "mental illness" is strongly influenced by social and structural forces in the training program. In fact, organizational forces play an important role in all aspects of psychiatric and medical education. Yet on the whole they had been ignored both by the training professionals and by social scientists who have studied the training and socialization experience. The former tend to overlook these forces because they are too close to their programs and take their structural features for granted. With some exceptions, social scientists have overlooked or minimized social and organizational forces because they have taken a social-psychological stance and because they have tended to assimilate the outlook of the medical programs they have studied (Light, 1982). In the case of psychiatry, both psychiatrists and many of the social scientists working with them suffer from the occupational hazard of incorporating a psychological framework for interpreting events around them. For example, training psychiatrists have often noted the high amount of stress and anxiety experienced by their residents, but they have almost uniformly attributed it to the emotional problems and neuroses of their residents rather than to the stress-inducing structure of the training experience (Light, 1980: chs. 11-12).

TYPES OF PSYCHIATRISTS
AND DIAGNOSTIC SYSTEMS

The training of psychiatrists can only be understood as an interaction between personality and social structure. For example, in learning to diagnose "mental illness," the resident's personal style of working with patients combines with the ideology of the training program and the structure of clinical and didactic experiences to incline him or her toward certain clusters of diagnostic terms. These clusters are themselves shaped by the social context in which psychiatric work takes place.

Let us examine this example more closely. Over the past 25 years, social scientists have attempted to identify types of residents by the ideologies they hold. However, this research has led to contradictions and artifacts of scaling that do not seem to reflect accurately the different approaches psychiatric residents reflect in their work with patients (Light, 1980: Appendix III). My research indicates that a better way to characterize trainees is by the working style in which they approach patients.

Therapeutic trainees tend to be those who want very much to help their patients and who will use whatever techniques promise results. In diagnosis and treatment they tend to emphasize the therapeutic issues at hand and not to be terribly ideological.

Managerial trainees do not become so personally concerned about their patients, but prefer an administrative approach to therapy. They are more inclined to use a therapeutic team and to think of the hospital and other staff as resources they employ to manage the patient's case.

Intellectual trainees approach patients as examples of interesting theoretical issues and tend to be the most ideological of the three types. Their goal is less to get the patient better than to understand what is going on. In the case of psychiatry they often are the early deciders who endured medical school so that could finally explore the intellectual world of psychiatry (Light, 1980: 52-56).

The differences among resident types are complemented by different clusters of diagnostic terms shaped by the social context in which residents are employed. There is, of course, overlap between the terms used in one diagnostic system and another, though the context and connotations are usually different. One cluster or diagnostic system concerns *therapeutic diagnosis* and serves the sociolinguistic function of enabling those treating the patient to talk about therapy. The terms are not the familiar legal terms but those that describe how the patient behaves or responds in therapy terms such as "rigid," "resisting," "working," "being in business," and "reality-testing."

Another cluster of terms concerns *managerial diagnosis*. These are obviously used more in a hospital than in outpatient care and are the terms most commonly shared between psychiatrists and those members of the staff running the wards. They include such terms as "agitated," "disorganized," "getting higher," "calming down," and "being depressed."

The third family of classifications constitutes *dynamic diagnosis*. It is the most intellectual and serves to enable psychiatrists to talk about the

psychoanalytic aspects of the patient. Here the language is rarely expressed
in brief terms, but rather in explanations of the patient's defenses and
ways of behaving. For example, a senior clinician summarized his diagnosis
by saying:

> Chronicity is the result of not resolving the first regression. Each
> subsequent one has the same elements. The ego wants to try to
> integrate the conflicting elements again and again. The death of her
> husband is not a loss, but has the tone of a sexual frustration. He left
> her sexually high and dry again. He abandoned her too [Light, 1980:
> 180-181].

Finally, there is the diagnostic system of terms embodied in the
Diagnostic and Statistical Manual. While these are what most outsiders
think of as psychiatric diagnoses, my research indicates that neither
psychiatrists nor residents take the terms very seriously even though they
have to use them daily for charts and legal purposes. However, they
constantly comment on how little a term such as "paranoid schizophrenic"
conveys about a case. Thus residents quickly learn to use these labels
without giving them serious thought, a point of significance for the
sociology of labelling. While this attitude may be changing with the far
more detailed and substantial classifications available in DSM-III, certainly
until the late 1970s these observations help to explain the facile application of official psychiatric labels by psychiatrists to patients.

THE SOCIOLOGY
OF DIAGNOSTIC TRAINING

Given this general framework of social structure, diagnostic systems,
and personal working styles, let us turn to the training structure in which
residents learn to diagnose. First, they arrive as competent physicians who
only a few weeks before were shouldering considerable responsibilities and
making numerous diagnoses over sometimes complex medical problems.
Suddenly they find themselves thrown into a bewildering new world,
where healthy-looking patients are "sick" and the nature of pathology has
an eerie, intangible quality. There is no time for ironic distance, and few
residency programs provide an academic review of diagnostic systems
along with the evidence for their efficacy. For example, at the time that
the residents I studied were learning the subtle complexities of dynamic
diagnoses, research psychiatrists issued a report showing that correct

diagnoses from dynamic formulations were no more likely to be accurate than chance variation (Light, 1980: 181-182). But the residents did not know about this study and, in general, research about the validity of diagnosis was not discussed. This is a chief flaw of psychiatric training, for, given the tenuous nature of the enterprise, there is a great need for the healthy skepticism of medical science rather than doctrinal instruction, confession, and the learning of catechisms. Only a few of the most creative psychiatrists, such as Leon Eisenberg (1979), have recognized the issues underlying psychiatric diagnosis and thought about them creatively.

In order to understand the social context of diagnosis and the pressures to label, sociologists of mental health must appreciate the situation in which residents find themselves. For example, in a residency program universally acknowledged to be one of the most distinguished, the chief of service gave out the assigned patients to residents on the first day and described them largely in terms of the problems they presented. The strengths of the patients were not mentioned, and several times he warned that a certain patient would be "a very difficult, if not impossible case." Another patient, he said, "sought to be psychopathic, but his MMPIs [psychological tests] showed he is schizophrenic." Another never had "a real relation" with her therapist. "Perhaps you can get into business with her," he said. Another was "a first-rate schizophrenic" and a "paranoid psychotic." After these assignments, the attending psychiatrist told the residents that they would feel like running away and that while a little running was expected, residents must learn to face the patients and their pain (Light, 1980: 67-68). Residents acutely felt the loss of objective medical bearings.

> *Adam:* We're looking for tests, like lab tests in medicine, which will tell us with reasonable reliability what is wrong, and we want to read all about the problems of our patients.
>
> *David:* Yes, it's very hard to go from medical school where there are reasonable lab tests.
>
> *Jeff:* We've talked among ourselves and we can't understand why we are so tired at night. We worked so much harder as interns [Light, 1980: 71].

Thus residents feel great pressure to know what they are doing, to have diagnostic labels that reassure them of their professional competence. It takes only a few weeks before residents begin to characterize the whole personality of their patients in terms of their diagnostic labels. The residents also intently watch the techniques of their mentors to learn as quickly as possible how to work with their patients. One technique these residents quickly picked up was not to ask open-ended questions, which patients could easily deny, but to ask instead questions that assumed the symptoms of the pathology they suspected. Instead of asking, "Do you have any trouble with your mother?" you say, "Tell me about your troubles with your mother." Framing the question that way guarantees that any response—including denial—is interesting and relevant. However, one effect of learning such lessons is that they accentuate the neurotic aspects of anyone, including oneself. Soon residents begin to perceive that they share some of the same problems as their patients. The concerns with contagion and with differentiating between oneself and one's patients are very real in this diagnostic context. To summarize, learning diagnosis involves four great issues: finding anchors of clarity in a sea of ambiguity, using diagnostic techniques as a means of controlling relations with patients, establishing professional confidence, and acculturating oneself to a psychiatric world view that applies to oneself as well as to patients. All of these incline psychiatrists to assimilate and use diagnostic labels uncritically.

Certain characteristics of the diagnostic enterprise stand out. First, residents learn to look for pathology rather than for mental health. This helps them in the trying circumstances described above to legitimize their new role. As Goffman (1961: 151-156) noted long ago, "The case record . . . is apparently not regularly used, however, to record occasions when the patient showed capacity to cope honorably and effectively with difficult life situations. Nor is the case record typically used to provide a rough average or sampling of this past conduct." Second, residents learn to characterize the whole patient by his or her diagnosis, so that the patient does not have *paranoid schizophrenia* but is a *paranoid schizophrenic*. This is a fundamental change from medical diagnosis and the rapidity with which residents incorporate this perspective is startling. Finally, residents learn to use their own personal styles and biases in making a diagnosis or treating a patient without feeling that this distorts information. Here, for example, is an excerpt from one of the seminars devoted to teaching the fine points of diagnostic skills, led by hand-picked members from the program's distinguished faculty. The patient, a 15-year-old girl who had been selected for the diagnostic seminar by members of the outpatient service, had been in therapy before but had stopped. A brief review of her family life was given, but no diagnosis, and just before she arrived the teaching psychiatrist said he would not introduce her to the four of us who sat in wooden chairs along the wall of a dim, bare, spacious office. The psychiatrist began in a cool, harsh tone:

What's your understanding [of this meeting]?

Girl: Diagnosing.

Psychiatrist: You're here to find out what's wrong.

Girl: I'm not—no.

Psychiatrist: [Pause, gaze] Who is?

[Silence]

Psychiatrist: Do you share responsibility?

Girl: It's partly my responsibility. Partly. I'm trying to find out.

Psychiatrist: You've been attributing responsibility to your family, responsibility for not finding help.

Girl: If it will help me, I'll accept responsibility.

Psychiatrist: We have no guarantee it will help. If you want only it, then we'll be in a stalemate.

[The tension had gotten quite high, at least for me.]

Girl: You're twisting my words.

[Silence—psychiatrist looks constantly at girl, who sometimes looks at him, at her lap, or around the room.]

Psychiatrist: What can we expect from you?

Girl: It's not a definite no (that I'll not cooperate). I want it for relief.

Psychiatrist: Of what?

[Long pause]

Girl: I just want to be happy.

Psychiatrist: You'll have to be more specific.

Girl: How?

Psychiatrist: [sarcastically] Take a try at it.

Girl: [looking down, shaken] You seem to have my attitude fixed before I came here. [Pause] I don't know what you mean by "more specific."

Psychiatrist: If you don't know, who does? [Light, 1980: 164-166.]

The exchange to this point took twenty minutes, and it continued in a similar manner for another thirty minutes. One resident thought the interview was great and remarked that you could only do such a forceful interview after you have much experience and confidence. Another resident questioned the accuracy of the material squeezed out of the girl when the psychiatrist pushed so hard to get it: "We have no idea how this girl behaves. We've only seen her under very unusual circumstances. I would let her be for a while and see what kind of person she is." Despite this reservation, in the end the residents decided among themselves that this psychiatrist used his anger very effectively in diagnosing mental illness. Although Thomas Scheff (1966) pointed out some time ago that "it is almost a truism, however, among social psychologists and students of language, that the meaning of behavior is not of property of the behavior itself, but of a relation between the behavior and the context in which it occurs," it is a truism that the psychiatrists we observed did not recognize. Rather, the behavior and information elicited was regarded as characteristic of the girl's personality rather than as the product of an unusual social context and a specific interaction with another powerful, hostile individual. From my own extensive experience with the same patients, I would estimate that most of them were "crazy" less than 10 percent of the time.

CONTROLLING UNCERTAINTIES[1]

Training for uncertainty involves five basic areas: uncertainties of knowledge, diagnosis, procedure or treatment, collegial relations, and client response. Residents learn techniques for controlling these areas of uncertainty that influence how they use psychiatric labels. We have already commented on how the ambiguities and uncertainties of psychiatric knowledge press residents to accept and use psychiatric terms. These terms also reduce uncertainties of diagnosis, though plenty of unclear situations remain that are ultimately resolved by deferring to those with more clinical experience. When applied generally as a professional norm, this deferring to clinical experience means that each resident collects his or her own stories and uses them as a basis for personal authority in resolving uncertainties of diagnosis and treatment. This norm has the secondary effect of insulating clinicians from criticism and creating a counter-scientific outlook toward professional work.

Complementing these two means of controlling uncertainty is the emphasis on technique as an end in itself. After a while, residents judge a therapeutic session by how well they technically managed it, and they no longer talk as they once had about the impact of the session on the patient's problems. This emphasis on technique is particularly useful for controlling uncertainties of treatment.

When colleagues have influence or power over a resident, collegial relations can become a problem. Residents look forward to gaining the professional autonomy that will eliminate the uncertainties of second-guessing those above them. The uncertainties of patient relations can be reduced by the opposite approach of maintaining a dominant (even as benevolent) stance and controlling what patients know about their diagnosis or treatment. In addition, this dominant relationship is institutionalized in legal powers and administrative prerogatives (Waitzkin and Waterman, 1974). These five means of controlling uncertainty complement each other and either encourage or facilitate the liberal use of psychiatric labels.

FUTURE TRENDS OF PSYCHIATRY AND MENTAL ILLNESS

In less than a decade, American psychiatry has undergone a sociological revolution, and with it the nature of "mental illness" has been altered. In the sixties, Freudian-based concepts of psychodynamics spawned dozens of psychotherapeutic schools, from scream therapy to encounter groups. Public awareness of and participation in therapeutic activities grew tremendously, proliferating psychodynamically oriented views of mental problems. In retrospect all of this activity appears more like the final burst of a dying star, for, within a short time, the leading departments of psychiatry left their imitators and camp followers behind as they forged a new professional identity around advances in biopsychiatry. This shift in professional self-image and public image was accompanied by the rise of Valium, Librium, and related drugs to an unmatched level of popularity. In addition, DSM-III was being written by members of the research-oriented segment of the profession, so that the very language of diagnosis was soon stripped of its psychodynamic garb. The public, always captivated by advances in medical science, has quickly accepted the new concept of "mental illness" that emphasizes chemical imbalances in the brain and genetic determinants rather than early childhood experiences with mother and father. Several factors account for this transformation.

First, the movement to create a national network of community mental health centers (CMHCs) represented an overextension of psychiatry and psychodynamic theory. According to one of its best chroniclers, "the CMHC program would be one of the federal government's first attempts to raise national mental health by improving the quality of general community life through expert knowledge, not merely by more effective treatment for the already ill" (Musto, 1977: 43). This entailed "the fantasy of an omnipotent and omniscient mental health technology that could thoroughly reform society" (Musto, 1977:50).

From a sociological point of view the community mental health movement appears to have been a strategy by leading activists in the profession to provide a new institutional base for public psychiatry to replace the expensive and embarrassing state mental hospitals, which had originally been the foundation on which the psychiatric profession had been built. The fatal error, however, was that too few psychiatrists showed an interest in running and controlling these centers, so that they rapidly became a new institutional base for psychiatry's nonphysician competitors (Light, 1980: 331-335). The community segment of the psychiatric profession never succeeded in mobilizing other segments, so that far fewer psychiatrists had an interest in community mental health than the proportion actually working in the community centers, and it was not long before the profession as a whole abandoned community psychiatry. Nevertheless, while members of the profession in the mid-1970s were declaring community psychiatry "dead," the profession and its allies had fundamentally transformed the delivery system of mental health care from heavily hospital-based institutions run by physicians to a far more differentiated network of outpatient and hospital arrangements in which mental health care was provided by a broad spectrum of nonphysician providers as well as doctors. In the eyes of many planners, such a transformation is in order for the rest of medicine.

A second factor was the rise of biopsychiatry to a place of political and financial dominance at the leading institutional psychiatric departments. For years psychiatric residents and practitioners had been using the fruits of pharmacology and biopsychiatry while ignoring the fundamentally different theory of mental illness they embodied. But a set of external events changed that situation. In the last flowering of psychodynamic psychiatry in the 1960s, the National Institute of Mental Health decided to devote nearly all of its research funds to projects in biopsychiatry. As a result of this shift in federal priorities, a generation of research psychiatrists emerged who had considerable institutional power and funds. When, in the early 1970s, support for psychiatric residency training dwindled, this professional segment and its allies had the prestige and resources to take over leading departments of psychiatry. This shift in power coincided with disillusionment over community psychiatry and the proliferation of psychotropic drugs.

This trend toward remedicalizing psychiatry has interesting implications for "mental illness" as a form of deviance. Psychiatry is not a unitary but a multifaceted profession that is constantly struggling with identity issues concerning whether its main focus is on the mind or the central nervous system and with how much either has to do with the rest of the body, which is medicine's domain. For example, while many European branches of psychiatry consider themselves principally concerned with neurology, American psychiatrists have felt about neurology the way medical students feel about biostatistics. For some time now neurology has developed apart from the rest of psychiatry (Ramsay, 1979). The recent explosion of knowledge in neurology has led to further compartmentalization, though there are signs of reintegration (Ramsay, 1979; Sandifer, 1980). At the same time, both psychiatrists and other physicians have tended to practice "decapitated" medicine, to the disadvantage of both sides. Until recently, psychiatrists have focused on mental problems without much attention to their significance in dealing with disorders of other organ systems, and medical students have shunned the psychological dimensions of medical problems. The development of liaison psychiatry on one side and a focus on primary care and family medicine on the other both promise to eliminate this false dualism that has injured both physicians and patients since the beginning of the century.

Nevertheless, there is still a long way to go (Schildkrout, 1980). So far, only psychiatry has developed an integrated biopsychosocial model of pathology and treatment (Engel, 1980; Eisenberg, 1979). In the coming period, when psychiatry must clarify its relationship to medicine and medicine must clarify its mission in an age of increasing competition and cost inflation, this integrated model is likely to receive greater emphasis. While it is possible that this will increase the range of behaviors considered as "mental illness," the effect may be to recognize the ubiquity of emotional problems in health care so that the stigma of "mental illness" and its specific domain will both diminish. But in the realm of social deviance, psychiatry will continue to play the ambivalent role of that profession which legitimates, with the esteemed values of medicine and science, social judgments of dubious medical and scientific merit.

NOTE

1. The material in this section is drawn from Chapter 13 of the author's book, *Becoming Psychiatrists* (Light, 1980).

REFERENCES

American Psychiatric Association (1980) Diagnostic and Statistical Manual of Mental Disorders. 3rd ed. Washington, DC: Author.

BECKER, H. S. (1970) Sociological Work: Method and Substance. Chicago: Aldine.

——— G. GREER, E. C. HUGHES, and A. STRAUSS (1961) Boys in White: Student Culture in Medical School. Chicago: University of Chicago Press.

BIEGEL, A. (1979) "Psychiatric education at the crossroads: issues and future directions." American Journal of Psychiatry 136 (December): 1525-1529.

BLAKEMORE, C. (1981) "The future of psychiatry in science and society." Psychological Medicine 11 (February): 27-37.

BRACELAND, F. J. (1981) "Psychiatry, medicine's erring sibling returns: a history and a prophecy." Medicine and History 3, Series V (September): 181-193.

BRIM, O. G., Jr. (1960) "Personality development as role learning," in I. Iscoe and H. W. Stevenson (eds.) Personality Development in Children. Austin: University of Texas Press.

EISENBERG, L. (1979) "Interfaces between medicine and psychiatry." Comprehensive Psychiatry 20 (January/February): 1-14.

ENGEL, G. L. (1980) "The clinical application of the biopsychosocial model." American Journal of Psychiatry 137 (May): 535-544.

GOFFMAN, E. (1961) Asylums. Garden City, NY: Doubleday.

GORDON, J. S. (1981) "Holistic medicine: toward a new medical model." Journal of Clinical Psychiatry 42 (March): 114-119.

GOVE, W. R. (1979) "The labeling versus the psychiatric explanation of mental illness: a debate that has become substantively irrelevant." Journal of Health and Social Behavior 20 (September): 301-304.

——— (1975) "The labelling theory of mental illness: a reply to Scheff." American Sociological Review 40 (April): 242-248.

——— (1970) "Societal reaction as an explanation of mental illness: an evaluation." American Sociological Review 35: 873-884.

HORWITZ, A. (1982) The Social Control of Mental Illness. New York: Academic.

——— (1979) "Models, muddles, and mental illness labelling." Journal of Health and Social Behavior 20 (September): 296-300.

KENDELL, R. E., J. COOPER, A. GOURLEY, and J. COPELAND (1971) "Diagnostic criteria of American and British psychiatrists." Archives of General Psychiatry 25: 123-130.

LANGSLEY, D. G. (1981) "President's address: today's teachers and tomorrow's psychiatrists." American Journal of Psychiatry 138 (August): 1013-1016.

LIGHT, D. (1982) "Medical and nursing education: surface behavior and deep structure," in D. Mechanic (ed.) Handbook of Health, Health Care, and the Health Professions. New York: Macmillan.

——— (1980) Becoming Psychiatrists: The Professional Transformation of Self. New York: W. W. Norton.

MUSTO, D. F. (1977) "What ever happened to community mental health?" Psychiatric Annals 7, 10: 30-55.

RAMSAY, R. A. (1979) "Neurology and psychiatry: interface and integration." Psychosomatics 20 (April): 269-277.

SANDIFER, M. G. (1980) "Psychiatry, the medical model, and primary care." Psychosomatics 21 (March): 187-188.

SCHEFF, T. J. (1979) "Reply to comment by Horwitz." Journal of Health and Social Behavior 20 (September): 305.

––– (1975) "Reply to Chauncy and Gove." American Sociological Review 40 (April): 252-257.

––– (1974) "The labelling theory of mental illness." American Sociological Review 39 (June): 444-452.

––– (1966) Being Mentally Ill. Chicago: Aldine.

SCHILDKROUT, E. (1980) "Medicine residents' difficulty in learning and utilizing a psychosocial perspective." Journal of Medical Education 55 (November): 962-964.

STROEBEL, C. F. (1981) "Biofeedback and behavioral medicine: a paradigm shift for psychiatry?" Psychiatric Annals 11 (February): 44-47.

SZASZ, T. S. (1977) Manufacture of Madness. New York: Harper & Row.

TOWNSEND, J. M. (1980) "Psychiatry versus societal reaction: a critical analysis." Journal of Health and Social Behavior 21 (September): 268-278.

WAITZKIN, H. B. and B. WATERMAN (1974) The Exploitation of Illness and Capitalist Society. New York: Bobbs-Merrill.

CULTURAL SHAPING AND MENTAL DISORDERS

JANE M. MURPHY

Over the past 50 years there has been sustained interest by the social and behavioral sciences in the idea that culture is an active agent in shaping many aspects of behavior relevant to mental disorders. A series of quotations serves as background to the themes of this chapter and demonstrates the progression of this idea:

Benedict, 1934

Most people are shaped to the form of their culture by the enormous malleability of their original endowment [p. 254].

Linton, 1956

Hysterical phenomena are everywhere very decidedly culturally patterned. In fact, if one knows a culture one can predict the form hysterias will take in that society, or pretty nearly so [p. 132].

Goffman, 1962

[The] perception of losing one's mind is based on culturally derived and socially engrained stereotypes as to the significance of symptoms such as hearing voices, losing temporal and spatial orientation, and sensing that one is being followed [p. 132].

Scheff, 1966

After exhausting these categories [categories of norm violations where the term is derived from the norm broken such as crime and drunkenness] there is always a residue of the most diverse kinds of violations for which the culture provides no explicit label. For example, although there is great cultural variation in what is defined as decent or real, each culture tends to reify its definition of decency and reality, and so provides no way of handling violations of its expectations in these areas. The typical norm governing decency or reality, therefore, literally "goes without saying" and its violation is unthinkable for most of its members. For the convenience of the society in construing those instances of unnamable rule-breaking which are called to its attention, these violations may be lumped together into a residual category: witchcraft, spirit possession, or, in our society, mental illness [pp. 33-34].

Silverman, 1967

Significant differences between acute schizophrenics and shamans [healers whose powers come from direct contact with the supernatural] are *not* found in the sequence of underlying psychological events that define their abnormal experiences [p. 21]. The essential difference between the psychosocial environments of the schizophrenic and the shaman lies in the pervasiveness of the anxiety that complicates each of their lives. The emotional supports and the modes of collective solutions to the basic problems of existence available to the shaman greatly alleviate the otherwise excruciatingly painful existence [p. 29]. In contrast to the shaman, the chances of the schizophrenic achieving a successful readaption are comparatively small [p. 29].

Rosenhan, 1973

Psychiatric diagnosis betrays little about the patient but much about the environment in which an observer finds him. . . . Diagnosis acts . . . as a self-fulfilling prophecy. Eventually the patient himself accepts the diagnosis with all its surplus meanings and expectations, and behaves accordingly [p. 254].

Waxler, 1977

Each society, through the responses of its members to the mentally ill person succeeds in molding the patient to meet its own expectations about what a mentally ill person should be [p. 233]. And that may be why mental illness is cured in traditional societies [p. 250].

The ideas embedded in these quotations are uniform in their emphasis on the shaping force of cultural expectations and the plasticity of human personality. Many of the ideas derive from studies carried out in relatively small, traditional, and homogeneous groups of people and take some of their strength from comparisons to large, modern, and complex societies.

If a chain of ideas were constructed from these themes it might take the following composition. Culture molds human personality to fit its expectations. Both normal and abnormal behavior are shaped by socially inherited stereotypes. Culturally normal behavior in one society may be culturally abnormal behavior in another society. Cultures vary in the degree to which they use and abuse the patterned forms of abnormality. Cultures vary in the degree to which they return abnormal behavior to normality. These ideas emphasize cultural relativity and many of them have been employed in the orientation described as the "social labelling theory" of mental illness (Scheff, 1966).

If this chain includes valid ideas, it holds a reservoir of solutions regarding the problems posed by mental disorders. It means that if cultures can be sorted out so that we know which ones create, prevent, cure, or reduce the disability of mental disorders it should be possible to engage the human capacity for learning so that a common culture of the future will dispel the burden of mental disorders. The purpose of this chapter is to suggest that the chain lacks the level of validity necessary for the task. It is not that the chain is altogether wrong, but rather that it is not sufficiently right. It is sorely in need of being complicated by information regarding other influences on the causes, courses, and outcomes of mental disorders. It needs to undergo the process Geertz (1973: 33) had in mind when he said that "scientific advancement commonly consists in the progressive complication of what once seemed a beautifully simple set of notions but now seems an unbearably simplistic one." It needs to take cognizance of the type of conclusion reached by the Whitings (1973: 59) in their study of altruistic and egotistic behavior of children in six cultures, in which they suggest "that the truth apparently lies between these two extremes and that both culture and personality have influence on children's behavior." Their work focused on essentially normal behavior. In expanding the area of interest to what may be abnormal behavior, the need for *looking between extremes* is, if anything, even greater.

MATERIALS

The data to be presented derive from studies carried out among peoples whose cultural heritages are diverse. Nevertheless, these peoples are often grouped together by words that dissociate them from Western culture. They are variously described as members of traditional, nonindustrialized, or developing societies. I will use my work among Eskimos and Yorubas as a point of departure, but will draw on a number of other studies of non-Western groups for purposes of comparison and to bring the themes of investigation to the present. These materials will be described in terms of their bearing on questions that stem from the chain of ideas about cultural patterning.

METHODS

The information from my work was gathered during a year spent in a village of Yupik-speaking Eskimos on an island in the Bering Sea in 1954-1955 and investigations among Egba Yorubas of Nigeria in 1961 and 1963. The island is icebound much of the year and is located just under the Arctic Circle. The area in Nigeria is tropical and somewhat above the equator. The Eskimos are a hunting and gathering group, while the Yorubas live in settled agricultural villages. The Eskimos are Oriental; the Yorubas are Black.

The fieldwork involved participant observation, interviewing key people, and daily recordings of events, comments, and observations. In the Eskimo study, some of the data came from a key person who was interviewed systematically regarding the life experiences of the 499 Eskimos who constituted a total village census for the 15 years previous to and including the year of investigation. These biographies were organized to cover birth, family of orientation, growth, education, travel, marriage, children, health, occupation, and so on. This procedure took 5 months, and during it I made use of a dictionary of Eskimo words for illness and deviance developed by Hughes (1960). The census also provided a structure for accumulating and coordinating comments and observations about these 499 individuals by a wide selection of Eskimos in addition to the key person who reviewed the whole census (Murphy, 1960; Murphy and Leighton, 1965).

The approach among the Yorubas was different in that I worked first with a group of 3 native healers and a member of an indigenous cult (Leighton and Murphy, 1964). These interviews were focused only on illness and deviance and they began at a more abstract level, our initial concern being an attempt to understand Yoruba concepts of abnormal behavior in a general way. It turned out to be more satisfying, however, to move to the specific mode characteristic of the Eskimo study. Most of what the Yoruba healers described concerned their actual patients and acquaintances. Following this period of interviewing, I participated in a larger study carried out with a group of Nigerian and U.S. colleagues in which we gathered data about 416 Yoruba adults, of whom 59 were patients in a mental hospital, 12 were patients of native healers, and the remainder were samples of the general population (Leighton et al., 1963).

In the Yoruba study we made use of a structured questionnaire that we developed for community studies of mental illness and that we had been gradually adapting for cross-cultural investigations. We had used such a technique in an exploratory way among the Eskimos (Murphy and Hughes, 1965). Because the interests here are Eskimo and Yoruba concepts of abnormality and how these groups label mental illness, only those sources in which an Eskimo described another Eskimo or a Yoruba described a Yoruba are used, rather than what anyone said about his or her own experiences and feelings in response to a questionnaire. A main resource for this approach in the Yoruba study was that we interviewed the *bale,* the headman, of each village about each sample member. This provided a systematic outside assessment of each sample member that can be considered a counterpart to the systematic census interviews among the Eskimos. To supplement the Eskimo-Eskimo and Yoruba-Yoruba information I have in some instances added my own observations about a person who was indigenously labelled as abnormal, or what such a person said to me in circumstances other than a questionnaire interview.

Thus the materials of this study can best be described as a collection of dossiers on specific individuals—observations by Eskimos about specific other Eskimos, and by Yorubas about specific other Yorubas. The focus was on indigenous meanings and native interpretations of behavior. Insofar as a general pattern of meaning emerged, it was revealed by sifting through a very large number of often small descriptions about particular individuals.

Often, but not always, meaning was conveyed by labels. Sometimes meaning was conveyed by actions taken in regard to a particular person described as exhibiting various behaviors. In Western societies, official recognition of abnormal behavior is conveyed by commitment of a person to a hospital or prison. Official native recognition of abnormality is equally conveyed in the action of taking a person to an Eskimo shaman or a Yoruba healer, or in taking a person to the village fathers for reprimand or punishment (among the Eskimos) or the native courts (among the Yorubas).

RESULTS AND DISCUSSION

This section is organized in terms of the following topics: (1) general descriptive concepts and labels; (2) specific content; (3) inclusion and exclusion of behavioral patterns; (4) social usability; (5) social abusability; (6) causes; (7) treatment; and (8) outcome.

General Descriptive Concepts and Labels

The questions of concern here are whether peoples in traditional societies have concepts and labels about psychological and behavioral differences that they describe in an abstract way and, if so, whether the descriptions bear resemblance to what in Western culture is meant by the concept of mental disorders.

The Eskimos and Yorubas clearly recognize differences among themselves and describe these in terms of what people do and what they say they feel and believe. Some of the differences arouse admiration, sympathy, or protection, while others elicit disapproval; some of them are called sickness and others strength, some are conceived as misconduct and others as good conduct. Some of them are described by a single word or nominative phrase. Other behaviors, which seem to have common features, are described in varying circumlocutions and sentences. If a word exists for a complex pattern of behavior it seems that the concept of that pattern has been crystallized out of a welter of specific attributes and that such a word qualifies as an explicit label.

Of first importance is whether or not the Yorubas and Eskimos conceptualize a distinction between body and mind and attribute differences in functioning to one or the other. The first indication of how this was viewed arose in the Eskimo census review, when early in the procedure one woman was described in these terms: "Her sickness is getting wild and out of mind . . . but she might have had sickness in her body too." "Getting wild" in this instance meant running out in the winter at night to the lake near the village and struggling with her son when he found her and tried to bring her home. "Going out of mind" meant not knowing where she was and accusing her family of things they did not do. In this and many other descriptions, it seemed that there was a distinction between mind and body.

To an Eskimo, a phenomenon that sometimes happens to the mind is *nuthkavihak,* a word which is translated as "crazy." It became clear from other descriptions that *nuthkavihak* refers to a complex pattern of multiple possible behavioral processes of which the hallmark is conceived to be that something inside the person—the soul, the spirit, the mind—is out of order. Descriptions of how *nuthkavihak* is manifest include such phenomena as "talking to oneself," "screaming at somebody who does not exist," "believing that a child or husband was murdered by witchcraft when nobody else believes it," "believing oneself to be an animal," "refusing to eat for fear it will kill the person," "refusing to talk," "running away," "getting lost," "hiding in strange places," "making strange grimaces," "drinking urine," "becoming strong and violent," "killing dogs," and "threatening people." Eskimos say that *nuthkavihak* means "being crazy."

There is a Yoruba word, *were*, which is also translated as insanity. The phenomena include "hearing voices and trying to get other people to see their source when other people cannot," "laughing when there is nothing to laugh at," "talking all the time or not talking at all," "asking oneself questions and answering them," "picking up sticks and leaves for no purpose except to put them in a pile," "throwing away food because it is thought to contain juju," "tearing off one's clothes," "setting fires," "defecating in public and then mushing around in the feces," "taking up a weapon and suddenly hitting someone," "breaking things in a state of being stronger than normal," and "believing that an odor is continuously being emitted from one's body."

It is of considerable significance that *were* and *nuthkavihak* were never used for a single attribute such as "hearing voices," but rather were applied to a pattern in which three or four phenomena existed together, even though no one person was described or observed as having the whole set of behaviors given above. I understand this to mean that a pattern or model of behaviors was in mind. No single person suffering from *nuthkavihak*, for example, fit the total pattern perfectly, but neither did any one sufferer have only one component. Since no one feature was considered sufficient reason for using the labels *were* and *nuthkavihak*, it is possible to examine the situations in which a person exhibited one or another of the components but was not labelled insane.

The ability to see things other people do not see and to look into the future and prophesy is a clearly recognized and highly valued trait in these groups. It is called "thinness" by Eskimos. This ability is used by numerous minor Eskimo diviners and is the outstanding characteristic of the shaman. If "thinness" is the Eskimo way of talking about what we would call "hallucinations," it alone does not constitute their stereotype of insanity since there were no instances when a "thin" person was also called *nuthkavihak*.

When a shaman undertakes a curing rite he becomes possessed by the spirit of an animal. He seems to believe that he is an animal, and we might say that he exhibits a "delusion." Consider this description, which concerns a female shaman among the Eskimos with whom I worked:

When my brother was sick, my grandmother who was a shamaness tried her best to get him well. She did all her part, acting as though a dog, singing some songs at night, but he died. While she was singing she fell down so hard on the floor, making a big noise. After about fifteen minutes later we heard the tappings of her fingers and her toes on the floor. Slowly she got up, already she had become like a dog. She looks awful. My grandfather told me that he used to hide his face with his drum just because she looks different, changed and awful like a dog, very scary. She used to crawl back and forth on the floor, making big noises. Even though my brother was afraid of her, he tried not to hide his face, he looked at her so that he would become well. Then my grandmother licked his mouth to try to pull up the cough and to blow it away. Then after half hour, she fell down so hard on the floor again [Murphy, 1964: 59].

Compare this to the case of a Baffin Island Eskimo, reported by Teicher (1954), who believed that a fox had entered her body. This was not associated with shamanizing, but was a continuous belief. She barked herself hoarse, tried to claw her husband, thought her feet were turning into fox paws, believed that the fox was moving up in her body, gagged because she thought she could feel its hair in her throat, lost control of her bowels at times, and finally became so excited that she was tied up and put into a coffin-like box with an opening at the head through which she could be fed. This woman was thought to be crazy, but the shamaness was not. One Eskimo summarized the distinction this way: *"When the shaman is healing he is out of his mind, but he is not crazy."*

This suggests that seeing, hearing, and believing things that are not seen, heard, and believed by all members of the group are sometimes linked to insanity and sometimes not. The distinction appears to be the degree to which they are controlled and utilized for a specific social function. The inability to control these processes is what is meant by a mind out of order, and when a mind is out of order it will not only fail to control sensory perception but also it will fail to control many other behaviors. Another Eskimo, on being asked to define *nuthkavihak,* said that it means "the mind does not control the person, *he is crazy."* I take this to indicate that volition is implicated and that hearing voices, for example, can be both voluntarily achieved and involuntarily manifest and that the involuntary aspect is what is associated with *were* and *nuthkavihak.*

When a person among the Eskimos or Yorubas behaved in the ways or said that he believed the kinds of things indicated in *nuthkavihak* or *were,* the course of action was to take him or her to a healer and have a curing rite performed. In fact, among the Yorubas some native healers specialize in the treatment of *were* (Prince, 1964).

Thus at the descriptive level these groups appear to have a concept that refers to something sufficiently unusual and at the same time often enough seen that a word has been formed so that they can easily communicate about it. The word is abstract in that it does not describe a particular individual but rather a class of individuals; it distinguishes between body and mind; it refers to a pattern, no one component of which is adequate for using the word; its components include phenomena that are similar to what in Western psychiatry have been described as hallucinations, delusions, and behavioral disorganization; it suggests that an important feature of the nature of this pattern is that the phenomena to which it refers are uncontrollable; and it seems to carry the meaning that a person who exhibits this behavior should be taken to a healer so that, if possible, the pattern can be changed.

A growing literature on this topic indicates that the concepts of insanity presented as reflecting Eskimo and Yoruba beliefs are common throughout many parts of the world. For example, Edgerton (1966), working with 4 tribal societies in East Africa, provides a list of 24 behaviors ascribed to psychosis by these groups, including such patterns as "serious assault," "arson," "abusing people verbally," "shouting, screaming, crying," "running wild," "going naked," "talking nonsense," "wandering aimlessly," "eating and smearing feces," and so on. Edgerton (1966: 413) noted that "the most obvious aspect of the many behaviors ascribed to 'psychosis' is the agreement between the four tribes." Comparing the African view of psychosis to that of the West, he wrote:

> It is remarkable how alike these African conceptions of psychosis are to the Western European psychoses, particularly to the constellation of reactions known as schizophrenia. The Africans of these four tribes do not regard a single behavior as psychotic which could not be so regarded in the West. That is, they do not produce symptoms which are understandable as psychotic only within the context of their own cultures. What is psychotic for them would be psychotic for us [Edgerton, 1966: 413].

Among the Serer of Senegal, Beiser et al. (1973: 883) identified a category defined as "illnesses of the spirit," one type of which is labeled *O'Dof,* a word that corresponds closely to "mad" or "crazy." This pattern of illness is illustrated by case descriptions, one of which concerns a farmer who awoke one night crying that someone had made his soul leave him. For the next two years he could not sit still. He sang and shouted and talked with spirits. He tried to run away many times and once he tried to hit his mother. Many healers were called in and they disagreed about the cause of the illness and the patient received numerous kinds of medications. At one point he spent four years living in a healer's compound. This seemed to his family to quiet him, but on returning home he rarely spoke, would work to exhaustion in the fields if not told to stop, often required urging to eat, would sometimes talk to spirits, and occasionally had angry outbursts, when he would tear up bedding.

Among the Zapotecs of Mexico, Selby (1974: 41) found that insanity was indigenously recognized and that the condition was defined as having "something to do with the soul and was symptomized by agitated motor behavior, . . . violent purposeless movement, and the inability to talk in ways that people could readily understand."

Among the Ainu of Japan, Ohnuki-Tierney (1980) reports that several illnesses that resemble Western concepts of mental disorder are vaguely conceived and do not lend themselves easily to classification. The best described involve the severest symptoms. One is considered to be insanity and is named *oyasi karape*. It involves, for example, "jumping, crying, and laughing for no reason," is "characterized by verbal aggression and physi-cal violence toward oneself and others," and the "stricken individual is often confined in a separate hut to protect others from being harmed" (Ohnuki-Tierney, 1980: 134). It is usually attributed to demon possession or to the estranged soul of a dead human who had similarly suffered from insanity.

In the Eskimo and Yoruba studies, I experienced some of the same difficulties regarding classification as pertained among the Ainu. While there were similarities between named concepts and what we think of as mental retardation, convulsions, and senility, I was unable to find a word that could be translated as a general reference to neurosis or words that directly parallel our meaning of anxiety and depression. On the other hand, the number of words for emotional responses that we might classify as manifestations of anxiety or depression constituted a very large vocab-ulary. The Yoruba concepts include, for example, "unrest of mind that prevents sleep," "fear of being among people," "tenseness and over-eagerness," and so on. The Eskimo ideas are "worrying too much until it makes a person sick," "too easy to get afraid," "crying with sadness, head down and rocking back and forth," "shaking and trembling all over," "afraid to stay indoors," and so on.

The point is that neither group has a single word or explicit label that lumps these phenomena together as constituting a general class of illness by virtue of their underlying similarities or as a pattern in which several components are usually found in association. There does not appear to be a well-developed abstract concept for these patterns, as there is for *nuthkavihak* and *were*. These emotional reactions do, however, exist.

People recognize them and try to do something about them. Some of them are conceived as minor ailments while others are severely disabling and have caused people to give up their work. One Eskimo stopped being the captain of a hunting boat on these grounds. Some of these reactions are transient episodes; others are lifelong characteristics.

Of special significance to the problem at hand is the fact that most of these emotional phenomena are definitely thought of as remediable illnesses for which the shaman and witchdoctor have an effective armamentarium of cures. The number of people who exhibit these patterns is considerably in excess of those labelled *were* and *nuthkavihak.* Among the Yorubas the ratio is approximately 12 to 1, and among the Eskimos 14 to 1. If one were to look at the clientele of an Eskimo shaman or a Yoruba healer, a healer who had *not* specialized in the treatment of *were,* a very large proportion would be those who come with patterns such as "unrest of mind that prevents sleep" or "shaking and trembling all the time."

These Eskimos and Yorubas thus point out a large number of psychological and behavioral phenomena that we would call neuroses but that they do not put together under such a rubric. The consequence is not, however, a reduction in the number of people who display the phenomena or a great difference in how they are treated. The fact that these peoples cannot categorically define someone as "a neurotic" appears mainly to be a classification difference, and these phenomena seem to exist independently of cultural stereotypes and labels.

These investigations, along with other studies (Field, 1960; Kaplan and Johnson, 1964; Prince, 1964; Cawte, 1972; Burton-Bradley, 1973; and Carstairs and Kapur, 1976), suggest that where studies have been carried out most peoples have been found to have an abstract descriptive concept and label for a pattern that seems to be congruent with the Western idea of psychosis, especially schizophrenia. In many of these groups there are a wide variety of emotional disturbances also recognized, but they are more variable in terms of how they are grouped together.

Specific Content

Thus far the focus has been on abstract concepts that refer to processes of thought, feeling, and behavior. The question now raised concerns whether "talking nonsense," "asking oneself questions and then answering them," and "talking in ways not readily understood," for example, have a content that can be predicted by knowing the culture in which it is found. Are psychotic thought productions and hysterias "decidedly culturally patterned"?

A number of researchers in the field of cross-cultural psychiatry take the position that the underlying processes of insanity are the same everywhere, but that the specific content varies between cultural groups (deReuck & Porter, 1965; Kiev, 1972; Yap, 1974). A psychotic person, it is thought, could not make use of the imagery of Christ if he or she had not been exposed to the Christian tradition, could not believe he or she was receiving messages from Mars if he or she had not heard something about the solar system, and could not elaborate ideas about the *wittiko* cannibalistic monster if he or she lacked knowledge of the Cree and Ojibwa Indian cultures. This position makes use of relativism in a modified fashion. It would seem that if a culture-specific stereotype of the content of psychosis exists in a group, it might have the kind of influence suggested by Benedict (1934) and Linton (1956) and elaborated in labelling theory as set forth by Scheff (1966). If the content stereotype were applied to the unstructured delusions of a psychotic, his or her thought products might be shaped and stabilized around the theme of that stereotype.

There have been several attempts to study phenomena such as *wittiko* (Parker, 1960; Teicher, 1960) and *pibloktoq* (Gussow, 1960). The former is thought of as the culturally defined content of a psychotic process in which a Cree or Ojibwa believes himself to be a cannibalistic monster; the latter as a culture-specific form of hysteria found in the Arctic. The evidence of their existence comes from early ethnographies, and it has been difficult in the contemporary period to locate people who have these illnesses. There are no recent reports of individuals exhibiting *wittiko,* and even the existing documentation from early investigations is open to question. After an extensive review of these materials, Honigmann (1967: 401) wrote, "I can't find one [case] that satisfactorily attests to someone being seriously obsessed by the idea of committing cannibalism."

Pibloktoq is a pattern of episodic and transient alteration of consciousness involving running away, jabbering in neologisms, making faces, and, lastly, a seizure. Scattered cases have been reported from Greenland across the Canadian archipelago to Alaska. Among the Eskimo group with whom I worked, I found only one description that was anything like the classical description, and it did not involve seizure. One woman was described as "once in a while having her face go every which way for short moments." People thought she might be on the verge of becoming a shamaness. She did not achieve this, but neither was she thought of as having an illness.

Foulks (1972) has carried out a much larger and more comprehensive study of Arctic hysteria. His conclusions are similar in that he found very few cases that could be said to match the prototype. Among 11,000 Innuit

Eskimos, 10 cases were located. These 10 appeared to be a heterogeneous group: Some had epilepsy, some were diagnosed as schizophrenic, and one was possibly alcoholic.

Other conditions that have been thought of as culturally specific mental disorders are *imu* among the Ainu (Winiarcz and Wilawski, 1936) and *latah*, found especially among Malayan groups (Yap, 1952). These follow much the same pattern as for the others. In a recent investigation of *latah*, for example, 13 cases were located in a population of 20,000 (Geertz, 1968). In reviewing this material, however, Neutra et al. (1977) suggest that only 2 cases are typical of the stereotype. Regarding *imu*, Ohnuki-Tierney (1980) indicates that although this pattern has attracted much attention from outside observers, the Ainu themselves do not consider it an illness.

Thus it appears that these highly particular, culturally patterned phenomena are exceedingly rare and not necessarily associated with illness. If they represent the influence of cultural shaping, the stereotype should have sustained the pattern, while in fact these content patterns seem to have largely disappeared.

Prominent in the descriptions of the images and behavior of people labelled *were* and *nuthkavihak* are cultural beliefs and practices as well as features of the natural environment. Eskimo ideation concerns Arctic animals and Eskimo people, Eskimo objects, and Eskimo spirits. The Yoruba ideation is based on tropical animals and Yoruba figures. The cultural variation is, in other words, general. There is no evidence that if a person were to become *were* or *nuthkavihak* he or she would reveal one specific delusion based on cultural mythology. The lack of cultural specificity was borne home to me when I was introduced to an illiterate psychotic Sudanese. He thought that he was Napoleon, an idea that I assume represented his knowledge of the history of the area but which was certainly not tightly linked to his own cultural tradition. In regard to specificity of content, I reach the same conclusion Brown (1973: 397) did when he set out to see how far labelling ideas would aid his understanding of hospitalized schizophrenics: "Delusions are as idiosyncratic as individual schizophrenics or normals. . . . There seems to be nothing like a standard set of heresies, but only endless variety."

Inclusion and Exclusion of Behavioral Patterns

It has now been suggested that most peoples have a concept of mental illness that is distinguished from physical illness, and that within the broad domain of mental illness, the identification of a pattern that resembles schizophrenia is usually the most well formulated, while other types are more variously crystallized as classes of phenomena. It often aids the task of understanding a system of beliefs to ask what kinds of patterns appear to be excluded from a given class. In other words, the definition of a "thing" is sometimes clarified by what it is not as much as by what it is. *Imu,* for example, was said not to be considered an illness by the Ainu. Thus the question of concern here is whether these groups have concepts of behavioral deviations that they do not consider to be among their mental illnesses.

The Eskimos and Yorubas have words for theft, cheating, lying, stinginess, drunkenness, and a large number of other behaviors that they consider to be specific acts of bad conduct. These, like the practice of witchcraft, are thought of as transgressions against social standards and are negatively sanctioned.

In addition, the Eskimos have a word, *kunlangeta,* which means "his mind knows what to do but he does not do it." This is an abstract term for the breaking of many rules when awareness of the rules is not in question. It might be applied to a person who, for example, repeatedly lies to people and thereby cheats them *and* steals things *and* does not go hunting *and,* when the men are out of the village, takes sexual advantage of many women; someone who does not pay attention to reprimands and who is always being brought to the elders for punishment. There was 1 Eskimo among the 499 who was called *kunlangeta.* When asked what would have happened to such a person traditionally, an Eskimo said that probably "somebody would have pushed him off the ice when nobody else was looking." This suggests that permissiveness has a limit even in a cultural group that in some other respects is quite lenient and tolerant. The Yorubas have a similarly abstract word, *arankan,* which means a person who always goes his own way regardless of others, uncooperative, full of malice, and bullheaded.

It appears, therefore, that these groups have a concept of behavior that is similar to what we call "deviance," and that these deviations are evaluated negatively. Further, there are parallels between *kunlangeta* and *arankan* and our concept of a "psychopath"—someone who consistently carries out multiple acts that violate the norms of society. Some of the specific acts of wrongdoing that they recognize might in our society be called evidence of "personality disorder." In Western psychiatry this term has traditionally referred to sexual deviations, excessive use of drugs or alcohol, and a variety of behaviors that primarily cause trouble for other people rather than for the wrongdoer.

It is of considerable interest that *kunlangeta* and *arankan* are not behaviors that the shamans and healers are believed to be able to cure or change. As a matter of fact, when I pressed this point with the Yoruba healers they denied that these patterns are illness. Both groups, however, believe that specific acts of wrongdoing may make an individual vulnerable to illness or other misfortune. Eskimos, for example, hold to a hunting ethic that prescribes ownership and sharing of animals. If a person cheats in reference to the hunting code, this is thought of as a potential cause of physical or mental illness. Although the social codes among the Yorubas are somewhat different, they also believe that breaking taboos can cause illness. Believing that transgression causes illness is nevertheless quite different from believing that transgression *is* illness.

Even though the Eskimos and Yorubas do not consider these norm violations to be illness and do not send people who exhibit them to healers, they do not lack means for dealing with misconduct. Among the Yorubas, bad conduct is dealt with at many levels, through the kinship system and in native courts. The channels of justice among the Eskimos, though somewhat less formal, follow a similar pattern.

The separation of illness from deviance was similarly reported by Selby (1974), whose work focused on witchcraft as a form of social deviance. While interpreting that his work supports labelling theory, he noted that after "talking about deviance for months" with his Zapotec informants, Selby realized that he had no information on mental illness. When he explored this topic separately he found that this group has the concept of insanity mentioned earlier. Thus it appears that the Zapotecs, like the Eskimos and Yorubas, do not classify mental illness in the same frame of reference with deviance.

While there does not appear to be very much cross-cultural information on the relationship between concepts of illness and concepts of deviance, what information exists suggests that concepts such as *were* and *nuthka-vihak* do not refer to "unnamable rule-breaking," which is simply a residual category after reference has been made to deviant patterns such as lying, cheating, and breaking taboos. Further, at least where the Eskimos and Yorubas are concerned, they exclude from the concept of illness certain patterns that Western psychiatry includes, such as personality disorders and alcohol abuse, and they do not believe that these forms of deviance are responsive to the techniques employed by shamans and healers.

Social Usability

It has been hypothesized by a number of researchers that individuals who fill the role of holy man, shaman, or witchdoctor are psychotic Benedict, 1934; Devereux, 1956; Linton, 1956; Silverman, 1967). Such people are rewarded for their mental illness by being the incumbents of highly regarded social roles. If this is the case, it means that in some cultures psychosis is noted for its social usability, in contrast to the social disability so often associated with it in ours.

The idea of social usability was germinated in descriptions of shamanistic seances such as given here. For example, the Eskimo shamaness mentioned earlier appeared to exhibit a delusion when she became possessed by the spirit of a dog. Another feature that has led to the idea that the healer is psychotic is that the trance state may involve magical flight. Under these circumstances, the healer appears to be hallucinating as he reports what he sees as he journeys into the spirit world to search for the soul whose loss has made his patient ill. "Shaman" is a Siberian term, but is used generally now for the types of healers found elsewhere who conduct curing during ecstatic states. The Bering Sea Eskimos whom I studied have a shamanistic tradition that involves both possession and magical flight. They seem, therefore, to be a group in which social usability might be prominent.

It can be recalled that the Eskimos do not believe the shaman is *nuthkavihak:* "When the shaman is healing he is out of his mind, but he is not crazy." Therefore, it cannot be insanity that, in their eyes, is being put to use in this prestigious role. It could be, however, that some other form of mental illness, possibly a neurotic disorder such as hysteria, is considered essential to what a shaman does, and therefore it is accorded the same respect that the role as a whole commands.

Among the 499 Eskimos, 18 had shamanized at some time in their lives. None of them was described as *nuthkavihak*. Similarly, no other personality characteristic or emotional response was given as typical of all of them. In these regards the shamans seemed to be a random sample of the whole group with no more and no less of the labelled phenomena than was true for those who did not shamanize. The only feature I was able to determine as common to the group was that they shamanized, and that with variable success.

It is important to note that this does not mean that a mad person has never become a shaman. I am sure this has happened sometimes. What seems interesting is that it did not occur among a group of Eskimos in which the shamans outnumbered the psychotics by better than 4 to 1 (if the minor diviners are included, the ratio can conservatively be estimated as 11 to 1) and where the group partakes of a cultural tradition that has been described as making extremely good use of its mentally disordered members. Even in this society, where a role exists that seems well suited to the characteristics of an insane person or a schizophrenic and where the

role is common enough to be open to a range of personalities, the fit
between individual psychopathology and useful social role did not take
place.

In a culture such as this Eskimo one, where clairvoyant kinds of mental
phenomena are encouraged and preternatural experiences are valued,
something similar to what we might call hallucinations and delusions can
probably be learned or simulated. A favorable social reaction is likely to
stabilize the performances of the people who fill the roles of fortune teller
and faith healer. For example, the shamaness whose spirit familiar was a
dog was unable to keep her patient alive, but her *performance* was
considered to have been well executed; she was said to have done "all her
part, acting like a *dog.*" The Eskimos believe that a person can *learn* to
become a shaman, and that the behaviors we might see as indicative of
psychosis are highly controlled and limited to the act of shamanizing.
Their view of *nuthkavihak* is of something that befalls the person, a
pattern of behavioral processes that is beyond voluntary control and that
can appear and disappear in unknown ways, lasting a long time with some
people and a short time with others.

Recently Peters and Price-Williams (1980) reviewed information on 42
cultures in which shamanism is or has been practiced. Their main purpose
was to provide a systematic overview of the characteristics of the altered
states of consciousness that occur during shamanistic rituals. They indicate
that the trance states are usually described as being under voluntary
control, that meaningful communication with spectators customarily takes
place during trance, and that in most instances the shaman has a clear
memory of what occurred. These features led them to the conclusion that
shamanistic trance states are not in and of themselves pathological.

Lending further support for this interpretation is a distinction drawn by
Bourguignon (1976: 38) between ritual trance and the type of dissociation
found in multiple personality: "The great difference between such a
patient and the characteristic Haitian cult initiate—is that these [multiple
personality] dissociations are purely idiosyncratic; the behavior is not
learned by following a cultural model" (emphasis added).

While the ecstatic state may not be pathological, the people who fill the
role may be differentially recruited from among the mentally ill. On this
point Peters and Price-Williams (1980) indicate from their review that
some individual shamans may be mentally ill but that *as a group* they
cannot be considered either abnormal or normal.

In Navajo ethnography considerable attention is given to patterns of
illness that involve seizure, and one of the highly rewarded social roles in
this society is that of the hand-trembler who functions as a diagnostician.

Neutra et al. (1977) studied the possibility of social usability of hysterical disorders by relating them to the hand-trembling role. For purposes of comparison their study also included epileptic disorders. A search of Indian Health Service records allowed 40 patients diagnosed in these 2 categories to be identified and located for investigation 11 years later. The hysterical patients were found to be free of symptoms, while the epileptic patients had continued to experience numerous problems and several had died. Among the combined group, only 2 hysterical patients had been pressed into hand-trembling by their families, but in each case it exacerbated rather than alleviated their symptoms and they eventually retired from the profession. Neutra et al. conclude that the social rewards of the role did not make them function better but rather that their incapacity made it impossible for them "to perform the role adequately if at all." Alternately, however, social stigma seemed to operate to the disadvantage of the epileptic patients in that they experienced significantly more abuse, such as being beaten or raped, and in turn participated in more violence.

Thus there appears to be considerable consensus that non-Western groups do not venerate mental illness by making it a requirement for selecting people into the prestigious roles of shaman and hand-trembler. The availability of these roles does little to channel any substantial numbers of mentally ill into these rewarding professions. When such recruitment sometimes takes place, it does not seem to have the effect of improving the patient's capacity to function.

Social Abusability

If there do not seem to be cultures in which a social role exists that regularly attracts psychotic individuals and in which role performance shapes them into functioning members of society, is the opposite true? Are there cultures that abuse, censure, stigmatize, or alienate their mentally ill in a specifically culturally patterned way? Numerous labelling-oriented reports indicate that degradation of the mentally ill is particularly characteristic of Western culture and that this attitude can be traced even as early as the medieval period, when lunatics were sometimes accused of being witches and were burned at the stake (Sarbin, 1969).

The witch fills a contemptible role in which he or she carries out magic-based acts intended to make other human beings ill or to cause them to die. To associate insanity with this role underscores the lengths to which cultural relativity can be carried. It suggests that the social definition of one pattern of behavior can mold it into such opposing roles as the defamed witch *or* the renowned shaman, the one who causes illness *or* the one who cures it.

Both the Yorubas and the Eskimos have a clearly defined role of witch. Though feared, the man or woman who is believed to use magic in this way is held in low esteem. Is insanity or other mental illness *prima facie* evidence that a person is a witch in these cultures, or at least that he or she will be so accused? If one tries to answer this by identifying the people labelled *were* or *nuthkavihak* and identifying the people labelled as witches and then comparing the two groups to see how much they overlap in membership, as I did regarding the shamans, a serious problem arises. The difficulty is in identifying the witches. Unlike shamanizing, which is a public act, the use of evil magic is exceedingly secretive, and there is not necessarily good agreement among people regarding whom they accuse of such acts.

Among the Eskimos I did note, however, that there was no correspondence between the group of Eskimos said to be insane at some point in their lives and the six people named as *auvinak* (witch) by at least one other Eskimo. The only circumstance that linked a type of mental disorder with witchcraft was that one *auvinak* was said to have persuaded a young mentally retarded Eskimo to gather nail parings and bits of hair from an intended victim so that the *auvinak* could boil them into a concoction which, as it boiled, would make the victim sicken and die. Thus having some kind of mental problem may create vulnerability to the accusation of being an accomplice to this demeaning role, but the relationship is far from uniform and invariant.

In the more general information from the Yoruba healers, it was evident that insanity is often believed to result from the use of evil magic, but that an insane person rarely uses magic against others. Thus my interpretation of whether mental illness is built into the negatively valued role of witch is similar to the view presented about the positively valued role of healer. Some insane people, or those mentally handicapped in other ways, have probably been accused of being witches, but this is by happenstance and not because witching and mental disorder are considered to be the same thing and equally stigmatized.

Another way in which a culture might institutionalize a negative view of mental illness is through a degradation ceremony or ritual slaying. Ceremony is a preservative of custom, and there is voluminous information on ceremonies whereby groups of people enact their negative and positive values. In view of the wide elaboration of different kinds of ceremonies, it is perhaps surprising that no groups seem to have developed the idea of *ceremonially* killing an insane person in the prime of life just because he or she is insane. Infanticide has sometimes been conducted when a child was born grossly abnormal in a way that might later have emerged as brain damage, and it is possible that senility might have been a contributing factor in the live burials practiced in some parts of the world (Rivers, 1926). Also there is no doubt but that insane people have sometimes been "done away with," but such is different from ritual sacrifice. There is no evidence as far as I can determine that killing the insane has ever been standardized as a custom.

There are, on the other hand, numerous indications from non-Western data that the ceremony appropriate for people labelled as mentally deranged is healing (Lambo, 1964; Kiev, 1968; Edgerton, 1969). Even the word "lunatic" associates the phenomena with healing, since it was usually the healer who was believed to have power over such cosmic forces as the lunar changes that were thought to cause insanity.

Regarding the problem of informal actions and attitudes toward the mentally ill, it is difficult to draw conclusions because there is evidence of a wide range of behaviors that can be conceptualized as social reactions. Insane people have been the objects of certain restrictive measures among both the Eskimos and the Yorubas. The Eskimos physically restrain people in violent phases, follow them around, and force them to return home if they run away; and there is one report of an insane man being killed in self-defense when, after killing several dogs, he turned on his family. In describing the Chukchee, a Siberian group known to these Bering Sea Eskimos, Bogoras (1904-1909) reports the case of an insane woman who was tied to a pole during periods of wildness. Teicher (1954) describes, in addition to the coffin-like box mentioned earlier, the use of an igloo with bars across the opening through which food could be passed.

The Yoruba healer of *were* often has 12 to 15 patients in custody at a time. Not infrequently he shackles those who are inclined to run off, and he may use various herbal concoctions for sedation. In Nigeria, where population is much denser than in the Arctic, it is not uncommon to see *were* people wandering about the city streets, sometimes naked, more often dressed in odd assortments of tattered clothing, almost always with long dirt-laden hair, talking to themselves, picking up objects to save.

Asuni (1968), a Yoruba psychiatrist trained in the West, made a study of such vagrant psychotics that bears on the topic of how such people are treated in a non-Western area. The study was motivated by the desire to determine what kinds of psychopathology the vagrant psychotics exhibited and whether they could be helped by modern psychiatric treatment. It involved, however, an effort to find out if there was an unusually high prevalence of such people in Abeokuta, which is the site of a psychiatric hospital complex as well as of several well-known native healers of *were*.

Asuni thought the vagrants might be attracted to the area on these accounts, but enumeration in several other towns suggested that the excess was only slight. The vagrants tended to collect in the central marketplace rather than in the residential areas. They slept in the market stalls at night and were either given food or stole it without the surrounding traders taking action against them unless they become violent. They were found on clinical examination to be mainly schizophrenic with depression unrepresented. Most of the 25 brought into the hospital improved rapidly with treatment but it was difficult to locate interested relatives who would take them back and even more difficult to keep in touch with them for follow-up. The relatives who accepted them were more likely to live in the countryside than in the city. Another census of vagrant psychotics was made in the same city 2 years later and none of the original group was among them, but a similar number of newly arrived vagrants was enumerated.

Asuni's (1968) investigation demonstrates the complexity of social responses to the mentally ill. It indicates that there was considerable tolerance on the part of strangers. Asuni suggests that because the schizophrenics had continued to mix with people, even in the disturbed ways of verbally abusing them and stealing food, they had been preserved from apathy and that this possibly contributed to their rapid improvement. On the other hand, the difficulty in finding relatives who would accept them, the successive generations of vagrant psychotics, and the fact that most towns and cities had a similar number suggest that some types of mentally ill people are not easily integrated with their families.

A case I encountered in Gambia also serves to illustrate that both compassion and rejection are sometimes engaged. The case is a man, identified as insane, who lived some 500 yards outside a village. The villagers lived in thatched mud houses while the madman lived on an abandoned anthill. It was about 2.5 meters long and 1.5 meters high and the top had been worn away to match the contours of his body. Except for occasional visits to the village, he remained on this platform through day and night in all weather. His behavior was said to have become odd when he was a young man, and when I saw him he had not spoken for years, although he sometimes made grunting sounds. In one sense he was as secluded and alienated from his society as back-ward patients are in ours. On the other hand, the villagers always put food out for him and gave him cigarettes. The latter act was accompanied by laughter because the insane man had a characteristic way of bouncing several leaps into the air to get away from anyone who came close to him. This was considered amusing. Once a year, however, someone would forceably bathe him and put new clothes on him.

If one thinks of social intolerance of mental illness as the use of confinement, restraint, or exclusion from the community (or allowing people to confine or exclude themselves), there does not appear to be a great deal of difference between Western and non-Western groups. Furthermore, there seems to be little that is distinctively cultural in the attitudes and actions directed toward the mentally ill, except in the obvious way that an abandoned anthill is not found in the Arctic nor a barred igloo in the tropics. There is apparently a common range of possible responses to the mentally ill person, and the portion of the range brought to bear regarding a particular person is determined more by the nature of his or her behavior than by a preexisting cultural set to respond in a uniform way to whatever is labelled mental illness. If the behavior indicates helplessness, help tends to be given, especially in food and clothes. If the behavior appears foolish or incongruous, even though obviously colored by the distinctive Eskimo and Yoruba views of what is humorous, laughter is the response. If the behavior is noisy and agitated, the response may be to quiet, sometimes by herbs and sometimes by other means. If the behavior is violent or threatening, the response is to restrain or subdue.

Causes

At the level of *describing* the symptomatic expressions of insanity and various other forms of mental disorders, there seems to be much similarity between Western and non-Western groups. The question here concerns the etiological explanations about what causes these patterns of illness. In this regard there is a wide cultural gap, in that non-Western groups regularly invoke causes that are very different from those involved in Western psychiatry.

The causal explanations found among both the Eskimo and Yoruba groups include beliefs that they share with many other non-Western groups. Some of these beliefs have already been mentioned, such as that the insane person has become possessed by a demon or that his or her soul has been taken away by the spirits. These can be thought of as the top layer of explanation, because they suggest the process that is occurring within the individual. Beneath these are deeper layers of explanations regarding why and how the process happens, such as that someone has put a hex on the patient through sorcery, the evil use of magic, or that he or she has broken a taboo and incurred the wrath of a deity or spirit.

Understanding the nature and distribution of these theories of illness was aided first by the work of Clements (1932), followed by numerous others, such as Rogers (1944) and Whiting and Child (1953) and recently by Murdock (1980). This work has established an important point: Most traditional societies lack an etiological system that is specific to mental disorders. Some groups may elaborate a particular idea as relevant to some form of mental disorder, but on the whole the causative frame of reference, especially the deeper layers, applies to all types of illnesses and sometimes equally well to other forms of misfortune.

To illustrate the variable level of specificity of these belief systems, it can be noted that another common idea about the process of illness is that a foreign object rather than a foreign spirit has been introduced into the patient's body. There seems to be some consistency to the explanations of the process of mental illnesses in that they tend to involve spirit intrusion or loss of soul rather than object intrusion. This suggests the commonsense notion that "object" relates to bodily ills while "spirit and soul" affiliate with mental illness. Even this, however, is rarely perfect in its specificity. Loss of soul, for example, is a common explanation for other patterns of illness among many groups.

There are also a few examples in which a specific deep cause, a specific process, and a specific pattern of symptomatology are linked together. *Ichaa* among the Navajo, for example, is a generalized convulsion believed to reflect the process of a moth fluttering in one's head—in this case an object—and being caused specifically by the act of incest (Kaplan and Johnson, 1964; Neutra et al., 1977). An interlocking set of specifications such as this one bears resemblance to the specificity achieved for some of the infectious diseases in Western medicine. On the whole, however, the evidence now available regarding non-Western theories emphasizes their general applicability to illnesses of various kinds.

From his world survey Murdock (1980: 20-26) has attempted to provide an overview of the most prominent and widespread causes in rank order. The first is the belief that illness is caused by the "hostile, arbitrary, or punitive action of some malevolent or affronted supernatural being" such as a ghost, spirit, or deity. Next is the belief that the cause resides in the "covert actions of an envious, affronted, or malicious human being" who uses magical means "either independently or with the assistance of a specialized magician." And third is the belief that the cause is "violation of some taboo or moral injunction" that is not mediated through a supernatural being. Thus repeated extensively throughout the ethnographic literature are the beliefs that illness generally is caused by an angry God, by the malevolence of a fellow human being, or by the transgressions carried out by the patient himself—in other words, "God," "other," or "self."

It is of interest that some of the patterns of illness that have usually been thought of as culture-bound, such as one that has been variously called *espanto* or *susto* and reported in various Latin American, Mexican, and southwest United States areas, has recently been re-presented as a theory rather than as a medical syndrome (Tousignant, 1979). It is a theory of the influence of spirits in causing illness and fits well with Murdock's formulation of the most prevalent explanation. The symptoms that have been associated with this presumed syndrome are as various as loss of appetite, pain in the ear, fever, and swollen feet. It seems appropriate to suggest that in the search for what is distinctively cultural, the theory was mistaken for an illness. This probably derives from the fact that the theories *are culturally patterned,* while the symptoms tend to take the same form everywhere. Because etiological explanations play such a crucial role in the way healers, patients, and others talk about illness, it may be that descriptive similarities in clusters of symptoms have at times been overlooked.

The inclination for patients to explain their illnesses in etiological terms was shown in a study of hypertension in a Western medical setting (Blumhagen, 1980). The patients tended to believe they suffered "Hyper-Tension" in which symptoms, process, and causes were linked together, with the causes being various kinds of social stresses, health behaviors, or constitutional proclivities to be high strung. The physicians and nurses, on the other hand, emphasized that hypertension is a disease of unknown etiology.

These observations about the cultural patterning of etiological explanations and the importance of theory in the way patients and native healers describe illness provide a way to emphasize what seems to be a starkly contrasting element between Western psychiatry at the present time and non-Western views. The classification systems that have evolved in the West emphasize the descriptive similarities of specific syndromes of mental disorders, and most of these categories are now formulated nonetiologically (American Psychiatric Association, 1980; Wing et al., 1974). The purpose of this atheoretical approach to classification is to lay the foundation for subsequent testing of theories. In contrast, the non-Western classification systems tend to place major emphasis on cause. While recognition of descriptive similarities is certainly not absent, the patterning of symptoms seems to play a lesser role. On the whole, the non-Western classifications are applied and interpreted as theory-confirming systems rather than as theory-testing systems.

Further, the etiological explanations seem to have a powerful influence generally on the way people talk and feel about their illnesses. Being able to explain seems to provide comfort. Whether believing that incest is what caused one to fall ill is right or wrong, whether believing that one's soul has been captured is valid or not—these questions are not the issue. The issue is only that these beliefs exemplify culture. They embody the learned social heritage of the group of people who enact them.

Kleinman (1977: 4) has suggested that disease is an explanatory model, not an entity. He suggests that in "comparing diseases one is always comparing explanations not entities." It is this orientation that leads him to conclude that "culture shapes disease first by shaping our explanations of disease." This review suggests a different conclusion. While culture shapes explanations, the patterns of symptoms that people describe as different types of mental disorders are more remarkable for their similarities across cultures than for their shaped differences.

Treatment

Like the causal framework, the patterns of treatment are strongly patterned by culture. By and large, what is done to cure a patient flows from what is believed to cause the illness. There is considerable evidence that indigenous healers have learned and practiced a number of treatments that are unrelated to the causal network, such as splinting, bone-setting, bandaging, and the use of herbs. Even these tend to occur, however, in settings where the causes outlined earlier are addressed and where ritual acts emphasizing the return of the patient to a state of health are highly elaborated.

The curing rituals employed in non-Western areas have been described extensively in the ethnographic literature and some elements have been discussed here in describing shamans and Yoruba healers. Of particular relevance is a study by Prince (1964) of 46 Yoruba healers who specialized in the treatment of mental disorders, especially *were,* and of 101 such cases cared for in 16 native treatment centers. He concludes that the treatment is often effective although relapses are frequent and patients tend to circulate between Western facilities and native healers.

Usually herbs of various types are employed. Rauwolfia is prominent among them, but others used include purgatives and various kinds of sedatives. These are combined with a wide variety of admission, treatment, and discharge ceremonies based on rituals that relate to the perceived cause. If the patient is not responding, the healer may change the medication. "He sometimes decides on the cause in this way; that is, he gives the patient *epe* (curse) medicine, and, if that does not cause improvement, he decides that it is *Sopono's* [the god of smallpox] work and applies *ero Sopono* (Prince, 1964: 98-99).

The main reason given by the Yoruba healers for their inability to cure some patients is that the fee has not been completely paid. The Eskimo shamans in my study also indicated that the common reason for therapeutic failure was that the specified fee, such as a special type of valuable bead, had not been forthcoming. This feature, along with changes in the healer's etiological interpretations over the course of treatment, indicates that these practices tend to be theory-confirming.

To indicate the therapeutic effectiveness of the ritual component of treatment, Prince reports the case of a severe neurotic. Over four years this patient had been treated without relief by several practitioners, both indigenous and Western. Following this he underwent a native treatment program, which involved only the ritual-based therapies of several sacrificial ceremonies and initiation into a healing cult. Over a subsequent thirteen-month period he remained asymptomatic.

In summarizing the psychotherapeutic elements that seem to be effective, Prince points first to the importance of suggestion, where, among other aspects, the discharge ceremony is organized to display ritually that the illness has passed out of the patient. Also significant is the role of direct command, as when the healer tells the patient: "Stop behaving like a madman!" "Be quiet!" "Don't be rude!" "Don't listen to those voices!" (Prince, 1964: 111.) Sacrifice of animals is the cornerstone of Yoruba healing, and Prince (1964: 113) reports that many patients remarked on their "ability to relax and have a good night's sleep following sacrifice ritual." Also important are recommendations regarding lifestyle, such as instructing a patient to move his or her location or change occupation in order to avoid contact with witches or sorcerers. Other elements concern ego-strengthening activities such as recommendations to join healing cults to prevent relapses, which also indicates that group support plays a prominent role in the therapeutic network.

This study is one of the most comprehensive in terms of its sampling of healers and patients and its effort to gain follow-up information. Nevertheless it shares with most of the studies of native healing the aspect that the effectiveness of treatment is only indirectly assessed. There do not appear to be any studies in which outcomes from one type of non-Western therapy have been systematically compared to another type, nor non-Western therapy compared systematically to Western therapy.

Outcome

While little quantitative information exists regarding the effectiveness of indigenous treatment in comparison to Western, a recent study of schizophrenia sponsored by the World Health Organization (1973, 1979; Sartorius et al., 1978) has pointed to marked contrasts in outcome between patients treated in Western psychiatric facilities in the developed as contrasted to the developing countries. This study took place in nine countries: China, Colombia, Czechoslovakia, Denmark, India, Nigeria, the Union of Soviet Socialist Republics, the United Kingdom, and the United States. It involved clinical diagnosis as well as standardized procedures for eliciting information about mental disorders. It contributes quite conclusive evidence that the pattern of psychiatric symptoms known as schizophrenia exists in all of these areas.

At the end of a 2-year follow-up, it was clear that more schizophrenic patients in the developing countries were in a favorable condition than those in the developed countries (Sartorius et al., 1978). While an equal number of patients—approximately one-quarter—from both the developed and developing countries were in a "very unfavorable" condition at this time, more than twice as many patients from developing countries were in a "very favorable" condition. The center that had by far the best outcome results was the mental hospital in Abeokuta, Nigeria.

The World Health Organization findings are not the only ones that indicate this difference. Murphy and Raman (1971) report that over a 12-year follow-up, schizophrenic patients of Indian and African origins treated in a mental hospital on the island of Mauritius were more likely to have a favorable outcome than a comparable sample in the United Kingdom, though in both sites approximately one-third of the patients remained chronically ill. Comparable information has been reported by Waxler (1977, 1979) for a group of schizophrenic patients followed over 5 years after receiving Western psychiatric treatment in Sri Lanka.

Against the background of work such as Asuni's (1968) concerning vagrant psychotics and Prince's (1964) concerning the frequent relapses of patients treated by native healers, it is of great interest that non-Western patients treated by Western-trained psychiatrists in Western psychiatric facilities should show a better prognosis than Western patients treated in Western facilities. The interest is heightened where Nigeria is concerned because the work of Asuni, Prince, and the World Health Organization study all took place in the same general area.

A question raised by studies that deal with hospital-treated cases is whether this type of patient population reflects a selection that is atypical of what would be found through a community epidemiological approach. Westermeyer (1980) reports a study carried out in Laos in which subjects identified as *baa*, the Lao term for insanity, were located in 27 villages. Case reports and photographic materials were rated independently later by U.S. psychiatrists who suggested that schizophrenia was the most common pattern among these cases, although a smaller number were thought to have organic or affective psychoses. Using a social rating scale, several village informants per case were asked about the current functioning of the *baa* people. Most of them were found to be dependent on other people for basic necessities and to have become "alienated from family and friends" and to have "ceased recreational and communal activities" (Westermeyer, 1980: 1393). These cases had not been treated in Western psychiatric facilities since there are none in Laos, and it was not reported whether or not they had received indigenous treatment.

A study such as this, which indicates a poor prognosis for indigenously identified psychotic cases not located through hospital services, highlights the importance of learning why schizophrenic patients in developing countries should have a better rate of improvement following Western hospital treatment than their counterparts in developed countries.

Waxler (1977, 1979) has suggested that the better prognosis of schizophrenic patients in nonindustrialized countries relates to cultural expectations. She suggests that "following social labelling theory and beginning with the assumption that mental illness is socially constructed and socially modeled, our attention is immediately directed to the qualities of these cultures themselves that influence the patient's illness career" (Waxler, 1979: 157). She suggests that the capacity of traditional societies to accomplish the molding of outcome lies in four factors: (1) the giving of messages that call for a quick return to normality, (2) the strength of family responsibility for accepting the patient, (3) the availability of alternate forms of therapy that allow the patient and his family to seek a healing approach compatible with their belief systems, and (4) the fact that mental illness is believed to be caused by external forces, such as in supernatural or natural events, rather than in the patient's personality or social past. In indicating the effectiveness of cultural expectations conveyed in messages to the effect that the patient should get well, Waxler notes that in Sri Lanka the cost of remaining chronically ill is much greater than in Western societies. The chronically ill "are threatened not only by barren lives but also, ultimately, by lack of food and shelter and, most significant, loss of family ties" (Waxler, 1977: 248). This suggests that if the outcome for patients is better in nonindustrialized societies it stems partly from the coercive influence of the threats incurred by noncompliance. Are these societies, perhaps, more strict and intolerant of a patient's behavior than Western society?

While one can question whether family responsibility can always be counted on, in view of the information on vagrancy, and whether mental illness is always believed to be caused by external sources, in view of the commonness of the transgression etiology, the weight of Waxler's argument is on the molding force of culturally patterned messages.

If a communication system of messages is to be called cultural, it must refer to the regular ways in which a group of people quite uniformly speak that distinguish them from other peoples. Benedict (1934), for example, thought of culture as the "unconscious canons of choice" that one learns as part of one's social heritage. Thus the question can be raised as to whether peoples of traditional societies automatically and with a sense of its embodying their laws and rules choose to give messages to ill people that are different from those in Western culture.

It seems well established that during the culturally patterned native curing rites, many messages are indeed given to the effect that the patient has been made well. These messages are supported by a thick symbolic structure that probably does much to strengthen their influence. Among the Eskimos, for example, one of the discharge acts is to give a patient, especially a child, a new name. Because names are considered to be souls and to be sex-linked, this sometimes means that the shaman prescribes that the patient, at least for a time, wear clothing and carry out the tasks of the opposite sex. These changes are believed to have the effect of fooling the evil spirit who sought to capture the former soul of the newly named person. It can be interpreted that this continuously enacted form of protection encourages the ex-patient and his or her family that health can now be sustained. Encouragement is probably very useful to the recovery process. It is possible that these kinds of "get well" messages also pervade the less structured everyday interactions of native peoples more than they do in the West. Perhaps the direct commands of the Yoruba healer, "Stop acting like a madman and don't listen to those voices," also carry over into informal interactions more commonly than in the West. Perhaps they, too, have a therapeutic effect, at least in some cases. It seems very doubtful, however, that they are culturally standardized in the way the rituals of curing and the beliefs about cause are. Can they be counted on the way one can count on most people being able to speak an intelligible version of their mother tongue?

If such messages are a regular and distinguishing pattern of communication in traditional societies and if they are effective in helping a schizophrenic patient to recover, why do they not have more universal influence? Not only is there the fact that a rather steady one-quarter to one-third of the schizophrenic patients treated in Western psychiatric facilities do not improve, no matter where they live, but also there is evidence that the messages, if they exist, seem to fail to speak to substantial numbers of people suffering from similar patterns of symptoms who are treated by the native healers of these traditional societies or who are not treated at all.

SUMMARY AND CONCLUSIONS

This chapter opened with a series of quotations about the molding force of culture, starting with that of Ruth Benedict about the malleability of human endowment and the relativity of abnormal behavior. A conclusion she drew from her studies is this:

> There can be no reasonable doubt that one of the most effective ways in which to deal with the staggering burden of psychopathic [sic] tragedies in America at the present time is by means of an educational program which fosters tolerance in society and a kind of self-respect and independence that is foreign to . . . our urban traditions [Benedict, 1934: 273-274].

The materials reported and reviewed here suggest that in the last 50 years the picture has been vastly complicated in the way that Geertz (1973) indicates is typical of scientific advancement. The interpretation I make of the evidence is that psychosis, especially a process such as schizophrenia, has remarkably similar features and is widely distributed around the world. This suggests that the causes of insanity, whether genetic or experiential, are ubiquitous in human groups. Because psychosis takes a rather similar form in all the diverse societies in which it is found, it seems to show less malleability to cultural molding than some other forms of behavior.

Everywhere investigated, this pattern of symptomatology seems to have been given a name. It does not appear, therefore, to be an unnamable affront against each culture's unique and reified standard of decency and reality. Even its manifestations of imagery and ideation, though colored by cultural patterns, are not inextricably bound to them in any standard way. By knowing a culture, it has not, in other words, proved possible to predict what form either schizophrenia or other patterns, such as hysteria, will take.

In addition to the fact that the patterns of mental disorders, especially the most severe ones, are similar across cultures, it has also become evident that irrespective of cultures the most common course of action is to take a person upon whom these afflictions have fallen to a healer. In this regard, too, insanity appears to be viewed in a different frame of reference from the deviance of rule breaking. Where evidence exists, it appears that deviance in this latter sense is not considered an illness and is not treated by traditional healers.

Social reactions to the phenomena of insanity appear in many cultures to be mixed, ambivalent, complex, and more determined by situational factors than by a culturally standardized pattern to respond one way rather than another. There is no evidence that a culture exists that can regularly recruit an insane person into a prestigious role and thereby shape him or her into a functioning member of society. Among the groups described here, psychosis seems commonly associated with social disability. While suggestive evidence exists that prognosis for schizophrenic patients treated in modern facilities may be better in developing than developed countries, evidence is lacking that in these societies culturally standardized messages are regularly able to cure the mentally ill.

The aspects of mental disorders that do show pronounced cultural molding are the beliefs held about what causes them and what the healer should do to cure them. These explanatory beliefs have patterned regularities that appear over and over again throughout traditional societies. This suggests that they have diffused widely and have been tenacious in their hold on the social heritage of many groups of peoples. They refer to a powerfully simple way of understanding misfortune. It must be God's fault; if it is not God's, it must be your fault; and if not your's, it must be my fault. Although it may be comforting to be able to offer such explanations, it seems doubtful that the problems posed by a disorder such as schizophrenia will be brought under control by actions that flow from these etiological orientations any more than by the patterns of tolerance recommended by Benedict.

REFERENCES

American Psychiatric Association (1980) Diagnostic and Statistical Manual of Mental Disorders. 3rd ed. Washington, DC: Author.

ASUNI, T. (1968) "Vagrant psychotics in Abeokuta." Deuxième Colloque Africain de Psychiatrie. Paris: Association Universitaire pour le Développement de l'Enseignement et de la Culture en Afrique et à Madagascar.

BEISER, M., W. BURR, J. RAVEL, and H. COLLOMB (1973) "Illnesses of the spirit among the Serer of Senegal." American Journal of Psychiatry 130: 881-886.
BENEDICT, R. (1934) Patterns of Culture. (Reprinted in 1959.) Boston: Houghton Mifflin.
BLUMHAGEN, D. (1980) "Hyper-Tension: a folk illness with a medical name." Culture, Medicine and Psychiatry 4: 197-227.
BOGORAS, W. (1904-1909) The Chukchee. New York: American Museum of Natural History.
BOURGUIGNON, E. (1976) Possession. San Francisco: Chandler and Sharp.
BROWN, R. (1973) "Schizophrenia, language, and reality." American Psychologist 28: 395-403.
BURTON-BRADLEY, B. G. (1973) Stone Age Crisis: A Psychiatric Appraisal. Nashville, TN: Vanderbilt University Press.
CARSTAIRS, G. M. and R. L. KAPUR (1976) The Great Universe of Kota: Stress, Change, and Mental Disorder in an Indian Village. Berkeley: University of California Press.
CAWTE, J. (1972) Cruel, Poor and Brutal Nations: The Assessment of Mental Health in an Australian Aboriginal Community. Honolulu: University of Hawaii Press.
CLEMENTS, F. (1932) Primitive Concepts of Disease. Berkeley: University of California Publications in American Archeology and Ethnology.
deREUCK, A. and R. PORTER [eds.] (1965) Transcultural Psychiatry: A Ciba Foundation Symposium. London: Churchill.
DEVEREUX, G. (1956) "Normal and abnormal: the key problem of psychiatric anthropology," in J. B. Casagrande and T. Gladwin (eds.) Some Uses of Anthropology: Theoretical and Applied. Washington, DC: Anthropological Society of Washington.
EDGERTON, R. B. (1969) "On the recognition of mental illness," in S. C. Plog and R. B. Edgerton (eds.) Changing Perspectives in Mental Illness. New York: Holt, Rinehart & Winston.
——— (1966) "Conceptions of psychosis in four East African societies." American Anthropologist 68: 408-425.
FIELD, M. J. (1960) Search for Security: An Ethnopsychiatric Study of Rural Ghana. Chicago: Northwestern University Press.
FOULKS, E. (1972) The Arctic Hysterias of the North Alaskan Eskimo. Washington, DC: American Anthropological Association.
GEERTZ, C. (1973) The Interpretation of Cultures. New York: Basic Books.
GEERTZ, H. (1968) "Latah in Java: a theoretical paradox." Indonesia 5: 93-104.
GOFFMAN, E. (1962) Asylums: Essays on the Social Situation of Mental Patients and Other Inmates. Chicago: Aldine.
GUSSOW, Z. (1960) " 'Pibloktoq' (hysteria) among polar Eskimos," in W. Muensterberger (ed.) Psychoanalysis and the Social Sciences. New York: International University Press.
HONIGMANN, J. (1967) Personality in Culture. New York: Harper & Row.
HUGHES, C. C. (1960) An Eskimo Village in the Modern World. Ithaca, NY: Cornell University Press.
KAPLAN, B. and D. JOHNSON (1964) "The social meaning of Navaho psychopathology and psychotherapy," in A. Kiev (ed.) Magic, Faith, and Healing. New York: Macmillan.

KENNEDY, D. (1961) "Key issues in the cross-cultural study of mental disorders,"
    in B. Kaplan (ed.) Studying Personality Cross-Culturally. New York: Row,
    Peterson.
KIEV, A. (1972) Transcultural Psychiatry. New York: Macmillan.
——— (1968) Curanderismo: Mexico-American Folk Psychiatry. New York:
    Macmillan.
KLEINMAN, A. (1977) "Depression, somatization and the 'new cross-cultural
    psychiatry.' " Social Science and Medicine 11: 3-10.
LAMBO, T. A. (1964) "Patterns of psychiatric care in developing African countries,"
    in A. Kiev (ed.) Magic, Faith, and Healing. New York: Macmillan.
LEIGHTON, A. H. and J. M. MURPHY (1964) "The problem of cultural distortion,"
    in R. M. Acheson (ed.) Comparability in International Epidemiology. New York:
    Milbank Memorial Fund.
LEIGHTON, A. H., T. A. LAMBO, C. C. HUGHES, D. C. LEIGHTON, J. M. MUR-
    PHY, and D. B. MACKLIN (1963) Psychiatric Disorder Among the Yoruba.
    Ithaca, NY: Cornell University Press.
LINTON, R. (1956) Culture and Mental Disorders. Springfield, IL: Charles C
    Thomas.
MURDOCK, G. (1980) Theories of Illness: A World Survey. Pittsburgh: University of
    Pittsburgh Press.
MURPHY, H. and A. RAMAN (1971) "The chronicity of schizophrenia in indigenous
    tropical peoples: results of a twelve-year follow-up survey in Mauritius." British
    Journal of Psychiatry 118: 489-497.
MURPHY, J. M. (1976) "Psychiatric labeling in cross-cultural perspective." Science
    191: 1019-1028.
——— (1964) "Psychotherapeutic aspects of shamanism on St. Lawrence Island,
    Alaska," in A. Kiev (ed.) Magic, Faith, and Healing. New York: Macmillan.
——— [formerly Hughes] (1960) "An epidemiological study of psychopathology in
    an Eskimo village." Ph.D. dissertation, Cornell University. University Microfilms
    60-6457.
MURPHY, J. M. and C. C. HUGHES (1965) "The use of psychophysiological
    symptoms as indicators of disorder among Eskimos," in J. M. Murphy and A. H.
    Leighton (eds.) Approaches to Cross-Cultural Psychiatry. Ithaca, NY: Cornell
    University Press.
MURPHY, J. M. and A. H. LEIGHTON (1965) "Native conceptions of psychiatric
    disorder," in J. M. Murphy and A. H. Leighton (eds.) Approaches to Cross-
    Cultural Psychiatry. Ithaca, NY: Cornell University Press.
NEUTRA, R., J. LEVY, and D. PARKER (1977) "Cultural expectations versus
    reality in Navajo seizure patterns and sick roles." Culture, Medicine and Psychi-
    atry 1: 255-275.
OHNUKI-TIERNEY, E. (1980) "Ainu illness and healing: a symbolic interpretation."
    American Ethnologist 7: 132-151.
PARKER, S. (1960) "The Wittiko psychosis in the context of Ojibwa personality and
    culture." American Anthropologist 62: 603-623.
PETERS, L. and D. PRICE-WILLIAMS (1980) "Towards an experiential analysis of
    shamanism." American Ethnologist 7: 397-418.
PRINCE, R. (1964) "Indigenous Yoruba psychiatry," in A. Kiev (ed.) Magic, Faith,
    and Healing. New York: Macmillan.

RIVERS, W.H.R. (1926) Psychology and Ethnology. New York: Harcourt Brace Jovanovich.

ROGERS, S. (1944) "Disease concepts in North America." American Anthropologist 46: 559-564.

ROSENHAN, D. L. (1973) "On being sane in insane places." Science 179: 250-258.

SARBIN, T. R. (1969) "The scientific status of the mental illness metaphor," in S. C. Plog and R. B. Edgerton (eds.) Changing Perspectives in Mental Illness. New York: Holt, Rinehart & Winston.

SARTORIUS, N., A. JABLENSKY, and R. SHAPIRO (1978) "Cross-cultural differences in the short-term prognosis of schizophrenic psychoses." Schizophrenia Bulletin 4: 102-113.

SCHEFF, T. J. (1966) Being Mentally Ill: A Sociological Theory. Chicago: Aldine.

SELBY, H. A. (1974) Zapotec Deviance: The Convergence of Folk and Modern Sociology. Austin: University of Texas Press.

SILVERMAN, J. (1967) "Shamans and acute schizophrenia." American Anthropologist 69: 21-31.

TEICHER, M. I. (1960) Windigo Psychosis. Seattle: American Ethnological Society.

––– (1954) "Three cases of psychosis among the Eskimos." Journal of Mental Science 100: 527-535.

TOUSIGNANT, M. (1979) "Espanto: a dialogue with the gods." Culture, Medicine and Psychiatry 3: 347-361.

WAXLER, N. (1979) "Is outcome for schizophrenia better in nonindustrialized societies? The case of Sri Lanka." Journal of Nervous and Mental Diseases 167: 144-158.

––– (1977) "Is mental illness cured in traditional societies? A theoretical analysis." Culture, Medicine and Psychiatry 1: 233-253.

WESTERMEYER, J. (1980) "Psychosis in a peasant society: social outcomes." American Journal of Psychiatry 137: 1390-1394.

WHITING, J. and I. CHILD (1953) Child Training and Personality. New Haven, CT: Yale University Press.

WHITING, J.W.M. and B. B. WHITING (1973) "Altruistic and egoistic behavior in six cultures," in L. Nader and T. W. Maretzki (eds.) Cultural Illness and Health. Washington, DC: American Anthropological Association.

WING, J., J. COOPER, and N. SARTORIUS (1974) The Measurement and Classification of Psychiatric Symptoms. London: Cambridge University Press.

WINIARCZ, W. and J. WILAWSKI (1936) "Imu." Psychoanalytic Review 23: 181-184.

World Health Organization (1979) Schizophrenia: An International Follow-Up Study. Sussex: John Wiley.

––– (1973) The International Pilot Study of Schizophrenia. Geneva: Author.

YAP, P. (1974) Comparative Psychiatry: A Theoretical Framework (M. P. Lau and A. B. Stokes, eds.). Toronto: University of Toronto Press.

––– (1952) "The Latah reaction: its pathodynamic and nosological position." Journal of Mental Science 98: 515-568.

LABELLING SOMEONE MENTALLY ILL
A Case Study

ANONYMOUS

This chapter explores the application of the label of mental illness to someone who knew about mental illness and thought it would never get personal.

The authors were raised in small towns of the South and West during the cold war years. We entered college with the civil rights movement of the 1960s, on the leading edge of the baby boom's emergence into politics. As with other youthful recruits to the national culture then, our adolescent fancies turned toward social "causes" of that age; and our WASPish heritage provided "education" as a magic social problem-solving tool (with incidental effects on middle-class mobility). We were among the mass of small-town kids who "went away to college" in the sixties, and there we discovered the social sciences.

We met in graduate school during the halcyon years of demonstrations and draft deferments, expanding enrollments, and plentiful fellowships. We married, received our Ph.D.s, published in respected journals, and accepted teaching positions at a modest university. We voted for student power, abandonment of grades, "relevance," and sometime socialists; against Nixon, pollution, and lethal food-like substances. We bought a house, planted a garden, raised a mongrel, and made granola, love, and friends. And with salaries greater than our parents ever knew, we drifted comfortably toward the nervous breakdown that came in our fourth year of marriage to dismember it: nightmares screaming through the daytime, nighttime, interminable years of nightmares, still, the central theme of which was murderous, raging, suicidal despair.

Literally millions of Americans were hospitalized for some type of mental breakdown during the 1970s. We are not unusual in coming to know how it feels. When perceived as the experience or fate of an individual, it feels like a breakdown in the psychological integrity or coherence of someone's "mind"—an organically healthy someone, usually, who is also (by a remarkable ratio of three to two in this society) a female. A woman's mind appears to crack. We are not unusual on that count, either. It was Elly who cracked.

When perceived as the shattering of normal routines, of families or other social systems in which a person might participate, one's "breakdown" appears in another guise. It appears that something greater than a single person cracks; and the integrity of some conscience more collective than a single mind breaks down. A marriage crumbles, a career disintegrates, friendships dissolve, and a thousand common hopes and expectations fade like unrecorded dreams. If we encountered a breakdown in this guise, we are not unusual in that either. The average mental patient is not simply female; she is intimately and crucially involved in social relationships. And her personal distress is often first perceived in the breaking down of those relationships.

If ours differed from other breakdowns of the day, the difference may lie in the academic preparations we carried on our way. Between us, we have consumed more course syllabi prepared by more certified psychologists and social scientists than one would want to count; we have accumulated several advanced degrees; we have offered college courses in social psychology, medical sociology, deviant behavior, women's studies, and other fields of possible relevance; and we have published as many academic articles in those areas. We have received tens of thousands of dollars for a single year's performances at accredited universities, as "professional" social scientists. We are experts, of a sort. And if we differ from others on this count, we report as experts now that it made no difference then.

We were completely unprepared for what happened to our lives; totally inadequate to the challenge of living with it or comprehending it. After seven years' possession of a breakdown and its aftermath, literally hundreds of consultations with psychiatrists, countless hours spent intellectualizing if not quite rationalizing the experience—after this mutual obsession and on top of a successful recovery, we cannot say what happened or why.

Coincidentally we find ourselves in the position of professionally trained participant-observers, recently emerged from years in the field. If our confusions in the face of mental abnormality are not precisely disciplinary, they nevertheless describe the "state of the art" in this field.

The following notes are culled from diaries, recorded conversations, and custom-tailored reminiscences. They are packaged here, but unrefined. The rawness of the data they present is suggested by dates, while pseudonyms identify our separate points of view. Here is the first entry in Elly's diary, written after nine months' gestation in psychotherapy. She addresses her therapist, exploring what he might call "transference," at a time when she felt (and sometimes thought) he might be turning to stone.

September 21, 1974
Elly (Saturday)

I am angry, because you treat me as my mother did. "Your headaches are not real," she would say. "Your problems are inventions. They're all in you head." And now you tell me I can ride the bus.

Nothing will happen, you say. "I'll be with you" (never in person, of course, but psychologically). My fears are irrational. Unreal. I think you do not know what it is to be afraid. It is real. And it makes me angry when you treat me as if I invented this all in my head.

Maybe it's that I see you as inhuman (like her). I tell you my reasons for killing myself, and you say that's "intriguing." I am afraid to get on a bus, and you don't understand. I wish you could be more human with me.

So I get angry, because you're like her. And I tell you I'm angry (although I can do it only indirectly). Then I'm terrified—because I know I wanted to hurt you. And even when I scream "I DON'T NEED YOU!" in your office, I am afraid I have pushed you away. I am overly demanding, no good, and difficult. And to protect yourself, you are turning into stone.

I am afraid I turned her to stone, and that I'm doing the same to you. I am sorry, very sorry—I don't want to turn you into stone. I am sorry. But I understand that you must do it to protect yourself. I know you hate me, and I don't blame you. I hate myself.

Ed

Does this sound crazy? Troubled, certainly. Dramatic, and perhaps extreme. But she has always had a flair for dramatizing things; and troubles abound.

Her psychiatrist told me she was "near psychotic" several weeks before she wrote this. She was a "very sick woman," he said, her childhood was a living hell. We had been living in limbo for some time by then, with occasional glimpses of what you might call hell. But the question we have never answered is whether she was crazy or not.

She could not ride the bus. That was a minor incapacity, becoming an issue in her therapy only when I brought it up. She could no longer drive. She could not enter a restaurant or a movie theater, and she found supermarkets difficult. She was working part time as a clerk in a health food store when she wrote this, and that was the only place outside the house where she could feel safe without me. The radius of "safe" journeys for her, even when encapsulated in the car and in my company, even when we waited until midnight to venture onto empty streets, extended perhaps five miles from the bedroom—where she spent much of her time alone, immersed in television or imaginary conversations with her therapist.

She had lost thirty pounds, a quarter of her normal body mass, while reliving in her waking life the emotional reality of innumerable nightmares by this time. She was feeling worse and more desperate, month by month. She had planned her suicide a hundred times. And with prodding from me, her therapist was beginning to discuss the possibility that she might more easily find help from someone else—an impossibility to her mind, in the light of her all-consuming dependency. To write that he was turning into stone may or may not have been intended metaphorically under the circumstances. The salient fact was that semantics hardly mattered now. Whether by Medusa's head or therapeutic alchemy, his transmutation threatened her with inexpressible loss.

Shall we call her "crazy," then? "Near psychotic" sounds technically accurate—until you try to define "psychotic" and wonder how "near" it is. Then it just sounds technical. Perhaps we might more simply label this "poetic license" in the dramatic portrayal of her childhood hell. The intensity and the drama of her feelings seem remarkable. But the feelings themselves are common enough in their different prosaic ways.

How was Elly different, then? She didn't look out of place sitting in a graduate seminar, the day I met her. What path was she following, before and after that day, to the point where one might reasonably ask whether to call her insane? We will approach these questions by organizing our remembrances to provide minimal descriptions of her family history, the onset of "symptoms" and development of symptomatology, the initiation and course of her "treatment," and the psychodynamics of her "illness" insofar as either of us has come to understand it.

These terms in quotes are marked to call attention to the medical model from which they derive. In describing Elly's case in these terms, we raise questions concerning the adequacy of that model to the conceptual problems we faced. Inevitably in the state and culture where we found ourselves, our definition of the situation involved the application of labels such as "mental illness" and related terms like "neurosis," "psychosis," etc. But it involved much more than this. It involved our attempt to define the *content* of such labels, too, in the process of using them. What does "illness" mean from day to day, to middle-class academicians in a situation providing neither germs nor organic disorders to focus on, when one of us (and sometimes both) is flipping out of her mind? What exactly does the "sick" role involve on a Saturday morning in September of 1974? And how did we decide?

We can do little more than pose these questions and document the process by which we defined our lives as we lived them, without abstracting them entirely from the context in which they broke down. Although current models of mental health and illness reflect the cultural presumption that life is lived by individuals, we lived it immersed in our relationship. On looking back it seems that terms like "illness," "breakdown," "symptom," even "treatment," refer to phenomena which might be conceptualized as properties of human relationships as well as individuals. Thus in putting together an account of our breakdown, we unavoidably describe the experience of a marriage as well as that of either one of us individually.

Our marriage at times seemed mentally, emotionally, spiritually ill. The symptoms of its illness consisted of interlocking behavioral patterns that if examined as the properties of Elly or me individually, looked "neurotic" or "psychotic" primarily because they failed so flagrantly as strategies in our relationship. If in other relationships one looks mentally "ill," this seems evidenced again by the games played; and the games are rarely solitary. To call such illness "mental" is perhaps correct. But in our experience it is certainly "relational" as well.

Although the form of our relationship and its fault lines were unique in some ways, we did not invent this marriage in our heads. These notes describe a single instance of an institutional form that is licensed by the state and embedded in a cultural milieu we have all experienced. Since our view of this particular breakdown remains obscured by our peculiar subjectivities, we cannot clearly conceptualize that general institutional form, its sicknesses and symptoms, or its breakdowns. But in juxtaposing individual subjectivities, we hope at least to suggest what a breakdown might look like when viewed as the objective experience of a relationship.

SOCIAL HISTORY

Elly

When I was little, I was really a ham. My father loved it. He would say, "Elly, show us what happens when the cowboy's wife dies," and I would take off my cowboy hat and roll it up, twisting it in my hands over my heart, and people would clap. He took me to see *Annie Get Your Gun* at the movies one time. There's a scene in it where Annie Oakley is polishing her gun, and this guy walks up and they fall in love. This is what I did for part of my act, I'd be polishing my gun. This guy in the movie says, "What're you doing?" and Annie says back, "Ain't you got eyes?" Then she looks up into these big blue eyes of his and she says, "Yeah, you got eyes." He sings to her then, "Be My Love." So I used to sing that in my act. My mother almost killed me at my relatives' in Baton Rouge. We visited them one time, and after I did my act I passed the hat around for them to put money in.

Starting in second grade, the teachers would have me ad lib stories at "rest time" for the other kids. I would get up in front of the class with no idea what I would say, and soon they'd be rolling in the aisles. In fourth grade, they would send me to the first-grade class if the teacher got sick, and I'd read stories to the younger kids and keep them occupied all day.

In this little school I went to, I had the same teacher in second, fourth, and seventh grades. In seventh grade I never said a word. If I thought about speaking, my heart would beat so fast I thought I would die. My teacher called by mother, she told me later, and said, "Something is wrong with Elly. What happened to her?" I don't know; but something went wrong around puberty.

I never had a boyfriend in high school, but everybody liked me. I don't know why. I was very self-conscious and often anxious, once I got to seventh grade; and then I started being afraid of thunderstorms. Ever since, whenever there's been a thunderstorm, I've had to go sit in a closet or a hallway where I couln't see the lightning. It's a long-standing phobia.

My father divorced my mother when I was seventeen, and it was a tremendous ordeal, a town scandal. I think I can truthfully say that I never loved my mother, ever. But I always loved my father. We were inseparable. My mother will now admit that she looked on me as a rival and was intimidated by me, even as a baby. My father would tell her that I was really special, smarter than she was, and you can imagine how she'd feel. She probably hated me.

When he left us, I completely broke off with him. I felt that my mother had been a victim, and that I owed her something because of that. In college I had a roommate who was very religious and kept telling me, "God wouldn't want you to hate your father," until one night I had a religious experience. I was kneeling down in church and I looked at one of these flickering candles they had all around, and then that candle flickered out. This might be called an hallucination, but it said to me, "You must get in touch with your father." So I ran back to my dorm and I cried and cried, and finally I wrote him a letter. He and his new wife came up to visit me that Christmas, but I broke if off after that. I refused to speak to him for six or seven years.

When I started teaching in 1970 my students really liked me, and I had one seminar that I truly enjoyed. But I lost weight that year, because I got so anxious that often I couldn't eat. I remember sometimes coming home, and if a student had sighed in class or implied some sort of rejection, I would cry. I wanted all of them to like me, all of the time. You can't teach that way, so it was difficult that year and I quit.

I didn't have a job the next year, and it felt pretty good. I helped set up a food co-op, learned some carpentry, spent time cooking and reading about nutrition, etc. But there were bad times, too, because I decided I wanted to have a baby and Ed decided he didn't.

That was the year I first began to experience actual "attacks" of anxiety. The first occurred in the spring at a friend's house, the day George Wallace was shot. They showed him being shot on TV, and I got really dizzy—racing pulse, lightheaded feeling, butterflies in my chest, churning stomach. I lay down on the couch because I thought I might pass out. I drank a coke to raise my blood sugar, but that didn't help. Ed took me home and I tried eating peanut butter for quick protein, but that didn't help either.

I knew a woman once who had described how it felt when her spleen was rupturing, and I felt like that. So we rushed to the emergency room in this little town we lived in. I remember sitting in the car saying, "Please go faster, I think I'm dying." They put me on a stretcher, took a urine sample and some blood to test, then gave me some pills for a bladder infection and sent me home. I felt better as soon as we left the hospital. It was my first anxiety attack, but I didn't know it then.

That summer we drove back home to visit my mother and father. My father had just married his third wife. He's on his fourth or fifth one now. When we got to my mother's house, I was so anxious that I couldn't eat. I stayed in bed for two days. Then we went to Memphis where my father had moved and we went to the zoo, my favorite place. In the middle of it I had an anxiety attack. "I feel like I'm dying," I said. "I've got to get out of here." It felt like my heart was running away. So we made an appointment with a first-rate cardiologist. After a thorough physical he said he couldn't find anything wrong and gave me Valium.

So everything was cool for a while. We drove back to Ohio and I found an administrative position in an agency I liked. I was popping Valium three times a day, 2 mg. tablets, and I thought that once I started work, now that I knew I was okay physically, everything else would be okay. But my anxiety got worse that year. It was no longer attached specifically to crowds or thunderstorms. It was interfering with my life. We tried to plan a Christmas vacation, but when the time came I just didn't feel like traveling. I began to see a therapist at a community mental health center in April, which only made it worse. He was intimidated by my Ph.D., and actually accentuated my anxiety.

Then Ed got a job offer he wanted to accept. We'd been planning to move from this town since the day we arrived, but I had grown to like it. I had friends and an interesting job, and I liked living in a small town without traffic or crowds.

When he got that offer, I felt like I was dead. I don't know how to explain it. If you've ever thought about dying, especially when you were younger, and you felt a very strange sensation because you just couldn't imagine what it's like to be dead, and you had nothing to go on—that's the way it felt. I could not believe we were leaving. I remember telling my friends that I'd never be able to get out of the closet once we moved, but no one took me seriously. I tried to tell Ed that this was a bad time for me, but he never understood. All I could say was that I was scared, but I didn't know why. So he took the job and we moved.

Ed

Looking back, it is clear: I made the decision to move, and it resulted in Elly's breakdown. If that's the question, we can be done with it for now. In my ignorance and selfishness I dealt her a devastating blow, and she very nearly lost her mind.

How guilty should I feel? There's a question of responsibility and control, here, which is only partly ethical. As an ethical question it's not a matter of looking back (or forward) and describing subsequent events; its a matter of our responsibilities to one another in that relationship. The question would be the same whether the move turned out to be right or wrong for her. And it's unclear what the social or psychological sciences offer in answering it. But as an empirical question about self-control and social responsibility, it goes to the heart of those sciences; and it poses a problem that as yet remains unsolved. The question is whether the locus of control in human affairs is to be sought within or without the individual; or more specifically, under what conditions does control of one's self reside in other hands.

My wife was approaching a breakdown. Was she "ill"? Might someone (like me) have assumed responsibility for looking after her? When she had confronted what we later called anxiety attacks, we had taken her to doctors; but that was for physical illnesses. We were barely beginning to think of her as "neurotic" in the spring of 1973—and no more so than most of our friends. She had a fear of thunderstorms, which she'd always had. She had frequent migraines, which she'd always had. And she was having periodic attacks of anxiety that seemed "exaggerated" when you considered their apparent cause (visiting her parents; being in crowds; traveling to strange places). But she had always been subject to anxiety. Like headaches and her lightning phobia, it almost seemed a part of her character.

If these traits that we later called "symptoms" never seemed entirely reasonable to me, neither did they seem abnormally deviant. We all have our quirks. One of Elly's was that she was melodramatic and high-strung. And as her friends would have told you, her quirks could be attractive, too. She was an energetic, joyful woman who could get truly excited over a picnic and thrilled by visiting relatives, if also sometimes scared by them. And she knew how to make a comedy out of sitting in the closet during a thunderstorm.

I thought of her as "normal" then. And as a normal wife she was getting to be a drag at times. She rarely went to parties any more, and when she did she often put a damper on the fun with her unreasoning malaise. Without premeditation or conscious intent, she sabotaged vacation plans. She complained about her job a lot. And she wanted to bring a child I didn't want into the midst of this, leaving me to support both of them in a tradition I viewed with uneasiness.

So the issues at the time seemed similar to those faced by any man and woman when his career conflicts with her domesticity. They had their own peculiar twist; but they didn't seem out of bounds. Feminism was being reinvented in the early 1970s, but it provided little guidance for a man who wanted his wife to pursue a career while she leaned toward the housewife role. The conventional solution provided by divorce had seemed like a real possibility earlier that winter; but after a week of sleeping in separate rooms, we both rejected it.

By springtime we were floating peacefully under partly sunny skies, just before the rapids about a quarter mile above the falls. I was looking for a better position; and if Elly discouraged my general pursuit, I did not notice it. I declined an invitation to be interviewed at an urban location when she expressed anxiety about the city. But then she advised, "You might as well go ahead and see if they offer you the job. You can always refuse."

So I did; and after I'd gone through the moves and gotten the treatment, when the offer finally came she told me finally, "I don't want to move." But she added, "It's up to you." I didn't want to stay at an alienating job in an uneventful town, and there were better opportunities for her in the city. The only argument for staying was her inexplicable anxiety. So I took the job and we moved.

BREAKDOWN

Elly

We left about 5:00 p.m. in July of 1973. The trip was one of horror for me. It was hot all the way, but I was freezing for two thousand miles. You know how your veins and capillaries constrict when you get cold feet— that's the way my whole body was. I was okay as long as the car kept moving, but whenever we stopped I became so anxious that I couldn't get out. One time I remember I had to go to the bathroom so bad it was either wet your pants or die. So I thought I'd rather be dead than humiliate myself, and I went to the john. I was sitting there and suddenly it felt like I was spinning around and the room was rocking back and forth. It scared me to death until I realized that the john wasn't bolted to the floor. It was actually wiggling. But I couldn't tell the difference between what was happening inside me and what was happening outside at that point.

You don't experience it as "anxiety" so much as plain physical symptoms. You feel light-headed, as if you're going to faint. Your heart is beating so fast you can't breathe very well. Sweating, diarrhea, nausea— you feel the physical symptoms of fear. And yet, objectively, there's nothing to be afraid of. That's what makes it so strange: There's nothing to focus on. I don't know how to describe it. To me it felt like I was going to die. That was my primary fear when I had an anxiety attack. I thought I was dying.

I remember the second or third time I saw my shrink he said, "Why don't we go to the coffee shop and have a cup of coffee?" I said, "No, I can't do it. I'm afraid of what those people will do to me. They'll kill me, or I'll die in front of them; and I don't want to die in front of them." He said, "You're not afraid of what they might do to you. You're afraid of what you might do to them." He was suggesting that my fear was really my own anger, projected onto them. That's a standard interpretation, but I rejected it. Because, consciously, I didn't feel like hurting anyone. I just felt terrified.

A very close friend of mine died about that time. He was only thirty-four, and he died of a heart attack. He'd called me the day we left Ohio, saying, "I love you. Please stay," and he died on my birthday six months later. After that I was very conscious of heart palpitations or missing a beat—premature ventricular contractions. I had a lot of those. And I heard ringing in my ears. Not constantly, but every single day. And not just ringing. Sometimes it would sound like a drum—thumpa-thump—as if my eardrums were being punched in and out. I thought it was from high blood pressure.

So I'd feel these heart contractions, and my pulse would be racing up around 180 anyway, and I'd hear what I thought was blood pressure noise, and I'd think, "Oh, my god, this is it, I'm dying now." That's why I was scared; I knew my heart couldn't take all the strain very long. Then I'd think, "Okay, I'm thirty-one. If John lived until he was thirty-four, I won't die for three more years." I carried that fantasy or delusion or whatever it was for a number of years: "I'll live until I'm thirty-four."

Ed

The first step toward labelling her "mentally ill" was taken on the long trip west. We didn't call it a "breakdown" then, but within a week it was clear that something unusual was happening. It wasn't quite a quantum leap from the past, since her experience was similar to previous attacks of anxiety (which themselves seemed familiar if nonetheless upsetting states of mind). But we were stepping into something different here. She couldn't get out of the house, even into the yard, for several days after we arrived. It was a week or more before she would walk through the backyard into the vacant field behind the house.

I found the names of three locally known psychiatrists, and suggested she make an appointment with one. I expected her to pull out of this as she had in the past, but I thought it might take professional help and more time than before. Originally I thought it might take several months. When she made no progress by the end of fall semester, and yet refused to initiate therapy, I began to withdraw semiconsciously. I felt pulled away from home by increasing demands at school, where I was teaching three courses I had never taught before (two of which I had never taken). And I was pushed from Elly by an increasing sense that she was choosing a lifestyle, rather than working her way through an emotional trauma.

I began to see her problems as a combination of incapacity and unwillingness. I could accept the larger incapacities as things beyond her power to influence then—such as her inability to get a job, or go to movies, parties, restaurants. But her failure to do little things, like gradually meeting people one by one, taking small steps to expand her realm of control, and especially her refusal to enter some form of psycho-therapy— I saw these as "willed" in some way. Not consciously willed; but nevertheless indicative of a style in which she was choosing to live.

I felt that, whether intended as "punishment" or not, her lifestyle served to demonstrate that I shouldn't have made that fateful decision to move. This made me defensive (or provoked an existing defensiveness, since I had in fact made the wrong move), and it angered me. I would tell her that she was "sick," itemizing the extent of her incapacity and demanding that she see a psychiatrist. She would cry that she wasn't "sick"; that she couldn't survive a session with a psychiatrist, and would not go; that I was the one who had dragged her west in the first place; that she was miserable, it was my fault, and she wished she had stayed behind where she had a job, self-respect, a livable life, and friends. I told her that I would prefer she had stayed in Ohio, a legitimate form of revenge for my move, rather than coming to live with me like this.

Elly

Ed has always been paranoid. He didn't understand what was happening. You can sympathize, but I don't know if you can empathize unless you've gone through it yourself. At times he wasn't even sympathetic. He was just angry, because it was happening. He tended to interpret my behavior as punishing him for something he had done, and that made things difficult. On one level there may have been some truth to that. But the further I got into it, the more I realized that on other levels something much broader and deeper was happening.

GETTING INTO IT

Elly

I kept trying to get up the courage to find help, but I was terrified. Once or twice I looked through the yellow pages for a psychiatrist, but just looking made me unbearably anxious. I began to fear that Ed would bring one home. But finally one Friday I picked out a name that I liked and told Ed that I'd see Turco if he would make the appointment. I went the next Monday at 3:00 p.m.

I almost always rejected his interpretations of my dreams. But I spent much of each session describing them. I always said I couldn't interpret them or free associate, leaving that for him to do. Then I would reject what he said; especially when it had to do with my mother. Or I would sit there smiling, sometimes giggling, like an idiot. It wasn't that I didn't take it seriously. It was deadly serious. But I was so overwhelmed that my defense was to make a joke of it. Even my dreams, sometimes, were about therapy sessions with comedians.

At times I would listen to him, though. During one of my early sessions I described a dream in which I was screaming at a troupe of drum majorettes and dancing girls. I kept shouting that they were all fools, that the world had been destroyed in the seventeenth century. Turco pointed out that I was seventeen years old when my father left my mother and me in a messy divorce. I was so surprised by the emotional impact of his interpretation that I became very wary of the things I told him after that. He also suggested that my anxiety might be based in latent homosexual feelings. And when I told him about the sexual aggressions I'd experienced from neighbor boys when I was four or five, he suggested that some repressed trauma might lie at the base of it all. So I would go home and think about those things: Maybe I do have homosexual feelings; or maybe I was raped, or seduced by my father; I don't know. But every time he said something about my mother I said, "Shut your mouth. You don't know what you're talking about."

Ed

As she developed a relationship with Turco, which she did fairly quickly, she became extremely dependent on him and she began to experience profoundly disturbing emotions. In psychoanalytic terms, she "transferred" onto her therapist much of the emotional baggage belonging to her parents. With my full and ignorant compliance, I think she made a similar transference onto me. Such emotional transference seems a normal part of any highly charged relationship, and in our marriage we had done it to each other in good as well as bad ways. I think this is how one comes to feel the complex of emotions labelled "love," among other intimacies. But the form it began to take at this point, and the dominant role it began to play in our relationship, destroyed much that remained in the marriage.

Her emotional turmoil reached the start of what became a continuing crisis during April or May. Turco had moved his office, which upset her very much. I thought her feelings of betrayal were related to our earlier move west; and further back, to the move she had been obliged to make in high school when her father left. In each of these cases she felt excluded from the decision that uprooted her, abandoned by the mainstay in her life.

Her torment took two forms. Either her sessions would arouse terrible feelings of alienation from her parents, or she would resist Turco's attempts to explore these feelings and conclude that he had turned against her for being unresponsive or obstinate. She was trapped between these crushing extremes—which, if Turco represented a "parent" in her emotional life, were really equivalent.

If she allowed herself to remember the despair evoked by her parents' betrayal, she would nearly drive herself mad with grief and horror at her mother's apparent wish to destroy her, her father's willingness to abandon her, and her simultaneous longing and hatred for them. She would come home to cover her head with her pillow and scream. Very loud, exhausting screams. Cries of "Mommy! Mommy!" and "Daddy!" and "NO! NO! NO!" Over and over again. I would go into the bedroom and sit with her, pet her, and she would beg me to tell her why they did it. At first I would ask her what it was they did, trying to verbalize what I thought she felt, and I'd think up answers to the question, "Why?" But it never mattered what I said. She would only cry out again, or beat the wall with her fists or head, and sob and scream. Most of the time I didn't know whether she wanted me there, to talk to her, to touch her, to leave her alone, or what.

Eventually, I learned how to prepare for classes in another room while she ripped herself inside-out, returning periodically to sit with her. One of the worst things that happened to me at this time is that I became capable of distancing myself from her agony. I just went to my desk and tried to turn my stomach off.

If she resisted therapy, refusing to feel such feelings toward her parents, Turco would chide her, I would let her know that half my salary was going down the drain, or she would castigate herself for failing to "work" at her therapy. In light of the pain she suffered when she did get into it, her resistance is completely understandable; and our attempts to pressure her seem not only cruel but terribly trivial alongside the forces that were tearing her apart.

She would come home feeling guilty when she'd "resisted," and begin a process of self-flagellation that sometimes stopped barely short of suicide. She would first feel depressed at her failure to "do" anything. Then she would feel devastated by Turco's presumed disgust with her. She needed his reassurance tremendously, but feared that he might turn away. In great fear and agitation, she would decide to risk calling him, to apologize. But she couldn't make a move. She would then become more apprehensive still, and want to call and have him verify at least that he wasn't leaving her. But again her fear of the phone prevented her from reaching out.

She would ask me to make the call. The first few times this happened, I refused. I felt that her relationship with her therapist was one she should handle for herself, without interference or protective covering. I thought her therapy depended on this. But my refusal of course upset her even more, focusing her feelings of rejection and abandonment on me.

Looking back, I am surprised at the coldness of my principled cruelty. I think in refusing her, I was punishing her subconsciously for behavior that distressed me. The principle on which I stood, that she and he as adults accept responsibility for their relationship, had been gutted months before in our own marriage. In standing on that principle, I was just rubbing her nose in its remains.

She would become frantic eventually, and even in my unacknowledged anger I would be so moved that eventually I'd give in. After the first few rehearsals of this scene we reached a standing compromise: I would dial the phone, following my symbolic resistance, and she would talk to him. Even talking to him was difficult for her, and usually we got to that point only late at night, after hours of increasing desperation and haggling. By that time it often happened that I could only leave a message with his answering service—after which an anxious period of waiting began.

Now she was in the position of having approached him. If he didn't return her call the next morning, her feelings changed from fear of his rejection to anger. She would decide to quit therapy, demanding that I call again, to cancel her next session. Typically she would then spend hours waiting for Turco to call. He was supposed to convince her that he wanted her to reschedule her appointment. If he didn't call her, it meant he didn't care about her progress or pain. This was a very distressing thought, and eventually it made her terribly angry. Et cetera, et cetera.

Sometimes this would continue for days. It was a battle that repeated itself every several weeks. Sometimes she would raise the ante and begin a slow process of drug overdose. She came close enough to suicide for an ambulance twice; close enough to scare me several times; and close enough to worry me a lot. The crucial elements as I eventually came to see them were her need for his approval and fear of his rejection; then grief, anger, guilt, anxiety; attempted extortions of support; depression, and self-hatred. It is probably unnecessary to note that her childhood relationship with her mother contained similar elements.

There was really no way out of this maze for Elly; and I don't know what to say about my own role in it. It might have been easier for her, and I might not have become identified with the source of her distress, if I had graciously acquiesced to her demands. In an objective sense, it would have been simple to make her phone calls and fight her other battles, too. But I wanted to treat her, and be treated by her, as an adult in an adult world.

I have to say that this wasn't a novel issue in our relationship. I had played the role of her protector and guardian in many ways before, assuming responsibility for both our lives while resenting the loneliness inherent in my prerogatives. It was precisely this familiarity with a fairly common sex-role relationship that made it easy as well as painful for me to be pulled into the process I have described. It was as if these patterns were truly a cancer in our relationship, constructed from the blood and marrow of a marriage which, before its malignant eruption, had always seemed quite "normal" and benign. Like a cancer it also devoured the good and healthy parts, and still demanded more.

Elly

For a long time, psychologically, I wasn't learning anything. I was getting out of the house more often during the first few months of therapy, and I was forced to find a job in May. Ed and I were having fights about money then, because when we discovered how expensive and long it would be, he wanted to switch to another psychiatrist. His insurance didn't cover the one I'd chosen originally, and it was taking over half his salary. But by then I had become so dependent on Turco that I just couldn't leave. So I got a part-time job at minimum wage, only six blocks from home. I was afraid to walk or drive that far by myself, so Ed always took me. But still it got me out of the house and put some structure in my life. Each time I got suicidal or really out of touch, I would remember that I had to go to work the next day, and I'd force myself out of it. So I was slowly finding ways to cope with my anxiety; but psychologically I wasn't learning anything.

Originally, I was being treated for a phobia. There was my fear of lightning, and what looked like agoraphobia, a fear of open places. After my first session Turco gave me a copy of some relaxation exercises and told me, "I don't think you're psychotic. I think we can handle this." We thought my therapy would be short term, and the strategy was behavioral modification through progressive conditioning. But as time went on, and the deeper we got into it, the worse I got.

My sessions began to trigger extremely powerful feelings, often anger. I fought it like crazy. Each insight was so bad that I could not handle it. Turco had a picture window in his office that he liked a lot, and I hated it. It was exposing me. I almost threw a coffee table through it once. And I began to have a lot more violent fantasies at home—being on top of a building and shooting people, killing them with grenades, that sort of thing.

I've always thought of myself as a pretty expressive person. I don't hold much in. But I never knew how angry I was. Today if I start feeling anxious for no reason, I know there's either anger or guilt behind it. So I start looking for one or the other and pretty soon there it is; I beat my pillow, and cry. But in the beginning I'd just come home from a session and fester and cry; or I'd do something like take this red shoe box of mine to the bedroom, where I'd stab it with a knife. "I'm going to kill you, kill you, kill you," I'd cry. Stab it, stab it, stab it! I would pretend the red was blood. And then it would be over, and I'd be sitting there sobbing with this mortally wounded box on the floor.

This Christmas I wanted something to mail some presents in, and I remembered that box. I looked for it in my closet, and when I saw it I thought, "Oh, my god! I put all those holes in my one good box." I keep it now for symbolic reasons. But in the beginning it didn't feel symbolic, and when all that anger started leaking out it nearly scared me to death.

LOOKING BACK

Elly

Soon after he moved his office last year, I wanted to give Turco something that would always be there, and be there from me. So I bought an air fern and a little vase to put it in. He put it on his desk, and at my next session he showed me some sketches he had made and told me I could pick one out. I wanted one, but I couldn't accept a thing from him. So I refused.

Later I began feeling as if I needed something to hold while seeing him. I would hold the sleeve of my coat and pretend it was a hand, a mother's hand. I asked him if I could bring a blanket and leave it in his office, so I could wrap myself up in a warm cocoon. That might make me feel less vulnerable. I thought I could work better, then, and resist the anxiety that prevented me from talking, sometimes, or hearing what he said. The next time I came, he gave me a little plastic doll to hold. I accepted it and cuddled it throughout my ensuing appointments.

Elly

There's nothing to it, you know? It's not dressed to be cute or anything like that. It's just a little dimestore doll. He has it in his office, still. Usually I don't hold it anymore. But usually, before I leave, I ask him, "Do you still have my doll?" It's something that I want to keep for the rest of my life, just to remind me—which is funny, because when I was a little girl I poked the eyes out of all my dolls.

All of my behavior during that period was very regressed. I didn't feel like an adult, I wasn't acting like an adult, and I couldn't do the things that adults do. I bought a baby's pacifier to keep in my room, and when I got upset I would sit in bed and suck on it. I went back to being a tiny infant, calling for its mother, with a rubber nipple in its mouth. I wanted Ed to read children's stories to me, too, and that would bother him. Once or twice he did, but generally he refused.

Another thing I did that was like my childhood was to engage in fantasy conversations with myself. When I was in junior high, I made up serial adventure stories about a pilot named Mike. I never said a thing about it, not to anyone. I would act out the roles in my imagination, where Mike was really me. Similarly, almost every day when I was in therapy, I constructed fantasy conversations with my doctor. I would say my lines out loud if Ed wasn't there; then I would say what Turco said back; then I'd respond, and on and on. I would spend three or four hours a day like that. Then I'd walk into his office and my mind would go blank, zip, all gone; I'd forget everthing I had said to myself. I'd sit through a session without saying a single word, and I'd think, "My god, what am I paying all this money for?"

Elly

I remember one session when Turco suggested I was a child, and asked me what the child wanted from her mother. I replied that she wanted to be held and rocked, and to hear stories read to her. Then he told me that my childhood was gone forever, and I could never get it back.

That made an indelible impression on me. I cried, "No, that's not right! Don't tell me that." I was fighting back, trying not to cry, getting sick and dizzy, and I felt like I was passing out. I'll never forget, ever, his telling me that. "Those things are gone forever." That was like—bam—someone kicking your face in, a brutal discovery.

I asked him to end the session then, but he went on. "What does the child want to do to her mother," he asked, "because she can't have those things?" This was after I had described some terrible dreams in which people were brutally murdered while I stood by helplessly; and the murdered person was sometimes my mother. I had also told him that my mother taught me to drink milk from a cup when I was three months old. I've always thought that was horrible, and so did he. For a baby, that whole sensation of being held, sucking and feeling the warmth—gone completely by the time I was three months old. It's indicative of my mother's attitude. "Does the child want to kill her mother?" he continued. "NO!" I cried. "No, my god, don't say such a thing!"

After that session he took me to the waiting room and told Ed that I might be more upset than usual that afternoon. I remember lying in bed once we got home, sobbing in horror and disbelief. Ed was in the kitchen, and I went out to him hysterically, trying to tell him that the child might want to kill her mother. "Please tell me—I'm not bad. Please, please, I don't want to kill her. I'm not bad, please tell me I'm not bad." It was overwhelming me. I couldn't entertain such a thought on any level, even hypothetically, much less feel that it might have been true of me. I couldn't stop crying for hours that night.

I frequently came home upset after therapy, crying, unable to stop. Often I called out for my mother when that happened. Sometimes I sat with a blanket and my pills in a closet upstairs, crying for my mother and father while taking Valium. More than once I took what I thought was an overdose.

Ed

I'm not sure how it started, but she began taking large doses of drugs; Valium at first, and later Thorazine. She would take her pills into the closet when she became upset with Turco, her parents, or me, trying to dull the pain. It rarely did much good.

She would sit in the closet for hours, sometimes, crying and sobbing into the night. Several times I went upstairs and thought I heard a voice; a high-pitched, little girl's voice. The first few times, it stopped when I approached. Later I could hear a small questioning voice calling "Mama?" High-pitched "Ma-Ma?" like a very young child just trying out the syllables. I looked in the open door one evening and Elly looked out with her head cocked girlishly, eyebrows raised, expectant face calling "Ma-ma?" "Da-Da?" Then with rising disappointment, "Da-Da!" as if to one who might not come. And then, desperately and frantically, "DA-DA?!" with a sob that might have been angry if she'd felt her cries had some validity. She was sitting on the closet floor with a blanket wrapped around her, as a child.

I would sit with her for a while when I found her there, holding onto her, but I really couldn't relate. If you've never seen your lover in a closet this way, try it sometime for a zinger of an experience. She was serious.

Elly

I had this dream once, shortly after I started therapy, where there was a very small baby and its mother, and they were trapped beneath a porch. It was cramped and scary and dark there, cement foundation walls on every side, with very small vents cut through the cement. The baby was frightened, and the mother was trying to get out. She managed to squeeze through one of those vents, somehow; but she left the baby behind. She left it buried in the dark, and it was terrified. I woke up with the baby still crying for her mother not to leave.

She deserted me, emotionally, not physically, when I was very, very young. And I've never . . . I've only recently begun to pick through the pieces and discover what my feelings were. When the baby is abandoned in that dream, it's a tiny infant that can't crawl out. It can't even crawl—that happened very young.

I can think of millions of reasons why she might have abandoned me. My brother was fifteen months old when I was born, so she had an infant and a kid barely walking. My father's an alcoholic, and dealing with an alcoholic is hard enough in itself. She's not very nurturing in the first place, never has been, didn't get much nurturance herself when she was young, and basically she doesn't like kids. I don't know what her story is; we've never talked about it. One reason I'm not using my real name here is that I never want her to realize what it felt like to me.

Whatever her side of it, I think I must have needed her and hated her at the same time. Then I felt I was evil for hating her, and I felt she was right in abandoning me. Throughout my childhood, with her help these feelings grew and grew. But they submerged and went underground. Just today when I saw Turco he said, "Why don't you take a break? You need a vacation." And the first thing that came to me was, "I can't, because she'll kill the babies." I couldn't believe I was saying that. When he asked who the babies were I said, "My brother and me. My mother will kill us if I try to leave." That was strange to hear myself saying that, because among other things my mother is nowhere around. I haven't seen her for months. She lives two thousand miles away, and yet I was saying that. When we first started therapy, it was so overwhelming that I couldn't even think such a thing.

Ed (1977)

I can't believe that I was actually teaching classes while these things went on. I asked students questions about assignments, posed problems, illustrated arguments, all as if they might be meaningful. I talked about "my wife," chatted casually with colleagues, and some of them probably tried to picture what my life, my wife, my evenings were like. What do they talk about when the lights are out? Do they go to movies, concerts, the drag strip, or plays? What does she do with her time?

One day I remember coming home for lunch, to see how she was. She was lying in bed crying, in very bad shape. I was worried and we were angry. I can't remember what the issue was, but when it came time to leave I delivered an ultimatum of some sort, walked into the kitchen, and instead of washing my glass I threw it against the wall. This was completely out of character for me. I was surprised at how easily I threw it, and how easily it broke. My heart was racing as I walked down the hall wondering if in five minutes I could step into class, sit down, and pretend I was a professor leading a seminar.

When I came home that afternoon there were broken glasses and plates all over the kitchen floor. Poor Sam was hanging around with his tail tucked away, looking very unsure of himself. The bedroom door was closed. I tried to open it, but I could move it only inches before it stopped against the chest of drawers lying face forward on the floor.

I pushed my way in and found Elly there looking sullen, calm, and silently proud. Every piece of clothing from both closets was strewn with the bedding on the floor. As I lifted the dresser up, the drawers fell out. After moving it out of the doorway I went upstairs feeling tense and uncertain, knowing I had established some precedent by throwing my glass at the wall. I thought from a distance that it might be good for her; but in my guts I didn't like it, and I didn't know what its boundaries were.

I was home the next time this happened, watching somewhat angrily, planning to stop her if real damage was done. Rip the clothes from the closet and throw them on the floor. Strain against the dresser, it's heavy, push its face to the floor. Throw pillows around. Then out to the kitchen to break a few things, and stomp through the house. This was connected to a suicide threat. She had taken a lot of Valium by the time I got home, and she said she would take the whole bottle, you bet she would, and there was enough to kill herself, she said. She continued taking pills throughout the evening, and when she reached what the pharmacologist had told me the danger point was, I went into the bedroom and demanded her pills. I had never taken it upon myself to "protect" her by taking them before. She angrily refused. I felt like hitting her. I grabbed her arm and hand, jerked her to me, pried open her fingers and took the pills. She threw herself at the bed, crying, "You hurt me," and raging at me as I walked out of sight.

More things thrown around, drawers slammed open, and doors. From the bathroom I heard her banging the dishwasher, full of dishes, across the kitchen floor toward the basement steps. As she slammed it into the doorframe at the top of the stairs I moved angrily toward her and slapped her in the face, surprising her. She held her hands up to protect herself, began to back away, and I slapped her again. "Cut it out!" I yelled. "CUT IT OUT!!" She ran away from me crying hysterically.

I was appalled that it had reached the point of my slapping her. I went to her, my heart still racing, and she cried at me and turned away. "You hit me! You hit me!" I tried to apologize, sorry and confused, but she just cried more.

Elly

There was more than one reason why I wanted to die. A lot of it was that everything I felt was so painful then, and my life was so miserable that it didn't seem worth living. It took so long to get better, you know. Since the symptoms first started, it's been six years. My god, that's so much time to lose. Now, I know that some day I'll be totally well; but when I was going through some really hard times and it looked like they would go on forever, I couldn't see any end except through killing myself.

The other reason was that I wanted to punish my mother, although it took me forever to realize that. I would tell Ed that if I killed myself I didn't want him to feel bad, that he would be rid of me and better off. I think he felt it was directed at him. But the one suicide note I wrote was to my mother.

Something happened just last year, where in talking to Dr. Turco I remembered a conversation with my mother that I'd never recalled before. When I was a child she told me that she wouldn't have cried at her own mother's funeral, except that she saw her father crying and her sister crying, and she thought that she should cry, too. I remembered that and I said to Dr. Turco, "I'm going to make her cry, by god. If I have to kill myself I'll make her cry. One time in her life, this woman will show some emotion for me." And I started shaking, then, and crying as I told him that.

"My god, that's it," I thought, and my stomach felt sick. "That's why I have to die." I realized I was killing myself for her. It doesn't sound like a very big thing but after that I've never felt like killing myself. It was incredible. For years I had thought about it almost every day. And now . . . I've thought about it a few times since, but never seriously. Once you realize why you're doing it, you don't have to do it anymore.

Ed

I remember taking my brother and sister to the train station on the third of July, in 1974. They had spent two weeks visiting, helping me fix up a rundown house we'd bought, then helping us move in. I hugged them goodbye at the gate, then walked to the parking lot, got in my car, and cried. It happened unexpectedly, the first time I'd cried since we made the trip west, and I sat there trying to understand the reasons before turning the key.

There were things I'd wanted to do with them, things we hadn't done, and I cried because they were leaving now while I drove home alone. We had never conceded that Elly was disabled enough to eliminate her from our travel plans, so only twice had we ventured out on short trips from home. She tried to come with us to the art museum, once, but her anxiety forced her back before we'd gone a mile. On the next trip she stayed home alone, crying while we went hiking and everyone felt bad for her. Both times I felt sorry, helpless, and completely frustrated.

It seems remarkable that at this point we were barely beginning to think of her as "mentally ill." In August, Turco told me she was "very sick," he said, "near psychotic"; and it hit me so that my legs and ribs shook uncontrollably. But this was still July.

I remember my feelings as I started the car and drove back toward the house. Although I know that route well, for some brief time it seemed less a fixed path than an unfolding web. Numbered cross streets spinning by me, asphalt threads connecting unseen destinies, strangers turning wheels at each corner I passed. Among these many intersecting lines, each one suggesting options that weren't open to my conscious mind, this car would travel a limited few. While the train slipped away on its rails, I in my car passed through unexplored mazeways, as if on a track to the house.

It's two-dimensional in my mind, flat and static, like an image from some alien picture book. Yellow painted wooden building, empty washed out frame in need of countless small repairs, unendingly tedious. Inside waits a lonely woman, thin and restless but inactive, slender hands becoming bony as she slowly gives up hoping for a better day. Once I return, I will stay in that house.

It's not that it's a dungeon I'm returning to, but a place where malignant forces converge, powerfully and invisibly. The atmosphere is thicker there, and heavier; more difficult to wade through, or suck through your lungs; containing less oxygen. And gravity is stronger there, draining blood and muscle from your legs and soul. It is the day before the Fourth of July; a family day of fireworks, cousins, and picnics when I was a child. My family is gone on the train, and I know that house with those forces will be there, and I will be in it, until my summer ends.

Let me be clear: Her condition is unbearable and getting worse. There is no diagnosis, no prognosis, but more fear and pain. Viewing the expert knowledge at our command, I can easily see why demonology might provide the simplest, most adequate and intuitively comprehensible image of this universe. It is not that my family has left, or that our house cries incessantly for attention and repair; that Elly is drowning, slowly strangling, or deserting me; that in her misery and her time of need I have failed to find the love and the strength to support her; that she is "mentally ill"; that our marriage has soured; that our life now is ugly and difficult. These words and others like them fail to grasp the central, indelible reality: This is an Evil place I am traveling toward; the home of forces Unknown, Powerful, and Bad.

NOTES FROM THE FIELD

October 1, 1974
Elly (Tuesday)

Please don't turn into stone. I need you—but I'm afraid. You might leave me or hurt me, even if you don't intend to.

It hurts to be sent away. Most of the time it feels like I'm being sent away when our session ends—like a bad child who doesn't do what mother wants.

I wanted to stay with you. It was warm, and I felt I needed you. But I feel like an egocentric infant who makes excessive demands. I want to call you—but I don't trust you. It terrifies me to call, even when I have a reason. And sometimes I just want to talk to you, with nothing to say.

I want you all for myself. It bothers me that you see other people. You can't possibly be what I want. I want too much. I am afraid my demands will drive you away.

October 2, 1974
Elly (Wednesday)

Why am I afraid to call? Sometimes when things seem not quite settled, I hope for something to happen so I can call you. Sometimes I think the things I do when I go bad are to legitimize my seeking you out. It is only legitimate to have you when I'm in "need," and not when I merely "want." I still don't understand.

October 3, 1974
Elly (Thursday)

Today I wanted to be read to—a child's story. Or to be told a story. My mother's birthday is coming, and I guess it reminds me that I'd like to be a child again. Mary Barnes had dolls and a teddy bear and books and her Ronnie. If I asked you to read me a story, would you? Maybe I'll try.

Ed

These notes were not written for an audience. They cannot provide a "report" of her first three days in October 1974. They were imaginary, personal conversations with her therapist. As such, they provide a glimpse and no more of that relationship from Elly's point of view.

Looking at these entries together with the preceding one for September 21, it appears that she *knows* she's experiencing "transference"; but she *feels* she's an insecure child. She wants to understand what is happening—but adult conceptual schemes are not at the forefront of her diary this week.

She asks two questions here. Not, "How did I learn to want and yet fear this man, with all the heart of a castaway child?" Not, "How do these wants and fears relate to my anger; that anger, and its illegitimacy, to my anxiety; this complex to my depression, self-hatred, and suicide?" She does not ask, in other words, "What patterns underlie my 'symptoms,' how did I learn them, and how might I master them?" She asks, "Why can't I call you when I want? And, would you read me a story, if only I could ask?"

October 5, 1974
Elly (Saturday Morning)

This morning Ed and I had an argument. He won. He always wins. My reasons are based on emotions and feelings. and his are always rational. So he makes me feel like a fool for defending my position. He doesn't want us to have a child.

I feel like a child, and I wanted him to read me a story. He refused. I accused him of hating children so much that he is intolerant of the child in me. He pointed out that I was wrong.

I need a daddy today. Sometimes I confuse Daddy with Doctor and I think they're the same. I wish they were.

I cried for my daddy today.

Elly (Saturday Evening)

I had very strong feelings, wanting to regress all day. I'd like to sit in a box, curled into a fetal position, safe and warm. I want to be read to, and played with—children's games.

Ed says he can't do those things for me, because he needs me as an adult. I want to start over; to be reborn. But this time with people who are warm and supporting, who care. Can we play games, and read stories? I'd like to be fed milk from a bottle once again.

October 6, 1974
Elly (Sunday)

Nightmares. I had three nightmares last night, the first time in weeks. When the tornado came there were two people I was struggling desperately to save—Ed, and a childhood friend who might have been Turco. I think maybe Turco is my third daddy.

There's a situation at work that has me upset. Money missing from the till, and me the scapegoat. I think I may get fired. Can't even make it in a menial job, when I try to do good work. Maybe that's why things are going so bad in my dreams.

Ed

Simple desires, expressed and denied. An argument, and angry dreams. I didn't want a child, but a wife. "Dear Elly, I miss you"—I tried to tell her in a positive way. But I think she had found a more compelling symbol for her own identity, much earlier, not as "wife" but as "unwanted child."

It took her most of Saturday to come to terms with my rejection of the father role. By Sunday her conscious thoughts sound more "adult." But from her notes it looks like a tornado was after my hide. And she decided, that day, to stop taking Thorazine. That's one of those drugs that replaced straightjackets in postwar mental hospitals, and in Elly's case it had a quieting effect.

October 9, 1974
Elly (Wednesday)

I really fought leaving my session on Monday. I was okay for a while when I got home, but then my headache came. Beginnings of a migraine, so I drank coffee as a vasoconstrictor.

I got anxious, then—the bad kind, not attached to anything. I was terrified. No reason. Unable to escape. I tried to call my doctor, but he wasn't home. I left a message for him to call emergency, and then I waited. I began to feel better before he called back, so I had Ed cancel my message.

Then things started to fall apart. My life disintegrates. Crying . . . can't stop. Don't know what is wrong. Call doctor again. He tells me to take my Thorazine, to help me settle down.

I'm still very anxious, two days afterwards. Everyone thinks it's because of my job—trouble at work. But why? It must be more than that. Too exaggerated a response from me. I really have thought about it, and I don't know why. I hope it doesn't happen again.

October 11, 1974
Elly (Friday)

Today was one of those down-in-a-hole days, everything's finished, nothing-will-ever-be-right-again days. Still not over. I feel hopeless. My job is alienating, meaningless, shit.

What does it matter?

I hate myself a lot today. Thought about ways to destroy myself. Fantasies of cutting my body to shreds with a knife. Considered jumping in front of a car. Accidentally knocked a flourescent tube off a shelf at work. It exploded and glass went flying everywhere, but it didn't even cut me. I found myself wishing it had smashed my face and eyes.

I'm tired of feeling rotten. Tired of crying. Tired of plodding on an endless trip. In the end at best we're all dead anyway, so why go on? I told Ed I'd rather die than live like this much longer. Maybe Alice will never get out of Wonderland.

October 15, 1974
Elly (Tuesday)

Bad session yesterday. Very angry! *Still* angry. I QUIT!!! Not sure why. Who cares?

Wanted to smash everything. Broke a lamp. Controlled it with drugs. Started taking my Thorazine regularly again, but no matter how bad it gets, I won't call. Goddamn it, I WON'T CALL! I don't need that goddamn doctor. Still hate his guts. But in semi-rational moments I think the anger is too much for what happened.

Shit, I don't even know what happened.

What more do I want from him? (How about, "You are worthwhile." How about, "I like you.") Shit, I don't care whether he hates me or not. I hate myself enough for everyone. I hate myself so much that death looks good.

But I don't want to be dead. The catch is, I don't want to be alive, either.

There are two options, Elly. Die. Or live the way you are, for the rest of your miserable life. What a choice.

I don't know whether I'll quit or not. I think he'd like to get rid of me anyway.

Ed

Anxiety attack. Depression, and suicidal fantasies. Rage. These entries span a week that might have been a year, as far as her symptomatology goes.

I remember the question, "Why?" We'd ask it before. Was her mother's birthday significant? Her fight with me about a child? Her fears of rejection on the job? Or had something come up in her sessions that we didn't know about? She'd found the nerve to ask Turco for a story, Monday (October 7), and he'd agreed. Thursday he brought in an annotated version of *Alice in Wonderland,* and he read to her on October tenth and fourteenth. Was there something in this event that set her off? The clue to it all might lie in knowing why.

Perhaps it was not an event, however, but an electrochemical imbalance in her brain. She hadn't been taking her daily Thorazine that week (October 6-13), with an unkown impact on her body chemistry. The phenothiazines, of which she had tried Thorazine and Stelazine by then, affect the brain's production of neurotransmitters—and presumably the internal transmission of "thoughts" through one's head. The details were unclear, concerning both whether and how it might work.

But suppose her problem were electrochemical. Would this mean her illness was a different one? We didn't really know. Should her treatment perhaps be chemical, rather than psychological? Experts disagreed. Would her prognosis be better, or worse? No one would say.

My wife was courting Death, and there was nothing to do but ask why. What kind of illness is near psychosis, anyway?

October 17, 1974
Elly (Thursday)

I guess I should mention the good things, too. Tuesday night Connie asked me over. I went and had a pleasant time. Then, last night, Ed and I went out to dinner for the first time in sixteen months. I was really scared, but it turned into fun.

I'm still angry at Turco, though. Still obsessed with thoughts of suicide. Not necessarily killing myself, but suicide in general. I collect bits and pieces of suicide data and store them away.

Ed says suicide is like my headaches when I was a child—a way of punishing myself and asking for comfort at the same time. When Turco acts like my mother, I get angry and then feel like hurting myself. Angry because when the session ends, he sends me away. Angry because he tells me I'm not progressing fast enough. Angry because when I asked him to read me a story, a stupid, silly childish one, I got a goddamn allegory instead. Is Alice really Elly? Isn't it interesting that Alice won't come out of the hole until they tell her who she is? So goddamn full of deeper meanings and shit—why can't things *mean* what they *are?*

Everything seems to have gotten worse since I stopped taking Thorazine. It's probably coincidence; but I feel safer when I'm taking it.

October 18, 1974
Elly (Friday)

I spent a long time at work today thinking about my anger. Remembered being angry as a child—early adolescence, junior high. I used to have an uncontrollable temper; violent episodes of stabbing knives and ice-picks into doors and walls, and tearing up my clothes. It was really frightening. I remember thinking I might kill someone someday, and deciding I had to control my outbursts.

I can't remember why I was angry then. Last time I saw my father, he told me I used to fight constantly with my mother. Everyone does, I think. But I don't remember it, and I don't trust his memory. Apparently most of that anger is still there today.

It was very difficult to ask Turco to read me a story. That was giving up a lot. Maybe I needed to push him away, to protect myself from inevitable rejection. I had felt my defenses slipping in the past few weeks.

I've also been thinking about my feelings toward my mother and father. For the past several months I've had very strong feelings about my father. I get upset about his leaving when they got divorced. Lots of tears and lots of despair. Lots of calling for Daddy aloud. I never knew that it hurt when he left. Now I wonder if I'll ever get over it.

A funny thing has happened, though. Today I told Ed that I'd never had any feelings about my mother but guilt, because I left her living all alone. But he tells me that before I ever called for Daddy, I used to call Mommy. I don't remember this. He says he heard me the first time I called for Daddy, and I'd been calling "Mommy" before. He says the Mama I called for (so I told him) was the Generalized Mother, not my own. This seems strange to me. I wonder what has happened to those feelings. Maybe I can feel just so much pain at once.

October 20, 1974
Elly (Sunday)

I tried to figure out today what happened last week to depress me so. I really don't know. Turco was reading *Alice in Wonderland,* and I think its allegorical indirectness reminds me of communications between my mother and me—never open or clear. At the same time I think I felt guilty for my anger, since I had asked him for a story and he went to some trouble to find one for me. That's all I can come up with.

I had lots of dreams last night—mostly strange dreams about animals. But I also dreamt I got a letter from my father. It said, "I hope Elly's mind gets straightened out soon." So does Elly.

Ed

It is hard to remember that this is a thirty-two year old woman, with a Ph.D. and published articles in the most prestigious journals of her discipline. Was she mentally ill? It should be clear that the question is largely academic. It is also largely mine. If it provides an organizing concept for a work like this, that accords with a traditional division of labor between us. Major issues, like where to live, or how to conceptualize our relationship, have tended to fall within masculine realms. Minor ones, like what it feels like to live and relate, have often been feminine. The reader is stuck with this. Elly had weightier things on her mind. As an academic question, I am asking whether to call her mentally ill.

Aside from its definition as a mental problem, the crucial term in the modern concept of mental "illness" suggests the undesired subjugation of an individual to some invited force. If "going crazy" in the backwater provinces from which Elly and I emerged suggests a yielding to that force, or even more active collusion, it is nevertheless viewed as involuntary. And "becoming mentally ill" among the educated describes a process for which one is rarely held responsible. That's what "illness" is.

If that label describes what happened to us, it does so primarily through this suggestion of helplessness and its legitimation of the sick role; not through its denotation of causes, genesis, or symptoms comparable to those of organic illnesses we knew about. In suggesting that the cause of her suffering was secular, its agencies uncontrolled by the individual, and its symptoms in the long run conquerable by licensed professionals, the label describes social constructions of reality, not anyone's body or mind.

Insofar as "illness" is the crucial term, then, it seems we were dealing with a social role, and not one individual's disease. But how does one inherit (or achieve) such a role? A more timely question is: How does one escape? If the individual is not responsible, is he or she not powerless as well?

In looking back on this October with the question "Why?" in mind, it seems some decisions were being made. A story was requested, and a child. Neurotransmitters were chemically stimulated by withdrawal of Thorazine; blood pressure and pulse by caffeine, perhaps. A fluorescent bulb was shattered, and therapy quit. If these were not "decisions," they were consequential acts. The question is, whose?

From a distance, the drama of that month almost flows with a predictable, rhythmic certainty: childish needs, and fear of rejection; hesitant approach, rejection, subterranean rage; reluctant withdrawal, anxiety, depression, self-mutilating fantasies and conscious rage; forced retreat to drugs and ruminating consciousness. We have seen this movie before. Elly knew the plot by heart. She came close to reciting it, September 21.

Would this make her responsible? We all have scripts from unwashed childhood days, and we act them out in dramatizations labelled "normal adult lives." I was raised to care for dependent women, if you want to hear about "normal" pathology; by a woman who loved me while punishing my eight-year-old masculinity with isolation (independence training) in a darkened cellar room. My WASP family's answer to *Oedipus Rex*. If this sounds like material for a drama involving a dependent woman I loved and could never call crazy, in an empty washed-out frame I called my home, let me add that there were demons in my childhood cellar; and my childish defense was to cover my eyes. We all replay the pirate tapes of childhood in our adult lives. Is this what mental illness is? Where are the germs?

COMING TO TERMS

February 7, 1975
Elly (Friday)

I was upset after my appointment, yesterday. It started as frustration because I couldn't "work." Then it turned to anger. Then despair; crying; begging for help, and feeling like I'll never make it. Then it turned to considering suicide.

I remember Turco's last question: "What happened to make you feel cheated and dumped on as a child?" There are things that come to mind—Mother not believing my headaches (or any illnesses) are real; Mother letting my teeth rot out; Father always drunk, so you can't bring anyone home and can never predict how things will be. I am angry for all of that. I feel it was unfair. I feel cheated out of my childhood.

I think suicide would hurt them, and it would let me escape. The ultimate answer. I had fantasies at work, all day, about shooting myself in the head, blood and brains all over everything. Wonder if I could get a gun. I've always been afraid of guns.

February 11, 1975
Elly (Tuesday)

Spent a whole session (almost) talking about suicide. I was obsessed with buying a gun last night—not so much so today. I see myself dead with a head blasted away, over and over again. I saw my mother dead. Still thinking of buying a gun; it has to be violent.

February 14, 1975
Elly (Friday)

Disoriented and disturbed after my session yesterday. Sat in the parking lot for 15 or 20 minutes, trying to pull myself together. Thought about staying there until Dr. Turco came out, so I could see him again. Then decided to get a gun. Drove to Mitchum's and looked at the hand guns. Very expensive. Lots of forms. Five day waiting time. I asked the price of what I thought was a .22 caliber hand gun but it only shoots blanks. That was the one I'd thought I might buy.

When I came home I still felt dazed. Went to another gun store, but afraid to stop. Drove to a parking lot and sat there for half an hour. Drove by the gun store again, but I was still afraid they would know why I wanted the gun. I wrote my suicide note when I got home.

Unsure what I should do today. Have to go to work—no time for guns.

Ed

Elly and I had discussed the question of labels early in the game, and with Turco's absolution we decided that "psychotic" wasn't it. I hadn't told her that she was "near psychotic" now. From my sketchy acquaintance with "labelling theory," I thought that was a bad idea. I knew that powerful institutions, manned by compelling ministers of mental "health," needed recruits and rites by which uncertain deviants might be confirmed in intuited sin, and then (sometimes) saved. I was convinced that the phenomenological status of "mental illness" was as murky as a long beclouded metaphor.

But whatever its phenomenological status, social functions, or value in the eyes of the gods, I felt at the base of my spine that all this was real. It was Valentine's Day, and Elly was planning to kill herself.

February 17, 1975
Elly (Monday)

Get a gun, get a gun, get a gun—need a gun. I'm supposed to try and figure out why. I would feel secure. It's paradoxical—I'd feel safe and secure with a gun, even though it's for self-destruction. I've always hated guns. I think they should be outlawed; but I need one. I drove to the Broadway Gun Store after my appointment today, but it was closed. Turco says he'll stop seeing me if I get one. I think it's a bluff. GET A GUN. What does it symbolize? I really don't know.

February 21, 1975
Elly (Friday)

I guess it's not a bluff. He says he won't see me if I buy a gun. Yet I can't stop thinking about it. I wrote a letter to him this morning. I didn't mail it, but maybe I should. It says a mother shouldn't desert her child, no matter how bad. You shouldn't just give up.

I knocked myself out with Thorazine and Valium last night. Ed is fed up. He says if I keep adding negative things to our relationship, he will leave. Christ, I wish I could figure it out. I just don't understand what is happening. Even in the dreams I am lost, except when I dream about getting a gun.

Ed

I never learned to live with her suicide threats. My best friend in college had killed himself, and it brought me great grief. I used every card in my hand to try and get her off that track, including the accusation that she was choosing between her mother and me: she was fighting lost battles, I claimed, with childhood tactics devised twenty years ago, at the cost of our marriage right then.

As things got worse, I faced the decision of staying home with her and abandoning my job, or trying to hold my own life together while behaving as if Elly's, in this very basic sense, were her responsibility. My hypocrisy in choosing the latter course was that I refused to grant her the right to destroy herself, under the conditions she defined. I felt our marriage contained an implicit social contract by which we had encouraged one another to invest emotions there; and by killing herself "unreasonably," she would betray that trust.

I don't know whether Durkheim would have termed it "anomic" or "egoistic" suicide—probably both. She had been severed from most of her roots: friends, career, neighborhood, family of origin. And the collective conscience of the minimal family we formed was torn by internal dissension, rendered by a secular protestantism which stood her alone, the captain of her sinking ship. The terms on which she might abandon it were secondary, though. My primary fear in these years was her death.

There was a time I remember when I came home from school and walked in the door, wondering if I'd find her dead on the floor; and I realized that I'd never have to fear that again if I did.

March 30, 1975
Elly (Saturday)

I had a dream about a gun last night. I got a good one. It has an ivory handle and holds ten bullets. But I took the bullets out before I held it to my head.

I feel depressed about Easter, a family holiday; depressed that I'm not Dr. Turco's child; that I myself don't have a child. I think that's why I have so many fantasies about Turco with his children. I wish I were one of them.

I told Ed I should set a death deadline—improve by June 1, or die. No more talking about it. Do it. Set everyone free.

Please help me, whoever it is. So little hope. Maybe I'll call Dr. Turco today. Please help. Please work. I don't want to die.

April 5, 1975
Elly (Friday)

Very depressed. No hope. Couldn't get out of bed. No reason to live. I'm a walking corpse. I might as well be dead. Called Dr. Turco—he said get out, but I can't.

April 10, 1975
Elly (Wednesday)

Up and down but mostly down. Turco's suggestion: take a vacation. Get away from it all. Get a new perspective. The trouble is, IT goes with me. I can't get away from IT. That's what I've been trying to do for two years now. I AM AFRAID. Afraid of leaving; afraid I'll never get back; afraid of being away from base. We talked about the hospital today. I want to go in. It's all so hopeless. June 1 is coming up fast, and nothing is changed.

Elly (1975)

April 15. Hospitalized. Going in; pack; not afraid. Looking forward—this may be the answer. Admitted at 10:15 a.m. People at the desk won't let me keep any money. Someone comes out to get me. The ward is locked. Ed and I go back. An aide takes my pulse and blood pressure. Then he takes me to a room and makes a bed for me. There is a woman asleep in another bed in the room. Ed stays a few minutes, then leaves. I am frightened; get in bed.

Ed

At the desk they addressed their questions to me, as if I were the guardian of some child who was standing there. I refused to do it that way. She was being "hospitalized," but she was doing it herself. As an adult. A woman in trouble—but a self-admitted human being, with enough command of the language to tell you what her name was if you asked, and when her birthday was. She was standing beside me with her suitcase, as we'd stood at the desks of so many motels.

April 15, 1975
Nurse's Notes

Thirty-two year old caucasian female, neatly dressed and groomed. Patient was very quiet and appeared guarded. Answered only a few questions during intake interview. Oriented as to day, place, and situation. When asked to cooperate with mental status exam, patient refused. Patient was read hospital rules and then taken to Room 306. After husband left, patient got into bed. She is there at this time.

Ed

It is generally agreed that professional diagnosticians exist whose job it is to distinguish mental "illness" from "normality." But each of us deviates from the ideal in our own peculiar way. We rarely know how to define that ideal precisely, or how much we deviate. How, then, does the man on the street know what behavior is acceptable in any given relationship; and what response is appropriate; and when? The answer Elly and I stumbled on is clear: We work it out.

Even in formal organizations with well-defined roles, we work it out. In intimate relationships we expose much more of our selves, and we work out more complex and private norms to govern those relationships. In doing so, we may be guided by cultural norms and perhaps by professionals; but the boundaries between "normal" and "abnormal" behavior are essentially defined by each of us in our day-to-day identification of the particular instances we label "deviant."

Durkheim suggests that identification in this social sense takes place through ceremonial recognition and ritual response to violations of normative boundaries. In the more outrageous cases, such as in the well-defined patterns of group response involved in a hanging, sentencing, lynching, etc., the response is an authoritative and public threat to the identity of the deviant. On occasions of less social significance, transgressions are identified in less formal and sometimes "private" ceremonies and rituals.

If the blunt existence of normative boundaries is signified by ceremonial recognition of transgressions, more precise demarcations are encoded in the specific rituals of "response." A question continuously at hand in *all* social relationships is, "What are the relevant norms here; to what extent is any transgression on any dimension taking place; and if there are transgressions, what or who is responsible?" And that complex question is continuously being answered through the meaningful responses of interdependent individuals to one another's actions. Elly and I do not differ from others in this respect. Close relationships are built on informal rituals that differ from the public rituals of "hospitalization," say, only in their informality.

Except in the case of perfect consensus, there must always be disagreement regarding the meanings of one another's actions and their legitimacy, and thus regarding the definition of the situation and its normative boundaries. As a result, the identification and definition of "deviant" behavior, as also the details of a "correct" diagnosis, are usually debatable and often debated. The ability to enforce the terms of ritual response to ritual transgressions becomes decisive in determining who has won and who has lost, and what debate. This is where informal as well as formal policing powers provided by outside forces become a social service for some, and an oppression for others.

In labelling Elly "mentally ill," her psychiatrist and the hospital formally ratified the existence of a general complex of normative boundaries that Elly and I had informally agreed she habitually transgressed. Within this general complex, more specifically defined lines remained to be drawn by differential diagnoses (such as "neurotic, "psychotic," and a variety of subclasses within each form). By convention and law, these designations rest on professional evaluations of symptomatology that are thought to have a scientific base. Violence, chronic unpredictability, and intransigence to treatment seem to be particularly critical symptoms, as are grossly indecent manners and unusually repulsive mannerisms. Intense personal discomfort seems important as a mitigating symptom and probably merits more lenient treatment, other symptoms being equal.

In Elly's case, her own discomfort was the primary presenting symptom, functioning both as self-punishment and as a plea for lenience. But she was violent sometimes, and over the course of two years she became a difficult case. She threatened to kill herself. The normative boundaries containing her marriage began to disintegrate. Was she mentally ill? When the insurance papers came for me to sign, I saw the terms in black and white: "Admitting Diagnosis: chronic undifferentiated schizophrenia." I knew immediately what specific form of illness that was—it means "very, very mentally ill."

Elly

I am now working at a job I like and do well. However, there are still lingering aspects of the label that stay with me, primarily because of the medication I take daily. Here's my standard spiel. I've had to give this three times so far, when medical doctors examine me. They walk in and ask, "What medications are you taking?" I say "I'm taking Stelazine," and they get a little nervous. "What are you taking that for?" they ask in this calm detached voice. I say, "They told me I was schizophrenic." And the doctor adds, "But you don't believe it," in a very neutral tone. He's hoping this isn't one of those classic cases where I think my insides are rotting out or something like that. "No," I say. And I've told this to the ophthalmologist, the neurologist, and the internist. "I used to be schizophrenic," I say, "until I learned how to control the inner workings of my organs with my mind." And then they go on to something else. Except for Dr. Rosenbaum. He tapped me on the head with his clipboard and laughed, "You don't look crazy to me."

THE MENTAL HOSPITAL FROM THE PATIENT'S POINT OF VIEW

RAYMOND M. WEINSTEIN

The mental hospital and the patients confined there have been the objects of intensive study by social scientists. Since the early 1950s a number of studies have appeared dealing with those characteristics of the hospital (such as formal structure, informal relations, staff behavior and ideology, and ward environment) that impinge upon mental patients and affect the course of their illness. Typically, portraits of the mental hospital from the patient's view have been painted with *qualitative* data, by scientists observing, interviewing, or masquerading as patients. Presented in Table 5.1 are examples of such studies, together with the attitudes toward or perceptions of hospitalization, staff, and treatment that were ascribed to patients.

Overwhelmingly, qualitative researchers have criticized the mental hospital or charged that it has a deleterious effect upon patients. Hospitalization is generally pictured in an authoritarian context, whereby patients are forced to define themselves as mentally ill, change their thinking and behavior, suffer humiliations, accept restrictions, and adjust to institutional life. Hospital staff are characterized, at best, as insensitive to patients' needs or unconcerned about their recovery,

TABLE 5.1 Qualitative Studies of Mental Hospitals from the Patient's View

Study	Type of Hospital	Hospitalization	Patients' Attitudes Toward or Perceptions of Staff	Treatment
Caudill et al. (1952)	private	patients feel "pressured" in the hospital to give up their defenses and relinquish normal social roles	patients believe doctors withhold information from them, feel compelled to counterpose staff	patients think psychotherapy is "endless one-way talk," are apprehensive about the lack of specific therapeutic goals
Dunham and Weinberg (1960)	state	patients deny being mentally ill, feel stigmatized, resent conforming to hospital norms	patients feel neglected by the doctors, feel coerced and abused by the attendants	patients dislike ECT because of its unpleasantness and adverse effects, resist psychotherapy because therapists try to change their ideas
Goffman (1961)	state	patients see hospital as an authoritarian structure and suffer restrictions on liberties, depersonalization, and loss of self esteem	patients have a keen sense of staff insensitivity and abuse via staff's avoidance of relationships, discreditations, and placement of derogatory information into the files	patients hate and fight psychiatrists in the course of psychotherapeutic relationships; they follow a "psychiatric line" in order to be judged as no longer in need of treatment

Pine and Levinson (1961)	state	patients see hospitalization as a "problem;" they must develop a new self-image, accept patient role, become reconciled to loss of freedom	patients feel powerless in the hands of doctors, fear the authority of the staff and retaliations by them	patients think talking about life difficulties is threatening; pressures to engage in psychotherapy conflict with their values, defenses, and character traits
Rosenhan (1973)	12 different hospitals	patients sense they have no legal rights, restricted freedoms, a loss of credibility, and lack of privacy in the hospital	patients believe staff are indifferent and avoid contact with them, dislike staff criticism in front of others	patients feel depersonalized by treatment due to the relatively short time spent in psychotherapy and the heavy reliance on psychotropic medication
Scheff (1966)	state	patients feel hospitalization forces them into a deviant social role and conform to the stereotyped behavior expected of them	patients resent the careless and hurried manner in which psychiatrists examine them, think psychiatrists hospitalize patients arbitrarily	patients become extremely indignant and angry when they are forcibly treated; treatment convinces patients they are "sick" and prolongs what may otherwise have been a transitory episode
Stanton and Schwartz (1954)	private	patients feel removed from society, experience loneliness and anxiety, and must conform to the informal organization of the hospital	patients believe no one in the hospital understands them, fear the power of the staff, and feel they act in contradictory manners	patients do not understand the purpose of psychotherapy, do not believe they benefit from it, and think there is an impersonal barrier in the therapeutic relationship

and, at worst, as physically abusive to patients or unjustly controlling their lives. Psychiatric treatments are described as unnecessary, emotionally threatening, and unsuccessful for many patients, while therapist-patient relationships are seen as strained and impersonal. In short, in the studies listed in Table 5.1 it is concluded that mental patients have negative views of hospitalization, staff, and treatment.

Not surprisingly, these conclusions drawn by the qualitative researchers, mainly sociologists, coincide with the societal reaction or "labelling theory" approach to mental illness and hospitalization. According to this approach persons who have been committed have been publicly labelled as "mentally ill" and become members of a deviant group (Gove, 1970). Because of society's adverse reaction to patients, they develop an ignominious self-image. Societal reaction theorists contend that institutionalization, rather than curing persons of their psychopathology, only serves to create a relatively permanent population of deviants (Roman, 1971). It is assumed that anything to do with mental hospitals is viewed negatively by patients and their relatives. Indeed, in recent years ex-mental patients have joined the ranks of the politically active, demanding improvements in the quality of institutional care and freedom from forced medication and shock treatments (Anspach, 1979).

Surprisingly, the traditional psychiatric perspective (generally the polar opposite of labelling theory) supports the idea that many patients harbor unfavorable attitudes toward hospitalization, staff, and treatment. Psychiatrists are well aware that patients frequently do not benefit from treatment and are released from mental hospitals without being "cured" (Clarke, 1979). Since treatment goals are often scaled down to limited resources, overburdened staff, and inadequate facilities, patients may return to the community less than satisfied with the outcome of their hospitalization. A basic tenet in psychiatry is that the patient need not like the doctor or believe in therapy, and open expressions of hostility are welcomed (Eaton and Peterson, 1969: 401). Therapists are often confronted with patients who manifest the "negative therapeutic reaction," Freud's formulation of a patient's sense of guilt, need for punishment, and moral masochism (Olinick, 1964). With this syndrome of negativism, patients vocalize defiant attitudes toward therapists because any improvement or temporary suspension of symptoms produces an exacerbation of their mental illness.

Some social scientists, however, have challenged the conclusions drawn from the qualitative studies and/or defended the mental hospital. Linn (1968) contends that observational data give us a one-sided and homogeneous conception of patienthood, and that a majority of patients in fact have positive attitudes because hospitalization helps them cope with their emotional and environmental problems. Gove and Fain (1973) claim that the mental hospital has a beneficial or benign effect, as most ex-patients show improvements in interpersonal relationships and community participation. To Townsend (1976) the impressionistic approach of the researchers in Table 5.1 has resulted in questionable interpretations of mental hospitalization, since empirical investigations of patients have consistently failed to reveal changes in their self-conceptions. A sociologist-patient confesses that before being committed he had feared hospitalization, anticipated abuse by staff, and envisioned such evils as ice baths, shock treatments, and straightjackets (Killian and Bloomberg, 1975). After discharge, by contrast, he felt that hospital treatment had facilitated rather than retarded his recovery and believed the experience had been a pleasant one.

The techniques employed in the qualitative studies have also been questioned. Descriptions of the mental hospital from the patient's perspective may be insightful and thought-provoking, but there are inherent limitations to the data. Reznikoff et al. (1959) point out that the accuracy of the observations cannot be appraised. The objectivity of the inferences reported is suspect since two or more observers with different backgrounds and training were not used. Moreover, Reznikoff et al. argue that subjective and experiential data are almost impossible to quantify for individual or group comparisons and perforce have limited applicability. Linn (1968) maintains that the patients interviewed or observed in the qualitative studies did not constitute representative samples. How typical the anecdotes and incidents cited were of the total hospital population remains a mystery. Linn is also critical of these researchers because they viewed patients as passive or powerless participants in the hospital system rather than as informants with useful opinions on the treatment process.

Studies of the kind listed in Table 5.1 tend to eclipse the relatively few *quantitative* reports in the literature dealing with the attitudes of hospitalized mental patients. Social scientists have seldom taken representative samples of patients, questioned them directly about the hospital or their illness, utilized objective tests or validated scales, and presented the findings in statistical format. Weinstein (1972) believes this neglect or lack of interest in patients' views is due to a "bias" among researchers, a tacit acceptance of the medical model of mental illness. Since the mentally ill (by definition) possess some kind of psychopathology, their opinions of themselves or their situation are assumed to be symptomatic of their illness and thus unreliable. Similarly, Sonn (1977) claims that patients' statements are deemed by psychiatrists to be unconscious distortions of reality and not to be taken at face value. In psychiatry patients are seen as objects of study rather than coinvestigators in the treatment process, and their views are discounted because of an incongruence with existing styles of therapy or research.

The handful of quantitative works concerning patients' views of mental hospitals does not constitute a unified body of knowledge. The few dozen studies are, for the most part, disjointed. Different scientists and investigative teams have largely focused on a specific patient attitude, and have not used the same or similar methodological techniques. The purpose of this chapter, therefore, is to review these quantitative studies of patient attitudes toward the mental hospital, to draw together the diverse methodologies, findings, and conclusions. The degree of patients' positiveness or favorableness is the theoretical focus around which the quantitative data are organized. Of key importance is the overall level of favorableness, that is, the number of studies in which patients perceived hospitalization, staff, and treatment favorably. Such a review, it is hoped, will complement the wealth of qualitative data already familiar to social scientists and shed light on the controversy between the critics and defenders of mental hospitals.

QUANTITATIVE STUDIES

The quantitative studies of interest to us (Table 5.2) cover a wide range of topics. These researchers tested various attitudes of patients toward hospitalization, staff, and treatment in general (for example, conceptions of a hospital's authoritarian control, staff roles, and therapeutic effectiveness) as well as specific opinions of their own institutions (evaluations of the benefits of hospitalization, helpfulness of staff, usefulness of treatment modalities). To measure these different attitudes, a wide variety of methodological techniques was utilized. Certain researchers favored objective tests with a small number of questions or statements, whereas others constructed questionnaire scales from scores or even hundreds of items. For each study, the different measures of patients' attitudes toward hospitalization, staff, and treatment were identified. These measures were based on patient responses to individual questions or statements, or the scaling of test items together.

For each measure of patients' attitudes in each study listed in Table 5.2, it was determined if hospitalization, staff, or treatment was viewed either favorably or unfavorably. In some studies, the measurement criteria listed were simply used. Researchers utilizing open-ended questions categorized the replies not only by content but purposefully to reflect a positive, neutral, or negative attitude. Researchers using multiple-choice

(text continues on page 131)

TABLE 5.2 Quantitative Studies of Mental Patients' Attitudes

Study	Type of Hospital	Patient Sample	Measurement Techniques	Number of Attitude Measures Favorable (F) or Unfavorable (U) Toward					
				Hospitalization		Staff		Treatment	
				F	U	F	U	F	U
Allen and Barton (1976)	university	95	open-ended questions	1	–	–	3	2	2
Almond et al. (1968)	university	66	agreement-disagreement scales					11	4
Backner and Kissinger (1963)	veterans	30	semantic differential			3	–		
Barton and Scheer (1975)	university	19	agreement-disagreement scales					10	6
Chastko et al. (1971)	university	47	open-ended questions, rating scale					2	–
Dowds and Fontana (1977)	veterans	54	rating scales					13	1
Ellsworth and Maroney (1972); Ellsworth et al. (1971)	veterans	1141	factor-analytic scales	3	–	2	–		
Freeman and Kendell (1980)	public	166	multiple-choice questions					11	2
Fryling and Fryling (1960)	state	48	open-ended questions	3	1			2	1
Giovannoni and Ullmann (1963)	veterans	35	semantic differential			1	–		
Goldman (1965)	veterans	139	multiple-choice questions	–	1				
Goldstein et al. (1972)	university	346	rating scales	5	1	7	–	7	1
Gordon and Groth (1961)	veterans	60	semantic differential	5	–	2	–		
Gould and Glick (1976)	university	44	rank orderings					15	5
Gove and Fain (1973)	state	429	multiple-choice questions	1	–			1	–
Gynther et al. (1963)	city	121	multiple-choice questions	1	–	1	–	1	–
Hamister (1955)	veterans	99	rank orderings			*			
Handler and Perlman (1973)	state	80	rating scales			*			
Hillard and Folger (1977)	state	32	multiple-choice questions,					5	2
	state	21	semantic differential					1	6

(continued)

TABLE 5.2 Continued

Study	Type of Hospital	Patient Sample	Measurement Techniques	Number of Attitude Measures Favorable (F) or Unfavorable (U) Toward					
				Hospitalization		Staff		Treatment	
				F	U	F	U	F	U
Imre (1962); Imre and Wolf (1962)	state	125	interval scale	1	—				
Ishiyama et al. (1962)	state	74	open-ended questions			2	—		
Jansen (1973); Jansen and Aldrich (1973)	state	205	multiple-choice questions, semantic differential			4	4	4	9
Jones et al. (1963)	university	54	agreement-disagreement scales	11	—	12	1	10	2
Kahn and Jones (1969);	state	42	factor-analytic scales	2	—			2	—
Kahn and Weber (1972)	veterans	43		2	—			2	—
	military	55		2	—			2	—
	university	56		2	—			2	—
Kahn et al. (1979)	city	50	factor-analytic scales	2	—			2	—
Keith-Spiegel et al. (1970)	veterans	360	open-ended questions	1	2			2	2
Kish (1971)	veterans	169	interval scales	2	2	2	1	4	1
Klass et al. (1977)	state	431	interval scales	1	1	1	2	3	2
Klopfer et al. (1956)	state	33	interval scales	1	—				
Konick (1971)	state	590	factor-analytic scales	6	3	4	2	2	—
Kotin and Schur (1969)	state	55	multiple-choice questions	1	—	3	—	1	4
Lee (1979)	private	76	multiple-choice questions			2	—	12	—
Leonard (1973)	university	96	rating scales						
Levinson and Gallagher (1964)	state	100	factor-analytic scales	1	1				

128

Study	Setting	N	Method/instrument						
Linn (1968)	state	185	open-ended questions	7				3	—
Lowenkopf and Greenstein (1972)	private	100	open-ended questions	5					
Luft et al. (1978)	city	183	multiple-choice questions	7				2	—
Mayer and Rosenblatt (1974)	state	220	agreement-disagreement scales, rank orderings	2		4	2	4	1
Mayo et al. (1971)	veterans	18	agreement-disagreement scales	1	1	—	1	4	1
Moos (1974)	state	1231	interval scales	1	1	—	3	4	1
	veterans	1687		2	—	1	2	3	2
	university	391		1	1	2	1	2	—
Morrow (1973)	state	64	rating scales	3		—	—	2	—
Pettit (1971)	provincial	50	semantic differential			1		1	—
Pierce et al. (1972)	general	17	interval scales	1	3	2	1	2	3
Polak (1970)	city	11	open-ended questions					—	1
	provincial	7						—	1
Reznikoff et al. (1960); Toomey et al. (1961)	private	142	picture test, incomplete statements, multiple-choice questions, interval scale	3	1	3	1	3	1
Roback and Snyder (1965)	state	101	interval scale	1	—				
	veterans	119		1	—				
Skodol et al. (1980)	city	30	agreement-disagreement scales	1	1			16	12
I. F. Small et al. (1965)	city	154	open-ended questions	1	—			—	5
J. G. Small et al. (1965)									
Souelem (1955)	state	103	interval scale	1	—				
Spencer (1977)	state	50	rating scale, multiple-choice questions	1	1			11	9
Spiegel and Younger (1972)	veterans	254	factor-analytic scales	1	1	—	1		

(continued)

TABLE 5.2   Continued

| | | | | Number of Attitude Measures Favorable (F) or Unfavorable (U) Toward | | | | | |
| | | | | Hospitalization | | Staff | | Treatment | |
Study	Type of Hospital	Patient Sample	Measurement Techniques	F	U	F	U	F	U
Townsend (1975)	state	110	semantic differential	1	1	1	–		1
Verinis and Flaherty (1978)	veterans	27	interval scales	1	1	3	–	4	1
Wing (1962)	public	256	open-ended question	–	1				
Wolfensberger (1958)	state	95	interval scale	1	–				
Zaslove et al. (1966, 1968)	university	93	open-ended questions	1	–	–	2	1	3

* Data for the total sample were not reported or could not be calculated. However, in these studies patient and staff attitudes toward staff in terms of favorableness were compared.

questions gave patients choices that signified the degree to which they were helped in the hospital, while those choosing rating scales or ranking procedures had the quality of favorableness built in to the different points. In the majority of studies, however, patients' attitudes were *not* analyzed in terms of favorableness and the data had to be interpreted in this context. Thus, on the agreement-disagreement scales the statements were dichotomized in terms of positive or negative descriptions of hospitalization, staff, or treatment. With the semantic differential technique, the adjectives rated suggested positions of approval or disapproval. On the factor-analytic and interval scales, favorableness was determined by the difference between the midpoint of the subscales and the patients' mean scores; subscale scores indicate the degree of endorsement of particular attitudes, the content of which denotes a favorable or unfavorable view.

It is important to comment on the data accuracy and sample representativeness of the quantitative studies, since some researchers have criticized the qualitative studies largely on these grounds. For almost all methods of measurement used in the studies in Table 5.2, the validity of the data (extent to which differences in test scores reflect true differences in patients' attitudes) was either demonstrated or presumed. Rating scales, rank orderings, agreement-disagreement scales, multiple-choice questions, and open-ended questions all have "face validity," are measures based directly on the attitude in question, and do not purport to measure any other attitude. The developers of the semantic differential demonstrated the validity of this technique. On the factor-analytic and interval scales, which purport to measure various abstractions, validational data were gathered. The reliability of these measurements (extent to which test scores do not reflect chance or random errors) was checked in most cases, via the consistency or stability of patient responses or scores. In the vast majority of quantitative studies, representative samples were taken. Some researchers selected all admissions over several weeks or months, others selected all discharges during a given time frame. Cross sections of a hospital's population were also obtained by random samples of patients or wards.

More detailed information on the validity, reliability, sample representativeness, and measures of favorableness of the studies in Table 5.2 can be found in earlier reports (Weinstein, 1979, 1981a, 1981b).

FAVORABLENESS OF PATIENTS' ATTITUDES

The overall favorableness of patients' attitudes was determined by counting the number of different hospital *samples,* separately for each of

the three types of attitudes, that had findings "in a favorable direction"—
more measures in the favorable than the unfavorable column. For each
sample judged to be attitudinally favorable, this meant that either (a) more
than half the mental patients viewed hospitalization, staff, or treatment
positively, or the total sample received a mean score on the better side of
the midpoint, when a single scoring technique was used by researchers, or
(b) there was a majority of positive responses or mean scores on the better
side of the midpoint when multiple questions, tests, or subscales were
used. These criteria appear to be the best means of assessing the issue of
attitudinal favorableness across the various studies, given the fact that
multiple measures were often used and patients sometimes tested at
different institutions. In each sample, findings in a favorable direction
imply that the patients exhibit a tendency, and not a unanimity, to view
hospitalization, staff, or treatment positively.

All Table 5.2 study samples were included in the overall determination
of favorableness except 2 (Hamister, 1955; Handler and Perlman, 1973).
Of the 39 Table 5.2 studies that tested patients' perceptions of hospitalization, 27, or 69 percent, had findings in a favorable direction. Patients were
unfavorable or ambivalent toward the mental hospital in the other 11
samples (Goldman, 1965; Keith-Spiegel et al., 1970; Kish, 1971; Klass et
al., 1977; Levinson and Gallagher, 1964: 75-79; Moos, 1974: 60—state and
university hospitals; Pierce et al., 1972; I. F. Small et al., 1965; Spiegel and
Younger, 1972; Verinis and Flaherty, 1978; Wing, 1962). Concerning
patients' attitudes toward staff, 20 of the 27 hospital samples (74 percent)
were positive, the rest either neutral or negative (Allen and Barton, 1976;
Jansen and Aldrich, 1973; Klass et al., 1977; Mayo et al., 1971; Moos,
1974: 60—state and veterans hospitals; Zaslove et al., 1968). Of the 44
different studies in Table 5.2 dealing with treatment, patients espoused
favorable views in 35, or 80 percent, of them. Here a majority of patients
in 9 samples were not on the positive side (Allen and Barton, 1976; Hillard
and Folger, 1977; Jansen, 1973; Lee, 1979; Pierce et al., 1972; Polak,
1970—both hospitals; I. F. Small et al., 1965; Zaslove et al., 1966).

The 39, 27, and 44 hospital samples, for the different attitudes listed in
Table 5.2, were cross tabulated in terms of favorableness with 3 characteristics pertaining to the quantitative studies or data reviewed that might
have had a bearing on patients' responses. These relationships are shown in
Table 5.3. It is clear that the frequency of favorable results varied considerably according to the orientation of the attitudes measured. In different
studies mental patients conceptualized hospitalization, staff, and treatment in general in a favorable context substantially more often than they
did their own institutional experiences. For example, 94 percent of those

TABLE 5.3 Favorableness of Patient Sample Attitudes, by Three Characteristics of the Quantitative Studies or Data Reviewed

	Patient Sample Attitudes Toward											
	Hospitalization				Staff				Treatment			
	Favorable		Unfavorable		Favorable		Unfavorable		Favorable		Unfavorable	
Study or Data Characteristics	N	%	N	%	N	%	N	%	N	%	N	%
Attitudinal Orientation												
Mental hospitals in general	16	94	1	6	8	100	–	–	14	100	–	–
Patients' own institution	11	50	11	50	12	63	7	37	21	70	9	30
Type of Hospital												
State or public	16	76	5	24	7	70	3	30	18	78	5	22
Veterans	5	50	5	50	7	78	2	22	6	100	–	–
University[a]	6	75	2	25	6	75	2	25	11	73	4	27
Time of Study[b]												
1950s	7	88	1	12	3	100	–	–	2	100	–	–
1960s	15	65	8	35	10	71	4	29	18	78	5	22
1970s	5	63	3	37	7	70	3	30	15	79	4	21

a. Includes the private hospitals and the psychiatric unit of a general hospital since all were short-term facilities with relatively young patient populations.
b. Denotes the time studies were conducted, not when published.

studies dealing with hospitalization in general met the criteria for favorableness, while 50 percent of the patient samples tested about their own hospitalization were in the favorable column. Findings did not vary according to the type of hospital sampled. It was anticipated that university hospital samples, with patients who tend to be less chronically ill and have shorter stays, would more often be positive in attitude, but this was not borne out by the data. Time of study likewise did not substantially affect patients' views. We expected that patients' test scores over the past 3 decades would reflect an increasing degree of favorableness, owing to the positive changes in hospital administration that have occurred (such as less custodialism, more milieu therapy, and shorter stays). However, the frequency of favorable attitudes toward hospitalization has, in fact, *decreased* somewhat over time, from 88 percent of the studies conducted in the 1950s to 63 percent of those in the 1970s.

An important issue is whether or not patients' opinions of the mental hospital *change* as a consequence of their commitment. Unfortunately, only a few of the researchers listed in Table 5.2 tested patients at 2 or more time periods, so this issue cannot be given the attention it deserves. Nevertheless, the data do suggest that patients' attitudes improve, or at least do not worsen, between admission and discharge. Of the 6 studies that measured attitudes toward hospitalization, 3 found that patients became more favorable over time (Allen and Barton, 1976; Pierce et al., 1972; I. F. Small et al., 1965) and 3 reported no changes (Gynther et al., 1963; Kahn and Weber, 1972; Reznikoff et al., 1960). Both studies concerned with staff discovered that patients registered positive changes (Pierce et al., 1972; Reznikoff et al., 1960). Of the 8 studies looking at treatment, patients' attitudes improved in 5 (Allen and Barton, 1976; Gynther et al., 1963; Pierce et al., 1972; Reznikoff et al., 1960; Verinis and Flaherty, 1978) and remained the same in 3 (Dowds and Fontana, 1977; Kahn and Weber, 1972; I. F. Small et al., 1965). Follow-up interviews 3-18 months after discharge revealed that patients espoused either the same (J. G. Small et al., 1965) or less favorable (Allen and Barton, 1976) attitudes toward both hospitalization and treatment.

Another important issue is whether patients are more or less favorable in their perceptions of the mental hospital than nonpatients. A number of Table 5.2 researchers compared patients' question, test, or subscale responses with those of hospital personnel, and an analysis of their data addresses this issue. The findings, however, do not disclose any clear-cut patterns. Patients were significantly *more* favorable toward hospitalization, staff, or treatment in 16 different comparisons (Dowds and Fontana, 1977; Goldstein et al., 1972; Hamister, 1955; Handler and Perlman, 1973;

Ishiyama et al., 1962; Leonard, 1973; Mayer and Rosenblatt, 1974; Pierce et al., 1972; Skodal et al., 1980; Verinis and Flaherty, 1978; Zaslove et al., 1966)[1] and *less* favorable in 19 (Goldman, 1965; Imre, 1962; Kahn and Weber, 1972; Kish, 1971; Klass et al., 1977; Levinson and Gallagher, 1964: 75; Mayer and Rosenblatt, 1974; Mayo et al., 1971; Moos, 1974: 57; Pierce et al., 1972; Polak, 1970; Spiegel and Younger, 1972). There were no significant differences between patients and various nonpatient groups in 12 cases (Ellsworth et al., 1971; Gould and Glick, 1976; Imre and Wolf, 1962; Kahn and Weber, 1972; Kahn et al., 1979; Kish, 1971; Klopfer et al., 1956; Mayer and Rosenblatt, 1974; Toomey et al., 1961). These inconsistencies in patient-nonpatient attitudes occurred in all types of hospitals and thus cannot be explained by the different treatment settings in which the studies were conducted.

Each study in Table 5.2 with data for the total sample contains one or more measures of attitudinal favorableness. The measures may be examined individually in terms of *content* to determine the particular characteristic or aspect of hospitalization, staff, or treatment that patients perceive either positively or negatively. The patient samples contain 116, 90, and 279 questions, tests, or subscales for the 3 types of attitudes, respectively. Each of these measures was thus content analyzed and placed into different categories. The favorableness of these measures, by category, was then tabulated for all study samples combined (Tables 5.4, 5.5, and 5.6).

From Table 5.4 it is clear that patients view most aspects of mental hospitalization quite favorably. A good proportion of the questions, tests, and subscales in almost all content categories were endorsed by various samples. Patients especially feel that the hospital is organized well and has a salutary atmosphere, and that institutionalization is beneficial, is not very restrictive, has a good effect on patients, and seldom stigmatizes patients. The data in Table 5.5 reveal that patients are rather pleased with the accessibility, receptivity, and support of staff (in general), and give high marks to psychiatrists and nurses. However, patients have negative opinions more often than positive toward staff's permissiveness and dominance, and are ambivalent about the helpfulness of attendants. As Table 5.6 depicts, not all characteristics of psychiatric treatment in general or specific therapies are viewed equally favorably by hospitalized patients. Patients are strongly positive in their orientations toward the hospital's therapeutic value, assistance with medical problems, restrictions, and environment, are ambivalent about its patient freedoms and responsibilities, and are negative toward its staff-patient relations. Individual and milieu therapies are perceived quite positively by patients, while occupa-

TABLE 5.4   Favorableness of Patient Sample Responses or Mean Scores
to Questions, Tests, and Subscales Dealing with Attitudes
Toward Hospitalization, by Content

| | Questions, Tests, and Subscales | | | |
| | Favorable | | Unfavorable | |
Content of Attitudes	N	%	N	%
Benefits of hospitalization[a]	26	84	5	16
Restrictiveness of hospitalization[b]	14	82	3	18
Organization of the hospital[c]	7	70	3	10
Amenities of the hospital[d]	5	56	4	44
Hospital's effect on patients[e]	19	70	8	30
Atmosphere of the hospital[f]	7	78	2	22
Stigma of hospitalization[g]	5	71	2	29
Expectations of hospitalization[h]	4	67	2	33
Total	87	75	29	25

a. Helpfulness of hospitalization, quality of patient care, general orientation toward mental hospitals.
b. Arbitrariness of restrictions, limitations imposed on patients, hospital's rules and regulations, difficulties in getting released, authoritarian character of the hospital.
c. Satisfaction with ward, orderliness of ward, cleanliness of ward, building safety, activities on ward.
d. Comforts of the hospital, meals, relaxation, escape from pressures, being alone at the hospital.
e. Hospital provides for patients' dependency needs, gives patients insight into problems, gets patients involved with other patients.
f. Hospital is entertaining, has programs to keep patients busy, raises patients' morale.
g. Hospital changes patients' reputation at home, family and friends betray patient to get him/her into the hospital, people reject ex-patients.
h. Acceptance of hospitalization, fears of commitment, motivation to go to the hospital.

tional, medication, activity, and electroconvulsive therapies are looked at somewhat positively. Patients are equally divided in their beliefs about the beneficial effects of group therapy.

DISCUSSION

The findings presented in this report lead us to conclude that the pictures of hospitalization, staff, and treatment drawn by patients bear little resemblance to the ones sketched by the critics of mental hospitals. Social scientists who have gathered qualitative data—by observing or interviewing patients informally or assuming the role of pseudopatient—have largely argued that patients are unfavorable in attitude because of their

TABLE 5.5   Favorableness of Patient Sample Responses or Mean Scores
to Questions, Tests, and Subscales Dealing with Attitudes
Toward Staff, by Content

	Questions, Tests, and Subscales			
	Favorable		Unfavorable	
Content of Attitudes	N	%	N	%
Accessibility of staff[a]	6	86	1	14
Receptivity of staff[b]	10	77	3	23
Permissiveness of staff[c]	4	44	5	56
Dominance of staff[d]	4	44	5	56
Support of staff[e]	5	71	2	29
Helpfulness of:				
Psychiatrists	17	89	2	11
Nurses	9	82	2	18
Attendants	2	50	2	50
Other staff groups	7	64	4	36
Total	64	71	26	29

a. Staff's attentiveness to patients, availability for consultation, activity with patients.
b. Staff's understanding of patients' problems, ability to communicate with the mentally ill, respect or concern for patients, expressions of kindness, acceptance of patients.
c. Staff's encouragement of patient-staff arguments, tolerance of patients' anger or aggressive behavior.
d. Staff's control over patients, enforcement of rules and regulations.
e. Staff's helpfulness to patients, encouragement to get well, therapeutic effectiveness.

fear of commitment, loss of freedom, social stigma, abuse by staff, sense of powerlessness, anxiety about treatment, poor relationships with therapists, problems in adjusting to institutional life, and lack of apparent "cures" for patients at the time of discharge. However, patients responding to formal interviews and questionnaires repeatedly stress the bright, not the dark, side of the mental hospital. This review of quantitative data for numerous samples representative of different types of hospital populations has revealed that a rather large majority of patients voice favorable attitudes toward mental hospitals in general as well as their own institutions. Patients often claim that they (or other patients) benefit from hospitalization, are not bothered by restrictions, sense no stigma, are helped by psychiatrists and nurses, are accepted by staff, get well as a result of treatment, are satisfied with ward conditions, and value different therapies. The evidence indicates that the defenders of mental hospitals have more accurately portrayed the views of patients than have the critics.

TABLE 5.6   Favorableness of Patient Sample Responses or Mean Scores
to Questions, Tests, and Subscales Dealing with Attitudes
Toward Treatment, by Content

	Questions, Tests, and Subscales			
	Favorable		Unfavorable	
Content of Attitudes	N	%	N	%
Treatment in General				
Therapeutic value[a]	22	79	6	21
Medical assistance[b]	10	100	–	–
Patient freedoms and responsibilities[c]	21	51	20	49
Staff/patient relations[d]	3	33	6	67
Ward restrictions[e]	10	91	1	9
Ward environment[f]	24	83	5	17
Specific Therapies				
Individual	13	81	3	19
Group	7	50	7	50
Occupational	10	59	7	41
Milieu	17	89	2	11
Medication	6	60	4	40
Activity	18	69	8	31
ECT	29	59	20	41
Total	190	68	89	32

a. Treatment is helpful, patients get well as a result of treatment.
b. Hospital provides medical treatment, helps with hearing aids and false teeth.
c. Treatment encourages patients to express themselves, act spontaneously, help
   care for other patients, seek out activities, cope with personal problems, become
   autonomous, help make decisions about ward activities and patient behavior.
d. Staff explain treatment to patients, act on patients' suggestions, communicate
   freely with patients, are friendly, are sociable.
e. Hospital pressures patients to conform, fails to discharge them on time, does not
   make ward rules known, has unclear program goals.
f. Hospital provides work programs, recreational activities, small group meetings,
   contacts with community agencies and family members, order and organization
   on the ward, practical assistance to patients.

That Table 5.1 researchers' descriptions of the meaning of hospitalization, staff, and treatment for patients deviate so markedly from the
meanings patients themselves ascribe to their hospital experiences is due,
in part, to certain methodological biases inherent in such qualitative
studies. The role of observer in the hospital, for example, can lead
researchers to misinterpret the patient's point of view. Linn (1968) notes
that when he observed patients on the ward he wondered how they could
tolerate such "deplorable conditions," but when he later formally interviewed these same patients he began to understand their social situation;

patients' favorableness toward the hospital seemed justified in light of the poverty, isolation, and disability from which many had come. The role of pseudopatient is not a satisfactory method of data collection either. Since the researchers are not mentally ill and are therefore not in a position to benefit from treatment, they cannot possibly perceive their experiences in the same manner as do bona fide patients. Caudill et al. (1952) openly state that the use of pseudopatients involves a subjectivity bias and discuss some of the disadvantages of this procedure. Similarly, Rosenhan (1973) admits that he and the other pseudopatients had distinctly "negative reactions" and do not pretend to describe the experiences of true patients. A third problem with the qualitative data on mental hospitals is the lack of representativeness. Informal interviews do not test attitudes in a systematic way, but instead are usually limited to topics that patients mention spontaneously, those most problematic to them at the time (Sonn, 1977). Such unstructured data tend to be collected via a nonprobability sampling of patients and are not interpreted within the context of a total hospital experience.

Qualitative researchers' theoretical biases also help to explain why the negative aspects of hospitalization, staff, and treatment have been exaggerated in their reports. It is clear that these scientists were not neutral toward patients or completely objective in their orientations. Goffman (1961: x) contends that his view of the mental hospital "is probably too much that of a middle-class male," that perhaps he "suffered vicariously about conditions that lower-class patients handle with little pain," and that unlike some patients he "came to the hospital with no great respect for the discipline of psychiatry." Qualitative researchers tended to identify with the disadvantaged patients, and were deeply concerned with their welfare although they had no direct responsibility toward them. These scientists were "outsiders" whose central aim was to analyze the mental hospital as a life setting for patients, as Levinson and Gallagher (1964: 9) put it, "with emphasis upon its pathogenic, ego-wounding, corrosive qualities." Another fault of the qualitative studies, according to Linn (1968), is the conceptual error of assuming that patients in mental hospitals have a homogeneous definition of their situation, that is, that they all view their institutionalization with embitterment, distrust, and hostility. He believes that in any mental hospital there are at least as many patients with favorable as unfavorable viewpoints, who see their treatment as a retreat from poor environmental conditions and a chance to begin a new life.

Findings from hospital studies other than those reviewed here offer clues as to why patients are so favorably disposed toward mental hospitals. Hudgens (1963) found that at the time of admission the patients' key motivations for entering treatment were to be protected or cared for permissively, to escape from the pressures of everyday life, to improve interpersonal relationships, and to establish control over feelings and behavior. Martin et al. (1977) observed that a very small minority of patients viewed their recovery as beyond their control and remained passive in treatment; most adopted an active role and endeavored to better their adjustment to the hospital. Gove and Fain (1977) contend that there is nothing intrinsic in the commitment process that is seriously debilitating; a follow-up study of committed and voluntary patients indicated that the situation and behavior (via employment, marriage, or relationships) of both groups improved after discharge. Studies of recidivism show that most patients return to the hospital voluntarily—because of poverty, deprivation, inactivity, or the lack of alternatives open to them (Rosenblatt and Mayer, 1974).

The assumptions of the labelling theory approach to mental illness and hospitalization vis-à-vis the attitudes of patients seem to apply to only a small proportion of them. We observed that a minority of patients in approximately three-fourths of the quantitative studies reviewed, and a majority in one-fourth, expressed negative or ambivalent opinions of hospitalization, staff, and treatment. These patients were especially critical of staff/patient relations, staff permissiveness, and staff control. These results underscore the fact that a good many patients still sense the coerciveness of mental hospitals, exactly as the qualitative researchers beginning in the 1950s so aptly described. Affirmative changes in hospital administration and growth of milieu therapy during the past two decades have apparently not completely assuaged the negative impressions of patients. Since the attitudes of the vast majority of patients in the Table 5.2 samples were positive, our observations are thus consistent with a growing number of studies in recent years that have found labelling theory to be a less than adequate framework for interpreting psychiatric phenomena (see Greenley, 1979; Quadagno and Antonio, 1976).

The traditional psychiatric perspective likewise does not adequately account for the attitudes of the majority of hospitalized patients. There is reason to presume that many patients would harbor negative feelings, since mental illness involves psychic pain, distress, and anxiety, and patients are sufficiently distraught by the time they reach the hospital. However, this potential for negativism is never realized for most patients. It may be that unfavorable attitudes are only characteristic of higher-class patients or those from environments that are more attractive than the hospital, a small percentage of the total psychiatric population at any given moment. Or perhaps the bulk of patients in institutions, regardless of class status or social situation, are favorably disposed to the hospital because it offers them the opportunity to relieve symptoms, learn to cope with life difficulties, overcome personal inadequacies, or correct behavioral problems. Whatever the reason, it seems that psychiatrists and other mental health professionals have misjudged how patients might feel about their illness, hospitalization, or treatment. This conclusion is substantiated by studies that have reported that staff often failed to accurately estimate patient attitudes (Kahn et al., 1979; Zaslove et al., 1966).

The patients and personnel of mental hospitals have been found, in various studies, to differ significantly in their perceptions of mental illness (Weinstein, 1977: 13). Patients have less general knowledge of psychiatry, adhere more to custodial ideology, and believe more in physical causation than do professional or treatment staff. It was anticipated, therefore, that patients would be less favorable toward hospitalization, staff, or treatment than hospital personnel, but this was borne out in only 19 of the 47 cases summarized that compared both groups. In the remaining cases patients were more favorable than staff slightly more often than they were similar to them. Thus, although in any mental hospital there are sharp differences between its patients and personnel in social status, role expectations, and personal experiences, such differences are not always manifested in terms of attitude.

Qualitative methods in social research are important means of obtaining data on human behavior and cultural patterns. Participant observations and informal interviews are especially useful for uncovering people's interpretations of social events and their own or someone else's behavior. One of the most important functions of qualitative methods is to stimulate or "set the stage" for later data collection via quantitative methods, and this is exactly what happened with studies of the mental hospital from the patient's view. Several Table 5.2 researchers (Levinson and Gallagher, 1964: 8-11; Linn, 1968; Reznikoff et al., 1959) reviewed the earlier qualitative studies and stated categorically that these works formed the backdrop for their quantitative studies of patients' attitudes. However, the data generated from the two types of methods differ greatly because by and large qualitative researchers failed to consider the *positive* experiences patients often encounter in the hospital. Studies of the kind given in Table 5.1 have overlooked the fact that the hospital provides various social and psychological opportunities for patients, the potential for rehabilitation, and at times a more protective environment than that enjoyed on the outside (Killian and Bloomberg, 1975). Much of this research has disregarded the restitutive processes that can occur inadvertently with mental hospitalization (such as for personal stability or family reintegration) and has instead focused on the debilitating processes (Gove, 1970). Unfortunately, it is the qualitative report of the mental hospital—with interesting, though one-sided, anecdotes and descriptions—that is more often read, quoted, and cited by mental health professionals.

The key observation of this study, that patients in about 75 percent of the hospital samples reviewed espoused favorable attitudes, was frankly quite surprising to us. We had anticipated that patients in perhaps 20-30 percent of the Table 5.2 studies would be positive, as we, too, pictured the mental hospital as a "total institution" with all the concomitant detriments the term implies. We can thus join ranks with other mental health researchers who have recently reported results that run counter to popular beliefs (Frank et al., 1978; Pearlin and Schooler, 1979). The facts concerning patients' degree of favorableness toward mental hospitals do not coincide with the myth about patients' attitudes.

NOTE

1. Some researchers made patient-nonpatient comparisons for 2-3 types of attitudes.

REFERENCES

ALLEN, J. C. and G. M. BARTON (1976) "Patient comments about hospitalization: implications for change." Comprehensive Psychiatry 17: 631-640.

ALMOND, R., K. KENISTON, and S. BOLTAX (1968) "The value system of a milieu therapy unit." Archives of General Psychiatry 19: 545-561.

ANSPACH, R. R. (1979) "From stigma to identity politics: political activism among the physically disabled and former mental patients." Social Science and Medicine 13A: 765-773.

BACKNER, B. L. and R. D. KISSINGER (1963) "Hospitalized patients' attitudes toward mental health professionals and mental patients." Journal of Nervous and Mental Disease 136: 72-75.

BARTON, G. M. and N. SCHEER (1975) "A measurement of attitudes about an activity program." American Journal of Occupational Therapy 29: 284-287.

CAUDILL, W., F. C. REDLICH, H. R. GILMORE, and E. B. BRODY (1952) "Social structure and interaction processes on a psychiatric ward." American Journal of Orthopsychiatry 22: 314-334.

CHASTKO, H. E., I. D. GLICK, E. GOULD, and W. A. HARGREAVES (1971) "Patients' posthospital evaluations of psychiatric nursing treatment." Nursing Research 20: 333-338.

CLARKE, G. J. (1979) "In defense of deinstitutionalization." Milbank Memorial Fund Quarterly 57: 461-469.

DOWDS, B. N. and A. F. FONTANA (1977) "Patients' and therapists' expectations and evaluations of hospital treatment: satisfactions and disappointments." Comprehensive Psychiatry 18: 295-300.

DUNHAM, H. W. and S. K. WEINBERG (1960) The Culture of the State Mental Hospital. Detroit: Wayne State University.

Raymond M. Weinstein 143

EATON, M. T. and M. H. PETERSON (1969) Psychiatry. Flushing, NY: Medical Examination Publishing.
ELLSWORTH, R. and R. MARONEY (1972) "Characteristics of psychiatric programs and their effects on patients' adjustment." Journal of Consulting and Clinical Psychology 39: 436-447.
――― W. KLETT, H. GORDON, and R. GUNN (1971) "Milieu characteristics of successful psychiatric treatment programs." American Journal of Orthopsychiatry 41: 427-441.
FRANK, A., S. EISENTHAL, and A. LAZARE (1978) "Are there social class differences in patients' treatment conceptions? Myths and facts." Archives of General Psychiatry 35: 61-69.
FREEMAN, C.P.L. and R. E. KENDELL (1980) "ECT: I. Patients' experiences and attitudes." British Journal of Psychiatry 137: 8-16.
FRYLING, V. B. and A. G. FRYLING (1960) "Patients' attitudes toward sociotherapy." Psychiatric Quarterly (Supplement) 34: 97-115.
GIOVANNONI, J. M. and L. P. ULLMANN (1963) "Conceptions of mental health held by psychiatric patients." Journal of Clinical Psychology 19: 398-400.
GOFFMAN, E. (1961) Asylums. Garden City, NY: Doubleday.
GOLDMAN, A. R. (1965) "Wanting to leave or stay in a mental hospital: incidence and correlates." Journal of Clinical Psychology 21: 317-322.
GOLDSTEIN, R. H., J. RACY, D. M. DRESSLER, R. A. CIOTTONE, and J. R. WILLIS (1972) "What benefits patients? An inquiry into the opinions of psychiatric inpatients and their residents." Psychiatric Quarterly 46: 49-80.
GORDON, H. L. and C. GROTH (1961) "Mental patients wanting to stay in the hospital." Archives of General Psychiatry 4: 124-130.
GOULD, E. and I. D. GLICK (1976) "Patient-staff judgments of treatment program helpfulness on a psychiatric ward." British Journal of Medical Psychology 49: 23-33.
GOVE, W. R. (1970) "Societal reaction as an explanation of mental illness: an evaluation." American Sociological Review 35: 873-884.
――― and T. FAIN (1977) "A comparison of voluntary and committed psychiatric patients." Archives of General Psychiatry 34: 669-676.
――― (1973) "The stigma of mental hospitalization: an attempt to evaluate its consequences." Archives of General Psychiatry 28: 494-500.
GREENLEY, J. R. (1979) "Familial expectations, posthospital adjustment, and the societal reaction perspective on mental illness." Journal of Health and Social Behavior 20: 217-227.
GYNTHER, M. D., M. REZNIKOFF, and M. FISHMAN (1963) "Attitudes of psychiatric patients toward treatment, psychiatrists and mental hospitals." Journal of Nervous and Mental Disease 136: 68-71.
HAMISTER, R. C. (1955) "An investigation of patient and staff opinions concerning the effectiveness of neuropsychiatric staff members." Journal of Social Psychology 41: 115-137.
HANDLER, L. and G. PERLMAN (1973) "The attitudes of patients and aides toward the role of the psychiatric aide." American Journal of Psychiatry 130: 322-325.
HILLARD, J. R. and R. FOLGER (1977) "Patients' attitudes and attributions to electroconvulsive shock therapy." Journal of Clinical Psychology 33: 855-861.
HUDGENS, R. W. (1963) "Psychiatric inpatients at a teaching hospital: an inquiry into reasons for admission and factors promoting clinical change." Archives of General Psychiatry 9: 384-389.

IMRE, P. D. (1962) "Attitudes of volunteers toward mental hospitals compared to patients and personnel." Journal of Clinical Psychology 18: 516.
——— and S. WOLF (1962) "Attitudes of patients and personnel toward mental hospitals." Journal of Clinical Psychology 18: 232-234.
ISHIYAMA, T., J. M. DENNY, R. PRADA, and R. VESPE (1962) "The role of the psychologist on mental hospital wards as defined by the expectant-others." Journal of Clinical Psychology 18: 3-10.
JANSEN, D. J. (1973) "What state hospital psychiatric patients want more of and less of in treatment." Journal of Consulting and Clinical Psychology 41: 317.
——— and M. W. ALDRICH (1973) "State hospital psychiatric patients evaluate their treatment teams." Hospital and Community Psychiatry 24: 768-770.
JONES, N. F., N. W. KAHN, and J. M. MacDONALD (1963) "Psychiatric patients' views of mental illness, hospitalization and treatment." Journal of Nervous and Mental Disease 136: 82-87.
KAHN, M. W. and N. F. JONES (1969) "A comparison of attitudes of mental patients from various mental hospital settings." Journal of Clinical Psychology 25: 312-316.
KAHN, M. W. and D. S. WEBER (1972) "Attitude variables associated with patient response to hospitalization." Journal of Consulting and Clinical Psychology 38: 150.
KAHN, M. W., L. OBSTFELD, and S. HEIMAN (1979) "Staff conceptions of patients' attitudes toward mental disorder and hospitalization as compared to patients' and staff's actual attitudes." Journal of Clinical Psychology 35: 415-420.
KEITH-SPIEGEL, P., H. M. GRAYSON, and D. SPIEGEL (1970) "Using the discharge interview to evaluate a psychiatric hospital." Mental Hygiene 54: 298-300.
KILLIAN, L. M. and S. BLOOMBERG (1975) "Rebirth in a therapeutic community: a case study." Psychiatry 38: 39-54.
KISH, G. B. (1971) "Evaluation of ward atmosphere." Hospital and Community Psychiatry 22: 159-161.
KLASS, D. B., G. A. GROWE, and M. STRIZICH (1977) "Ward treatment milieu and posthospital functioning." Archives of General Psychiatry 34: 1047-1052.
KLOPFER, W. G., A. L. WYLIE, and J. S. HILLSON (1956) "Attitudes towards mental hospitals." Journal of Clinical Psychology 12: 361-365.
KONICK, D. (1971) "A summary of patients' responses on four hospital milieu scales." Intramural Report IX, Cleveland Psychiatric Institute.
KOTIN, J. and J. M. SCHUR (1969) "Attitudes of discharged mental patients toward their hospital experiences." Journal of Nervous and Mental Disease 149: 408-414.
LEE, H. S. (1979) "Patients' comments on psychiatric inpatient treatment experiences: patient-therapist relationships and their implications for treatment outcome." Psychiatric Quarterly 51: 39-54.
LEONARD, C. V. (1973) "What helps most about hospitalization?" Comprehensive Psychiatry 14: 365-369.
LEVINSON, D. J. and E. B. GALLAGHER (1964) Patienthood in the Mental Hospital. Boston: Houghton Mifflin.
LINN, L. S. (1968) "The mental hospital from the patient perspective." Psychiatry 31: 213-223.
LOWENKOPF, E. and M. GREENSTEIN (1972) "How state hospital patients view their illness." Diseases of the Nervous System 33: 679-683.
LUFT, L. L., K. SMITH, and M. KACE (1978) "Therapists', patients', and inpatient staff's views of treatment modes and outcomes." Hospital and Community Psychiatry 29: 505-511.

MARTIN, P. J., M. H. FRIEDMEYER, J. E. MOORE, and R. A. CLAVEAUX (1977) "Patients' expectancies and improvement in treatment: the shape of the link." Journal of Clinical Psychology 33: 827-833.

MAYER, J. E. and A. ROSENBLATT (1974) "Clash in perspective between mental patients and staff." American Journal of Orthopsychiatry 44: 432-441.

MAYO, C., R. G. HAVELOCK, and D. L. SIMPSON (1971) "Attitudes toward mental illness among psychiatric patients and their wives." Journal of Clinical Psychology 27: 128-132.

MOOS, R. H. (1974) Evaluating Treatment Environments: A Social Ecological Approach. New York: John Wiley.

MORROW, W. R. (1973) "Effects of a nursing home visit on state hospital patients' attitudes toward nursing home placement." Journal of Geriatric Psychiatry 6: 122-133.

OLINICK, S. L. (1964) "The negative therapeutic reaction." International Journal of Psychoanalysis 45: 540-548.

PEARLIN, L. I. and C. SCHOOLER (1979) "Some extensions of 'the structure of coping.'" Journal of Health and Social Behavior 20: 202-205.

PETTIT, D. E. (1971) "Patients' attitudes toward ECT—not the 'shocker' we think?" Canadian Psychiatric Association Journal 16: 365-366.

PIERCE, W. D., E. J. TRICKETT, and R. H. MOOS (1972) "Changing ward atmosphere through staff discussion of the perceived ward environment." Archives of General Psychiatry 26: 35-41.

PINE, F. and D. J. LEVINSON (1961) "A sociopsychological conception of patient-hood." International Journal of Social Psychiatry 7: 106-123.

POLAK, P. (1970) "Patterns of discord: goals of patients, therapists, and community members." Archives of General Psychiatry 23: 277-283.

QUADAGNO, J. S. and R. J. ANTONIO (1976) "Labeling theory as an oversocialized conception of man: the case of mental illness." Sociology and Social Research 60: 33-45.

REZNIKOFF, M., J. P. BRADY, and W. W. ZELLER (1959) "The psychiatric attitudes battery: a procedure for assessing attitudes toward psychiatric treatment and hospitals." Journal of Clinical Psychology 15: 260-265.

——— and L. C. TOOMEY (1960) "Attitudinal change in hospitalized psychiatric patients." Journal of Clinical and Experimental Psychopathology 21: 309-314.

ROBACK, H. and W. U. SNYDER (1965) "A comparison of hospitalized mental patients' adjustment with their attitudes toward psychiatric hospitals." Journal of Clinical Psychology 21: 228-230.

ROMAN, P. M. (1971) "Labeling theory and community psychiatry: the impact of psychiatric sociology on ideology and practice in American psychiatry." Psychiatry 34: 378-390.

ROSENBLATT, A. and J. E. MAYER (1974) "The recidivism of mental patients: a review of past studies." American Journal of Orthopsychiatry 44: 697-706.

ROSENHAN, D. L. (1973) "On being sane in insane places." Science 179: 250-258.

SCHEFF, T. J. (1966) Being Mentally Ill: A Sociological Theory. Chicago: Aldine.

SKODOL, A. E., R. PLUTCHIK, and T. B. KARASU (1980) "Expectations of hospital treatment: conflicting views of patients and staff." Journal of Nervous and Mental Disease 168: 70-74.

SMALL, I. F., J. G. SMALL, and R. GONZALEZ (1965) "The clinical correlates of attitudinal change during psychiatric treatment." American Journal of Psychotherapy 19: 66-74.

SMALL, J. G., I. F. SMALL, and M. P. HAYDEN (1965) "Prognosis and change in attitude: the importance of shifts of opinion in psychiatric patients." Journal of Nervous and Mental Disease 140: 215-217.

SONN, M. (1977) "Patients' subjective experiences of psychiatric hospitalization," pp. 245-264 in T. C. Manschreck and A. M. Kleinman (eds.) Renewal in Psychiatry. New York: John Wiley.

SOUELEM, O. (1955) "Mental patients' attitudes toward mental hospitals." Journal of Clinical Psychology 11: 181-185.

SPENCER, J. (1977) "Psychiatry and convulsant therapy." Medical Journal of Australia 1: 844-847.

SPIEGEL, D. and J. B. YOUNGER (1972) "Ward climate and community stay of psychiatric patients." Journal of Consulting and Clinical Psychology 39: 62-69.

STANTON, A. H. and M. S. SCHWARTZ (1954) The Mental Hospital. New York: Basic Books.

TOOMEY, L. C., M. REZNIKOFF, J. P. BRADY, and D. W. SCHUMANN (1961) "Attitudes of nursing students toward psychiatric treatment and hospitals." Mental Hygiene 45: 589-602.

TOWNSEND, J. M. (1976) "Self-concept and the institutionalization of mental patients: an overview and critique." Journal of Health and Social Behavior 17: 263-271.

——— (1975) "Cultural conceptions and mental illness: a controlled comparison of Germany and America." Journal of Nervous and Mental Disease 160: 409-421.

VERINIS, J. S. and J. A. FLAHERTY (1978) "Using the Ward Atmosphere Scale to help change the treatment environment." Hospital and Community Psychiatry 29: 238-240.

WEINSTEIN, R. M. (1981a) "Mental patients' attitudes toward hospital staff: a review of quantitative research." Archives of General Psychiatry 38: 483-489.

——— (1981b) "Attitudes toward psychiatric treatment among hospitalized patients: a review of quantitative research." Social Science and Medicine 15E: 301-314.

——— (1979) "Patient attitudes toward mental hospitalization: a review of quantitative research." Journal of Health and Social Behavior 20: 237-258.

——— (1977) "Patient attitudes toward mental illness and the mentally ill." Current Concepts in Psychiatry 3: 7-13.

——— (1972) "Patients' perceptions of mental illness: paradigms for analysis." Journal of Health and Social Behavior 13: 38-47.

WING, J. K. (1962) "Institutionalism in mental hospitals." British Journal of Social and Clinical Psychology 1: 38-51.

WOLFENSBERGER, W. P. (1958) "Attitudes of alcoholics toward mental hospitals." Quarterly Journal of Studies of Alcohol 19: 447-451.

ZASLOVE, M. O., J. T. UNGERLEIDER, and M. C. FULLER (1968) "The importance of the psychiatric nurse: views of physicians, patients, and nurses." American Journal of Psychiatry 125: 482-486.

——— (1966) "How psychiatric hospitalization helps: patient views vs. staff views." Journal of Nervous and Mental Disease 142: 568-576.

DEINSTITU-
TIONALIZING
THE
MENTALLY ILL
Process,
Outcomes, and
New Directions

JOSEPH P. MORRISSEY

AUTHOR'S NOTE: The state mental hospital data cited here were assembled with the assistance of Michael Witkin and Laura Sayer, Division of Biometry and Epidemiology, NIMH; Kathy Fagerstrom and Penny O'Daniels, California Department of Mental Health; Abbott Weinstein and Al Maiwald, New York State Department of Mental Hygiene; and Doris Pearsall, Massachusetts Department of Mental Health. The comments of Howard Goldman, Phil Brown, and Henry Steadman on an earlier version of this chapter are also gratefully acknowledged.

The history of public intervention in America on behalf of the sick, the poor, and the disabled reveals a cyclical pattern of policy initiatives spawned by transitory social reform movements. Sporadic exposés and demands for reform have led to short-lived programs intended to upgrade existing conditions to a decent level of humane care. The residue of each reform set the stage for the next generation of innovators, with little cumulative impact on the fundamental nature of the social problems to which the reforms were addressed. Nowhere is this pattern better illustrated than in public provisions for the care and treatment of the mentally ill (Morrissey et al., 1980).

The development of state mental hospitals in the early part of the nineteenth century represented the first formal system of public care for the mentally ill in this country (Grob, 1966, 1973; Caplan, 1969; Rothman, 1971). These hospitals were founded during an era of social reform in response to the failures of "outdoor relief" and the practice of incarcerating the insane in local almshouses and jails. In contrast to the pattern of physical abuse, neglect, and ridicule that characterized these settings, the early mental hospitals were championed as repositories of hope and humane care for the mentally ill. Under the aegis of "moral treatment," the first state mental hospitals claimed high rates of recovery for persons brought under early care (Bockoven, 1972). Quick success fueled the reformist zeal of social activist groups whose lobbying efforts before state legislatures led to the proliferation of publicly supported mental hospitals throughout the country. The optimism of this era soon dissipated, however, in the throes of massive waves of immigration, the accumulation of chronic patients, and the growing belief in the incurability of insanity.

What started out as a limited-purpose institution was transformed in the late nineteenth century into a general-purpose solution for the social welfare burdens of a society undergoing rapid industrialization and stratification along social class and ethnic lines (Grob, 1973; Scull, 1977). With the death or retirement of the early moral therapists, the new generation of psychiatrists passively accepted the social role of these hospitals while actively attending to their own professionalization. In time, both hospital staff and local communities accepted as fact that the majority of patients committed to state hospitals were destined to reside there for years. With overcrowding and staff shortages, the hospitals imposed a uniform custodial routine on all patients, leading to their "institutionalization," or total dependency on the hospital (Wing, 1962; Gruenberg, 1974). Almost within a generation of their widespread introduction, therefore, state mental hospitals were changed from small, intimate, therapeutically oriented "asylums" to large, impersonal, custodially oriented "warehouses," filled primarily with members of the lower classes who suffered from a bewildering array of physical, mental, and social "ills."

For the last two or three decades, another major reform in public mental health services has held sway under the aegis of "community mental health." A central thrust of this reform movement has been *deinstitutionalization:* an effort to dismantle and close state mental hospitals and to relocate their clientele in a new network of community-based mental health services (Bachrach, 1976, 1978). This dual objective was made plausible by the discovery and widespread use of psychotropic drugs[1] in the mid-1950s, by changes in psychosocial treatment approaches, and by the growing availability of nursing homes and general hospital-based psychiatric services. The near-term accomplishments of this movement seemingly rival the success claims advanced for the early mental hospitals. Between 1955 and 1980, for example, the resident population of state mental hospitals was reduced by more than 75 percent, or approximately 420,000 occupied beds, and, since the mid-1960s, over 700 community mental health centers (CMHCs) serving catchment areas representing 50 percent of the U.S. population have been created with the massive financial support of the federal government.

Upon closer examination, however, there is clear and convincing evidence that the "bold new approach" embodied in this latest reform has yet to supplant the state hospitals, and that it may even have created as many problems as it attempted to solve (Bassuk and Gerson, 1978; Rose, 1979; Gruenberg and Archer, 1979). In a number of respects, therefore, the deinstitutionalization movement has followed the cyclical course of earlier reforms (Morrissey et al., 1980) and its aftermath has set the stage for a new round of planning and program development in an effort to remedy the failings of public mental health policy during the past decade (Scherl and Macht, 1980).

While there are a number of parallels in the processes and outcomes of deinstitutionalization in various parts of the country, there are important between-state differences as well. The similarities reside in the two distinct phases through which this reform movement was carried out; the role of ideological, legal, and fiscal interests in initiating and accelerating this movement; and the enduring functions of state mental hospitals in the contemporary mental health system. The between-state differences, in turn, reside in the timing and pace of change in each phase; the size-composition of the residual populations still served by these institutions; and the fiscal-administrative structures for the delivery of public mental health services in each state.

This chapter will present an overview of these similarities and differences, identify new programmatic directions currently being pursued in the aftermath of more than a decade of rapid deinstitutionalization, and suggest a number of policy research issues that warrant careful study in the years ahead. The presentation will rely on the experiences of California, Massachusetts, and New York—three states that have been in the forefront of the deinstitutionalization movement in the United States.

PROCESSES OF STATE HOSPITAL DEINSTITUTIONALIZATION

Although the term "deinstitutionalization" only came into popular use in the mid-1970s, its core ideal—the phase-out of state mental hospitals—had been the subject of continuous policy debates since the early 1950s (Mechanic, 1969). These debates were sustained by two essentially antagonistic ideologies, one rooted in institutional psychiatry and the other in community mental health. The first called for a regeneration of state mental hospitals as the hub of the mental health services network, while the second called instead for the early demise of state hospitals and their replacement by a new community-based and community-controlled mental health services delivery system.

During the 1950s and early 1960s, state government policy makers fostered both models of care. While most legislatures expanded appropriations for improvements in state hospital facilities and for increased staffing ratios, several also initiated support for the growth of community-based programs. New York, for example, enacted the nation's first community mental health legislation in 1954 (Hunt and Forstenzer, 1957) and California enacted similar provisions in the Short-Doyle Act of 1957 (Jacobson, 1973; Segal and Aviram, 1978). In both states, the legislation authorized the establishment of county mental health boards to plan and supervise the development of community mental health services. State reimbursements to counties were authorized on a 50/50 state-to-local matching basis. These funds provided the initial impetus for the expansion of local outpatient services and the development of short-term inpatient units for voluntary patients in general hospitals. Responsibility for providing long-term treatment and custodial care, however, continued to be assumed by state government. The vast majority of patients in the state hospitals were hospitalized on involuntary legal statuses, and admissions were secured primarily through civil petitions and court commitment procedures (Robitscher, 1978).

At the outset, the upgrading of state hospitals and the expansion of community mental health services worked to the mutual advantage of the opposing interest groups. In order to transform state hospitals into active treatment institutions, for example, the overcrowding had to be reduced by resocialization and community placement programs and, if newly admitted patients were to be returned to their community of origin as quickly as possible, then expanded community aftercare programs had to be supported. Similarly, since the new community mental health ideology advocated the eventual repatriation of institutionalized patients, the improvement of state hospital programs that would foster their rehabilitation and release was both necessary and desirable.

In 1955 the resident patient census of state mental hospitals in the United States reached its maximum of 558,922 persons (Table 6.1). During that year there were 185,597 admissions, for a combined total of 744,519 patient care episodes.[2] While the year 1955 is often cited as the peak of state hospital use in this country, the number of patient care episodes in these facilities continued to expand each year for the next decade. In 1964 they reached an all-time high of 807,113, or 8.4 percent

TABLE 6.1   Trends in State Mental Hospital Deinstitutionalization, 1950-1980

	United States Totals[a]				California[b]				Massachusetts[c]				New York[d]			
Year	Resident Patients	Total Admissions	Patient Care Episodes (PCE)	% Change PCE	Resident Patients	Total Admissions	Patient Care Episodes (PCE)	% Change PCE	Resident Patients	Total Admissions	Patient Care Episodes (PCE)	% Change PCE	Resident Patients	Total Admissions	Patient Care Episodes (PCE)	% Change PCE
1950	512,501	152,079	664,580	—	32,430	14,768	47,198	—	23,657	7,208	30,865	—	82,971	20,929	103,900	—
1955	558,922	185,597	744,519	+12.0	36,927	17,073	54,000	+14.4	23,302	7,853	31,155	+ 0.9	93,379	21,925	115,304	+11.0
1960	535,540	252,742	788,282	+ 5.9	36,853	23,790	60,643	+12.3	22,174	10,485	32,659	+ 5.8	88,824	27,676	116,500	+ 1.0
1965	475,202	328,564	803,766	+ 2.0	30,193	26,799	57,424	− 5.3	21,406	11,737	33,143	+ 1.5	84,859	36,466	121,325	+ 4.1
1970	337,619	402,472	740,091	− 8.0	12,671	42,040	54,711	− 4.7	18,508	12,988	31,496	− 5.0	64,257	35,742	99,999	−17.6
1975	193,436	376,156	569,592	−23.0	6,468	27,735	34,203	−37.5	6,767	8,438	15,205	−48.3	33,292	26,861	60,153	−39.8
1980	137,810	332,920	470,730[e]	−17.4	5,209	18,893	24,102	−29.5	2,213[f]	6,038	8,251[f]	−45.7	24,961	22,897	47,858	−20.4

a. United States data were obtained from *Provisional Patient Movement and Administrative Data on State and County Mental Hospitals: 1950-1979*, Division of Biometry and Epidemiology, National Institute of Mental Health.

b. California data were obtained from *Annual Statistical Reports*, California Department of Mental Health.

c. Massachusetts data for 1950-1959 were obtained from NIMH patient movement files (see note a). For 1960-1980, data were obtained from *Annual Statistical Summary for Inpatient Facilities*, Massachusetts Department of Mental Health.

d. New York data were obtained from the Office of Statistical and Clinical Information Systems, New York State Office of Mental Health.

e. Estimate based on resident patients at end of fiscal year 1979 and admissions during fiscal year 1979.

f. This figure represents the average daily census for the fiscal year ending June 30, 1980.

more than in 1955. For the nation as a whole this growth was occasioned by rapid increases in annual admissions (+71 percent over 1955), which offset the gradual annual decrease in resident patients (-12 percent over 1955). These national trends, however, mask a number of important differences at the state level.

The starting conditions for the 3 states listed in Table 6.1, as indexed by the sheer magnitude and composition of their state hospital populations, were markedly different. In 1955, New York's resident patient census (93,379) was 4 times as large as the state hospital census in Massachusetts (23,302) and 2.5 times as large as the state hospital census in California (36,927). Moreover, long-stay patients composed a much larger proportion of the resident caseload in New York and Massachusetts than in California. Of the 93,379 resident patients in New York in 1955, over 60 percent had a length of stay of at least 5 years and roughly 33 percent had been continuously hospitalized for 15 years or longer (Weinstein, 1971). The only comparable datum for California is "time of record" of resident patients in 1960, which is biased toward an inflated length-of-stay profile.[3] Of the 36,556 resident patients in 1960, nonetheless, about 45 percent had been hospitalized for 5 years or longer and only about 14 percent for 15 years or longer. While precise data are not available for Massachusetts, it had the smallest resident census of the 3 states in 1955 and its length-of-stay profile fell between those of New York and California.

Over the period 1955-1960, Massachusetts closely paralleled the national trends with a 5 percent census reduction, a 34 percent growth in admissions, and a net increase of 6 percent in patient care episodes.[4] New York also experienced a 5 percent hospital census reduction, but the admissions increase was slower at 26 percent, for a net growth of only 1 percent in patient care episodes. California, in contrast, had a more rapidly expanding mental hospital system during the late 1950s. While its resident census had reached a plateau and remained relatively stable, admissions experienced a 39 percent increase and patient care episodes grew by 12 percent.

The first consistent drop in California's resident census did not occur until 1960, but it soon began to catch up, and to quickly exceed, the trend in other states. Between 1960 and 1965 the resident census decreased by 18 percent, admissions increased by 13 percent, and patient care episodes fell by 5 percent. (The initial decline in California's episodes of care occurred in 1964, after reaching a peak of nearly 62,000.) It was the first of these states to reduce overall patient care episodes in state hospitals. In New York and Massachusetts the resident census declines over the same interval were only 5 percent and 4 percent, respectively. With a continued annual increase in admissions, episodes of care edged upward in both states.

Throughout this period, policies governing state mental hospital utilization were based on a benign form of deinstitutionalization that led to "opening the back doors" of these institutions for the release of chronic patients and for the early discharge of newly admitted patients. As long as "revolving door" patients could be easily returned to these hospitals by local agencies or police authorities, deinstitutionalization was not a major political issue. State hospitals provided back-up for the fledgling community mental health programs, which were able, in turn, to concentrate on the development of services for less disabled clients in the community.

The fiscal structure of mental health services contributed to the heightened use of state mental hospitals and the gradual emergence of a dual system of services. In California, under the Short-Doyle legislation, state funds supported the total cost of treating patients in state hospitals, but only a fraction of the cost of treating them in local programs. This legislation thereby created fiscal incentives for local programs to hospitalize patients: "Treating patients in the community resulted in a local tax burden while state hospital confinement did not add to it" (Urmer, 1978: 144). Similarly, Bodin et al. (1972: 942) noted that in New York "when a patient enters a state institution, his local community no longer assumes any responsibility for his support. As a result, there is a tendency to remove patients from their communities and confine them in remote state institutions."

The differential trends that began to emerge in the early 1960s reflected historical legacies as well as the administrative policies that state mental hospital authorities adopted in each state. Massachusetts and New York had been in the forefront of the institutional psychiatry movement since the mid-nineteenth century. In 1955, there were 14 state mental hospitals in Massachusetts and 23 in New York (NIMH, 1955: 6). The residue of a large network of geographically dispersed institutions in each state represented a "sunk cost" (Stinchcombe, 1965: 168) and a reality constraint on efforts to embrace the new community mental health philosophy. As a result, reformers in Massachusetts and New York relied upon a strategy of transforming state mental institutions into community-oriented "open hospitals" providing intensive inpatient care and strengthened "aftercare" services. State hospitals, in several instances, began to function as "community mental health centers" offering day care, night care, aftercare, and emergency services in addition to both short-term and long-term inpatient treatment (Morrissey et al., 1980; Hunt et al., 1961;

Gruenberg, 1966). Moreover, the intensity of efforts to reinstitute active psychosocial treatment and to shorten length of stay with the aid of psychoactive drugs was matched by a readiness to readmit patients who deteriorated after being placed in family-care and other community settings. In these respects both states followed administrative policies modeled upon the British mental hospital experience of the early 1950s (Gruenberg, 1974; Bennett, 1979). By focusing upon state hospital-based outreach programs and encouraging more flexible use of state hospital inpatient services, administrators in Massachusetts and New York were attempting to adapt institutional psychiatry to a new set of social conditions.

California, in contrast, pursued a different course. At the start of World War II, California operated only seven state mental hospitals. In 1947, with the beginnings of its post-World War II population boom, California sought temporary relief from the overcrowded conditions in these facilities by acquiring two surplus military hospitals built during the war in DeWitt and Modesto (Bardach, 1972: 135). In 1954, a tenth facility was opened in Atascadero for mentally ill offenders. Community mental health advocacy and lobbying throughout the 1950s, however, led to the formulation of long-range plans for the location of all new services in the community rather than in the state hospital system (Segal and Aviram, 1978: 33-50). The immense capital investment necessary to refurbish the state hospital system and to expand it closer to the areas of new population growth was judged to be neither politically nor economically feasible. Instead, these plans called for a "depopulation project" designed to reduce the state hospital patient census without additional state appropriations.

A combination of factors facilitated the implementation of these plans. In 1962 the U.S. Department of Health, Education and Welfare revised its policy toward mental patients so that persons on conditional release from mental hospitals were no longer barred from eligibility for state public-assistance programs by lack of matching federal funds. California capitalized on this opportunity by instituting a public-assistance program for the mentally handicapped in the following year, thereby creating economic incentives for local communities to care for former patients (Segal and Aviram, 1978). In 1963 a Geriatric Screening Project was also initiated to reduce admissions and to find alternative income maintenance and medical services for those aged who otherwise would have been committed to state institutions (Aviram et al., 1976). With the enactment of the Medicaid-Medicare amendments to the U.S. Social Security Act in 1965, mental patients also became eligible for expanded medical services and nursing home care. These income maintenance and administrative reforms led to the growth of the nursing home industry in California and the beginnings of the rapid census decline in its state mental hospitals.

With the rise of civil libertarianism in the mid-1960s, however, forces were set in motion that radically altered the character and pace of deinstitutionalization in each state. Initially, the focus of these concerns was on the state hospital commitment process and its gross violation of the patient's due process rights (Robitscher, 1978). In 1965, the laws affecting admissions to New York state mental hospitals were revised and updated. These reforms, characterized as "the most revolutionary in this country in the field of mental health in a century" (Wiley, 1965: 2722), encouraged increased use of voluntary admission procedures and required the conversion of all involuntary patients in treatment facilities (who were so suitable) to a voluntary or informal status. This legislation abolished court certification of involuntary hospitalization (the primary means of state hospitalization prior to its enactment) and established a system of initial admissions based upon medical judgment (two physician's certificates) with constitutional safeguards of notice and right to judicial hearings on the need for hospitalization and its extension beyond 60 days. The new law also established the Mental Health Information Service, as an adjunct of the New York State Supreme Court, to oversee the protection of these rights and procedures.

In California, community mental health advocates joined forces with civil libertarians and fiscal conservatives in an effort to gain legislative support for the phase-out of the entire state hospital system.[5] In 1966 the Assembly Subcommittee on Mental Health Services issued a report concluding that "the commitment process was the most critical factor shaping the California mental health system" because it "fostered the public's erroneous equation of mental illness with dangerousness, controlled the major treatment process by funneling most of the state's mental health budget into the state hospital system, and, thus, perpetuated a singular treatment approach that was frequently inappropriate and unsuccessful" (Urmer, 1978: 139). Characterizing the report as "an ideological instrument carefully constructed to put forth a particular point of view," Cameron (1978: 314) notes that:

> if the Subcommittee had centered its attention on termination of the state hospitals, it would have faced considerable resistance. Abolition of involuntary commitment would, however, achieve essentially the same purpose since the hospital clientele was predominantly this category of patient. By concentrating on the commitment issue, and capitalizing on the ideological thrust toward non-

institutional community-based care, the Subcommittee successfully
generated enough moral indignation to alter the system radically.

This report, in conjunction with the skillful lobbying and proselytizing
efforts of "a small group of citizens" (Jacobson, 1973: 55), led to the
formulation of the Lanterman-Petris-Short (LPS) Act, which was passed in
1967 and became effective July 1, 1969 (also see Bardach, 1972). Similar
to that in New York, this legislation extensively revised the criteria and
procedures for involuntary hospitalization while ensuring the legal and
civil rights of persons so detained.[6] The unique feature of the LPS
legislation, however, was the transfer of responsibility for all clients in the
mental health system to local communities (Jacobson, 1973). To assist
counties in meeting these new responsibilities, a Community Mental
Health Services Act was passed in 1968. It revised the Short-Doyle Act and
stipulated that all services to the mentally disordered had to be provided
through a single system of care financed by a single appropriation on a
90/10 percent state/local basis. Responsibility for the mental health service system (both state hospitals and county programs) was assigned to
county mental health directors, who would have the authority to designate
which agencies would carry out which responsibilities according to the
service priorities established by law. In effect, the new laws made the
criteria for involuntary commitment much more stringent, and removed
the fiscal incentives for using state hospitals that were engendered by the
original Short-Doyle Act.

In 1970, following the precedents established in New York and California, the Massachusetts legislature enacted mental health law reforms that
limited the criteria and intent of involuntary hospitalization and encouraged the use of voluntary admissions to state hospitals.[7] Unlike that in
California, however, this legislation did not affect the fiscal structure of
the public mental health system. As in New York, the bulk of state
appropriations for mental health services still flowed to the state hospitals,
which served as the primary vehicle for delivery of inpatient as well as
outpatient and rehabilitation services.

In each state, with the "voluntarization" of the admissions process and
the tightening of the criteria for involuntary hospitalization, state mental
hospital authorities for the first time acquired a legal basis for reversing the
community "dumping" process that contributed to the rise of the custodial mental hospital in the latter half of the nineteenth century (Morrissey
and Tessler, 1981). The rise of right to treatment litigation in the late
1960s contributed to the enforcement of these legislative provisions and
an abrupt change in the pace and character of deinsitutionalization. The

earlier strategy of "opening the back doors" was complemented with a newer strategy of "closing the front doors" of state hospitals. This litigation clearly implied that states either had to phase out their mental hospitals or invest considerable sums of money in bringing them up to court-ordered standards (Robitscher, 1976). The fiscal crises that began to envelope the states during the early 1970s created pressures to meet this judicial challenge by resorting to the rapid phase-down of state institutions. In the process, deinstitutionalization practices shifted from a benign reform to a radical program of census run-downs. The remainder of this section will highlight the sequence of events in each state.

In New York, state hospital admissions continued to increase after the passage of the new commitment laws in 1965 (Table 6.1). For the 5 years prior to its enactment (1961-1965), voluntary admissions averaged 27.8 percent of the annual total (Weinstein and Maiwald, 1974: 19). By the end of fiscal year 1966 (March 31, 1966) voluntary admissions rose to 33.4 percent and, within 5 years, they rose to 47.8 percent of the total. The most immediate impact of this legislation, however, was on the resident census. From 1966 to 1968 the decrease exceeded 2,000 patients each year compared to an average reduction of 850 per year from 1955 to 1965 (Weinstein and Maiwald, 1974: 13). While the cumulative census reduction over this 3-year period amounted to 8.3 percent, admission increases led to a continued growth in patient care episodes that reached an all-time high of 124,337 during fiscal year 1968.

At that time, 40 percent of the patients in New York state hospitals were over 65 years of age—half of these had aged into geriatric status and half had been admitted in old age (Markson et al., 1971). In June 1968 the Department of Mental Hygiene announced a new policy concerning the screening of geriatric admissions to state mental hospitals. Citing provisions in the 1965 law that indicated that "the need for hospitalization shall be *confirmed* by the receiving hospital," the department's directive stated that individuals would not be accepted for state hospital admission "if care and treatment would more appropriately be given by another facility. . . . Patients would not be admitted when their problems are primarily social, medical, or financial or for the convenience of some other care facility" (Cumming, 1968: 2). Similar to the earlier geriatric screening projects in California, this policy had a twofold objective of reducing inappropriate admissions (targeted at 4000 by the end of fiscal 1969) and encouraging local communities to develop more adequate services for the aged. Treatment teams were established to screen, to refer individuals for appropriate services, and to provide follow-up reviews of those not admitted to state hospitals (Markson et al., 1971).

The vigorous enforcement of this policy accounted for 30 percent of the overall census reduction between 1969 and 1972 (Weinstein and Maiwald, 1974: 15). The overall reduction within the first year this policy was in effect amounted to 7,295 (9.4 percent), and by the end of fiscal 1972, the cumulative reduction was 30,503 (39.1 percent). The reversal in trend and rapid decline of admissions to New York state hospitals also correspond to the implementation of this policy.[8] In 1969, there were 9 percent fewer admissions than in the previous year and, by 1972, there were 39 percent fewer. By the end of fiscal year 1975 the census was down to 33,292 residents, admissions were reduced to 26,861, and patient care episodes had fallen to 60,153 (Table 6.1). From 1976 to 1980, however, the annual rate of census decline slowed considerably (from 11 percent to less than 4 percent), suggesting that the resident patient population had begun to level off with a core of long-stay patients having limited placement potential (Weinstein, 1980).

In California, the combination of statutory changes in state hospital admissions procedures and the fiscal reorganization of service delivery had abrupt ramifications throughout the mental health system (Jacobson, 1973). Emergency screening for state hospital admissions was transferred to local agencies that had little prior experience with these processes. The initial result was a rise in state hospital admissions but, with the statutory restrictions on length of stay, the average duration of stay was sharply reduced. Urmer (1978: 143), for example, reports that "in the first two years post-LPS, the average treatment duration of *involuntary patients* dropped from 180 days to 15 days, while (unexpectedly) the average duration of *voluntary patients* dropped from 75 to 23 days." Moreover, Cameron (1978: 315) points out that

> the new law was followed by a vigourous effort to deinstitutionalize. Within three years after LPS took effect the resident population had been sliced in half. The multiple incentives designed to depopulate state hospitals and increase local mental health services led to a massive increase in expenditures for local mental health programs. Between fiscal years 1968 and 1973 local programs jumped from 21% to 64% of the state mental health budget. The closure of California's state hospitals began with the implementation of the new law. Between 1970 and 1973, five state hospitals closed their doors to the mentally ill. (One of them continues to admit penal code commitments only.)

Admissions to California state hospitals reached a peak of 42,040 during 1971 and then began a precipitous decline. Over the next 3 years admissions were reduced by 16,408, or 39 percent. In 1973, by announcing plans to close all of California's state mental hospitals, Governor Reagan's administration made it clear that it intended to "get out of the mental health business" (Cameron, 1978: 302). These plans generated widespread opposition among county mental health personnel, legislators, and the general public. This opposition was led by interest groups for the mentally retarded and it effectively blunted the unilateral movement toward further hospital closings. The rapid decline in admissions was also reversed temporarily. Admissions increased by 8 percent in 1975 and 1976, but they were reduced by 14 percent in 1977. Similar to that in New York, the resident census decline in California slowed considerably (from 8 percent to less than 1 percent) between 1978 and 1980. By the end of fiscal year 1980 the census count was 5,209 residents, admissions totaled 18,893, and patient care episodes amounted to 24,102 (Table 6.1).

In Massachusetts, the legislation revising commitment codes became effective in July 1971. It has been characterized as "the *sine qua non* that led to deinstitutionalization" (Myerson, 1975: 8) and "more directly responsible than any other factor for the accelerated census decline evident in our state mental hospitals" (United Community Planning Corporation, 1973: 14). Within its first year of operation, involuntary admissions were reduced from 76 percent to 27 percent, prolonged civil commitments were reduced by 40 percent, and pretrial court commitments were decreased by 50 percent.

> Not only has there been a shift in the proportion of involuntary to voluntary commitments, the [new law] also has tended to reduce the absolute number of admissions to state hospitals. Because of the legislation's more stringent requirements for admissions, mental health personnel throughout the state have demonstrated an increasing reluctance to admit patients, even on a voluntary basis, unless there are compelling reasons to do so" [United Community Planning Corporation, 1973: 14].

In the 2 years following implementation of the revised commitment statutes, the resident census was reduced by 23 percent, total admissions by 24 percent, and patient care episodes by 22 percent. By July 1975 (4 years after the new law became effective), the resident census had been reduced by 59 percent—a rate of reduction that exceeds slightly the 56 percent census decline in the California system during the first 4 years of LPS.

The economic downturn of the mid-1970s led to a fiscal crisis in Massachusetts government and a movement away from the mental health policies of the 1960s. A cap was placed on state expenditures and a policy of dismantling state hospital budgets and programs was implemented (Morrissey et al., 1980). Of 11 state hospitals, 3 were closed and funds were reallocated to area mental health programs. The geographic units at the 8 remaining state hospitals were gradually placed under the control of area program directors and a policy of services contracting with local vendors was established. These administrative and policy changes reinforced the census trends precipitated by the earlier legal reforms. Between 1975 and 1980, patient care episodes were reduced by 46 percent as a result of both resident patient and admission declines amounting to 67 percent and 28 percent, respectively (Table 6.1).

OUTCOMES OF STATE HOSPITAL DEINSTITUTIONALIZATION

As the above synopsis indicates, the character of state hospital deinstitutionalization underwent an abrupt shift in the late 1960s and early 1970s from "opening the back doors" to "closing the front doors" of these institutions. Although the timing of this shift varied in different states, it was the coalescing of diverse interest groups—community mental health advocates, civil libertarians, and fiscal conservatives—that ultimately led to the rapid phase-down of state mental hospitals across the country.

The outcomes of this depopulation process are well known to even casual readers of the recent popular and professional literature: In the past decade, thousands of patients were returned to communities across the country, where they often encountered the hostility and rejection of the general public and the reluctance of community mental health and welfare agencies to assume responsibility for their care.

For years, the latent social function of state hospitals was to serve as a "dumping ground" for residual social problem cases that were burdensome to their families, rejected by other health and welfare agencies, or otherwise regarded as "public nuisances" in their local communities (Belknap, 1956; Strauss and Sabshin, 1961; Fowlkes, 1975). The prospect that these patients would be suddenly "returned home," or (less euphemistically) released en masse, stimulated the economic worries and social prejudices rather than the humanitarian concerns of their fellow citizens (Kirk and Therrien, 1975; Segal et al., 1980). Community groups began to lobby for the restrictive zoning of residential areas while actively blocking the creation of group homes for ex-patients (Segal and Aviram, 1978). Moreover, in many parts of the country, state hospitals represented major sources of employment and a prime market for locally produced goods and services. The closing of these hospitals was seen as posing severe economic burdens on neighboring communities both in terms of lost income and expansion of welfare rolls. Civil service unions also actively lobbied against any hint of job cutbacks or employee transfers that would be necessitated by state hospital phase-downs (Santiestevan, 1975). Stereotypic fears of madmen on the streets also heightened concerns for neighborhood safety and public decency (Siegel, 1978).

The rapid depopulation of state hospitals was also undertaken without careful planning with federally funded community mental health centers (CMHCs) to develop the support services needed for the maintenance of large numbers of severely disabled patients outside institutional settings. From its inception in the mid-1960s, the CMHC program had grown up largely as a separate delivery system without formal linkages to state hospitals (Chu and Trotter, 1974; Musto, 1975). These centers were oriented primarily toward new or "underserved" constituencies in their local communities (Windle and Scully, 1976). Many were still on the drawing boards at the time of the initial influx of deinstitutionalized patients (Bassuk and Gerson, 1978). The first generation of CMHCs soon encountered severe financial crises of their own, and the claims that total community-based care would be more cost-effective than institutional care have yet to be fully demonstrated (Arnhoff, 1975; Braun et al., 1981). Although federal guidelines now mandate twelve essential services (including some forms of partial care), few of these CMHCs have a well-developed spectrum of services for the care of chronic patients, such as halfway houses, group homes, foster-care programs, and other residential units.

In California, despite the explosive increase in the delivery of local mental health services, most communities were not prepared to provide care for the chronically mentally ill (Jacobson, 1973; Urmer, 1978; Cameron, 1978). Few intermediate care facilities were available and most patients were either placed in inadequate board and care homes or left to find their own living arrangements. The expansion of outpatient services had been directed toward a new population of mental health consumers for whom few services were available prior to California's Community Mental Health Services Act of 1968. Cameron (1978: 323), for example, notes that

the focus of attention . . . shifted to a new and more professionally interesting clientele—voluntary patients, those who are more likely to be amenable to service. In one sense, what has occurred is an institutionally prescribed and ideologically sanctioned "creaming" effect in which those who are the easiest to treat are the ones receiving service. The severely mentally ill, on the other hand, are more professionally frustrating; treating them has been largely eschewed with the reorganization of the mental health system.

Similar to the aftermath of deinstitutionalization in California, the burden of caring for the multitude of released patients in New York State fell on the local welfare system. The Department of Mental Hygiene was attacked for "dumping" chronic patients on the community without regard for their aftercare and sustenance needs. The policy of rapid deinstitutionalization became a major political issue in New York, and the news media drew widespread attention to the plight of the mentally ill in local communities (Rivera, 1972; Koenig, 1978).

In a widely publicized article, for example, Reich and Siegel (1973) charged that

> rooming houses, foster homes, nursing homes, and run-down hotels [in New York City] take the place of former back wards. Here, the discharged patients are frequently clustered—unsupervised, unmedicated, uncared for, frequently the prey of unscrupulous and criminal elements. The mass transfer of patients from state care to diverse city and private accommodations has been without benefit, and often with detriment, to the patients themselves. The state hospital back ward may be no worse, and is in some respects better, than a coffin-like room at a deteriorated inner-city hotel or Bowery flophouse.

Thus, rather than "deinstitutionalization," a process of *transinstitutionalization* has occurred for many patients over the past two decades. Thousands of former patients are now living in nursing homes, board and care homes, adult homes, and other institutional settings in the community (Schmidt et al., 1977; Segal and Aviram, 1978; Lamb, 1979; Shadish and Bootzin, 1981). These mostly private, profit-making concerns now serve custody, asylum, and treatment functions for the mentally ill that were once performed almost exclusively by state mental hospitals. The growth of what Warren (1981) has characterized as "social control entrepreneurialism" has thereby perpetuated the segregation of the chronically mentally ill in a new ecological arrangement in the community. Numerous reports also indicate that many other patients are now incarcerated in local jails and correctional facilities (Abrahamson, 1972; Stelovich, 1979; Whitmer, 1980). The transfer of patients from the "backwards to the back alleys" (Aviram and Segal, 1973) has led to widespread concerns that the states have abdicated their responsibilities to the mentally ill (Gruenberg and Archer, 1979; Rose, 1979; Brown, 1980).

In contrast to one of the prevailing "Myths" in this field, the rapid expansion of mental health and other protective services in the United States since 1955 has diminished but not supplanted the role of state mental hospitals (Goldman, Adams, et al., 1981). Whereas inpatient services of state mental hospitals accounted for nearly 50 percent of the total episodes of care in 1955, their "market share" dropped to 31 percent in 1965, to 19 percent in 1971, and to only 9 percent in 1975 (Regier et al., 1978). Rather than signaling the virtual elimination of state hospital use, these figures reflect the sizable expansion of new caseloads in outpatient psychiatric clinics, general hospital psychiatric units, and CMHCs. A much better appreciation of the current role of state hospitals can be gleaned from estimates of the volume of inpatient services still provided by these institutions. In 1980 there were approximately 138,000 resident patients in state mental hospitals, about 333,000 admissions, for a total of nearly 471,000 patient care episodes (Table 6.1).[9] What these numbers mean is that patient care episodes in 1980 were only 37 percent less than they were in 1955. A major difference between these 2 years, of course, lies in the relative mix of resident patients and admissions; resident patients accounted for 75 percent of the episodes in 1955, whereas they accounted for only 29 percent in 1980. Yet, in contrast to the widespread belief that deinstitutionalization has all but eliminated the use of state hospitals, it is clear from these episodes of care figures that they continue to serve a substantial patient caseload (Goldman et al., forthcoming).

The enduring functions of state hospitals involve custody, social control, and treatment for many of the most disturbed and most troublesome patients in the U.S. mental health system (Morrissey et al., 1980). The private psychiatry sector has accepted responsibility for the more acute, less disturbed, voluntary patients, leaving state hospitals to serve as a 24-hour back-up and institution of last resort and ultimate responsibility. The growth of the nursing home and community residence industries has reduced the number of long-stay patients who once languished on the wards of state hospitals. But many others remain in these institutions because they are "Inappropriate" (too disturbed or too disturbing) for current types of residential alternatives or because alternatives are not available.

The scope and mix of these residual functions vary considerably in different states. In New York, long-stay patients constitute the largest segment of the state hospital inpatient census. Of the total census on March 31, 1980 (24,961), 61 percent had been hospitalized 5 years or longer and over 53 percent for 15 years or longer (Weinstein, 1981). A Massachusetts survey conducted in 1977, in contrast, estimated that nearly 50 percent of the resident patients were hospitalized less than 1 year, 25 percent for 1 to 10 years, and 25 percent for over 10 years (Blue Ribbon Commission, 1981: 62). California's length-of-stay data are even more striking. Of the total census on June 30, 1981 (5,645), 64 percent had been hospitalized less than 1 year, 31 percent from 1 to 5 years, and only 5 percent for longer than 5 years.

On the basis of these admittedly sketchy data, it would appear that acute (short-stay) patients account for a much larger proportion of the episodes of care in California and Massachusetts, while chronic (long-stay) patients continue to dominate the caseload in New York. Moreover, the large majority of admissions to each state system (63 percent in New York, 68 percent in Massachusetts, and 78 percent in California) now consists of involuntary patients[10] who are considered to be "dangerous" to self or others. Thus, while custodial functions vary considerably between states, social control functions remain as a prominent feature of hospital use in each state.

In spite of over two decades of deinstitutionalization, therefore, state mental hospitals continue to serve their historic functions, albeit at a reduced level. The mental health system has expanded and become much more diversified both in terms of the mix of inpatient-outpatient services and the mix of public-private providers. Persons suffering from the milder and more acute forms of mental disorder have been the primary beneficiaries of these changes in the organization and locus of mental health care. Many of these persons are now able to receive appropriate care in general hospitals and outpatient settings. Those who suffer from more chronic conditions, the violent and more disturbing, as well as those who are socially incapacitated, still reside in state hospitals or alternative institutional settings in the community. Still others have been released to the community, where they live marginal existences in single-room occupancy hotels, often with only minimal support from local health and welfare agencies.

NEW DIRECTIONS

In the late 1970s, the deinstitutionalization movement entered a transitional phase. The change was occasioned by the political "backlash" to several years of rapid census run-downs and a fuller realization that the abrupt closure of state hospitals was premature. In November 1977 the

General Accounting Office issued the final report of a year-long study of state mental hospital deinstitutionalization (GAO, 1977). While the report contained little new information on the consequences of the rapid phase-down of state mental hospitals, it offered a devastating critique of the federal support for this policy and called for immediate efforts to deal with the needs of the thousands of chronic patients released to local communities without adequate provision for their care. The following year the President's Commission on Mental Health (1978) presented a similar assessment and called for a national mental health policy focused, in part, on the chronically mentally ill.

In response to this new wave of criticism, the National Institute of Mental Health launched a community support program (CSP) designed "to improve services for one particularly vulnerable population—adult psychiatric patients whose disabilities are severe and persistent but for whom long-term skilled or semi-skilled nursing care is inappropriate" (Turner and TenHoor, 1978: 319). A total of $3.5 million was allocated to contracts with 19 states for 3-year pilot demonstration programs involving crisis care services, psychosocial rehabilitation services, supporting living and working arrangements, medical and mental health care, and case management for the chronically mentally ill (Tessler and Goldman, 1982).

The needs of the CSP population, currently estimated at between 0.8 million and 1.5 million persons (Goldman, Gattozzi, et al., 1981), also formed a core part of the Mental Health Systems Act (P.L. 96-398), which was signed into law by President Carter in September 1980. While reaffirming the basic principles of the CMHC program, this legislation highlighted the need for a more flexible mental health service delivery system focusing on the chronically mentally ill and other underserved populations such as children and youth, the elderly, and minorities. The preamble to the act called for "a comprehensive and coordinated array of appropriate private and public mental health and support services for all people in need within specific geographic areas based upon a cooperative local-state-federal partnership."

In New York, the recent planning activities of the Office of Mental Health have been based on the premise that "the deinstitutionalization era is past" (NYSOMH, 1981: 6). Programming has emphasized improvement in the quality of care provided to patients in the state psychiatric centers (state hospitals) and the expansion of community services for patients discharged after extended periods of hospitalization. In 1978, a statewide community support system (CSS) was inaugurated through purchase of service contracts with local governmental units, voluntary agencies, and state psychiatric center programs. For fiscal year 1981-1982 approximately $50 million were allocated to CSS services. Plans were also announced for the closing and consolidation of 2 state hospitals by 1983 and the functional reorganization of the other psychiatric centers into acute care, skilled nursing care, and domiciliary units. In addition, as a longer-term goal, the plan called for the consolidation of state-local financing mechanisms and the development of a unified system for the administration of state and local government mental health services.[11] Pilot projects in the Rochester and Elmira areas were developed in 1981 to serve as local demonstrations of a single service system. Statewide efforts, however, had concentrated only on the integration of state-local management information systems and uniform budget reports.

In the late 1970s, the Massachusetts Department of Mental Health (1977: 163) also accelerated the switch from state hospital-based programs to a service-contracting model, both to promote the expansion of community services and "to avoid the rigidities of the state personnel system and to lessen the demand for State employees in the provision of [highly skilled, costly, and innovative] services." The accelerated reallocation of funds from institutional accounts to purchase of service contracts, however, created widespread concerns that the quality of care had deteriorated in the state hospitals and that census run-down had proceeded too rapidly. In the face of growing political controversy, the Commissioner of Mental Health created a Blue Ribbon Commission to make recommendations on the future use of the state mental hospitals. The core recommendation presented in the commission's final report (issued in May 1981) states that "within the immediate future, a network of alternative care should be developed so that the regional state mental hospitals can be closed" (Blue Ribbon Commission, 1981: 2). The report emphasized that the restructuring of the care-giving system could only be accomplished by a new system of financing and contracting for services in the private sector (see Schaeffer, 1981). It also strongly recommended against patient transfers until a preferable alternative system of care is available.

Thus, mental health planners in New York and Massachusetts (among other states) are now attempting to create fiscal and administrative structures analogous to those incorporated in the reorganization of the California mental health system in the late 1960s. Unlike the implementation of fiscal changes in California, however, these efforts are not predicated on the abrupt closure of state mental hospitals. The experiences of the last several years have convinced many public officials and mental health professionals that in order for deinstitutionalization to be truly effective census reductions and hospital closures must be preceded by the development of appropriate clinical, social, and environmental supports in the community.

POLICY RESEARCH IMPLICATIONS

This context presents a number of exciting opportunities and challenges for social research on the changing patterns of mental health service delivery in the United States. The future role of state mental hospitals—how they will function, for whom, and for what purpose—needs to be examined carefully. It is clear from the data considered in this chapter, however, that there will be no single or uniform answer to these questions in each state. The homogeneity of state mental hospitals that was fostered by more than a century of institutionalization practices has now been disrupted. While these institutions continue to perform their historic social functions, they do so in a mix that reveals considerable variability within as well as between states. The shifting responsibilities among federal, state, and local governments and the growing "privatization" of mental health and related human services are also areas that warrant close and comparative attention in the years ahead.

Much of the recent social science research in the mental health field has focused on state hospital *outputs*, or the problems and prospects for relocating mental patients in alternative settings, to the relative neglect of hospital *inputs*, or the forces that continue to generate a demand population for these institutions. To understand the future role of state hospitals, however, increased attention must be focused on the admissions process (Morrissey and Tessler, 1981). By gathering data on the social, clinical, and situational characteristics of persons presented for admission, insights can be obtained about the ways in which communities continue to use these hospitals. Analyses of the similarities and differences between those "selected in" (admitted) and those "selected out" (diverted) can also reveal the operative criteria now used for state hospitalization (for example, see Volo et al., 1980; Solomon, 1981).

Comparative research across a range of state hospitals and decision contexts would also yield important insights into the organizational and interorganizational correlates of admission diversion programs. For example, some state hospitals continue to do their own screening, while for others prescreening occurs in the community. The extent to which the organizational auspices of admissions screening affect the criteria and outcome of the decision process is an important topic for further research. Does community-based screening, for example, lead to the use of less restrictive criteria and a higher probability of admission than hospital-based screening?

In addition to focusing on the admissions process itself, research should be directed at the subsequent fates of persons who are considered for state hospitalization. The stripping away of the historic case mix problems of the state hospital seems to be leaving a residual of younger, male, aggressive patients (Urmer, 1978; Steadman et al., 1979). If the state hospital is to have a future as an acute treatment institution, then this is the population for which distinctive competence must be demonstrated.

Many of these young male patients enter state hospitals on involuntary legal statuses through civil or criminal commitment procedures. Whether there has been an actual growth in such commitments in recent years, or whether such patients are simply becoming more dominant with the reduction of patients hospitalized on voluntary statuses, are questions that deserve close scrutiny. One issue here is the extent to which the psychiatric-judicial-correctional systems are in the process of realigning their historic partnership and respective roles in the segregation and control of deviants (Steadman, 1981; Lister and Geller, 1980; Brown, 1980).

An even more crucial group for follow-up research in the context of the issues discussed in this chapter are the "seen but not admitted" (Morrissey et al., 1979), or those persons who are denied admission and referred/diverted elsewhere. The subsequent fates of these persons in the community, especially their continuity of care from alternative service providers, offer a basis for assessing current deinstitutionalization policies in the mental health field. One of the principal issues in this regard is whether receipt of community-based care obviates the need for state hospitalization.

As an alternative to state hospitals, efforts are now under way to create community support programs for the thousands of mental patients who have been released from state mental hospitals across the country. In the short run, these programs seek to fill the service gaps attendant upon the dual system of state hospitals and community-based services. As part of the growing trend for government at both the federal and state levels to disengage from the provision of direct patient services, these new programs are financed by purchase-of-service contracts between state mental health authorities and local service vendors (both public and private). The underlying rationale is that a system of incentives will thereby be created to induce local agencies to take responsibility for chronically disabled patients. In the longer run, the development of a network of community support services is seen as allowing for the complete phase-out of state hospitals and the emergence of a totally community-based and community-controlled mental health service delivery system.

Whether the reliance on marketplace mechanisms in the mental health arena will actually lead to a more responsive and comprehensive mental health service delivery system remains to be evaluated carefully (Rose, 1979; Lamb, 1981). An opposite effect is equally plausible: Namely, confronted with year-to-year performance contracts, vendor agencies may resort to "creaming" practices (Miller et al., 1970; Greenley and Kirk, 1973; McKinley, 1975), whereby the tough problem cases are rejected in favor of those clients who will show up as "successes" in end-of-year performance reviews (see Young, 1974, 1978). In other words, purchase-of-service arrangements may operate as *disincentives* for taking on chronic patients who require disproportionate amounts of staff time and effort relative to the probability of ever demonstrating successful outcomes.

With regard to promoting a comprehensive array of local services, contracting and purchase-of-service arrangements may also yield contrary results. Recent experiences in New Jersey, for example, suggest that contracting actually widens the gap between resource-rich and resource-poor areas. [12] In the last few years, analysts have noted an increasing discrepancy between areas targeted for local mental health services on the basis of need (usually rural and suburban) and those areas that are successful in obtaining service contracts (usually urban). In other words, current procurement mechanisms seemingly *disadvantage* communities lacking "grantsmanship" or proposal-writing skills that are common among providers in resource-rich areas. The implication is that purchase-of-service models that are inattentive to the skill factor and the geographic maldistribution of services may exacerbate rather than mitigate the inequities in the current mental health system.

Moreover, these initiatives are being launched at a time when the resource base for mental health and human services is shrinking. Given the press of other social problems that have received even fewer of our societal resources to date and the citizens' tax revolt now sweeping the country (Herbers, 1979), the goal of a totally community-based mental health system seems even more remote than it did in the recent past. New uncertainties for the viability of these programs have been introduced by the massive human services cuts engineered by the Reagan administration in the 1981-1982 federal budgets. One of the first casualties of the shift from categorical funding to block grants occurred with the repeal of the Mental Health Systems Act, which had placed high priority on serving the chronically mentally ill. Ironically, the transfer of responsibility from federal to state and local agencies without secure, long-term funding may leave the severely mentally disabled more vulnerable to the capriciousness of public opinion on the question of who and what deserves to be funded from the public treasury (Morrissey et al., 1980; Tessler and Goldman, 1982).

In no small measure, the current climate of public opinion mirrors the socioeconomic forces that eroded the support base of the early state mental hospitals in the nineteenth century. Its impact on the growth of community mental health services in the next several years will determine whether a truly humane system of care for the chronically mentally ill will finally emerge from the cycles of reform in the mental health field.

NOTES

1. The causal role of psychotropic drugs in the decline of state mental hospital populations has been a controversial issue in the mental health literature. For opposing views see Brill and Patton (1957) and Scull (1977: 79-94).

2. The numbers in Table 6.1 are based on fiscal year transactions in each state, as follows: California and Massachusetts (July 1-June 30) and New York (April 1-March 31). The *resident patient* figures are end-of-year counts (unduplicated) that include all patients resident in state mental hospitals on that day, plus those patients on short-term leave who are expected to return within a few days. *Admissions* represent a duplicated count of persons entering state mental hospitals within the reporting year. *Patient care episodes* are typically computed by adding total admissions to the beginning-of-year resident patient counts (NIMH, 1977: 4). However, for present purposes, the end-of-year resident counts were used to compute this index. To adjust for proper time sequencing, the end of year count for year x–1 (prior year) was added to the total admissions for year x (current year) in the computation of patient care episodes. This approximation may result in slight distortions in the resultant estimates, since the end-of-year resident count at each hospital is taken the day before the beginning-of-(next)-year count. As the admission component of this index is based on a duplicated count, patient care episodes are also a duplicated count; in this case, of persons served during each fiscal year.

3. The "time on record" estimates are based on the time difference between each resident patient's date of first admission to a California state mental hospital and the date of the survey (June 30, 1960) without discounting time out of hospital on release or trial visit. Thus these estimates are biased toward much longer length of stay (Personal communication of November 23, 1981, from Penny O'Daniels, California Department of Mental Health, Sacramento, CA).

4. The resident patient census in Massachusetts state mental hospitals had reached a plateau in 1950-1951 and fluctuated around the 23,000 figure through 1955. This stabilization of the long-term trend of annual increases in resident patients occurred prior to the widespread use of the phenothiazines in state mental hospitals. As similar reversals occurred at facilities in other states, these experiences suggest that factors other than drugs were involved in the nationwide census reductions that began in 1955 (see Gruenberg, 1974).

5. Segal and Aviram (1978: 46) report that these legal reforms in California were "supported by what has been called an unholy alliance of liberals and conservatives. The liberals saw in the law an opportunity to guarantee patients' civil liberties and to improve treatment. The conservatives thought it would lead to a reduction of state expenditures in areas that should be the responsibility of the local community. Many mental health professionals supported the law because they saw in it an opportunity to provide better treatment based on local care for the mentally ill."

6. The major commitment provisions of the Lanterman-Petris-Short Act include: (1) only persons determined to be dangerous to self or others and those found

to be gravely disabled as a function of their mental disorder can be involuntarily hospitalized; (2) the burden of proof is on the applicant agency and at least observational evidence of dangerousness or disability is required; (3) such persons can be involuntarily held for treatment on the certification of 2 mental health professionals without court review for a maximum of 17 days; and (4) such persons retain the right to judicial review (including a habeas corpus hearing) as well as other legal and civil rights (for further details, see Urmer, 1978; Jacobson, 1973; Segal and Aviram, 1978).

7. The revised commitment statutes in Massachusetts stipulate that no person can be involuntarily hospitalized unless there is a finding (by a qualified physician) that the failure to hospitalize would result in a substantial risk of physical harm to self or others as evidenced by suicidal, homicidal, or other violent behavior or impaired judgment leading to the inability to protect oneself, or obtain reasonable protection in the community (see Bayle, 1971).

8. By limiting the number of admissions (especially from geriatric age groups) this policy sharply reduced the build-up of new long-stay patients. As a result, the population of aged patients in the institutions began to decline rapidly as a function of natural deaths and discharges to nursing homes and other settings. A revealing analysis of the long-term impact of this policy change has recently been completed by Weinstein (1981). The study involved a 15-year follow-up of the 85,012 patients who were resident in New York state mental hospitals as of March 31, 1965. The results indicate that 45 percent died in residence, 36 percent were discharged, 2 percent were placed in family care, and 16 percent were still in residence on March 31, 1980. The last group accounted for 53 percent of the 24,961 patients resident in New York State mental hospitals on that date.

9. If returns from extended leave were added to these figures, the episodes of care would be much higher. For the nation as a whole, "additions" (admissions and returns from extended leave) are approximately 18 percent larger than the admission counts cited in the text (personal communication from Michael Witkin, Division of Biometry and Epidemiology, NIMH).

10. The estimates of the proportion of involuntary admissions to state mental hospitals in New York (fiscal year 1980) and Massachusetts (fiscal year 1981) were obtained from the statistical reporting systems maintained by their respective departments of mental health. The California estimate is based on the proportion of involuntary admissions in 1977-1978 as reported by Lamb et al. (1981). The dramatic increase in the percentage of involuntary admissions to each state mental hospital system represents a relative rather than an absolute increase. The legal reform of commitment codes in each state had the effect of initially increasing the relative percentage of voluntary admissions. However, as more stringent "dangerousness" standards were applied, the number of voluntary admissions was sharply reduced. As the base number declined, the relative percentage of involuntary admissions increased dramatically. Even so, Lamb et al. (1981) have suggested that, when considered in terms of rates per 100,000 population, involuntary admissions have actually increased in the California mental health system since the passage of LPS.

11. The 1980 Annual Report of the New York State Office of Mental Health (NYSOMH, 1981) states that "the overall service delivery system [in New York] encompasses two discrete funding methods which in essence result in two separate service delivery systems—one financed and operated by the state and one indirectly financed in part by the state through state aid to local governmental units and

voluntary provider agencies. The latter, locally operated system is further segregated into a number of service delivery subsystems by the existence of various funding mechanisms with their own unique patient eligibility criteria and state-local cost-sharing formula."

12. Personal communication of November 23, 1981, from Jonas Waizer, Assistant Director, New Jersey Division of Mental Health and Hospitals, Trenton, NJ.

REFERENCES

ABRAHAMSON, M. (1972) "The criminalization of mentally disordered behavior: a possible side effect of a new mental health law." Hospital and Community Psychiatry 23: 101-105.

ARNHOFF, F. (1975) "Social consequences of policy towards mental illness." Science 188: 1277-1281.

AVIRAM, U. and S. SEGAL (1977) "From hospital to community care: the change in the mental health treatment system in California." Community Mental Health Journal 13: 158-167.

——— (1973) "Exclusion of the mentally ill: reflections on an old problem in a new context." Archives of General Psychiatry 29: 126-131.

AVIRAM, U., S. SYME, and J. COHEN (1976) "The effects of policies and programs on reduction of mental hospitalization." Social Science and Medicine 10: 571-577.

BACHRACH, L. (1978) "A conceptual approach to deinstitutionalization." Hospital and Community Psychiatry 29 (September): 573-578.

——— (1976) Deinstitutionalization: An Analytical Review and Sociological Perspective. Rockville, MD: National Institute of Mental Health.

BARDACH, E. (1972) The Skill Factor in Politics: Repealing the Mental Commitment Laws in California. Berkeley: University of California Press.

BASSUK, E. L. and J. GERSON (1978) "Deinstitutionalization and mental health services." Scientific American 238: 46-53.

BAYLE, S. (1971) "Chapter 888." Massachusetts Journal of Mental Health 1 (Winter): 1-4.

BELKNAP, I. (1956) Human Problems of a State Mental Hospital. New York: McGraw-Hill.

BENNETT, D. (1979) "Deinstitutionalization in two cultures." Milbank Memorial Fund Quarterly/Health and Society 57: 516-532.

Blue Ribbon Commission (1981) Mental Health Crossroads: The Report of the Blue Ribbon Commission on the Future of Public Inpatient Mental Health Services in Massachusetts. Boston: Center for Law and Health Sciences, Boston University.

BOCKOVEN, J. S. (1972) Moral Treatment in Community Mental Health. New York: Springer.

BODIN, L., T. CARROLL, A. LEE, and S. STOUT (1972) "Financing mental health services in the State of New York." Operations Research 5 (September/October): 942-954.

BRAUN, P., G. KOCHANSKY, R. SHAPIRO, et al. (1981) "Overview: deinstitutionalization of psychiatric patients, a critical review of outcome studies." American Journal of Psychiatry 138: 736-749.

BRILL, H. and R. PATTON (1957) "Analysis of 1955-56 population fall in New York State mental hospitals during the first year of large-scale use of tranquilizing drugs." American Journal of Psychiatry 114: 509-517.

BROWN, P. (1980) "Social implications of deinstitutionalization." Journal of Community Psychology 8: 314-322.

CAMERON, J. M. (1978) "Ideology and policy termination: restructuring California's mental health system," pp. 301-328 in J. V. May and A. B. Wildavsky (eds.) The Policy Cycle. Beverly Hills, CA: Sage.

CAPLAN, R. (1969) Psychiatry and the Community in Nineteenth Century America. New York: Basic Books.

CHU, F. and S. TROTTER (1974) The Madness Establishment. New York: Grossman.

CUMMING, J. (1968) "Screening of admissions." Memorandum 68-27, Division of Mental Health, New York State Department of Mental Hygiene.

FELDMAN, S. (1971) "Community mental health centers in the United States: an overview." International Journal of Nursing Studies 8 (September): 247-257.

FOWLKES, M. (1975) "Business as usual—at the state mental hospital." Psychiatry 38: 55-64.

General Accounting Office [GAO] (1977) Returning the Mentally Disabled to the Community: Government Needs to Do More. Washington, DC: Author.

GOLDMAN, H., N. ADAMS, and C. TAUBE (1981) "Deinstitutionalization data demythologized." Langley Porter Institute, University of California Medical Center. (unpublished)

GOLDMAN, H., A. GATTOZZI, and C. TAUBE (1981) "Defining and counting the chronically mentally ill." Hospital and Community Psychiatry 32: 21-27.

GOLDMAN, H., C. TAUBE, D. REGIER, and M. WITKIN (forthcoming) "The multiple functions of the state mental hospital." American Journal of Psychiatry.

GREENLEY, J. and S. KIRK (1973) "Organizational characteristics of agencies and the distribution of services to applicants." Journal of Health and Social Behavior 14 (March): 70-79.

GROB, G. (1973) Mental Institutions in America: Social Policy to 1875. New York: Macmillan.

——— (1966) The State and the Mentally Ill· A History of Worcester State Hospital in Massachusetts 1830-1920. Chapel Hill: University of North Carolina Press.

GRUENBERG, E. (1974) "The social breakdown syndrome and its prevention," pp. 697-711 in S. Arieti (ed.) American Handbook of Psychiatry. New York: Basic Books.

——— (1966) "Evaluating the effectiveness of community mental health services." Milbank Memorial Fund Quarterly 44, Part 2.

——— and J. ARCHER (1979) "Abandonment of responsibility for the seriously mentally ill." Milbank Memorial Fund Quarterly/Health and Society 57: 485-506.

HERBERS, J. (1979) "State's trying a variety of ways to reduce taxes and spending." New York Times (February 25): 1, 25.

HUNT, R. and H. FORSTENZER (1957). "The New York State Community Mental Health Services Act: its birth and early development." American Journal of Psychiatry 113: 680-685.

HUNT, R., E. GRUENBERG, E. HACKEN, and M. HUXLEY (1961) 'A comprehensive hospital-community service in a state hospital." American Journal of Psychiatry 117: 817-821.

JACOBSON, D. S. (1973) "From protective custody to treatment in a hurry." Social Work (March): 55-64.

KIRK, S. and M. E. THERRIEN (1975) "Community mental health myths and the fate of former hospitalized patients." Psychiatry 38: 209-217.

KOENIG, P. (1978) "The problem that cannot be tranquilized." New York Times Magazine (May 21): 14-17.

LAMB, H. R. (1981) "What did we really expect from deinstitutionalization?" Hospital and Community Psychiatry 32: 105-109.

――― (1979) "The new asylums in the community." Archives of General Psychiatry 36: 129-134.

――― A. SORKIN, and J. ZUSMAN (1981) "Legislating social control of the mentally ill in California." American Journal of Psychiatry 138: 334-339.

LISTER, E. and J. GELLER (1980) "Crossing organizational boundaries: pretrial commitment for psychiatric evaluation," pp. 143-160 in J. Morrissey et al., The Enduring Asylum. New York: Grune & Stratton.

McKINLEY, J. (1975) "Clients and organizations," pp. 339-378 in J. McKinley (ed.) Processing People: Cases in Organizational Behavior. New York: Holt, Rinehart & Winston.

MARKSON, E., A. KWOH, J. CUMMING, and E. CUMMING (1971) "Alternatives to hospitalization for psychiatrically ill geriatric patients." American Journal of Psychiatry 127 (February): 1057-1062.

Massachusetts Department of Mental Health [MDMH] (1977) The Five Year State Plan for Mental Health Services. Boston: Author.

MECHANIC, D. (1969) Mental Health and Social Policy. Englewood Cliffs, NJ: Prentice-Hall.

MILLER, S. M., P. ROBY, and A. STEENWIJK (1970) "Creaming the poor." Transaction 7 (June): 38-45.

MORRISSEY, J. and R. TESSLER (1981) "Selection processes in state mental hospitalization: policy issues and research directions," in M. Lewis (ed.) Social Problems and Public Policy: A Research Annual, Vol. II. Greenwich, CT: JAI.

――― and L. FARRIN (1979) "Being seen but not admitted: a note on some neglected aspects of state hospital deinstitutionalization." American Journal of Orthopsychiatry 49 (January): 153-156.

MORRISSEY, J., H. GOLDMAN, L. KLERMAN, and Associates (1980) The Enduring Asylum: Cycles of Institutional Reform at Worcester State Hospital. New York: Grune & Stratton.

MUSTO, D. (1975) "Whatever happened to community mental health?" Public Interest 39: 53-79.

MYERSON, D. (1975) "Does history have to repeat itself? A study of reforms at the Worcester State Hospital." Worcester, MA: Worcester State Hospital.

National Institute of Mental Health [NIMH] (1977) Additions and Resident Patients at End of Year State and County Mental Hospitals by Age and Diagnosis, by State, United States 1975. Rockville, MD: Author.

――― (1955) Patients in Mental Institutions 1955, Part II: Public Hospitals for the Mentally Ill. Rockville, MD: Author.

New York State Office of Mental Health [NYSOMH] (1981) Annual Report, 1980. Albany, NY: Author.

――― (1978) Five Year Comprehensive Plan for Services to Mentally Ill Persons in New York State. Albany, NY: Author.

President's Commission on Mental Health (1978) Report to the President from the President's Commission on Mental Health. Washington, DC: Government Printing Office.

REICH, R. and L. SIEGEL (1973) "Psychiatry under siege: the chronically mentally ill shuffle to oblivion." Psychiatric Annals 3 (November): 35-55.

REGIER, D., I. GOLDBERG, and C. TAUBE (1978) "The defacto mental health services system." Archives of General Psychiatry 34: 615-693.

RIVERA, G. (1972) Willowbrooke: A Report on How It Is and Why It Doesn't Have to Be That Way. New York: Random House.

ROBITSCHER, J. (1978) "Legal standards and their implications regarding civil commitment procedures," pp. 61-82 in C. J. Frederick (ed.) Dangerous Behavior: A Problem in Law and Mental Health. Rockville, MD: Center for Studies of Crime and Delinquency, National Institute of Mental Health.

——— (1976) "Moving patients out of hospitals—In whose interest?" pp. 141-176 in P. Ahmed and S. C. Plog (eds.) State Mental Hospitals: What Happens When They Close. New York: Plenum.

ROSE, S. (1979) "Deciphering deinstitutionalization: complexities in policy and program analysis." Millbank Memorial Fund Quarterly/Health and Society 57 (Fall): 429-60.

ROTHMAN, D. J. (1971) The Discovery of the Asylum. Boston: Little, Brown.

SANTIESTEVAN, H. (1975) Deinstitutionalization: Out of Their Beds and into the Streets. Washington, DC: American Federation of State, County, and Municipal Employees.

SCHAEFFER, P. (1981) "Massachusetts to place inpatient care in hands of private sector." Clinical Psychiatry News 9: 6-7.

SCHERL, D. and L. MACHT (1980) "Deinstitutionalization in the absence of consensus." Hospital and Community Psychiatry 30: 599-604.

SCHMIDT, L., A. REINHARDT, R. KANE, and D. OLSEN (1977) "The mentally ill in nursing homes: new backwards in the community." Archives of General Psychiatry 34: 687-691.

SCULL, A. (1977) Decarceration: Community Treatment and the Deviant—A Radical View. Englewood Cliffs, NJ: Prentice-Hall.

SEGAL, S. and U. AVIRAM (1978) The Mentally Ill in Community-Based Sheltered Care. New York: John Wiley.

SEGAL, S., J. BAUMAHL, and E. MOULES (1980) "Neighborhood types and community reaction to the mentally ill: a paradox of intensity." Journal of Health and Social Behavior 21: 345-359.

SHADISH, W. and R. BOOTZIN (1981) "Nursing homes and chronic mental patients." Schizophrenia Bulletin 7: 488-98.

SIEGEL, M. (1978) "Safeguards urged on mental patients." New York Times (April 2): 43.

SOLOMON, P. (1981) "The admissions process in two state psychiatric hospitals." Hospital and Community Psychiatry 32: 405-408.

STEADMAN, H. (1981) "From bedlam to Bastille?: The confinement of the mentally ill in U.S. prisons." Presented at the annual meeting of the American Sociological Association, Toronto, Ontario.

——— J. BRAFF, R. CASTELLANI, R. INGALLS, and A. WEINSTEIN (1979) "Staff perceptions of factors affecting changes in New York State psychiatric center inpatient census trends." Bureau of Special Projects Research, New York State Department of Mental Hygiene. (unpublished)

STELOVICH, S. (1979) "From the hospital to the prison: a step forward in deinstitutionalization?" Hospital and Community Psychiatry 30: 618-620.

STINCHCOMBE, A. (1965) "Social structure and organization," pp. 142-193 in J. G. March (ed.) Handbook of Organizations. Skokie, IL: Rand-McNally.

STRAUSS, A. and M. SABSHIN (1961) "Large state hospitals: social values and societal resources." Archives of General Psychiatry 5: 75-87.

TESSLER, R. and H. GOLDMAN (1982) The Chronically Mentally Ill: Assessing Community Support Programs. Cambridge, MA: Ballinger.

TURNER, J. and W. TenHOOR (1978) "The NIMH community support program: pilot approach to a needed social reform." Schizophrenia Bulletin 4: 319-348.

United Community Planning Corporation (1973) Community Mental Health and the Mental Hospital: Final Report of the Massachusetts Mental Hospital Planning Project. Boston: Author.

URMER, A. (1978) "An assessment of California's mental health program: implications for mental health delivery systems," pp. 137-152 in C. J. Frederick (ed.) Dangerous Behavior: A Problem in Law and Mental Health. Rockville, MD: Center for Studies of Crime and Delinquency, National Institute of Mental Health.

VOLO, A., W. FURMAN, and C. REGULA (1980) "Who gets admitted and why." Journal of Psychiatric Treatment and Evaluation 2: 165-178.

WARREN, C. (1981) "New forms of social control: the myth of deinstitutionalization." American Behavioral Scientist 6 (July/August): 724-740.

WEINSTEIN, A. (1981) "Whatever happened to the class of '65?" Statistical Report, New York State Office of Mental Health. (unpublished)

——— (1980) "The pace of the resident patient decrease is slowing down." Statistical Report, New York State Office of Mental Health. (unpublished)

——— (1971) "Notes regarding comparisons between New York and California." Memorandum, New York State Department of Mental Hygiene. (unpublished)

——— and A. MAIWALD (1974) "Trends in New York State mental hospital admission and length of stay," pp. 11-21 in The State Hospital—Past and Present. Hanover, NJ: Sandoz Pharmaceuticals.

WHITMER, G. (1980) "From hospitals to jails: the fate of California's deinstitutionalized mentally ill." American Journal of Orthopsychiatry 50: 65-75.

WILEY, E. (1965) "Legislation affecting psychiatry and mental health." New York State Journal of Medicine 65 (November): 2718-2728.

WINDLE, C. and D. SCULLY (1976) "Community mental health centers and the decreasing use of state mental hospitals." Community Mental Health Journal 12: 239-243.

WING, J. (1962) "Institutionalism in mental hospitals." Journal of Social and Clinical Psychology 1 (February): 38-51.

YOUNG, D. (1978) "Contracting out for services," pp. 67-78 in M. J. Murphy and T. Glynn (eds.) Human Service Management: Priorities for Research. Washington, DC: International City Management Association.

——— (1974) "Referral and placement in child care: the New York City purchase of service system." Public Policy 22.

THE PSYCHIATRIC REVOLUTION OF THE PAST TWENTY-FIVE YEARS

GERALD L. KLERMAN

The past two and one-half decades have witnessed several important trends in mental health care: a decline in the resident census in public mental health hospitals, an increase in outpatient treatment and facilities, relative stability in the number of hospitalization episodes per 100,000 population, and briefer duration of hospitalization. The combined result of these trends is increased pluralism, diversity, and deinstitutionalization in mental health care. The changes are primarily the consequence of the success of psychopharmacologic agents, new forms of psychotherapy, changing attitudes of the public, and increased financial support by the federal government.

During that same 25 years, there have been significant advances in the scientific status of psychiatry. Research in genetics, psychopathology, and psychopharmacology have contributed to a better empirical and experimental basis for the diagnosis and treatment of psychiatric disorders. Moreover, advances in social science and epidemiology have provided better data as to the scope of the problem and the magnitude of mental illness.

This chapter will review some of the significant changes, particularly those in the utilization of mental health services. These changes will be interpreted in the context of a broadening definition of the scope of psychiatry. The overall data indicate that there has been at least a sixfold increase in the utilization of psychiatric and other mental health services by the population during the last 25 years. It is important to emphasize that this marked expansion in utilization of mental health services should not be interpreted as any indication of an increase in the incidence or prevalence of mental illness. On the contrary, the available evidence indicates that the prevalence of mental illness has remained fairly constant in North America over recent decades. The change that has occurred is in the attitude of the public toward regarding mental illness as treatable and the willingness of increasing segments of the population with emotional and psychological problems to seek professional help from psychiatrists and other mental health professionals. Even with this tremendous expansion, only a minority of individuals with any form of mental illness are treated for that condition by a mental health professional. As will be described later, the current epidemiologic evidence indicates that about 15 percent of the population, or 30 million individuals, have a diagnosable psychiatric disorder. Of this number, only about 20 to 25 percent seek help from a psychiatrist or other mental health professional. The remainder are treated in the general health care system, but by mental health specialists.

CHANGES IN UTILIZATION
OF MENTAL HEALTH SERVICES,
1955-1980

The critical year for understanding the revolutionary changes in psychiatry and the mental health system is 1955. In that year, there were close to 600,000 patients in public mental hospitals. These hospitals were the main facilities for mental illness treatment. There were very few private hospitals, mainly for wealthy and upper-middle-class people, and less than 10,000 psychiatrists and other professionals in private practice. Only a small number of outpatient clinics and child-guidance centers provided ambulatory treatment in addition to that provided by private practitioners.

In 1955, there was a dramatic change in hospitalization rates; for the first time in over a century, the census of public mental hospitals showed a decline, rather than an increase. Over the subsequent 25 years the mental health system experienced a major shift, from almost total reliance on a system of involuntary incarceration in public institutions to a voluntaristic and pluralistic system.

Until the 1950s, the delivery of mental health services was almost exclusively monopolized by large public institutions. Since that time, there has been not only a dramatic shift in the primary locus of treatment from institutional to community settings, but also a radical reapportioning of services among the different types of psychiatric facilities (Klerman, 1977).

Current trends toward pluralism, diversity, and deinstitutionalization in mental health care are in sharp contrast to the centralization, isolation, and institutionalization that characterized the first half of this century. These changes are primarily the result of new forms of technology—both pharmacological and psychological—coupled with increasing support by the federal government. However, despite effective new treatments and the emergence of progressive alternatives to institutional care, many patients become "better," but not "well."

In the 1950s, two major developments occurred that revolutionized the treatment of severe mental illness. The first was the introduction of the phenothiazines. These new drugs contributed to the effective treatment and symptomatic management of many severely psychotic patients. They also led to a reduction in the duration of hospitalization and to an increase in the percentage of patients discharged from hospitals.

New psychosocial methods of treatment began to emerge prior to the introduction of the phenothiazines. In the 1940s, a shift in the philosophical attitudes of the hospital keepers began to take place in response to criticisms of their institutions. Efforts at internal hospital reform included avoiding seclusion and restraint, implementing open-door policies, improving internal power relations, and breaking down administrative and other barriers between the hospital and the community.

Psychosocial reform and reconstruction efforts quickly affected the mental health professions and were symbolized in theory and research as "social psychiatry" and in practice as the "therapeutic community." Major efforts at therapeutic reform were first initiated in Britain but were rapidly extended to the United States, where they escalated during the 1950s and 1960s. These reforms were crystallized in the ideal of the therapeutic community, which coupled the belief in the human potential for change with techniques of group dynamics to improve interpersonal communication and behavior.

In the early to mid-1960s, the social psychiatrist reformers were joined by civil libertarians, conservative budget advisors, and the federal government in support of deinstitutionalization policies in state and local mental health programs. While their theoretical rationales differed dramatically, these diverse groups developed a short-lived consensus on matters of mental health care. Lawyers argued that institutions deprived patients not only of their health, but also of their civil rights. Conservative budget advisors, pressured by strong economic forces, eagerly joined the push toward deinstitutionalization because it provided an opportunity to shift the burden of financing from the state to the national level. Federal efforts to address the management of mental illness culminated in 1963, when the federal government established a series of programs to stimulate and support community services as alternatives to institutional care.

The consequences of new public policies, changing community attitudes, altered professional practices, and new forms of therapy were dramatic. There was a marked shift in the care of the mentally ill from institutional to community settings, from inpatient to ambulatory facilities, and from the public to the private sector.

The Dramatic Decline of Institutional Care

Statistical data reflecting the changing trends of the past quarter century show not only the shift in locus of care from public mental hospitals to community, but also changes in the distribution of care provided by the various types of inpatient facilities. The most dramatic change in mental health care has been the sharp decline in the public mental hospital resident census from a national peak of 559,000 persons in 1955 to less than 200,000 in 1975, a 65 percent decrease (Kramer, 1977).

As the population of institutions decreased, there was an increase in outpatient treatment facilities in the community. Currently the largest area of growth in mental health care is in outpatient and ambulatory facilities. There has been rapid expansion in outpatient and ambulatory services of all kinds—free-standing outpatient services as well as those affiliated with psychiatric and general hospitals, public and private facilities, and adult child care. To illustrate, in 1955 inpatient services accounted for 77 percent of the episodes of care, while 28 percent were handled in outpatient settings. By 1975 that trend had reversed, with inpatient settings accounting for 27 percent of the patient care episodes, outpatient settings for 70 percent, and day-care settings for 3 percent (Taube and Redlick, 1977).

Between 1955 and 1975, the total number of patient care episodes climbed from 1.7 million to 6.9 million, but in 1975 the majority of patients were treated in outpatient settings. When the absolute numbers are converted to number of patient care episodes per 100,000 population, the diverging trends between inpatient and outpatient care become even more evident. The rate for inpatients has remained relatively stable at about 800 episodes per 100,000 population. In contrast, utilization of outpatient services has increased significantly, from around 1,100 per 100,000 population in 1955 to around 2,000 per 100,000 population in 1971.

The psychiatric case register in Monroe County, New York, maintained since 1960 by the University of Rochester Department of Psychiatry, provides a unique picture of the rates and patterns of utilization of psychiatric services by the resident population of a large community. These data offer further evidence of changing trends. Among the residents of Monroe County, the number of persons who received psychiatric services of all types rose steadily over a 10-year period, from 18.4 per 1000 population in 1962 to 25.1 per 1000 population in 1971. The rise in utilization was due to the increasing rate of persons receiving outpatient services only. The rate of persons who had at least 1 inpatient episode during each year fell to a level of 7.8 per 1000 population in 1971 from a rate of 8.6 per 1000 in 1962 (NIMH, 1976).

As noted earlier, the rate of inpatient care episodes has remained relatively stable since 1955. This stability is a consequence of a reduction of residential patients combined with increased admission rates. Although the rate has remained stable, there has been a radical redistribution among the different types of psychiatric facilities. State and county hospitals handled about 33 percent of the 1.8 million episodes of inpatient care in 1971, compared to 63 percent of the 1.3 million inpatient episodes in 1955. During the same period, the proportion of inpatient care episodes handled by general hospital psychiatric units greatly increased, from 21 percent in 1955 to 32 percent in 1975. Community mental health centers, which were nonexistent in 1955, have become a critical factor in the changing distribution of services, accounting for 14 percent of the inpatient episodes in 1975.

The downward population trend in public institutions is attributed largely to a decrease in average duration of hospitalization. Unpublished data from the National Institute of Mental Health indicate that for the period between 1971 and 1975 there was a 41 percent decline in length of stay for admissions (excluding those who died) to state and county psychiatric hospitals. This translates to a decrease in the median stay for admissions from 44 days in 1971 to 26 days in 1975.

The Problems of Deinstitutionalization

The combined result of these trends has been the movement out of the mental hospital and into the community. Mental health institutions have undergone a steady reduction in resident populations and a radical puncturing of their delivery systems (Greenblatt and Glazier, 1975). However, just as there are critics of institutionalization, so too there are critics of deinstitutionalization and its concomitants. Some feel that the pharmacological and psychological technology that originally facilitated the shift in locus of treatment has now become too extreme and represents a degree of behavior control that is unacceptable. The quality of care received by patients released from institutions to community facilities is another area of concern. It is important to note, however, that patients may have a positive response to new locations, even when they are considered inferior to the hospital setting by professionals.

The creation of community mental health facilities has introduced its own set of problems, including unrealistic expectations of their capabilities, lack of sufficient funding to achieve their goals, the development of an uncoordinated network of community resources, and inadequate planning for patient release, referral, and follow-up. Problems arise when patients are discharged from institutions into crowded, substandard, or inappropriate facilities. On the other hand, many other mentally ill persons enter, reenter, or remain in public institutions when they could be treated in the community.

The Changing Federal Role

Federal efforts to reform the delivery of mental health services were initiated in the 1950s when Congress established the Joint Commission on Mental Illness and Health. The resulting report and its recommendations led to President Kennedy's landmark 1963 address to Congress on mental illness and mental retardation. Federal efforts at reform culminated in 1963 with the passage of the Mental Retardation Facilities and Community Mental Health Centers Construction Act, which established guidelines and promised federal funding for community facilities to treat mentally ill patients. This legislation marked a dramatic shift in treatment ideology that resulted in a radical change in the locus of care.

The goal of caring for and treating the mentally ill in community facilities rather than in mental institutions has been endorsed over the years by four presidents and the Congress. The federal role in mental health has grown substantially in recent times. The amount and types of financial assistance the federal government provides, and the requirements, standards, and restrictions imposed, as well as the policies of federal agencies, have significantly influenced both the progress and problems encountered in deinstitutionalization efforts.

One important role of the federal government has been to provide funds for mental health services, and not (except for the Department of

Defense and VA hospitals) to run them. Most of the federal health dollar is used to provide health insurance—including Medicaid and Medicare—and to fund community mental health centers. These efforts have radically changed the structure of the delivery system toward pluralism by increasing the number of treatment alternatives available to patients.

Furthermore, the portion of federal funds devoted to support of research has resulted in enormous benefits to psychiatric patients. Research led to the two major technological advances that were directly responsible for the shift away from institutional toward community care. Psychopharmacology is most visible, but significant advances in psychosocial treatment techniques have also occurred. Together, these technological achievements have contributed to reduced length of hospital stays, control of psychoses, and advances in community care.

With the coming of the Reagan administration, major changes have been initiated. The funding of community programs with federal dollars is about to cease, and what federal monies will be appropriated will be administered through the states via the new program of block grants. The full impact of these changes in federal policy is unclear, but it is likely that the public support of community mental health programs will diminish.

The Evolving Pluralistic System

A shift has occurred as increasing numbers of patients have been given the choice of site of treatment via their health insurance. The system is becoming increasingly pluralistic as patients have more options regarding the type of treatment they will receive. No longer is the mental health system a state-owned and state-operated monopoly. The availability of increased numbers of individual practitioners, nonprofit hospitals, and voluntary agencies has greatly increased the number of treatment alternatives. The availability of the voucher system, in the form of health insurance, has given the individual patient and his or her family increasing degrees of freedom. The care and treatment of mentally ill people in the community has become an alternative to institutional care, but with uncertain financing and lack of community facilities, the progress made thus far could falter in the 1980s.

THE EXPANDING USE
OF THE PSYCHOTHERAPIES
IN AMERICAN SOCIETY

The preceding section has documented the shifts in patterns of utilization of mental health services, particularly the use of inpatient institutions. Parallel with these changes in inpatient utilization has been a tremendous expansion of ambulatory services, including psychotropic drugs and psychotherapy.

In 1955, about 1 percent of the population saw some form of mental health professional, almost exclusively a psychiatrist. The majority of episodes of mental health care were in hospitals. Approximately .8 percent of the population had some hospitalization for mental illness during that year, mostly in public mental hospitals, usually state, county, and VA. Over the ensuing 25 years, overall utilization increased so that by 1980 approximately 6 percent of the population saw a mental health practitioner. The percentage of the population hospitalized for psychiatric or mental illness has remained fairly constant, at below 1 percent of the population. However, whereas in 1955 inpatient care was almost always provided in the public sector, today psychiatric units in general hospitals and private hospitals account for more than half of all admissions to inpatient care.

The greatest growth has been in the outpatient ambulatory sector. While there has been a tremendous increase in outpatient utilization, psychiatrists now represent only about one-quarter of all contacts. Another index is the increasing reimbursement of nonpsychiatric practitioners by various third-party payments. It is currently estimated that for ambulatory mental health benefits provided by third-party payment, particularly Blue Cross-Blue Shield, only about 50 percent is given to the psychiatrist, the remainder going to psychologists, social workers, and other practitioners, depending on the state level of licensure and certification.

The Growth of the Psychotherapies[1]

The field of psychotherapy now has more definition, more specifiable application, and more predictable results than it has ever had. There has been a profusion of new psychotherapeutic schools, and new techniques continue to increase. The scientific procedures for evaluating the efficacy of psychotherapeutic outcomes are also improving, so that it is increasingly possible to cite evidence about the psychotherapies and potentially to disseminate it to the professions and to the public.

New psychotherapeutic techniques have been invented, taught, and practiced; multiple professions have become involved in the practice of psychotherapy; the number of practitioners has increased; the number of schools, institutes, and training programs for teaching people to practice psychotherapy has multiplied; and public attention has increased immensely.

The money spent on psychotherapy has also increased. Extrapolating only from the conservative estimates by the Group for the Advancement of Psychiatry (GAP, 1975), the direct cost of psychotherapy in the United States exceeds a billion dollars per year, "an order of magnitude comparable to that of the pharmacotherapy industry."

The Scope of the Psychotherapies

It is difficult to catalogue neatly all the different activities that can be included as psychotherapy. There is no universally accepted terminology covering the many kinds of psychological treatment used for emotional problems, alcoholism, drug abuse, developmental disabilities, and other mental health problems. The vast majority of psychotherapies involve face-to-face exchange between a professional administering the treatment (the psychotherapist) and the person who receives it (the patient or client).

The largest class of psychotherapies is made up of those that rely on verbal dialogues. This class includes counseling, case work, insight therapy, psychoanalysis, client-centered or nondirective therapy, psychiatric or psychological interviews or consultations, encounter groups, humanistic or existential therapy, rational-emotive therapy, transactional analysis, and most forms of group psychotherapy and behavior therapy.

A second class also uses verbal interaction as the main technique of treatment, but in more dramatic or unusual forms, often combined with specific behavioral methods of rehearsal or with altered states of consciousness. This category includes psychodrama, gestalt therapy, desensitization, implosive therapy, behavior shaping or operant conditioning, and hypnosis.

A third class of treatments makes active use of chemical or physical manipulation of the body. Included here are aversion therapies, biofeedback, bioenergetic therapy, and rolfing. One form of aversion therapy involves the treatment of alcoholism by emetic agents.

The above classes do not include all the named forms of psychotherapies. Estimates vary up to 200 or more "brand names" (Parloff, 1976). These classes do, however, include most kinds of psychological treatment used by psychiatrists, psychologists, social workers, nurses, counselors, and other professionals who claim expertise in this domain. Since there is no single term that adequately covers the field, I shall use the term "psychotherapy" to refer to treatment methods and classes otherwise called "mental treatment," "psychological treatment," and "therapy."

Drugs and Other Biological Treatments

It is important to note the growth of the use of drugs and other biological treatments. Beginning in 1952-1955, a large number of new and effective psychopharmacologic agents became available in North America. The first of these were the tranquilizers, particularly chlorpromazine and other drugs useful in the treatment of psychoses and major mental illnesses such as schizophrenia and manic depressive illness. Meprobamate, marketed as Miltown and Equanil, was the first of the antianxiety or minor tranquilizers. In the 1960s came the introduction of Valium and Librium and a large number of similar derivatives. The extent of the use of these drugs has caused considerable controversy. In any given year, between 10 and 12 percent of the general population receives a prescription for some psychoactive drug, most often Valium, Librium, or one of the other antianxiety agents. The antidepressant and antipsychotic drugs valuable in the treatment of hospitalized patients and patients with serious mental illnesses represent only a small fraction of the total prescriptions.

As will be discussed below, not all patients who receive psychopharmacologic agents have diagnosable mental illnesses. Many of them have symptoms of anxiety, depression, tension, and insomnia associated with medical illnesses such as arthritis, cardiovascular disease, or gastrointestinal disease. A large number are also experiencing symptoms in response to life stress. They seek help in coping with these stresses from the medical and health care system, where they often receive a prescription for minor tranquilizers.

Increasing Numbers and Types
of Mental Health Practitioners

At the same time as there has been a proliferation of a large number of therapies, there has been a parallel expansion in the number of practitioners. In 1955, soon after the Korean war but before the development of the community mental health centers program and the expansion of social programs as part of the "war on poverty" and "great society" eras, there were about 10,000 psychiatrists, half of whom were in clinical practice or private practice. There were a small number of clinical psychologists in private practice and an even smaller number of social workers. Over the ensuing 25 years the number and types of practitioners have increased greatly. My estimate is that there are now about 100,000 practitioners of psychotherapy. These break down as follows:

Psychiatrists: There are about 33,000 psychiatrists. Let us assume that two-thirds of them do some sort of private practice or institutional practice of psychotherapy. This would yield between 20,000 and 25,000.

Psychologists: There are about 55,000 psychologists, of whom approximately one-half are clinical psychologists. If we add to this school psychologists, we have another 30,000.

Psychiatric Social Workers: There are about 70,000 psychiatric social workers with masters degrees, and of this group it is estimated that about one-quarter are involved in some form of private practice, yielding about 20,000.

There are an increasing number of psychiatric nurses with masters degrees and marriage and family counselors, plus an increasing number of pastoral counselors and clergy who have taken formal training in counseling or psychotherapy.

What is characteristic of the recent trend is not only an absolute growth in the number of practitioners of psychotherapy, but the diversity of their professional backgrounds. Whereas at the end of World War II the psychotherapy situation was dominated by the psychiatrists, and among the psychiatrists by the psychoanalysts, today the psychiatrist in general, and psychoanalyst in particular, is in the minority.

The Social Context

The tremendous expansion of ambulatory mental health services, particularly with drugs and psychotherapy, has taken place in an era of rising economic well-being, increasing education of the population, the experience of the cohort of children born during the "baby boom," who are now in their young adulthood, and the growth of values around individualism, self-determination, self-fulfillment, and the increasing legitimization of the search for personal happiness, including artistic and creative expression, increasing sexual freedom, and greater mobility.

Within the context of these larger historical changes, periods of stress and distress are increasingly coped with through the health care system. The traditional social supports that buttress people against life stress have been the family, the church and religion, and the immediate neighborhood. All of these are increasingly less available to modern men and women as they cope with the demands for personal happiness and the ethic of self-fulfillment. In this context, psychotherapy is rational, it is modern, it promises individual fulfillment, and it reinforces the general tendency toward personalism.

THE SCIENTIFIC BASIS OF PSYCHIATRY

Most readers of this volume will be familiar with the advances in social science relevant to mental illness, particularly from sociology, social psychology, and anthropology. At the same time, there have been important advances in psychiatric research, particularly psychopharmacology, genetics, psychopathology, and neurobiology. The development in these fields has led to advances in validity and reliability of diagnoses and to a strengthening of the evidence for biological factors in the etiology of mental illness, both contributing to the redefinition of the traditional "medical" model as being relevant to psychiatry, and, therefore, to psychiatric epidemiology.

Advances in Genetics and Neurobiology

Research in genetics strengthened evidence for the biological as well as the psychosocial factors in the causation of mental illness. The studies by Heston (1966), and those done in Scandinavia by Mednick et al. (1974) and Rosenthal and Kety (1968), using the cross-rearing adoptive technique, established the high likelihood that genetic factors were involved in schizophrenia. In the 1960s, independent research groups in the United States, Europe, and Scandinavia studied primary affective disorders and found that by dividing their population into unipolar and bipolar groups based on the presence of a history of manic episodes, strong familial association could be found that supported a genetic transmission for the primary affective disorders, especially bipolar forms.

Evidence for biological factors in psychiatric disorders also emanated from studies in mental retardation, where the classical medical strategy led to discovery of new nosological subclasses. Using laboratory methods, the large group of mental retardations could be divided on the basis of origin, particularly subclasses due to aminoacidurias and to chromosomal abnormalities. However, in the other mental disorders, particularly schizophrenia, affective states, and anxiety states, evidence for biological factors has been slower to emerge and what evidence there is derives indirectly from psychopharamacology. In studies of the modes of action of these drugs, the neurotransmitters, particularly the catecholamines, have been implicated in the pathogenesis of various disorders.

Advances in Psychopharmacology

The introduction of psychotropic drugs in the mid-1950s led to changes in both the scientific investigation and the treatment of psychiatric disorders. The initial contribution of modern psychopharmacology was to stimulate the development of methodology for systematic assessment of patients' symptoms, social function, and diagnosis. Case reports and clinical experience could no longer be relied on to evaluate the flood of new agents that followed the introduction of chlorpromazine. The need to establish efficacy led to controlled clinical trials. Randomized designs, double-blind techniques, and placebo controls became the standards for therapeutic evaluation. These studies demonstrated that the new drugs, which had been shown to have varying neuropharmacologic modes of action, had different patterns of clinical efficacy, explainable partially by diagnostic type, for example, schizophrenic patients responded to phenothiazines whereas depressed patients responded to tricyclic antidepressants, and the bipolar subtype of affected patients showed response to lithium carbonate. These findings supported the concept that psychiatric disorders were discrete and heterogeneous and prompted reevaluation of diagnosis.

Advances in Psychopathology

By the mid-1960s, there was growing awareness among clinicians and researchers that the absence of an objective and reliable system for description of psychopathology and for psychiatric diagnosis was limiting research. In 1965, the National Institute of Mental Health, Psychopharmacology Research Branch, sponsored a conference on classification in psychiatry, taking note of the problem created by inadequate diagnosis and classification. In the decade since that conference, there have been major achievements in three areas: understanding sources of cross-national differences in diagnostic practices, improving their precision and reliability, and developing methods for their validation.

Cross-national differences in diagnosis. Two major studies clarified diagnostic practices and led to comparable data on mental disorders in different countries. The first, the U.S.-United Kingdom study organized by Kramer (1969) and Zubin (1969), investigated whether reported differences in diagnostic distribution between patients admitted to mental hospitals in the United States and the United Kingdom were real or artifacts due to different diagnostic criteria. The findings showed that the reported large differences between American and British rates of depression and schizophrenia were mainly a function of different diagnostic usage. American psychiatrists tended to diagnose as schizophrenic patients who would be considered as depressed or manic by British psychiatrists (Kramer, 1975).

Stimulated in part by the findings of the U.S.-U.K. study, the World Health Organization (WHO) undertook a study to determine whether comparable cases of schizophrenia could be identified in various nations with different political and social characteristics (Wing et al., 1974). The results of the U.S.-U.K. and WHO studies demonstrated that criteria and methods could be developed for the collection of reliable, uniform, and comparable diagnoses under varying conditions.

Reliability of diagnosis. Considerable progress in psychopathology research helped to identify sources of variance and contributed to unreliability of diagnosis between clinicians. Five sources of variance in the diagnostic process were identified (Spitzer et al., 1975): subject—the patient actually has different conditions at different times; occasion—the patient is in a different stage of the same condition at different times; information—the clinicians have different sources of information; observation—clinicians presented with the same stimuli differ in what they observe; and criteria—the formal inclusion and exclusion criteria that clinicians use to summarize patient data into psychiatric diagnosis differ.

Methods were evolved to reduce these sources of variance. A structured clinical interview was developed to elicit the patient's signs and symptoms in a systematic fasion and to reduce that portion of variance due to differing interviewing styles and coverage (Endicott and Spitzer, 1977). A set of operational definitions, with specific inclusion and exclusion criteria for a variety of nosological groups, was developed for reducing the criterion variance that was shown to account for the largest source of error (Feighner et al., 1972; Robins and Guze, 1972).

The research diagnostic criteria evolved from a decade of research on diagnosis, particularly by the group at Washington University, St. Louis. The conditions included were usually chosen because they had the most evidence of validity in terms of clinical descriptions, consistency over time, and increased familial incidence.

Spitzer et al. (1975), Wing et al. (1974), and others have shown convincingly that the use of these methods increases the reliability of psychiatric diagnosis. Although the approach of the research diagnostic criteria has received attention in the United States, parallel work in Great Britain, Scandinavia, and continental Europe, particularly by the Wing group, led to similar efforts to improve reliability. These efforts demonstrated that reasonable concordance in psychiatric diagnosis among clinicians and researchers could be achieved.

Validity of diagnosis. Whereas the validity of a classification is limited by its reliability per se does not establish validity. Validity of nosological classes in psychiatry requires correlation of the clinical phenomena with other domains of variables, such as long-term outcome, responses to treatment, familial association, and so on.

The usual approach to validity in psychiatry has been to base diagnostic classification on the best clinical judgment of experienced psychiatrists largely based on a priori principle rather than on systematic study. Robins and Guze (1970) put forth methods for establishing diagnostic validity in psychiatry on a scientific basis. The methods identified were careful clinical description, delimitation from other disorders, laboratory studies, follow-up studies, family and genetic studies, response to treatment, and correlation with independent psychological or social variables.

THE SCOPE OF PSYCHIATRY
AND MENTAL HEALTH

As stated earlier this chapter, the tremendous expansion in utilization of mental health services should not be interpreted as an increase in the incidence and prevalence of mental illness. Although there is much speculation about the increasing mental health problems of urban living and the consequences of the rapid pace of social change, the available epidemiological evidence indicates that the incidence and prevalence of mental illness in North America and indeed in most Western European nations has remained fairly constant. What has changed is the willingness of the public to utilize mental health services. Nevertheless the questions arise as to what is the magnitude and scope of psychiatric problems in the population in general and what are the appropriate conditions under which psychiatry and mental health services should be used. It should be noted that these two questions are different in nature. The first is a question as to fact, namely, the extent to which there are mental illnesses of various sorts, by some objective criteria, in the population. The second question is one of value and social policy, namely, what is legitimate and what is appropriate as to the use of psychiatry and other mental health services.

Psychiatry emerged in the mid-nineteenth century as a medical specialty. Psychotherapy began as a medical health procedure. Freud, Prince, and others in the late nineteenth century and early twentieth century who began writing about psychotherapy regarded it as a medical treatment for illnesses, usually hysteria, neurasthenia, and other neuropsychiatric conditions. The word's root, "therapy," indicates treatment, implying treatment of some condition that is implicit or otherwise regarded as "illness," "sickness," "disease," or "pathology." In this context, discussion about psychiatry and mental health usually involves debates about "the medical

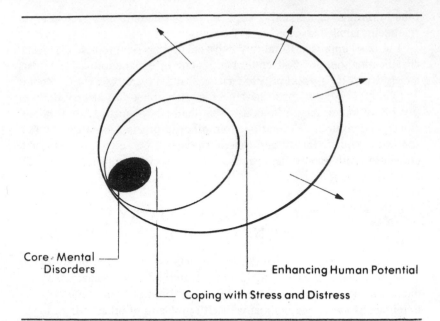

Core - Mental Disorders

Coping with Stress and Distress

Enhancing Human Potential

Figure 7.1   Boundaries Between Mental Illness and Mental Health

model" and the legitimacy of psychiatric activities. As an alternative to the usual debates about the limits of the medical model, I propose approaching the issues of legitimacy of psychiatry from an epidemiologic point of view—inquiring as to which segments of the population would meet alternative criteria of appropriateness. As shown in Figure 7.1, I identify three populations for whom psychiatric services are actually used and potentially legitimate. These are:

(1) A "core" group of people with definable mental illness, about 15 percent of the population, or approximately 30-35 million individuals.

(2) A large number of individuals who cope with various adverse life events and who experience distressing emotional symptoms but not necessarily a definable and diagnosable mental illness, approximately 50 million per year.

(3) The large number of individuals with problems of living who have the desire to enhance their personal happiness and satisfaction—this group is potentially unlimited.

The Core—Persons with Mental Disorders

For the "core" group, those with definable mental illnesses, there seems little at issue as to the legitimacy of psychiatric treatment. There is a growing consensus among policy makers, mental health professionals, and the public at large that treatment is appropriate for individuals who suffer from a diagnosable disorder using the criteria of the American Psychiatric Association's *Diagnostic and Statistical Manual of Mental Disorders III* (DSM-III) or the World Health Organization's *International Classification of Diseases* (ICD). While there is still some lingering debate around the "myth" of mental illness or the validity of many diagnostic categories, this controversy seems to have subsided. There is an increasing acceptance of the concept of multiple mental disorders that operationally can be diagnosed reliably by the type of criteria embodied in DSM-III (Weissman and Klerman, 1978). Epidemiologic evidence from Scandanavia, the United Kingdom (Robins, 1978), and North America indicates that about 15 to 20 percent of the population have such illnesses and that the majority of these illnesses are nonpsychotic, involving anxiety, depressive states, and alcoholism (Regier et al., 1978; Weissman and Myers, 1978).

For psychotherapies for patients in this large core group, the issue is not legitimacy or appropriateness but evidence for safety or efficacy. The use of psychotherapy for these individuals is within the health model— treatment for disorder that renders patients distressed and potentially disabled and at a higher risk for various forms of mortality and medical morbidity.

Persons Coping with Stress

One of the major advances in mental health research since World War II has been a growing recognition of the role of adverse life events and other stressors as precipitants of changes in the individual's health state, including his or her mental health. The evidence is increasingly conclusive that individuals experiencing these stressful life events potentially or actually suffer health problems in two stages: immediately after and during the period of adjustment, and later on. During the period of adjustment in coping with life events there is evidence of increased emotional symptoms such as depression, anxiety, and tension and associated bodily changes in sleep, appetite, level of activity, and sexual performance. Moreover, people coping with these events make greater use of the health care system and increase their use of alcohol, tobacco, and various sedatives. Antianxiety drugs such as Valium, Librium, and other bensodiazepines are often used

TABLE 7.1   Epidemiology of Life Stress

Stressful Life Event	Estimated Prevalence of Persons Directly Affected	Estimated Prevalence of Number Indirectly Affected per Year
Death	1.5 million	4 million
Divorce	3 million	6 million
Retirement	10 million	20 million
Unemployment	7 million	20 million
Chronic medical illness	10 million	20 million
Others ?	?	?

by individuals attempting to cope with these stressful events (Uhlenhuth et al., 1978).

As shown in Table 7.1, there may be approximately 50 million people a year who cope with various forms of adverse life events. Treatment is appropriate in these circumstances to assist people in the reduction of distress during the period of coping and adaptation and as a preventive measure to reduce the risk for the development of overt psychiatric or medical illnesses.

The use of psychotherapy and related treatments to assist people who are coping with life stress can be justified both as direct treatment and as a measure to offset the likelihood for the development of adverse health consequences that research has increasingly documented.

Persons Seeking Enhancement of Personal Potential

Since the Korean war there have been a large number of psychotherapies advocating the enhancement of personal potential. This trend has been crystallized in the fields of humanistic psychology and the "human potential movement." The people in this group, however, are those that are most problematic from the point of view of public policy and conceptualization. Most of the proponents of humanistic psychology and of the human potential movement explicitly reject the health model.

Many of the leaders of the field, such as Maslow (1954) and Rogers and Dymond (1954), criticize the psychopathology model as emphasizing symptoms and the negative aspects of personality rather than enhancing human potential. From their point of view, the legitimacy of psychotherapy is *not* as a health intervention, but for enhancement of human potential and promotion of general satisfaction. However, within this definition, there are no limits to the number of persons for whom some form of psychotherapy might be appropriate. Who among us has not wished to be more productive or more sexually attractive, to have a better memory, play better tennis, lose weight, or delay the onset of aging? The promise of psychotherapy is that it will do all of these things without any adverse side effects. The social issues included in the use of psychotherapy for these goals are similar to those that arise with the use of drugs for the enhancement of performance by athletes, the use of stimulant drugs by college students preparing for examinations, the process of football players getting "psyched up" for Sunday afternoon events, the use of LSD and other hallucinogens for expansion of consciousness, or the use of cocaine or cannabis derivatives by musicians.

CONCLUSIONS

This chapter has illustrated the trends in increasing utilization of mental health services. These trends parallel the general increase in utilization of the health care system. In the past the health care system was mainly devoted to the prevention of death and the extension of life. Now, increasingly, the health care system is called upon to remove distress where distress is defined, not only in terms of physical pain but also in terms of emotional discomfort and the ability to cope with life's vicissitudes and social change.

The increase in utilization of mental health services comes at a time when there is also an increasing demand for restriction of the mental hospitalization system. As the public's interest in relieving anxiety, depression, and other emotional distresses through various psychiatric services has expanded, debate has ensued as to the legitimacy of treatment of personal distress as medical disease. The discussion centers on which individuals are entitled to care in the medical system. Many people who are distressed due to anxiety or depression seek help through their general physicians, who then prescribe psychoactive drugs and offer some form of counseling. This inclusion of neurosis in the health care model since the turn of the century may be part of a new social definition or it may be due to the current conceptualization of disease.

Concomitant with the widening of mental health services has been the expanded use of psychoactive drugs, especially antianxiety agents. This has led to a dispute over the question of whether we have become an overmedicated society.

The dilemma facing the health care system is one of definitions. The health care system used to be devoted to the extension of life and the prevention of death. Currently it is being called upon to provide for the enhancement of life, emotional comfort, and the ability to cope with life's vicissitudes. The increased use of Valium and Librium heralds this new trend toward alleviation of distressing symptoms via the medical profession. The Declaration of Independence did not promise absence of anxiety, guilt, and insomnia, but rather the guarantee of life, liberty, and the pursuit of happiness. The change in definition for utilization of health care services will most likely promote an increase in care through the medical care system.

The urban industrial society of today, with its secular orientation and geographic mobility, relies less on social supports of family, church, and neighbors and more on the health care system. Geographic mobility means fewer friends and family are called upon for support when individuals find themselves lonely, disabled, or distressed. In a time when religion and social supports are lacking, people turn increasingly to what is available, namely, the health care system. It is effective and specialized and, most important, provides a financial base of support, the insurance system. The health care system, in addition to prolonging life, maintains and expands the size and quality of the population through reduction of mortality and morbidity, maintains an effective labor force by reducing disability due to illness, and promotes cohesion by regulating social control. This last function includes not only the extreme case of the use of psychiatry for the control of political dissidents in the Soviet Union but also the incarceration of socially disruptive and handicapped individuals, as has been the practice in the United States. In some societies the health system serves as a socializing force for the acculturation of new population groups, as in the case of Israel. Increasingly in the United States and other industrialized societies it provides a system to aid in the coping of individuals and families with distress and life tensions and with the enhancement of personal performance and happiness.

Thus the expansion of mental health services and the inclusion of neurotic distress, including anxiety and depression, as legitimate objects for psychiatric attention, or for the provision of services by other members of the health care system, provide a quasi-experimental case for defining the limits of the extent to which health and illness are socially defined and the extent to which the health care system is called upon to deal with quality of life in addition to its prolongation.

NOTE

1. For extended discussion of issues related to psychotherapy, see London and Klerman (forthcoming).

REFERENCES

ENDICOTT, J. and R. L. SPITZER (1977) "A diagnostic interview: the schedule for affective disorders and schizophrenia." Presented at the annual meeting of the American Psychiatric Association, Toronto, May.

FEIGHNER, J. P., E. ROBINS, S. B. GUZE, et al. (1972) "Diagnostic criteria for use in psychiatric research." Archives of General Psychiatry 26: 57-63.

GREENBLATT, M. and E. GLAZIER (1975) "The phasing out of mental hospitals in the United States." American Journal of Psychiatry 132: 1135-1140.

Group for the Advancement of Psychiatry (1975) Pharmacotherapy and Psychotherapy: Paradoxes, Problems and Progress, Vol. 9 New York: Author.

HESTON, L. L. (1966) "Psychiatric disorders in foster home reared children of schizophrenic mothers." British Journal of Psychiatry 112: 819-825.

KLERMAN, G. L. (1977) "Better but not well: social and ethical issues in the deinstitutionalization of the mentally ill." Schizophrenia Bulletin 3, 4: 617-631.

KRAMER, M. (1977) Psychiatric Services and the Changing Institutional Scene, 1950-1985. Rockville, MD: National Institute of Mental Health.

——— (1975) "Diagnosis and classification in epidemiological and health services research," pp. 66-83 in N. Hobbes (ed.) Issues in the Classification of Children, Vol. 1. San Francisco: Jossey-Bass.

——— (1969) "Cross-national study of diagnoses of the mental disorders: origin of the problem." American Journal of Psychiatry 125 (supplement): 1-11.

LONDON, P. (1977) Behavior Control. New York: New American Library.

——— (1964) The Modes and Morals of Psychotherapy. New York: Holt, Rinehart & Winston.

——— and G. L. KLERMAN (forthcoming) "Evaluating psychotherapy." American Journal of Psychiatry.

MASLOW, A. H. (1954) Motivation and Personality. New York: Harper & Row.

MEDNICK, S. A., F. SCHULSENGER, J. HIGGINS, et al. [eds.] (1974) Genetics, Environment and Psychopathology. New York: North Holland.

National Institute of Mental Health [NIMH] (1976) Draft Report: The Financing, Utilization, and Quality of Mental Health Care in the United States. Rockville, MD: Author.

PARLOFF, M. B. (1976) "Shopping for the right therapy." Saturday Review: 14-20.

REGIER, D. A., I. D. GOLDBERG, and C. A. TAUBE (1978) "The de facto U.S. mental health services system." Archives of General Psychiatry 35: 685-693.

ROBINS, E. and S. B. GUZE (1972) "Classification of affective disorders: the primary-secondary, the endogenous-reactive, and the neurotic-psychotic concepts," pp. 283-293 in T. A. Williams et al. (eds.) Recent Advances in the Psychobiology of the Depressive Illness. Washington, DC: Government Printing Office.

——— (1970) "Establishment of diagnostic validity in psychiatric illness: its application to schizophrenia." American Journal of Psychiatry 126: 107-111.

ROBINS, L. (1978) "Psychiatric epidemiology." Archives of General Psychiatry 35: 697-702.

ROGERS, C. R. and R. F. DYMOND [eds.] (1954) Psychotherapy and Personality Change. Chicago: University of Chicago Press.

ROSENTHAL, D. and S. S. KETY (1968) The Transmission of Schizophrenia. New York: Pergamon.

SPITZER, R., J. ENDICOTT, and E. ROBINS (1975) "Clinical criteria for psychiatric diagnoses and the DSM-II." American Journal of Psychiatry 132: 1187-1192.

TAUBE, C. A. and R. W. REDLICK (1977) Provisional Data on Patient Care Episodes in Mental Health Facilities, 1975. Statistical Note 139. Rockville, MD: National Institute of Mental Health.

UHLENHUTH, E. H., M. B. BALTER, and R. S. LIPMAN (1978) "Minor tranquilizers clinical correlates of use in an urban population." Archives of General Psychiatry 35: 650-655.

WEISSMAN, M. M. and G. L. KLERMAN (1978) "Epidemiology of mental disorders." Archives of General Psychiatry 35: 705-712.

WEISSMAN, M. M. and J. K. MYERS (1978) "Affective disorders in a U.S. urban community." Archives of General Psychiatry 35: 1304-1311.

WING, J. K., J. E. COOPER, and N. SARTORIUS (1974) The Measurement and Classification of Psychiatric Symptoms. London: Cambridge University Press.

ZUBIN, J. (1969) "Cross-national study of diagnosis of the mental disorders: methodology and planning." American Journal of Psychiatry 125 (supplement): 12-20.

ANTI-PSYCHIATRY FROM THE SIXTIES TO THE EIGHTIES

PETER SEDGWICK

AUTHOR'S NOTE: The author wishes to thank Mark Beeson and David Goldberg for calling his attention to some important references.

The thinkers discussed in this chapter are all identified by a large reading public as the major proponents of a school of thought known as "antipsychiatry." I shall use the term "antipsychiatry" and its collaterals "antipsychiatrist" and "antipsychiatric" as if they were relatively unproblematic, even though one of the authors discussed, R. D. Laing, has been at pains to state "I have never called myself an anti-psychiatrist" (Laing, 1972), and another, Thomas S. Szasz, has composed an acrimonious polemic dismissing antipsychiatry as an "imprecise, misleading and cheaply self-aggrandizing" concept and the antipsychiatrists (in his view, Laing and David Cooper) as being "all self-declared socialists, communists, or at least anti-capitalists and collectivists" (Szasz, 1979b: 49). For purposes of my analysis, I shall take "antipsychiatry" to be the view, expressed by Laing and Szasz at various times, as well as by Erving Goffman and (more recently) by David Rosenhan, that the subject matter in which psychiatry claims to deal— the various mental illnesses—is suspect and indeed improper, since these illnesses have no status other than that of convenient social fictions. Antipsychiatry amounts to the denial of a valid object for psychiatry. Reduced to these simple, bald terms, it is a position that has enjoyed a considerable and continuous vogue from the late fifties down to the present day, surviving a large number of social and intellectual changes in the context that has given it support over the years.

GOFFMAN AND THE RISE OF ANTIPSYCHIATRY

The proposition that the symptoms of mental illness are the construction of various social institutions and agencies may be put in either a strong or a weak form. The less sweeping version of the case would have it that, *in addition to* any features of mental illness arising from a biologically based disease condition, the progress of a psychiatric infirmity may be worsened or sharpened by the social handling of the patient in diagnosis or treatment. The more drastic, or stronger, version argues that the attribution of mental illness solely involves the power relationships between a weaker party (the person or persons singled out by society as being "mentally ill") and one or more dominant parties—the family of the patient, the medical establishment, and force of general public opinion, with its demeaning stereotypes of what constitutes mental deviance.

To be sure, the strong version of the antipsychiatric case need not ignore the possibility that some attributions of mental illness have a certain point of origin, in particular morbid inner processes or outward behaviors that are truly characteristic of the individual adjudged as "mentally ill" (and are thus not simply properties arising from the social process of adverse categorization surrounding him or her). But the supporters of strong antipsychiatry are insistent that these individual characteristics of the mental patient are quite marginal in determining the onset and course of society's adjudication of a psychiatric pathology. As demonstrated by one sociologist, Thomas J. Scheff, who has developed an antipsychiatric position with some striking resemblances to that of Goffman, the initial deviation displayed personally by the patient may be any of a very wide range of rule violations whose heterogeneous, rag-bag character renders them ineligible for systematic definition and study (Scheff, 1966).

Goffman himself has developed the strong antipsychiatric thesis in a number of tests composed some time ago (Goffman, 1963, 1967, 1972); but these discussions of the nature of psychiatric symptoms now appear as no more than stopping points in a search across a much broader set of themes that have little to do with the debate between psychiatry and antipsychiatry. It is true that Goffman's version of the strong case is a particularly strong and sweeping one: It involves the claim that mental symptoms are basically no more than "situational improprieties," infractions of the small-scale rules of demeanor and decorum that govern face-to-face interaction in small settings. Nevertheless, Goffman's subsequent *oeuvre* has bypassed the issues in the social framing of psychiatric pathology that were raised in these early papers; and it is rare for either defenders or opponents of the strong case in antipsychiatry to refer to them at all. Indeed, apart from allowing his name to appear as a sponsor on the letterhead of the American Association for the Abolition of Involuntary Mental Hospitalization—a body opposing all involuntary psychiatric interventions of whatever kind—Goffman cannot personally be identified with the theoretical or propagandistic backing of any of the large number of campaigns against psychiatric practices that have sprung up from the latter sixties to the present day. Indeed, the Association for the Abolition of Involutary Mental Hospitalization has achieved, in contrast to many other mental health lobbies pursuing a similar libertarian line, scarcely any prominence at all, apart from the individual writings of Goffman's distinguished colleague in the direction of its affairs, Thomas S. Szasz himself.

Goffman's claim to celebrity in the origins of antipsychiatry rests, in fact, on his early essays "On the Characteristics of Total Institutions," "The Moral Career of the Mental Patient," "The Underlife of a Public Institution: A Study of Ways of Making Out in a Mental Hospital," and "The Medical Model and Mental Hospitalization," all of which were gathered to compose the book *Asylums: Essays on the Social Situation of Mental Patients and Other Inmates,* which was published in 1961. During the preparation of these essays Goffman was an extremely close observer of the psychiatric practices current in the late fifties. The asylum method of disposal for persons with virtually any degree of mental derangement ranging from the moderate to the severe then reigned unchallenged by any rival perspectives of psychiatric care: 1955, the year in which Goffman began an unobtrusive spell of participant observation, in the guise of an assistant in sporting activities, on the wards of a vast and depersonalized mental institution in Washington, D.C. was also the year in which the total of inpatients in public mental hospitals in the United States reached its all-time maximum. Indeed, at this point "the public mental hospital population had quadrupled during the previous half century, whereas the general population had only doubled" (Joint Commission on Mental Illness and Health, cited in Scull, 1977: 66).

At the same time, Goffman was a key figure in the active current of medical, sociological, and administrative opinion which, from the mid-fifties onward, would evolve a substantial critique of the asylum solution for the mentally ill, a critique which would soon, in the hands of most of its authors, eventuate in the devising of powerful alternative policies to replace the mental hospital as the prime route of treatment in psychiatry. The author of *Asylums* himself took a stance of fatalism, indeed near nihilism, toward any suggestion that the inhuman practices toward mental patients so vividly depicted in his text might be susceptible to reform: There were, in his view, " 'good functional reasons' for the deprivations and horrors of the total institution"; and he discounted any claim that he could "suggest some better way of handling persons called mental patients," since "in our society . . . mental hospitals are found because there is a market for them" (Goffman, 1968: 115, 334). The terms of this "market" were undergoing considerable change in the very years when Goffman was drawing these conclusions as to their immutability: The wave of community mental health reforms symbolized by the passing of the "Kennedy Act" of 1963 was preceded by a multitude of initiatives in social theory and social policy, some of them stemming from the late fifties and involving a critical scrutiny of the regimen and relationships on mental hospital wards, often from a sociological or anthropological perspective bringing new insights to supplement or correct a narrow medical-individualistic appreciation. To take a couple of examples: It was at the Symposium on Preventive and Social Psychiatry convened in 1957 by the Walter Reed Army Institute of Research that Goffman presented his first version of the classic "On the Characteristics of Total Institutions"; the conference included several other pioneering statements in social psychiatry, from a more reformist, social engineering standpoint than Goffman's own, but still with a strong cutting edge in the criticism of institutional life in the mass asylum (Walter Reed Army Institute, 1958). Again in 1961, the year in which Goffman's *Asylums* was first published, a study of ward life in British mental hospitals was produced jointly by a sociologist and a psychiatrist, who inquired in considerable detail into the regimen to which patients were subjected. For example, an inventory of the personal possessions of each patient was drawn up, down to the last comb or nail file (of the chronic female schizophrenic patients at one hospital, 55 percent lacked combs of their own and 92 percent had no personal scissors or nail files); each ward was allotted a numerical score of the degree to which patients' free activity was restricted (for example, by being denied facilities to make their own cups of tea); a time-budget measuring the extent to which inmates were active or inactive in the course of their day was also drawn up; and, finally, these quantitative measures of the social atmosphere on the ward were compared with clinical indices of withdrawal or disturbance in the patients, with results that indicated how an impoverished social environment in the hospital could worsen the illness of the patient (Wing and Brown, 1961).

A comparison between this early study by Wing and Brown and the much more complex text produced by Goffman as a ward observer is quite revealing. Wing and Brown here display little of the conceptual fluency and magniloquent irony that make *Asylums* such a compelling document even for readers of the present day. They did, however, manage to work within a "weak" version of antipsychiatry, labelling theory, or societal reaction theory, which is particularly serviceable in practical work with the mentally ill. Goffman assumes (rather than argues) that he is describing constant, "functional" features of life in total institutions: Wing and Brown not only emphasize the variability of institutional environments but stress the fateful consequences for ward patients if hospital administrators, doctors, and nurses choose to arrange the life of the institution in one way rather than another. The starting point for Goffman appears to be a well-elaborated theoretical construction about the nature of the self and its need and desire to protect itself from engulfment by the institutional or societal totality: There is a striking affiliation here—to some extent acknowledged by Goffman in his reference to Czeslaw Milosz's study of Polish Stalinism, *The Captive Mind* (mentioned in the penultimate paragraph of one of the essays in *Asylums*)—between the Goffmanesque antiposition of "self" and "total institution" and the stark antithesis, so common in postwar Western political theorizing, between "individual liberty" and "totalitarianism." Wing and Brown, like other students of mental hospital living patterns from a critical-empirical perspective, start less from any such large historical canvas than from the minutiae of specific patients' lives in highly specific circumstances: The counting of articles of underwear on a crummy back ward may seem an unpromising beginning for an ambitious social investigation, but one may suggest that this hard-nosed, unromantic form of inquiry may prove a better pointer to theory as well as to policy than is the tragic eloquence of Goffman even at his best.

For, in the first place, the rigorous and specific detailing of patients' living conditions must be an indispensable prelude to any project of a public inspection and control over the fate of the hospitalized. Goffman's anatomization of the degradation rituals, the privilege systems, and other forms of staff manipulation for purposes of control will also constitute part of the understanding necessary in any such civic accounting of patients' institutional careers. But his category of the "total institution" evades any possibility of posing the question of how such institutions, where they are unavoidable, can be rendered *less* "total" and more human in quality as well as in scale. And his celebration of the stratagems for personal survival pursued so adeptly by the victims of the institution runs the risk that these isolated, individual "secondary adjustments" of permanent opposition will be presented as if no further *collective* prosecution of patients' rights, whether from inside the institution or with the help of philanthropic pressure groups outside it, is even worth discussing. Certainly few of the mortifications and other insults to the personality of patients described in *Asylums* are outlined in such a way that a program of demands could be framed in order to reduce or abolish them.

On a more theoretical plane, Goffman's conceptions of stigma and patient career, and his development for purposes of institutional analysis of the Meadian concept of the socially constituted self, are permanent and invaluable tools for the understanding of the situation of mental patients. Although these and kindred ideas have been codified and extended within the strong version of antipsychiatry or labelling theory, particularly in the work of Howard Becker, Thomas Scheff, and similar sociologists of deviance, there is no reason such Goffmanesque concepts should be seen as applicable solely to the strong rather than to the diluted version of this broad approach. Most of the analysis in *Asylums* need not imply the further position that all mental illness is *merely* a social construction around the self, even though the separate papers by Goffman mentioned earlier do take roughly that standpoint. Indeed, it is becoming less and less useful to speak of a *general* "moral career of the mental patient": Acute phases of illness behavior and transient hospitalizations nowadays complicate the picture of a permanent or chronic institutional career portrayed for the epoch when *Asylums* was drafted. Further, not all illness conditions are compatible with all possible phases of the socially constructed destiny of the mental patient as depicted by Goffman and other societal reaction theorists. The degree of chronicity in hospital stays and the level of social impoverishment in the ward setting are both likely to be affected by the sort of illness the patient has: A depressive or even a schizophrenic is liable to have shorter spells of admission, into more active and sociable facilities, than is the case with a sufferer from Alzheimer's disease or Huntington's chorea, with the pessimistic prognosis associated with those particular "labels."

An effective use of Goffman's contribution in the field of mental health must therefore tend in the direction of empiricism, and of a certain eclecticism in drawing on more biologistic or medical models of pathology as well as on sociological approaches. Such, at any rate, was the orientation pursued by the two observers of the British asylum whose humdrum counting of the patients' combs and nail files we mentioned earlier. The psychiatrist of that small team, John Wing, has gone on to produce a series of seminal texts on the nature of schizophrenic illnesses, with a due sensitivity to such social elements as family reactions, the role of industrial rehabilitation, and the "extrinsic" impairments—in addition to the "primary" and "secondary" deviance described by societal reaction theorists—which arise from such mundane, extramedical (and even unethnomethodological) factors as lack of money or a permanent address (Wing, 1978a, 1978b). Sociologist George W. Brown has over a number of years achieved eminence as the director of a research team whose work has shed unprecedented light on the social determinants of depressive illness, challenging that fatalistic view of an "endogenous" (as opposed to "reactive") variety of severe depression that has been part of the received wisdom of many psychiatrists (Brown and Harris, 1977). In these sociologically informed but medically specific researches of a rival empirical tradition, the insights of a Goffman still stand as an important reference-point, but creative work in social psychiatry has surely moved on from the crudities of labelling theory.

LAING AND THE LABELLING OF SCHIZOPHRENIA

It might be thought that the contribution in the sixties of R. D. Laing, a slightly later influence in the stream of strong antipsychiatry, would escape this criticism of an excessive generality. After all, Laing and his coworkers, David Cooper and Aaron Esterson, devoted their entire output to the study of one particular diagnostic category in psychopathology, namely, schizophrenia. Unfortunately, however, the activity of the Laing school (in the period when it was both productive and prominent) was characterized by a number of tendencies, which, taken together and also individually, were fated to terminate in a more or less complete dead end.

As most veterans of the radical sixties and seventies will recall, Laingian theorizing about mental derangement was imbued with a highly romantic vision of the nature of psychosis. This romanticism, attaching a kind of privilege to the fragmented alienation typical of some psychotic states, accorded well with the contemporary counter culture's emphasis on personal authenticity and heightened awareness. For a time, the Laingians' "politics of experience"—schizophrenic experience—synthesized with the Western youth revolt and its "politics of ecstasy": The psychotic became blurred with the psychedelic, and the schizophrenic became the latest inheritor of the long lineage of the suffering servant, at once victim and prophet. The more conservative era that has followed the withering of flower power has removed the cultural substrate for the popularity of the Laingian vision of psychosis. The pursuit of ecstasy has been channeled into the multifarious markets of the encounter group, bioenergetics, and Esalen-type movements, who avoid having much to do with psychotic patients (not least because the latter cannot afford the fees for these latter-day transcendent rituals).

But the specific approaches to schizophrenia pioneered (or at least publicized) by Laing and his collaborators have also failed to withstand the pressures of scrutiny and debate from other researchers in the field of schizophrenia. The phenomenological approach to aberrant mental states offered by Laing in *The Divided Self* and *Self and Others* appears for the moment to be in abeyance among clinical observers. There is some reason to suppose that Laing's particular descriptions of "ontological insecurity" and "false self systems" in these earlier works may be good approximations to the inner experience of patients with difficulties (such as severe depression or character disorder) lying outside the usual diagnostic framework for schizophrenia. Certainly such sympatheic interpretative writing, attempting to enter the world of the patient from the inside, deserves to be studied carefully by all those who have to do with the care of the mentally distressed: I personally recall a note being handed up to the platform following a public meeting addressed by Laing, in which an experienced psychiatric nurse confessed that he had not understood the humanity of the patients in his charge until he had read Laing's work. Nevertheless, an alternative approach to the clinician's phenomenology can be worked out satisfactorily by encouraging patients themselves to write about their own states of mind (see, for example, Wing, 1975).

The theorizing of the Laingian school about two further aspects of schizophrenia has also met with singularly little issue. The incrimination of the schizophrenic patient's family in the genesis of his or her illness was perhaps the most influential element in Laingian teaching, coinciding as it did with the arrival of a substantial body of social-psychological research into disturbed communication within the families of schizophrenics. Illustrations from the late fifties and sixties include Bateson's "double bind" theory of schizophrenia's origins, the emphasis in Theodore Lidz's work on pathogenic "schism" and "skew" in the patient's household, and the remarkable performance of Lyman Wynne and Margaret Singer in discriminating schizophrenics' families from normal families by a blind study of the transcripts of their conversations together. More recently, however, quite apart from the virtual disappearance of the Laingian school itself from this field of inquiry, there has been a noticeable tapering off of general research interest in such matters as the "double bind" and similar allegedly schizophrenia-producing material from families (Liem, 1980). In a careful study of possible abnormalities in the communication patterns of families of schizophrenics, Hirsch and Leff (1975) failed to replicate the clear-cut distinctions between these households and the families of nonschizophrenics (whether neurotic or normal); and it may be noted that the members of the Wynne team who had managed these successful blind discriminations by themselves were unable to train a further set of observers, suitably indoctrinated in the original team's coding system, to discern schizophrenics' families from other folk (Palombo et al., 1967). The oddity of communication in the families of certain schizophrenic patients, and even the researcher's capacity to judge an oddness when it arises, remains an elusive topic. Such findings as exist are certainly not firm enough to discredit a biological or even genetic model for the causation of schizophrenia: Laing himself has never published the control material from observations of nonschizophrenic families gathered in the period when he and Esterson were working on *Sanity, Madness and the Family* (apparently because of "major methodological difficulties in making comparisons between group processes"; Laing, 1976a: 30) and a few years ago he let it be known, through an indirect source, that it was "quite possible that the central elements of schizophrenia will eventually be shown to have a partly 'medical' (i.e., somatic) basis for their existence rather than an entirely social one" (Laing, personal communication, 1978, in Taylor, 1979: 9).

The other main orientation on schizophrenic psychosis that has been seen as characteristically Laingian is the idea that periods of madness may constitute a benign form of experience, "breakthrough" rather than solely "breakdown," provided that the psychotic's voyage of inner discovery is not suppressed or sidetracked through medical interference. The last ten years have seen an extraordinary dearth of cases with this benign outcome reported by Laing and his collaborators. Actually, it has never been hard to come across schizophrenic episodes of a one-time character, terminating without further sequel in the patient's life. What was unusual in the Laing School's presentation was their statement that these benign psychotic interludes displayed a lawful progression, a kind of inner integration within their own terms, so to speak, that could be watched and supported at each stage by sympathetic onlookers. This influential perspective on psychosis was actually supported by extremely few case studies; the principal piece of evidence was the fate of Laing's patient Mary Barnes, a study of whose career in the Laingian commune of Kingsley Hall was published in 1971 by herself and a therapist from that center (Barnes and Berke, 1971). Despite the evaporation of Laingian interest in benign psychotic episodes, at any rate in terms of published work, a series of

interesting studies has appeared from Soteria House, a community household for young schizophrenics in the Bay Area of San Francisco that offers
support to its residents during their florid phases of psychosis with a
minimal use of drugs and an extensive use of medically unsophisticated
nonprofessionals as the prime helpers (for example, see Mosher and Menn,
1975, 1978; Hirschfeld et al., 1977). These studies include a tentative but
positive controlled two-year follow-up of the patients and a study of the
personality characteristics required in helpers of schizophrenics. It would
be a pity if the oblivion into which the writings of the Laing school have
currently fallen were also to affect the public reception of the Soteria
project's reports. These are all the more noteworthy because one of their
coauthors is a particularly distinguished psychiatrist, Dr. Loren Mosher,
who, in another capacity, edits the *Schizophrenia Bulletin* of the National
Institute for Mental Health in an eclectic spirit open to all serious
approaches, medicobiological as well as social, in the study of schizophrenia. Some of the more valid concerns of Laingian therapy thus have
their continuation in a more objective tradition of social psychiatry.

It must be said that, with the abandoning of his former radical excesses,
Laing has ceased for some time to be productive of any sociologically
focused work of a detailed description. His clinical practice continues in
London with various group households around the Philadelphia Association. His theoretical pronouncements in matters touching his old interests
have become both sparse and generalized. A few years ago an apparent
defense of the helping role of the psychiatrist by Laing, in the course of a
review in which he accused Thomas Szasz of "making . . . a scapegoat out
of psychiatry" (Laing, 1979), provoked a shocked reaction from a therapist who, as an ardent protagonist both of Szasz and of Laing's earlier
work, concluded that "Dr Laing's present position clearly implies that he
now believes his work of 1964 to be gravely mistaken." The disappointed
Laingian publicly requested clarification as to "what reasons have led him
to this remarkable conclusion?" (Stadlen, 1979).

Laing did not take up this challenge, which many of his old disciples
must have thought of putting to him. We are left to infer both the
motivation and the logic of his retraction from the various hints he has
given about his new position (see Sedgwick, 1982: ch. 3). For example, in
a 1975 interview with a Spanish sympathizer, he distanced himself again
from Szasz and the radical psychiatrists of America and Europe, to whom
he ascribed the view that "madness is fabricated by psychiatrists and . . .
the majority of the signs and symptoms of the so-called mental illnesses
are iatrogenic." On this position, Laing put it simply, "I do not go so far."
As "a traditionalist rather than an innovator," he now harked back to an

older humanistic vein in psychiatry, of "non-interference and respect for the patient," going "back to the origins of psychiatry" but continuing still in the first years of his own psychiatric training in the forties and early fifties. "Within this tradition there were psychiatrists who refused to give electro-shocks, who abstained from recommending lobotomies, who rejected excessive medication for their patients, who tried to listen." For the present "technological generation" of psychiatrists, "I am a relic from a period before this era." But there are "a small number of old psychiatrists who think as I do," and from these he has had a cordial reception (Laing, 1976b). We must leave this Laing of an explicitly Hippocratic tradition, of professional peership, and—apparently—of moderate medication, in order to consider the destinies of an antipsychiatry he has now repudiated.

THOMAS SZASZ: THE UNMAKING OF A MYTH

Szasz's own attack on the antipsychiatry of the Laing school is based on the charge that Laingian therapeutic interventions, of the sort conducted with Mary Barnes and other inhabitants of Kingsley Hall-type communes, actually constitute a disguised form of psychiatry. The intensity of Szasz's diatribe may be gauged from his analogy between the violence of coercion in the traditional state mental institution and the imposition on the tax paying public that he claims is the inevitable consequence of the welfare assistance received by the residents of Laingian group households: "It does not follow logically or morally that such persons are entitled to services extracted by force or fraud from others—whether these 'others' be indentured torturers in old-fashioned state hospitals or indentured tax-payers in new-fashioned welfare states" (Szasz, 1979b: 52).

It should be clear from the above summary, and from a scrutiny of his recent works, that Szasz, virtually alone among the old root-and-branch opponents of the medical model in psychiatry, has pursued a consistent course of argument from the sixties to the present day. His critique of the Laingian variant of antipsychiatry rests on the belief (which, as we have seen from Laing's recent statements, may be partially justified) that it is not antipsychiatric *enough,* since its practice and precept amounts to a shamefaced, covert capitulation to psychiatry itself. Despite his own disclaimer of the term "antipsychiatry" as a description of his own viewpoint—a disavowal that appears to arise from the logic of his dispute with Laing and the Laingian antipsychiatrists—Szasz can be regarded as the foremost proponent of antipsychiatry, taken in the strong sense of the concept outlined earlier. For Szasz (1979b: 49), psychiatry is a "specialty ... not of medicine but of mythology" since the object of its investigation, mental illness, is itself a myth. While at one point he claims that "I am not against voluntary psychiatry, or psychiatric relations between consenting adults," it is clear that this suspension of opposition to certain types of psychiatric practice is possible only on the premise that "people are entitled to their mythologies," psychiatry being one variety of myth making or "ersatz religion" (Szasz, 1979b: 49).

The mythical character of mental illness and consequently of psychiatric treatment is argued by Szasz on the basis of identical considerations in the whole series of his works, beginning with his paper "The Myth of Mental Illness," published over twenty years ago (Szasz, 1960) and proceeding to such recent treatments of the same issues as "Psychiatry: The Model of the Syphilitic Mind" (1979b: 1-44) and the introductory pages to *The Myth of Psychotherapy* (1979a: xi-xviii). (Szasz's discovery of a further myth in psychotherapy, as distinct from psychiatry, is slightly confusing since he has long contended that an entirely valid form of psychotherapy is possible—namely, the "autonomous psychotherapy" practiced within private two-person contracts resembling his own therapeutic work with clients; Szasz, 1974.) In an essay such as the present chapter, which is intended to focus on shifts and changes in the world of antipsychiatry from the sixties to the eighties, it would be wrong to devote much space to Szasz's persisting arguments on the inapplicability of illness concepts to the problems of psychic distress. It is enough to note that in Szasz's recent works as in his earlier texts, these arguments rest in large part on the postulate that "illness" or "disease," when applied to the phenomena of mental distress or malfunctioning, constitute no more than metaphors whose real and literal meaning is to be found in physical lesions or disturbances affecting the human body. It is proper, therefore, to use "illness" and "disease" as terms applicable to physical ailments, since in these disorders an abnormal variation of anatomy or physiology is implicated in the definition of what is wrong. No such anatomical or physiological abnormalities, in contrast, have been plausibly identified for the so-called mental illnesses, and therefore any schema of diagnosis or treatment for these forms of distress amounts to an illogical and invalid enterprise, even apart from the specific examples of maltreatment and pseudo-diagnosis that can be alleged against the practice of psychiatrists.

While Szasz's position on the metaphorical, indeed, mythological character of the mental illnesses has remained intact over the years (although with some fresh turns of argument in, for example, Szasz, 1978), debate around this question among other authors concerned with this question has undergone a number of striking and related developments. With the mounting crisis in general health care provision that has characterized advanced Western societies in the current period of industrial recession and state-directed cutbacks in welfare spending, the attention of social critics in matters diagnostic and remedial has moved away from the pretensions of psychiatry to the claims of medicine itself as a purveyor of the common good. Although in the sixties, as Ehrenreich and Ehrenreich (1978: 40) have put it, "medical services themselves were seen as politically neutral; the need for them was biologically ordained; their precise content was technologically determined," the critique that was already in this period directed against psychiatry by the mass force of labelling theory and antipsychiatry has proven, in the seventies and now, to be the opening engagement in a much larger war that encompasses gynecological as well as psychiatric diagnosis, the technology of the forceps as well as of the tranquillizer, the social control exerted by the profession of surgery as a whole, no less in mastectomy than in lobotomy. The public warning against "the triumph of the therapeutic" is nowadays as much in evidence against purportedly therapeutic practices in somatic doctoring as against the psychoanalysts and their intellectual abettors who were the target of Philip Rieff's celebrated obloquy when he first coined the slogan during the mid-sixties.

This broad development in the critique of general medicine over recent years, along with the growth of protest and self-help groups in the sphere of somatic as well as of mental health, has an unwelcome implication for that large train of antipsychiatric thought, symbolized by Szasz though not pioneered exclusively by him, that attempted to discredit the enterprise of psychiatry by posing it as an invalid rival or pretender to the legitimate lineage of biological medicine itself. Despite the failure of Szasz or any of the other leading antipsychiatric writers to take stock of this new appreciation of general medical goals and practices, the demotion of psychiatry's own critique from the status of an autonomous intellectual current to that of a component (albeit an important one) in a broadly skeptical view of medicine is likely to be long-lasting.

The more recent politicization of psychiatric issues has, indeed, been framed less in the dualistic approach that separates psychopathology from somatic causation than in the terms of a psychophysical monism that draws on a certain amount of biological knowledge among campaigners. Whereas some years ago it was fashionable to dismiss the concepts of behavior disorder and hyperactivity among schoolchildren as a mere artifact of repressive social labelling (see Schrag and Divoky, 1975), the ecological militancy of our own epoch has displayed little or no reluctance in drawing upon these and similar "labels" in their incrimination of chemical additives to food, or lead additives to gasoline, as causative elements in the genesis of childhood maldevelopment. Where in the sixties the advent of mental derangement or psychosis was seen as society's violation of a pristine self, which, freed of repressive institutions, would run blissfully free, we are now more likely to be given notice of the perils of alcohol-induced dementia or of the various psychoses that are misleadingly (but physiologically) grouped as "senile" or "presenile." If Mary Barnes was the chosen spectacle of psychosis in the sixties, it is Rita Hayworth, lapsing into confusion and incoherence through a reported degeneration of her brain cells in Alzheimer's disease, who strikes nearer home in the eighties. In the new alliance between the critique of psychiatric provision and the critique of somatic medicine, popular concern with psychiatric questions has itself become somatized.   Apart from these pragmatic public responses, a number of tendencies within theoretical and academic discussion have also been at odds with any sharp distinction between a biologically defined bodily pathology and a socially (or even politically) construed psychopathology. Among both sociological and medical theorists, illness and disease, in a sense encompassing both physical ailments and psychiatric disabilities, are being seen as problematic social constructions, rather than as self-evident biological givens. Some sociologists working at the level of everyday, commonsensical ascriptions of illness by ordinary members of the public have produced valuable reports or theorizations on illness as a social construct, in a vein of inquiry that has clearly drawn on the older labelling theory approach that was applied solely to attributions of mental illness. Robert Dingwall's (1976) and David Locker's (1981) work may be mentioned as powerful examples of this continuing trend.

Meanwhile, apart from the illness-ascribing behavior of the lay public, doctors and medical scientists have themselves been forced to face the highly ambiguous and even at times subjective character of what they choose to categorize as diseases. The position espoused by Thomas Szasz, to the effect that disease consists of a pathological site in the body, and, indeed, can even occur in bodies which, like cadavers, are thoroughly dead (as in Szasz, 1979b: 34), is nowadays contested and debated in a host of quarters (for example Scadding, 1967; Kendell, 1975; Pies, 1979). There remains a tendency among writers in the United States, particularly, to reserve the term "disease" to cover pathoanatomic changes of the type referred to by Szasz, while keeping the term "illness" to refer to the personal and social consequences of such biological abnormalities (Fabrega, 1972; Boorse, 1975; see also the discussion in Kraüpl Taylor, 1981).

The merits of using "disease" in this narrower, more technical sense cannot be properly discussed in this chapter: I, for one, find it strange that a word in the English language that has been in common usage for centuries, with its root meaning thoroughly embedded in a reference to some kind of discomfort or "disease," should be seen as acquiring a technical connotation that is supposed to have no bearing on illnesses, as distinct from lesions, or on persons, as distinct from bodies. Nevertheless, it should be clear from this brief account of the debate that the theoretical arguments for antipsychiatry no longer can be justified, as Szasz and other authors have done (see Sedgwick, 1982: chs. 1 and 2), by contrasting mental illness with a supposedly more objective and obvious physical disease state or illness category. Illness has turned out to be more sociologically interesting than that; and a more philosophical biology has weakened the magisterial confidence, characteristic of the Virchowian school of the nineteenth century, whereby disease was as securely "in there" (in the patient's body) as matter and its fundamental constituents were "out there" (in atoms, electrons, or the ether).

PSYCHIATRY'S COUNTERATTACK

In short, the heat that blistered psychiatry twenty or so years ago is now warming the backside of other targets. Antipsychiatry has lost the theoretical and political initiative, and has failed to renew its ideas or its audience. Moreover, in an epoch, like our own, typified by growing macroeconomic and megamilitaristic tensions or despondencies, fewer and fewer members of the public are likely to relish a view of the human condition that pronounces the psychiatric sequelae of, for example, unemployment to be of no clinical interest, or the mental casualties of war to be untreatable compared with its more strictly anatomical traumas. If in the affluent sixties the intrusions of the psychiatrist or the social worker could form a principal topic of the intelligentsia's anxiety, it is nowadays the absence of therapeutic and welfare services rather than any excess of their presence or availability that tends to impinge on a previously sheltered middle class. The books of the antipsychiatrists, of course, enjoy a circulation, but their titles are mere reprints of what has already been said or (in the case of Thomas Szasz) a preamble to reworded but broadly similar arguments, past which the currents of modern controversy have swirled and moved on.

As we have argued, a weak version of societal reaction or labelling theory can be incroporated quite easily within a liberalized medical framework, and a number of psychiatric writers have taken the opportunity to strengthen their own case with inputs drawn from a scrutiny of antipsychiatric arguments. John Wing's *Reasoning About Madness* (1978a), while amounting in part to an ardent plea for the focusing of medical attention upon technically conceived disease entities, also develops a view of the socially caused handicaps consequent on mental illness in a vocabulary explicitly indebted to Edwin Lemert's pioneering contributions to societal reaction theory in the study of deviance (Wing, 1978a). Anthony Clare's (1976) potent and well-argued book not only takes up many of the practical issues first campaigned for by antipsychiatric militants (such as psychosurgery, electro-convulsive therapy, the uncertainties of psychiatric diagnosis), but attacks the biologistic, "organicist" orientation that still governs much of clinical practice in psychiatry. Clare's insistence on the importance of an integrated medicosocial approach to the treatment of mental illnesses is hostile to labelling theory, but at the same time influenced by many of the labelling theorists' insights into the vicissitudes of the mental patient's career.

From the ranks of biological psychiatry itself, Professor H. M. van Praag has mounted a forceful and intricate polemic against the postulates of antipsychiatric labelling theory (van Praag, 1978). If at times his defense of current psychiatric procedures seems to err in the direction of a certain complacency (as in his blanket endorsement of the therapeutic value of psychotropic drugs, without reference to the problems of side effects or of the patient's dependency), it is still clear that in order for these primarily biochemical researchers to have marshalled this attack large concessions were necessary: first, in the positive appraisal of sociological theories of mental illness outside labelling theory (the work of Walter Gove being cited with particular approbation) and, second, in van Praag's final admission that antipsychiatry has performed a constructive "sensitizing" function in assisting with the generation of more humane policies toward mental patients. From the examples of Wing, Clare, and van Praag, it could be argued that antipsychiatry has operated as psychiatry's own necessary baptism of fire, tempering the excesses of biologism and fusing the Aesculapian with the Socratic tradition to forge some kind of synthesis between a critical sociology and a positivist medicine.

Nevertheless, as some critics of Anthony Clare's medicosocial approach have argued, the net effect of this apparently nondogmatic eclecticism is to reassert the hegemony of the psychiatrist's own expertise and the paramountcy of a medical monopoly in the understanding of mental distress. The biologism of the medically trained psychiatrist is ingrained: Whatever lip service is paid to the sociological and psychological dimensions that should be "taken into account," the remedy offered to the sufferer is likely to be some dosage of psychotropic medication, "which of course only a psychiatrist can prescribe" (Treacher and Baruch, 1981: 123). How realistic is it to suppose that, on top of his or her arduous accumulation of skills in medicobiological disciplines, the psychiatrist is going to be an insightful and up-to-date social scientist as well—in Treacher and Baruch's (1981: 123) words a sort of "master detective—a veritable Sherlock Holmes who takes into account all the myriad aspects of the patient, by drawing on every known science which has relevance to human behaviour"?

There are those of us who feel that, however difficult the task may be of integrating a biological with a social approach in the interpretation of mental disorders, such a synthesis remains the only possible ideal. The problems of an oversophisticated and overinclusive psychiatric ethic seem less daunting than any venture in therapy that refuses to reckon with the contribution made by any particular branch of the relevant sciences. But it may be more fruitful to equip socially orientated therapists with some biological and natural-scientific knowledge than to turn medically qualified physicians into suitable practitioners of a social psychiatry which, however eclectic and many-sided, retains a near-monopolistic hegemony in its assumption of "clinical responsibility."

ENTER THE PSEUDOPATIENTS

In any case, the supposition is scarcely tenable that the progress of debate and practice in psychopathological medicine would come to resemble one of those fortunate Hegelian triads of conceptual movement whose *thesis* would be psychiatry, its *antithesis* antipsychiatry, with a culminating synthesis in an *anti-antipsychiatry* incorporating the best of all previous contentions. The irruption of critical tendencies of thought into an area as ambiguous and as highly charged as psychopathology cannot fail to be sensational, and at times even catastrophic in import. As a final example of the continuing reverberations of antipsychiatry in the contemporary public consciousness, we will recount the history of D. L. Rosenhan's (1973a) study, "On Being Sane in Insane Places."

Spasm One: Publication

The appearance of Rosenhan's paper, with its evidence for the inability of psychiatrists and nursing staff in twelve different mental hospitals to discover the deception (in the simulation of hallucinatory experience) practiced on them by Rosenhan himself and several confederates—the "pseudopatients" of the study—created immediate consternation. Appearing as it did in a medium (the journal of the American Association for the Advancement of Science) that is both highly reputable and a frequent reference point for nonspecialists interested in public questions of science, it received early and excited attention in a wider press. The very details of its textual form are revealing: It contains no significance tests, inferences from multivariate design, theoretical neologisms, or other arcane accompaniments of the sort that typify the style of reports in experimental social psychology. The introduction of statistical or quantitative material is carefully rationed, data being nearly always introduced sparsely but effectively within the natural flow of the argument. At once a popularization and a scientific intervention in its own right, with a plainness in conception and execution that cannot conceal the ingenuity and artfulness of its author, "On Being Sane in Insane Places" has become a deservedly famous contribution to psychiatric controversy.

Spasm Two: Rebuttal and Restatement

Following its publication of Rosenhan's study, the correspondence section of *Science* received a considerable number of letters from psychiatrists and other professionals who objected to various features of the paper and (usually) defended either current psychiatric diagnosis or current mental hospital procedures. Of these protesting arguments, fifteen were collected in a subsequent issue of the journal, along with a substantial reply by Rosenhan (Science, 1973; Rosenhan, 1973b). In 1975 one of the specialized journals of the American Psychological Association printed further papers analyzing Rosenhan's study in a distinctly critical vein, along with a British psychiatrist's comment endorsing his work. Rosenhan again replied to his critics in the same issue (Weiner, 1975; Spitzer, 1975; Crown, 1975; Millon, 1975; Rosenhan, 1975).

The interplay between the contestants in this dispute is quite revealing, particularly as Rosenhan appears to amend some of his positions as the exchange progresses. While the 1973 *Science* article could easily be classed as a vindication of the strong variant in antipsychiatry (since here Rosenhan refused any validity to the diagnostic procedures of psychiatry as distinct from those of medicine), in 1975 he merely argues that future diagnostic systems should be validated "in a variety of settings" (Rosenhan, 1975: 473), that is, sampling the patient's behavior outside the special context of the mental hospital ward. Rosenhan (1973b: 368) even excused the admitting physicians in the twelve hospitals of any blame by stating that, given their acceptance of the veracity of the pseudopatients, hospitalizing them was "the only humane thing to do"—this conclusion of Rosenhan's being somewhat at variance with the appraisal of those psychiatrists who were alarmed at his report precisely because "a complaint of auditory hallucinations of the sort described would seem to be readily manageable with outpatient psychiatric care" (Burr, 1973). What is perhaps more surprising is that the issue of the admitting physicians' competence remained an unresolved question among Rosenhan's many critics. Some (like his three opponents in the *Journal of Abnormal Psychology* controversy) produced a defense of the diagnostic handling of the pseudopatients, arguing that a diagnosis of schizophrenia (performed by eleven out of the twelve admitting hospitals) was actually a reasonable and competent differential diagnosis in the circumstances. Some of the correspondents in *Science,* on the other hand, admitted that the diagnosis was botched: But even though "incompetent evaluators" with a "poor quality of practice" had been operating in the admissions units of the twelve hospitals, existing diagnostic systems were quite capable of dealing with the dilemmas of pseudopatienthood provided that psychiatrists acted competently within the current criteria and procedures.

The defense of modern psychiatry's diagnostic framework that was mounted against Rosenhan actually, therefore, tended to increase the uncertainties surrounding current clinical practice. Moreover, the large and complex range of issues spurred by Rosenhan's 1973 paper—which included some very sensitive discussion about the depersonalized "labelling" tendencies inside mental hospitals—was narrowed down in the course of the debate to the question of the propriety of the admitting diagnosis. Even Rosenhan (1973b: 366-367) concentrated his counterargument on "the diagnostic leap" made by the admitting physicians from "the single presenting symptom" of auditory hallucination to the fullblown disease category of (usually) schizophrenia: This issue, he insisted, was "the heart of the matter." Rosenhan's own proposal for a reformed diagnosis, that is, the production of a new system of classificatory labels based on simple surface behaviors such as auditory hallucination, formed a lame as well as an unrealistic conclusion to the pungent debate his study had initiated.

The impetus and daring of Rosenhan's initiative was soon lost within a formal and research-oriented debate in which few of the contenders displayed much sense or even knowledge of the practical issues affecting the welfare of patients. Rosenhan's persistent assumption, for example, that psychiatric labelling induces an irreversible mental patient identity was never challenged by the obvious point that schizophrenic patients, to take the category principally targeted in the controversy, nowadays drop out of the diagnostic enterprise, and its attendant medical facilities, with considerable ease—to be affixed with far more "irreversible" labels such as that of the aged pauper or the ignominious corpse. There are places even more insane than the unfeeling, bureaucratized psychiatric wards that Rosenhan and his fellow researchers entered as voluntary victims, and it is these depositories for the dehospitalized, the flophouses and lockups and guilt-ridden nuclear families, that are tending to multiply as the residences for those in mental torment, at any rate in this age of the greater insanity of government-induced cutbacks and cheapening, worsening welfare services.

Spasm Three: The Contented Pseudopatient

As Rosenhan always made clear in his 1973 report and subsequent discussion, there was a ninth pseudopatient who underwent the full ordeal of feigned hallucination and actual hospitalization, but whose experiences were omitted from the analysis of data. This subject had violated the canon of deception imposed on all participants by falsifying aspects of his personal background at the admission interview (denying, for example, that he was married). Even though his sanity went undetected by the hospital and "his data ... were consistent with the data from another pseudopatient," the variability in experimental procedure adopted by this person was considered enough to justify the erasure of his results (Rosenhan, 1973a: 258; 1975: 469).

Three years after his exclusion from the Rosenhan report, this missing subject published his own account of his part in the project (Lando, 1976). Dr. Harry A. Lando produced what was a very considerable qualification of the negative evaluations reached by Rosenhan and his colleagues on modern American mental hospital treatment. The large public insitution to which he was summarily admitted after a 45-minute psychiatric interview had "excellent" and "attractive" facilities, with ample recreation choices, and an excellent staff-patient ratio. While nursing staff did tend to misinterpret, in a pathological sense, Lando's rational activities, such as note-taking on the ward, their principal attitudes are described as warm, positive, and care-giving. "The powerlessness and depersonalization of patients so strongly emphasized by Rosenhan simply did not exist in this setting" (Lando, 1976: 50). Lando was discharged after 19 days, having argued his case for release. The initial diagnosis given to Lando was the serious one of "chronic undifferentiated schizophrenia," a label powerful enough to pathologize the staff's perceptions of his everyday actions—but not enough, it seems, to condemn him to a longer hospitalization. In this case, as with Rosenhan's other pseudopatients, the social processes on the ward whereby staff members come to perceive the patients's behavior as satisfactory for discharge purposes, rather than as essentially pathological, remain unexplored.

The Last Spasm: The Criminal as Pseudopatient

The most sensational sequel to the Rosenhan affair took place during May 1981, at the Old Bailey, London's Central Criminal Court. Peter William Sutcliffe, who had terrorized cities in the North of England by killing thirteen women (often with sadistic mutilation) over a period of five years, attempted to evade conviction on charges of murder by claiming a "diminished responsibility" by reason of mental disorder. Sutcliffe gave an elaborate account of his belief in a personal divine mission to purify society by killing prostitutes (the last group of his victims were not in fact prostitutes), and his defending counsel summoned the evidence of three psychiatrists who testified to the truthfulness of the accused's description of his mental state and confirmed their diagnosis of paranoid schizophrenia.

The conduct of the trial was particularly remarkable because, until the judge insisted that the defense case must be cross-examined before a jury, the prosecution (led by the British attorney-general, Sir Michael Havers) was prepared to accept the diminished responsibility plea, which would have led to a conviction of manslaughter rather than murder. Six days after arguing before the judge that the psychiatric evidence from the defense was satisfactory, Havers was opening a prosecution case that involved a vigorous attempt to discredit the defense diagnosticians by showing that Sutcliffe's reports of his hallucinations and delusions were deliberately fabricated by him. During his cross-examination of a defense psychiatrist, the attorney-general asked whether the witness had heard about "an experiment in the United States" in which eight pseudopatients had persuaded doctors to diagnose them as schizophrenic by claiming to hear voices. The psychiatrist said that he had indeed read about the Rosenhan study and "agreed that, ideally, a doctor would find outside corroboration for his diagnosis" (*Guardian* report, May 19, 1981).

The defense's psychiatric testimony was effectively undermined when it became transparent that the medical witnesses had failed to cross-check Sutcliffe's statements to them against the confessions he had made to the police, or against the detailed material that was available about his sadistic sexual gratification in killing women. One of the defense psychiatrists had no answer to this latter patent evidence, and retracted part of his sworn statement while in the witness box (*Guardian* report, May 15, 1981). The jury, not surprisingly, rejected the defendant's plea of diminished responsibility—which was rendered even more paradoxical by his insistence, on cross-examination by his defense lawyer (whom, presumably, he had instructed), that his sense of a divine mission was not a pathological symptom but a response to the voice of God (London *Times* report, May 13, 1981). In finding the accused guilty of murder on all thirteen counts, the jurors repudiated the diagnostic competence of three experienced and trained psychiatrists and, in effect, placed Sutcliffe in the role of successful pseudopatient that had been suggested to them by the prosecution.

The discrediting of their colleagues' testimony was by a further paradox "a relief to psychiatrists and all working in mental health," as the London *Times* medical correspondent put it (Smith, 1981), since public sympathy toward the plight of schizophrenics would have been rendered even more precarious if so atrocious and well known a killer had been tagged with this label. As in the American medical reaction to the Rosenhan case, a local incompetence in the diagnostic skills, or perhaps only in the forensic naivety, of particular doctors was held to excuse the general methodology of the profession itself.

Within the wider public response to the Sutcliffe trial, it is worth noting the suspicion of feminists as to the validity of a psychopathological approach to these horrific killings. Feminists refused to interpret Sutcliffe's actions in the circumscribed terms of an individual pathology focusing on delusions about prostitutes, on the lines offered by the defense with its appeal to a medical expertise of diagnosing such pathology. To some extent the feminist critique of Sutcliffe's claim to be mentally ill matched the arguments of the prosecuting counsel, who suggested that the accused was wicked rather than schizophrenic and a woman-hater rather than a prostitute-hater. One feminist writer on the Sutcliffe trial expressed a preference for viewing the defendant as "bad," since such a label would require an understanding "of the moral, that is the social, content of the acts" as distinct from diagnosing him as "mad," a label that "avoids seeing the link between the individual and society" (Holloway, 1981: 35). While the "badness" of Sutcliffe was construed in different ways by feminists and by the Tory (and male) attorney-general of Britain (the former seeing this killer's viciousness as evidence in an incrimination of male sexuality, the latter working with a conception of "plain evil, plain bad" probably deriving from an unanalyzed Christianity), the discomfiture of psychiatry was in both cases the necessary prelude to a reassertion of moral judgment.

CONCLUSION

The debate between psychiatry and its antidiagnostic critics has lasted now more than two decades. Its terms may shift as psychiatry becomes more skilled in dialectic and as the public ignorance of the conditions usually called mental illnesses becomes gradually lessened through education and exposure. Nevertheless, the refutation of some of the central propositions of antipsychiatric or labelling theory will not terminate the contest between mental medicine and its interrogators. In its claims to veracity both in the diagnoses declared by its clinicians and in the symptoms offered by its clients; in its work of custody, guardianship, and behavioral control, where an unthinking paternalism is often the easiest way out; above all, in its hegemony over systems of care, where often its role should be that of an adjutant among concerned helpers—in all these aspects psychiatry invites a continuing interrogation. It is to be hoped that the future arguments of an antipsychiatry that is an essential pole to this contest will display a greater sensitivity both to facts and to issues than did the labelling theorists with whom this chapter has been principally concerned.

REFERENCES

BARNES, M. and J. BERKE (1971) Mary Barnes: Two Accounts of a Journey Through Madness. London: Macgibbon & Kee.

BOORSE, C. (1975) "On the distinction between disease and illness." Philosophy and Public Affairs 5: 49-68.

BROWN, G. W. and T. HARRIS (1977) Social Origins of Depression. London: Tavistock.

BURR, W. A. (1973) Letter. Science 179: 358.

CLARE, A. (1976) Psychiatry in Dissent: Controversial Issues in Thought and Practice. London: Tavistock.

CROWN, S. (1975) " 'On being sane in insane places': a comment from England." Journal of Abnormal Psychology 84: 453-455.

DINGWALL, R. (1976) Aspects of Illness. London: Martin Robertson.

EHRENREICH, B. and J. EHRENREICH (1978) "Medicine and social control," pp. 39-79 in J. Ehrenreich (ed.) The Cultural Crisis of Modern Medicine. New York and London: Monthly Review Press.

FABREGA, H., Jr. (1972) "Concepts of disease: logical features and social implications." Perspectives in Biology and Medicine 15, 4: 538-617.

GOFFMAN, E. (1972) "The insanity of place," pp. 389-450 in E. Goffman, Relations in Public. Harmondsworth: Penguin.

——— (1968) Asylums: Essays on the Social Situation of Mental Patients and Other Inmates. Harmondsworth: Penguin.

—— (1967) "Mental symptoms and public order," pp. 137-148 in E. Goffman, Interaction Ritual. Garden City, NY: Doubleday.
—— (1963) Behavior in Public Places. New York: Macmillan.
HIRSCH, S. R. and J. P. LEFF (1975) Abnormalities in the Parents of Schizophrenics: A Review of the Literature and an Investigation of Communication Defects and Deviance. London: Oxford University Press and Institute of Psychiatry.
HIRSCHFELD, R. M., S. M. MATTHEWS, L. R. MOSHER, and A. Z. MENN (1977) "Being with madness: personality characteristics of three treatment staffs." Hospital and Community Psychiatry 28: 267-273.
HOLLOWAY, W. (1981) " 'I just wanted to kill a woman.' Why? The Ripper and male sexuality." Feminist Studies 9: 33-40.
KENDELL, R. E. (1975) "The concept of disease and its implications for psychiatry." British Journal of Psychiatry 127: 305-315.
KRAÜPL TAYLOR, F. (1981) "Disease concepts and the logic of classes." British Journal of Medical Psychology 54: 277-286.
LAING, R. D. (1979) "Round the bend." New Statesman (July 20).
—— (1976a) Interview, pp. 22-31 in R. I. Evans, R. D. Laing: The Man and His Ideas. New York: Dutton.
—— (1976b) "Entrevista con R. D. Laing," pp. 44-55 in J. L. Fábregas and A. Calafat, Politica de la Psiquiatria: Charlando con Laing. Bilbao: Zero.
—— (1972) Interview. London Times (October 4).
LANDO, H. A. (1976) "On being sane in insane places: a supplemental report." Professional Psychology (February): 46-51.
LIEM, J. H. (1980) "Family studies of schizophrenia: an update and commentary." Schizophrenia Bulletin 6: 429-455.
LOCKER, D. (1981) Symptoms and Illness: The Cognitive Organization of Disorder. London: Tavistock.
MILLON, T. (1975) "Reflections on Rosenhan's 'On being sane in insane places.' " Journal of Abnormal Psychology 84: 456-461.
MOSHER, L. R. and A. Z. MENN (1978) "Community residential treatment for schizophrenia: two-year follow-up." Hospital and Community Psychiatry 29: 715-723.
—— (1975) "Soteria: an alternative to hospitalization for schizophrenia," pp. 287-296 in J. H. Masserman (ed.) Current Psychiatric Therapies, Vol. 15. New York: Grune & Stratton.
PALOMBO, S. R., J. MERRIFIELD, W. WEIGERT, G. O. MORRIS, and L. C. WYNNE (1967) "Recognition of parents of schizophrenics from excerpts of family therapy interviews." Psychiatry 30: 405-412.
PIES, R. (1979) "On myths and countermyths: more on Szaszian fallacies." Archives of General Psychiatry 36: 139-144.
ROSENHAN, D. D. (1975) "The contextual nature of psychiatric diagnosis." Journal of Abnormal Psychology 84: 462-474.
—— (1973a) "On being sane in insane places." Science 179: 250-258.
—— (1973b) Reply to letters. Science 179: 365-369.
SCADDING, J. G. (1967) "Diagnosis: the disease and the computer." Lancet 2: 877-882.

SCHEFF, T. J. (1966) Being Mentally Ill: A Sociological Theory. Chicage: Aldine.
SCHRAG, J. and D. DIVOKY (1975) The Myth of the Hyperactive Child. New York: Pantheon.
Science (1973) Letters. Science 179: 356-365, 1116.
SCULL, A. T. (1977) Decarceration: Community Treatment of the Deviant. A Radical View. Englewood Cliffs, NJ: Prentice-Hall.
SEDGWICK, P. (1982) Psycho-Politics. New York: Harper & Row.
SMITH, T. (1981) "A sigh of relief from the psychiatrists." London Times (May 23).
SPITZER, R. L. (1975) "On pseudoscience, logic in remission, and psychiatric diagnosis: a critique of Rosenhan's 'On being sane in insane places.' " Journal of Abnormal Psychology 84: 442-452.
STADLEN, A. (1979) Letter. New Statesman (August 17).
SZASZ, T. S. (1979a) The Myth of Psychotherapy. Oxford: Oxford University Press.
——— (1979b) Schizophrenia: The Sacred Symbol of Psychiatry. Oxford: Oxford University Press.
——— (1978) "The concept of mental illness: explanation or justification," pp. 235-250 in H. T. Engelhardt, Jr., and S. F. Spicker (eds.) Mental Health: Philosophical Perspectives. Dordrecht: Reidel.
——— (1974) The Ethics of Psychoanalysis. London: Routledge & Kegan Paul.
——— (1960) "The myth of mental illness." American Psychologist 15: 113-118.
TAYLOR, D. (1979) Schizophrenia: Biochemical Impairments: Social Handicaps? London: Office of Health Economics.
TREACHER, A. and G. BARUCH (1981) "Towards a critical history of the psychiatric profession," pp. 120-149 in D. Ingleby (ed.) Critical Psychiatry. Harmondsworth: Penguin.
van PRAAG, H. M. (1978) "The scientific foundations of anti-psychiatry." Acta Psychologica Scandinavica 58: 113-141.
Walter Reed Army Institute (1958) Symposium on Preventive and Social Psychiatry, April 15-17, 1957. Washington, DC: Author.
WEINER, B. (1975) " 'On being sane in insane places': A process (attributional) analysis and critique." Journal of Abnormal Psychology 84: 433-441.
WING, J. K. (1978a) Reasoning About Madness. Oxford: Oxford University Press.
——— (1978b) Schizophrenia: Towards a New Synthesis. New York and London: Academic.
——— (1975) Schizophrenia from Within. Surbiton: National Schizophrenia Fellowship.
——— and G. W. BROWN (1961) "Social treatment of chronic schizophrenics: a comparative study of three mental hospitals." Journal of Mental Science 107: 847-861.

9

THE IMAGE OF MENTAL ILLNESS IN THE MASS MEDIA

CHARLES WINICK

Mental illness has been a continuing subject of mass media for decades. It is intrinsically interesting and has been of concern to artists working in practically all of the art and other forms of media in the twentieth century. The subject attracts audiences and consumers on several different levels. Audiences can learn about people whose lives are very different from their own. By exposure to presentations of mental illness, users of the media may obtain insight into their own problems and those of their relatives. Audiences can feel cathartic release, in the Aristotelian sense, from experience with the kinds of extreme behavior involved in many forms of mental illness, and thus obtain symbolic mastery over such behavior. Audience members may obtain information on a subject of continuing conversational and personal interest, since approximately one out of every ten Americans will be afflicted by mental illness at some time.

In the discussion that follows, the presentation of mental illness in newspapers, magazines, comic books, fiction, self-help books, media accounts of celebrities as mentally ill persons, jokes, television, radio, and movies will be reviewed, and some functions of the media presentation of mental illness will be considered. We shall only be considering mass media that have attracted large audiences, because such materials may be presumed to be, for whatever reasons, meeting various needs of their audiences. The dimension of appeal to audiences may or may not be related to the aesthetic qualities of the media. Special attention will be paid to the degrees to which the image of mental illness reflects reality and a stigmatizing condition.

NEWSPAPERS

The approximately 1800 daily newspapers in the United States can influence attitudes toward mental illness by their decisions on whether to run stories on the subject and the prominence of such stories. Particular aspects of newspaper stories can also be influential; for example, they can refer to persons charged with serious crime as "former mental patients" or identify social achievers, such as athletes, in the same way.

Newspapers publicized the 1972 dismissal by Democratic presidential candidate George McGovern of his running mate, Senator Thomas Eagleton, because of the latter's history of psychiatric treatment for depression. Millions of newspaper readers surely derived very negative impressions of emotional illness from the reams of copy devoted to Eagleton's dismissal.

In 1977, the New York mass murderer known as the Son of Sam received nationwide headlines. A study of this and related crimes covered by newspapers concluded that "nothing sells newspapers like an insane . . . killer on the loose" (Kalbfleisch, 1979). Another investigator asked respondents to identify some "criminally insane" people; all those identified were murderers, although only a small proportion of the "criminally insane" have been accused of murder (Steadman and Cocozza, 1977-1978).

Newspapers reporting on famous recent criminals such as mass murderers Richard Speck, Charles Manson, and the Boston Strangler often stressed their "insanity." Since an "ordinary" murder is unlikely to command much media attention, the frequency with which such noted "insane" killers are mentioned may create an erroneous impression about the link between murder and insanity. Enormous newspaper attention paid to the comments of attorneys or other defense representatives of heavily publicized murderers such as Sirhan Sirhan, who killed Senator Robert Kennedy, and Lee Oswald, who presumably killed President Kennedy, further extend this conviction.

To some extent, such links are balanced by the many newspaper columnists who give advice on personal problems, such as Dr. Joyce

Brothers, Ann Landers, or Abigail Van Buren. These widely syndicated columnists generally offer commonsense guidance on how to handle a variety of emotional problems and convey the notion that such problems represent understandable aspects of daily living. The problems thus are likely to be perceived as being relatively less bizarre and more manageable. Most people seeking help from these syndicated columnists for their emotional problems are given specific directions on how to handle the matter; some are referred to various professional resources.

More and more newspapers have "lifestyle" pages or sections that often feature people with unusual qualities or living situations. Increasingly, such story subjects may be persons who are or were mentally ill. The attitudes of trust and confidence that most readers have toward the newspapers they read regularly make such material likely to have considerable impact. By and large, however, most accounts of mental illness in newspapers tend to be concerned with the bizarre and reinforce conventional stigmatizing stereotypes.

MAGAZINES

The thousands of magazines published today provide content that is relatively predictable by their readers. One reason a consumer buys a magazine is that he or she has a fairly good idea of what will be appearing in any issue. Magazine readers thus tend to be loyal to their publications.

One investigation of trends in the amount of magazine space devoted to mental illness and related subjects concluded that articles on these themes increase in times of war and prosperity but fall during depressions and recessions (Gerbner, 1961). We may speculate that in times of economic difficulty, readers are too concerned about survival to be thinking about matters of mental health, which may be regarded as luxuries.

There are only a few general magazines with a significant amount of content devoted to mental illness, such as *Psychology Today*, which is professionally oriented and extremely successful. However, practically every issue of the major women's service magazines, such as *Family Circle, Women's Day, McCall's*, and *Ladies' Home Journal*, or of fashion magazines, such as *Harper's Bazaar* and *Vogue*, or of age-specific magazines, such as *Seventeen* or *Modern Maturity*, contains at least one article on mental illness ("Living with a Schizophrenic," "Managing Your Mid-Life Crisis," "How to Deal with Depression"). The tone of such articles is reassuring and positive and their frequency has probably helped to make mental illness less of a frightening prospect to the general public.

Similarly, many women's service magazines have carried regular columns by psychiatrists such as Theodore I. Rubin and Renatus Hartogs. Such columns tend to deal with questions from readers on various aspects of emotional illness, and they are generally positive and reassuring. In the few paragraphs allotted most of these columns it is difficult to be very complex, so that the image of mental illness communicated in them tends to be simple.

Magazines have been a primary medium for disseminating information about the antipsychotic drugs that have been emptying state mental hospitals since 1954. Practically every month, some magazine will carry a glowing report on the utility and power of these drugs. The steady flow of such articles has probably contributed to the public's growing perception of mental illness as a condition that can be managed pharmacologically even if it cannot be cured.

In recent years, weekly tabloid magazines such as the *Enquirer* and the *Star* have developed huge circulations. They regularly carry articles on a "new cure for mental illness," which is almost always a drug. Readers of such articles may get the impression that little is known about mental illness and that a magical "cure" is being discovered every few weeks.

In general, the more sophisticated the readers of a magazine, the more professional, cautious, and nonstereotypical and nonstigmatizing is its mental illness content. The more broad-based the circulation of a magazine, the less professional and more extravagant, stereotyped, and stigmatizing its content related to mental illness.

COMIC BOOKS

Since the 1930s, comic-format magazines, universally called "comic books," have represented a significant kind of media exposure for pre-adolescents. The publications increasingly may have a strand of mental illness woven into larger themes or, in some cases, whole stories may be devoted to the subject.

The first comic book entirely devoted to mental illness was published in 1955. Called *Psychoanalysis*, it presented the introductory meetings of a young analyst with each of three patients. One patient was a 15-year-old kleptomaniac who was brought to the session by his parents. The second was a 19-year-old girl who resented her sister. The third was a 28-year-old male television writer with disturbed fantasies. The need to present complex material in a relatively small number of comic panels made the presentation of the cases somewhat oversimplified and staccato, with the analyst taking an unusually active role. Subsequent issues of the publication presented the details of treatment of each case.

Since 1955, there have been a number of other comic books dealing with psychosis and/or neurosis. The availability of such material in comic-book format is noteworthy because the representative reader of such material is between 7 and 11 years old, an age at which the sense of right and wrong is just beginning to emerge. Also, preadolescents are beginning to sort out and evaluate specific character traits so that comparative judgments are possible, and they project and participate on several levels vis-à-vis others (Winick and Winick, 1970: 94-110).

In general, the presentation of mental illness content in comic books is fair, accurate, nonstigmatizing, nonsterotypical, and in accordance with current professional thinking. Such content is important for many reasons, not the least of which is the comic book's role in a vast swapping and collecting activity that does not exist in any other medium. Millions of young people read and collect comic books and will probably continue to do so into the future.

FICTION

Fiction that reaches very large audiences must meet audience needs for some form of identification with its characters (Lesser, 1959). Novels have assumed a significant role among mass media, especially since the beginning of large-scale paperback publishing in 1939. A successful novel may become a mass market paperback, remain in print for years, and be adapted for movies and television. The novelist is under no formal restraints in terms of subject matter and can present any dimensions of mental illness that are of interest to him or her.

Many great European masters of the novel, such as Flaubert, Tolstoy, Dickens, Lawrence, Proust, Mann, and Joyce, were centrally concerned with mental illness. The subject has also figured centrally in American serious novels, such as Fitzgerald's (1934) *Tender Is the Night.* It also appeared in many American novels by popular, if less "literary," writers. One such novel, which was the first major best seller with a mental patient as the main character, was Mary Jane Ward's (1946) *The Snake Pit,* which presents its amnesic character very sympathetically and the title of which has entered the language.

During the 1960s, two novels that contributed to the decade's unique ideology and political atmosphere were Joseph Heller's (1961) *Catch-22* and Ken Kesey's (1962) *One Flew Over the Cuckoo's Nest.* Heller's book deals with the difference between mental illness and mental health, as its hero tries to feign illness in order to get out of military service in World War II. Similarly, the hero of Kesey's book pretends to be mentally ill as a way of getting out of prison. In both novels, mental illness is presented as one end product of a power struggle between people and "the system" or "the Combine," as Kesey calls it.

In these two novels, which were among the decade's most popular fiction among young adults and sold many millions of copies, the mentally ill are seen as heroic and intelligent, and, in Kesey's book, almost Christ-like, crushed by a capricious society. Both novels were made into success-ful movies, and *One Flew Over the Cuckoo's Nest* was the most profitable movie of 1975, as well as the winner of several Academy Awards.

The relationship between psychosis and genius has been suggested in many novels. Probably because of the notoriety surrounding its author's suicide by placing her head in an oven, Sylvia Plath's (1971) *The Bell Jar* has received much attention and many sympathetic readers. The book deals, in a thinly disguised autobiographical manner, with the problems of a writer in maintaining her sanity in the face of problems posed by her work and family.

Another first-person account by a schizophrenic, Hannah Green's (1964) *I Never Promised You a Rose Garden,* helped millions of readers to enter the narrator's "kingdom" of the psychotic. Green's heroine recovers, as does Janet Frame's (1961) protagonist, who also conveys the solitude of slow madness and the difficulties of treatment. Such extreme cases are likely to represent material of special interest to the novelist, so that lesser forms of mental illness are not likely to get as much attention (Winick, 1963a). The mental illness-related content of such novels dealing with psychosis may have substantial impact because of their readers' involve-ment with the characters.

Every season brings novels about psychotics or other emotionally ill persons; they now represent an established genre. No novel in recent years has had the impact of those mentioned earlier, but many of the latter represent staples of library and school reading lists and are reaching new generations of readers. Every book about mental illness that has become a best seller represents the protagonist in a very sympathetic and under-standing way, whether or not he or she is portrayed as being in treatment. The tone of most recent fiction concerned with mental illness is nonstereo-typical and nonstigmatizing.

SELF-HELP BOOKS

The self-help book has assumed new importance in recent years because of the paperback revolution and because of the tremendous exposure the authors of these books may get on television talk shows, so that an author of such a book can be read by millions and seen by tens of millions.

Modern self-help books are the descendants of earlier volumes such as Ernest Dimnet's (1929) *The Art of Thinking,* Dale Carnegie's (1937) *How to Win Friends and Influence People,* and Norman Vincent Peale's (1954) *The Power of Positive Thinking.*

The modern books of this genre include Berkowitz and Newman's (1973) *How to Be Your Own Best Friend,* Dyer's (1976) *Your Erroneous Zones,* Harris's (1969) *I'm OK, You're OK,* and Monsky's (1974) *Looking Out for Number One.* Such books, which sell in the tens of millions of copies, defuse anxiety about mental illness by encouraging the reader to assess and treat his or her symptoms via bibliotherapy. Their implicit message is that everybody is somewhat disturbed, but that such problems in adaptation are part of living and can be handled relatively easily.

A hazard of such "psychobabble" is that some persons who have serious emotional problems will attempt to engage in self-treatment, with uncertain likelihood of success. Another hazard is that each season brings a new such book to the best-seller lists, and the regular purchaser of such materials could be trying a new technique every few months.

Relatively few professionals in mental health are sanguine about the substantial number of people with emotional problems who treat themselves by procedures acquired from popular books. The genus, however, seems to continue to grow in popularity, and every year sees such titles being bought by large numbers of people. By stressing the malleability of the person with problems, self-help books only minimally communicate notions of stereotype and stigma.

MEDIA ACCOUNTS OF CELEBRITIES AS MENTALLY ILL PERSONS

When a well-known person or someone with a substantial status in our society indicates that he or she is or was mentally ill, such information often is likely to be widely disseminated via several media. The general public is likely to be very interested in full details of the celebrity's illness, how it affected his or her work and personal relationships, and whether the symptoms ultimately increased, declined, or vanished. Up to recently, most of the famous people who have written of their mental illnesses have reported that they emerged fairly symptom-free from their conditions.

One effect of such reports is that they reinforce the notion of mental illness as a condition that can be finite in duration and responsive to treatment. Perhaps the first substantial and widely read report of mental illness by the ill person was Clifford Beers's (1907) best-selling autobiography, *A Mind That Found Itself.* This report by a depressive had enormous impact and is generally credited with being the major spur to the nascent mental hygiene movement. Beers became a celebrity because of the book.

Reports by prominent persons on their mental illnesses began to emerge with special frequency again in the 1950s, sparked to a considerable extent by a best-selling book on her neurosis by a well-known reporter for the *New York Times* (Freeman, 1951). It was part of the book's appeal that the author came from a very distinguished and wealthy family and had achieved substantial success in her chosen career, but was still extremely neurotic and unhappy and did not know why her life had turned out so badly. The book ends on a fairly optimistic note, as the author attributes the disappearance of many of her symptoms to psychoanalytic treatment.

During the 1950s, a number of famous movie and television stars used print media to publicize their serious neuroses and, more importantly, how they had overcome their symptoms and conditions. Comedian Sid Caesar (1956) discussed how it was impossible for him to be happy although his marriage was successful and he was earning enormous amounts of money as the star of the country's top television show. His co-star, Nanette Fabray (1956) collapsed emotionally. Among her symptoms were the inability to decide what dress to wear and the inability to function either professionally or as a wife. Both stars recovered, and their program remained one of the most popular on television. Their great visibility and success in overcoming emotional problems provided additional weight for their stories.

Another miserably unhappy television and movie star, Tony Curtis, told interviewer Mike Wallace (1957) that he had been overly aggressive because he felt inferior. However, he was able to reassure his fans that he had lost these symptoms. Many other celebrities rushed into print. Kitty Kallen (1960), who had just been voted Singer of the Year, lost her voice and left the stage for five years as the result of phobic fears. Unlike many celebrities who reported on their conditions, she did not get much help from her psychiatrist. So many famous people have since discussed their emotional pain, symptoms, and problems with mental illness that there have been at least two popular anthologies of such reports (Freeman, 1967; Steltzer, 1977). Some celebrities, like entertainer Orson Bean (1971), have written whole books about their neuroses.

A few celebrities have written books about their mental illnesses that presented less optimistic reports but which also have become best sellers. The most unusual such book was the autobiography of Frances Farmer (1972), a major movie actress of the 1930s, who spent eight years in a state mental hospital. She was a sensitive and gifted woman who could not convince the hospital staff that she was not psychotic. The book, which received enormous attention because of the author's death before the book was published, her appearance as the star of 19 movies in 7 years, and her beauty, implicitly argues that it is almost chance that leads a person to be designated mentally ill. Her attack on the state mental hospital system is riveting and persuasive.

The iatrogenic origin of much mental illness is the central theme of Barbara Gordon's (1979) *I'm Dancing as Fast as I Can,* an autobiography by a successful television producer who reports on the tension and anxiety associated with her work. Seeking relief from such symptoms, she consulted doctors whose treatment, and especially the drugs they prescribed, plunged her into devastating mental illness. The books by Farmer and Gordon argue that the pressure associated with some entertainment vocations can almost inexorably lead a person to become mentally ill.

A number of people famous in political life have made known to the media their experiences with mental illness. Innumerable magazine stories have dealt with the depression experienced by Betty Ford, wife of the former president, and Joan Kennedy, wife of the Massachusetts senator. President John F. Kennedy gave many interviews in which he said that his own family's experience with mental illness had been so significant that he was sponsoring legislation to deal with it. The troubles of the famous, in sports, entertainment, or politics, are of continuing interest to the general public.

There appears to be a large market for such celebrity self-reports on mental illness. Part of their appeal is that of gossip; part is fascination with the troubles of famous people (Winick, 1962). As more famous people identify themselves as having been mentally ill, via reports in magazines and books, the stigma connected with mental illness could decline, and ordinary citizens will likely be less embarrassed about identifying their own problems.

JOKES

Jokes about mental illness are frequently repeated on television, printed in newspaper columns, told in movies, and collected in anthologies and magazine columns (Winick, 1976; Ragaway, 1974). Jokes can convey underlying attitudes because they are usually told to friends in fairly intimate social situations in which social control is minimal, with the joke representing a kind of shared secret.

Jokes about mental illness generally communicate the notion that the illness is a relatively lighthearted, unimportant condition. Thus:

Man: I think I'm going crazy. What should I do?

Friend: Why don't you go down to Washington? No one will notice it there.

Or:

Woman: I don't know what to do about my husband—he thinks he's a parking meter.

Friend: Why doesn't he say something?

Woman: He can't, not with all those dimes and nickels in his mouth.

Such stories reflect a casual attitude toward mental illness. Their importance can be seen in the consistently large number of orally communicated jokes that deal with mental illness (Winick, 1963b). It is possible that these jokes provide a vehicle by which people can come to terms with the concept of emotional disturbance, by establishing distance from it. Such jokes usually convey stigma and stereotypy. Similarly, cartoons in magazines and newspapers can permit the audience to feel superior to the mentally ill and to scoff at the procedures for dealing with them (Redlich, 1950). Both jokes and cartoons may serve the function of permitting the audience to express its hostility toward the mentally ill in a socially approved and nonthreatening manner. The baring of the teeth involved in a smile could, in such cases, have additional symbolic value.

Another function of humor about mental illness is to enable people to deal with their fears about the subject. Laughing at something that is disturbing is one way of dealing with the subject.

TELEVISION

Television is viewed in the average American home for over 6 hours daily. Preschoolers, who are the most impressionable of all age groups, are the heaviest viewers. Children aged 2 to 11 view television for an average of 4 hours a day. By the end of high school, the typical young American will have spent 15,000 hours watching television, compared to 12,000 hours in the classroom. In terms of time, television is our most important medium; its content concerned with mental illness could be especially significant.

Mental illness on television has been presented in many different kinds of programs. By and large, entertainment programs that deal with the mentally ill are prepared in cooperation with professionals in psychiatry and/or psychology and reflect currently valid information on the different psychoses, neuroses, and other conditions. However, the demands of entertainment programs for colorful characters, conflict, and the requirements of continuing series for tension maintenance may impinge on accuracy of portrayal. Continuing series, such as daily soap operas or weekly programs with recurrent characters, are especially likely to have some impact on audiences because viewers build up strong feelings of identification and involvement.

A long-term analysis of the content of evening prime-time television programs concluded that 17 percent involve some significant depiction of mental illness (Gerbner et al., forthcoming). About 3 percent of the major characters are or have been mentally ill. Mentally ill people depicted on television are especially prone to engage in violence and to be victimized. Two-fifths of "normals" but 73 percent of the mentally ill are violent; 44 percent of "normals" but 81 percent of the mentally ill are victims of violence. In daytime serials, women are frequently mentally ill, often because of guilt, trauma, or anxiety (Cassata et al., 1979).

During the early 1960s, there occurred the medium's first concentration of day and evening program series on mental illness, and such series became established genres, like the western or private detective programs that represented the most popular program formats of the time. This peak in popularity for mental illness material has never reappeared, although such material has returned in individual programs.

In 1960-1961, the afternoon daily serial or soap opera *Road to Reality* (ABC) dealt with a psychotherapy group, which was presumably based on a real group. All the parts were, of course, played by professional actors. A very wide range of neurotics were presented very sympathetically in this program, which surely helped to hasten public acceptance of group therapy, which was then a relatively unfamiliar modality.

During the early 1960s, there were three general medical drama series that enjoyed great popularity. These series (*Ben Casey,* 1960-1966; *Dr. Kildare,* 1961-1965; and *The Nurses,* 1962-1964) may have created an audience climate that was receptive to the two pioneering prime-time evening series that dealt with mental illness and experienced great success with audiences. They were *The Eleventh Hour* (NBC), which ran from 1962 through 1964, and *The Breaking Point* (ABC), which ran from 1963 through 1964. Although both programs were built around the cases seen by the psychiatrists who appeared every week, considerable skill and imagination went into the plot depictions of almost every form of psychosis, neurosis, and especially psychopathy and "acting out" behavior (in which the patient behaved in a manner directly reflecting unconscious needs, usually to his or her disadvantage).

Early in the next decade (1971-1973), a similar nonnetwork program, *Paul Bernard, Psychiatrist,* was syndicated. In all three of these programs, there was a high probability of the mentally ill characters recovering enough to function effectively and reasonably in the family, work, and community settings in which they found themselves. The mentally ill were usually shown as ordinary people who were expressing the end products of a variety of biological, social, interpersonal, situational, familial, and related pressures. Mental illness in these series was usually plausible, understandable, multifactorial in origin, nonstigmatizing, and nonstereotyping.

A much quirkier and less realistic version of mental illness was on view during the six years (1972-1978) that the *Bob Newhart Show* (CBS) was presented. In this half-hour program, Newhart, who had previously been a very successful comedian, played a Chicago psychologist in private practice. His patients were usually not people with very serious problems, or, if serious, they were more comic than weighty.

In one typical episode, a patient visits Bob to complain that his son is trying to kill him. Bob invites the son to tell his side of the story and the son discloses that he had indeed tried to poison his father in order to inherit the latter's business. The father then tells Bob that he himself inherited the business by killing his own father! Other episodes similarly deal with unreal and/or strange behavior, which is very seldom handled seriously. This series is currently in syndication and can be expected to be a feature of television stations in America for many years to come, via reruns. Its lighthearted approach to mental illness may be expected to remove some of the subject's stigma and was probably responsible for its being on the air so long. It will probably contribute to greater public acceptance of psychologists' treating the mentally ill.

Mental illness is an occasional subject for network documentary programs, which usually attract only a fraction of the audiences of the entertainment series. In 1978, for example, *Escape from Madness* (NBC) summarized the changes in the treatment of psychoses since 1954. In

1975, five one-hour specials provided a textbook overview of the different kinds of mental illness (Public Broadcasting System).

Individual stations have also presented documentaries on subjects of special interest. Thus, KABC in Los Angeles aired a miniseries on compulsions in 1978, and the subject of depression received a five-part report on Philadelphia's KYW in 1976.

Individual stations, station groups, and networks have, since the very beginnings of television, presented eccentric and bizarre people as guests on interview and talk shows, in which a host engaged in conversation with various guests. Generally, the symptoms of such guests are presented as "interesting" and the guests' ability to function effectively in the world is stressed.

Most talk shows have a number of psychiatrists and psychologists as recurrent guests who discuss emotional problems in a reassuring way and suggest, implicitly or explicitly, that mental illness is a condition that should be viewed matter-of-factly and can be successfully treated. Guests like psychologist Joyce Brothers and psychiatrist David Reuben are convincing and empathetic persons who avoid jargon and convey positive role models of mental health. Such doctors also convey a nonjudgmental attitude toward mental illness, which is reinforced because hosts like Mike Douglas, Johnny Carson, and Merv Griffin usually are supportive of such openness toward mental illness.

Entertainment programs sometimes contain significant prosocial content dealing with the mentally ill, although such material is not the main program theme. Producer Norman Lear, who is concerned about the treatment of the mentally ill, has dealt positively with such material in such very popular (CBS) programs as *All in the Family* and *Archie Bunker's Place* (1971-), *Maude* (1972-1978), and *One Day at a Time* (1975-). A presidential commission on mental health cited these programs as examples of how entertainment materials can help to convey realistic and valid portraits of the mentally ill (Allen, 1977). Other (ABC) entertainment programs, such as *Family* (1976-1980) and *Eight Is Enough* (1977-1981), and the series *Little House on the Prairie* (NBC, 1974-), with huge audiences, regularly present aspects of mental illness in a valid and nonstigmatizing manner.

Programs specifically directed to children and shown on Saturday mornings also may contain specific prosocial material concerned with mental health. Thus, a program might convey the notion that a child who looks and talks strangely should not be made to feel ashamed or embarrassed because he or she is different in some way. Such content is integrated into the script. Follow-up studies have demonstrated that prosocial content is understood by a substantial proportion of children (Office of Social Research, CBS, 1976).

In the early days of television it was not uncommon for the mentally ill to be the butt of jokes. Today such treatment would be inconceivable, and television has progressed from occasional references to people as "nuts" and "crazy" to a realistic and accurate approach to the subject. Many stations regularly carry public service announcements on behalf of various mental health and social health groups, conveying information about mental illness that is responsible and helpful.

In spite of such positive developments, there have been and still are some organizations and groups that have objected to mental illness as the subject of commercial television programs. The time constraints of television, it is sometimes alleged, require oversimplification of complex material. Also, the ubiquity of commercials is said to detract from the seriousness of the theme of mental illness. The American Psychological Association complained that the problem of mental illness was too large to be used as entertainment for "selling mouthwash" and other commercial products (Harrison, 1962). Some groups believe that the seriousness of a program about mental illness is contradicted by the minidramas presented in commercials, which often clearly suggest that a person will be happy only if a particular product is used.

Because of the power and reach of television, few groups or agencies will refuse to cooperate in a program or series about mental illness. Whatever directions will be developed by cable and other new technologies, television will continue to be a significant contributor to the public's perceptions of mental illness.

RADIO

During the early days of radio, a number of network programs, such as *John J. Anthony* and *The Answer Man,* featured paraprofessionals and lay persons giving advice on emotional and other personal problems. These programs, which were broadcast from the 1930s through the early 1950s, conveyed commonsense information and guidance on a variety of kinds of neurotic and interpersonal difficulties. They were jargon-free.

Other radio programs featured professional psychologists and social workers, such as Lee Steiner and Rose Franzblau, who dealt in a serious and cautious way with problems submitted by listeners. In general, these programs conveyed the notion that interpersonal problems were part of ordinary living, that no stigma need be attached to them, and that most such problems would yield to rational examination.

Since the 1960s, the popularity of local and network live call-in radio programs, in which hosts like Long John Nebel and Larry King chatted with a wide variety of callers, many of whom were eccentric, exposed listeners not only to eccentrics but also to psychologists and psychiatrists who gave advice on dealing with emotional problems. In recent years, a number of stations have given psychotherapists their own programs. Since 1974, for example, psychiatrist Lloyd Moglen has had a radio call-in program in San Francisco, and since 1978, psychologist Toni Grant has hosted a similar program in Los Angeles. Troubled people telephone about their problems and the professional deals directly with the caller. California, traditionally the pioneer in self-expression, was the first state to present such programs, which will probably further contribute to the general public's willingness to deal with mental illness without undue anxiety. Many of the all-news radio stations regularly carry segments featuring local psychologists and psychiatrists. Stations with a variety of celebrity interviews, news, and other talk-format programs usually find that the program concerned with personal and emotional difficulties is their single most popular program. Thus on WOR in New York, an all-talk station, the single most popular program is that of Dr. Bernard Meltzer, who gives advice on personal problems. Such programs tend to reflect current professional thinking and avoid stereotypy and stigma.

MOVIES

Movies represented the central leisure activity of Americans for several decades, from the 1920s through the 1940s. Even now, some movies attract millions of adults and children in their original theatrical releases and many other millions who wait to see the movies on television. The core of the movie audience today consists of young adults, from 13 to 25, who may be relatively impressionable and may still be developing attitudes toward mental illness as they experiment with the roles of adulthood.

Movies are uniquely able to render the world of the mentally ill because skillful directing and editing may present imagery of the unconscious, hallucinations, multiple personalities, and fantasies, and may move characters forward, backward, and sideways in time. Movies can show material that violates the established laws of cause and effect and that conveys what Freud called "the primary process," the action of the unconscious. The combination of sight and sound, perceived while sharing an experience with many other people in a darkened theater, can have an effect that is potentially more powerful than that of any other medium (Schneider, 1977).

Movies significantly concerned with the mentally ill have been popular in America since *The Cabinet of Dr. Caligari,* a German import, was released in 1919. They assumed more momentum in the 1920s and 1930s. During the decade of the 1940s, every single year had at least one very successul film concerned with mental illness. In the 1950s, every year but 1953 had at least one such film. By the 1960s, there was an average of five such films annually. The decade of the 1970s saw an average of three films dealing with the mentally ill released each year.

It is useful to divide the movies dealing with the mentally ill into two groups: those released before and after 1968. Before 1968, the production code to which the major studios subscribed required that every movie receive a seal of approval, which was not given to a film that focused on an insane or extremely neurotic or psychopathetic person unless such a person were a criminal or other villain. Thus an admirable mentally ill character could not be the main character of a pre-1968 movie. After 1968, when the rating system replaced the seal of approval, almost any kind of presentation of the mentally ill was possible, including their appearance as sympathetic principal characters (Winick, 1978).

One type of movie that flourished after 1968 was the genre that argued that in our dehumanized and irrational world the person who is "insane" is admirable and ought to be emulated. It is better, these films argue, to be "insane" than sane in our sick world. This is the theme of *The Rocky Horror Picture Show* (1975), a widely discussed film that began as a cult favorite and blossomed into a national phenomenon (Austin, 1981). It is also the theme of the melodrama *Equus* (1977), which juxtaposes the wisdom of a psychotic stablehand with the rigidity and anxiety of a middle-class psychiatrist, the adaptation of the Kesey novel, *One Flew Over the Cuckoo's Nest* (1975), and *Outrageous* (1977), which is about a "crazy" who is effective, intelligent, and able to cope creatively with the world.

The heroine of *Near and Far Away* (1978) is named Mania, as if to underscore the contrast between the sensitivity of the psychotic and the coldness of the rest of the world. Dudley Moore, as the 42-year-old millionaire songwriter in *10* (1979) with an obsessive fixation on a young married woman, is presented more sympathetically than his psychotherapist or the other "straight" people with whom he interacts. All of these movies about emotionally disturbed persons who are presented sympathetically were critical and box-office successes.

It is noteworthy that this theme can attract fiction and movie audiences now, but when the same argument was made in the magazine *Neurotica,* edited by G. Legman and published between 1948 and 1951, it could not attract any significant number of followers. The magazine was "a literary exposition, defense, and correlation . . . of the . . . neurotic" (Legman, 1948). This credo is a reminder of some of the great European writers, such as the French poet Arthur Rimbaud, who argued that we achieve sanity by becoming mad, or Fyodor Dostoyevsky, whose title character in *The Idiot* was so pure that he appeared to be mad.

The only characters who were "crazy" but with whom audiences could identify positively, in pre-1968 movies, were comic. Thus, Jerry Lewis's eccentricity was close to madness but was acceptable because he was funny, as in *The Nutty Professor* (1963). Harpo Marx's zaniness could similarly be tolerated because he was a divine fool, just as Ed Wynn was "the Perfect Fool." Tolerance of the madman as hero was slow in coming to the movies, as can be inferred from the 13 years that *One Flew Over the Cuckoo's Nest* took to get to the screen, in spite of its enormous success as a novel.

Taking all commercially successful movies released in the United States since 1919 with significant mental illness content, one-half the mentally ill persons shown are male, two-fifths are female, and one-tenth involve both sexes (Winick, 1978). In terms of socioeconomic status, middle-class persons are most often (40 percent) presented, upper-class persons next most frequently (32 percent), and lower-class persons least (11 percent), with a considerable number (17 percent) having no identifiable class affiliation.

About four-fifths of the persons who are shown with symptoms of mental illness are depicted as being treated by some professional practitioner or agency. Thus movies strongly communicate the notion that mental illness is a condition that ought to be treated. About half the persons in treatment in movies improve, compared with the one-third who are likely to improve in real life. To the extent that diagnoses can be made of the emotionally disturbed characters in movies, the 5 most frequent conditions are: schizophrenia (10 percent), psychosis and violent behavior (9 percent), neurosis (7 percent), psychopathy (6 percent), and work-related problems (6 percent). Although reliable national figures on the prevalence of different kinds of mental illness are not available, it is highly unlikely that these 5 conditions are present in the same proportions in the actual population. We can assume that writers and producers will choose conditions and symptoms that lend themselves to the filmic visualization of conflict. Thus it is likely that the more bizarre or unusual aspects of mental illness will be shown in movies.

Movies have also presented relatively bizarre treatments for emotional distress. Thus, *Bob and Carol and Ted and Alice* (1969) and *Semi-Tough*

(1977) mocked the newer Esalen and EST-type fad therapies. Hardly any movie, however, presents an emotionally ill person recovering without some professional assistance, perhaps because therapist-patient interaction can lend itself to interesting film visualization, from comedy to tragedy.

One change in movie content that reflects a more serious approach to mental illness is the decline of the "screwball" or "crazy" comedy since the 1930s. In this kind of movie, adults, who are usually quite wealthy, behave in a bizarre, irresponsible, and very eccentric way that often approaches psychosis. Films such as *Theodora Goes Wild* (1936), *My Man Godfrey* (1936), *The Awful Truth* (1937), *You Can't Take It with You* (1938), and *Bringing Up Baby* (1938) established the genre. At the time of the economic depression of the 1930s, there may have been some social function served by presenting heros and heroines who were both wealthy and mad. This theme has since become far less acceptable, reappearing very seldom in comedies such as *What's Up, Doc?* (1972) with Barbra Streisand and *Arthur* (1981) with Dudley Moore, which did not enjoy the great success of their predecessors. It is probable that the decline of the "screwball" comedy reflects movies' greater caution about presenting mental illness stereotypically, as well as changed social conditions and different audience needs.

SOME FUNCTIONS OF THE MEDIA PRESENTATION OF MENTAL ILLNESS

Mental illness is so pervasive a theme in the media that it is likely to be meeting important needs of audiences. There is no way in which the public can be forced to devote its attention to a subject in which it is not interested.

Gerbner (n.d.) has speculated that the mentally ill, on television, represent a stigmatized group that attracts accumulated insecurities and demonstrates the moral and physical price to be paid for deviance. Such a mechanism, he believes, stems from deeply rooted dynamics that help to maintain the social structure. It is possible that the same kind of mechanism may operate in all the mass media. However, there is every reason to believe that the degree of stigma associated with mental illness in the mass media has been declining, reflecting a decline in negative stereotyping of the mentally ill in other aspects of American life.

A generation ago, the first substantial investigation of the subject concluded that the mass media present an image of the mentally ill that tends to reinforce traditional prejudices rather than to communicate the group's characteristics as they have been established by professionals in mental health (Nunnally, 1961). Today, such a sweeping conclusion would probably be less valid. It might be argued that one reason for Congress's willingness to pass the Community Mental Health Act in 1964, which set up a national network of treatment, was the confluence of mass media content dealing with mental illness. In the early 1960s there were more successful movies concerned with the subject than ever before or since; famous entertainers and other celebrity and political figures were appearing in the mass media to discuss their emotional problems; three major network series on television dealt with the treatment of the mentally ill; and a number of best-selling novels were published dealing with the subject. This concentration of media activity may have provided a critical mass of content that helped to domesticate the subject of mental illness and make it more acceptable, more of a condition that can be dealt with rather than an overwhelming and negative pathology that is salient to the person. Since the 1950s, Americans have learned a lot about mental illness and are more realistic about it (Crocetti et al., 1974).

The various media are addressed to different audiences and are subject to varying degrees of social control. Television probably has reflected the most sensitive and professionally oriented images of the mentally ill, which have evolved over the several decades in which the medium has become the dominant factor in American leisure. One reason for this is the existence of a formal mechanism of social control via the continuity acceptance departments of stations and networks (Gerbner, 1959; Winick, 1959, 1961). These departments, among their many duties, monitor script content for accuracy and the manner in which it presents subgroups in the population, such as the mentally ill. Comic books also have a voluntary system of self-regulation of content, which ensures that mental illness-related material will be accurate and contemporary.

Newspapers probably have been much less responsive to social changes, and many papers still carry headlines about "crazed killers" or "psychopathic rapists." Jokes similarly reflect deep-rooted prejudices and provide vehicles for expressing such stereotypes.

Radio has reflected television's modern approach to the mentally ill, perhaps because it has industrywide voluntary machinery for social control similar to that of television, and both radio and television stations must have their licenses renewed by the federal government every three years and are thus ultimately accountable for their program content.

Although magazines are not, of course, regulated in any way, they have tended to reflect conventional professional views of mental illness. More

than any other medium, they have disseminated established current thinking on the subject with a minimum of stigma.

Pre-1968 movies usually dealt with the mentally ill as patients and as
deviants. Post-1968 movies have reflected considerable freedom in their
portraits of the psychotic, neurotic, and psychopath, sometimes extolling
the virtues of being deviant and denouncing the establishment of psychiatrists, psychologists, and social workers, both in private practice and
institutional settings. While some recent movies have argued that madness
is the true root of human vitality, there have been more such as *The
President's Analyst* (1967), which noted that even the president of the
United States is disturbed enough to require some professional easing of
his anxieties.

It is not surprising, in the current media climate, that the president
should be shown as a psychiatric patient, because movies since the 1960s
have minimally communicated stigma connected with mental illness and
have generally presented psychotherapy as a reasonable activity. Celebrities being interviewed on television and radio talk shows or in newspapers
in recent years, or accepting Oscar or Emmy or other awards, regularly
refer to their psychotherapists and the help the latter have provided.

Books are most likely to reflect the individual author's vision and
personality. Some works of fiction and nonfiction have directly reflected
conventional professional thinking on mental illness and other books have
ridiculed and attacked psychiatric labelling. Self-help books have suggested
that the average person can treat his or her own problems. By and large,
books have quite sensitively reflected the destigmatizing of mental illness
over the last several decades.

In all of the media there has been a growing tendency in recent decades
to present the mentally ill person in the home and community, rather than
in an institution, reflecting what is actually happening in the society.
Overall, the mentally ill are much less likely to be seen as institutionalized
patients today than they were two or three decades ago.

There are, however, some countervailing forces at work. Heterodoxies
of the psychiatric establishment such as those of Szasz (1974), Eysenck
and Rachman (1965), and Torrey (1975) have not had much impact on
mass media. Their persistence may, however, ultimately lead the media to
pay more heed to their views.

Another consideration is that various current conservative pressure
groups, such as the Moral Majority, may be able to influence television to
present less material that is regarded as "unwholesome" or overly concerned with deviance. If television advertisers are responsive to such
pressures, the proportion of program time devoted to mental illness could

diminish. It is not clear how much pressure could be applied by mental health professionals and the viewing public to combat such a trend. However, television is only one medium, and it is important to be aware of the segmentation of the audiences for different media. Although the various mass media usually move on a parallel basis in terms of content, it is possible that, even if television has less program content dealing with mental illness, the other media might decide that the subject warrants substantial attention. The other media will be responsive to the kinds of economic, social, and political forces that, in interaction with consumers' needs, have always contributed to the content of the popular arts.

REFERENCES

ALLEN, S. (1977) "Some notes on TV's responsibility to America's mental health." Television Quarterly 14: 27-33.
AUSTIN, B. A. (1981) "Portrait of a cult film audience: The Rocky Horror Picture Show." Journal of Communication 31: 43-54.
BEAN, O. (1971) Me and the Orgone. New York: St. Martin's.
BEERS, C. (1907) A Mind that Found Itself. Garden City, NY: Doubleday.
BERKOWITZ, B. and M. NEWMAN (1973) How to Be Your Own Best Friend. New York: Random House.
CAESAR, S. (1956) "What psychoanalysis did for me." Look (October 2): 49-52.
CARNEGIE, D. (1937) How to Win Friends and Influence People. New York: Simon & Schuster.
CASSATA, M. B., T. D. SKILL, and S. O. BOADU (1979) "In sickness and in health." Journal of Communication 29: 73-80.
CROCETTI, G. M., H. R. SPIRO, and I. SIASSI (1974) Contemporary Attitudes Toward Mental Illness. Pittsburgh: University of Pittsburgh Press.
DIMNET, E. (1929) The Art of Thinking. New York: Folcroft.
DYER, W. (1976) Your Erroneous Zones. New York: Funk & Wagnalls.
EYSENCK, H. J. and S. RACHMAN (1965) Causes and Cures of Neurosis. New York: Knapp.
FABRAY, N. (1956) "My fight with Nanette." This Week (December 9).
FARMER, F. (1972) Will There Ever Be a Morning? New York: G. P. Putnam.
FITZGERALD, F. S. (1934) Tender Is the Night. New York: Scribner.
FRAME, J. (1961) Faces in the Water. New York: Braziller.
FREEMAN, L. (1967) Celebrities on the Couch. Los Angeles: Price/Stern/Sloan.
——— (1951) Fight Against Fears. New York: Crown.
GERBNER, G. (1961) "Psychology, psychiatry and mental illness in the mass media: a study of trends, 1900-1959." Mental Hygiene 45: 89-93.
——— (1959) "Mental illness on television: a study of censorship." Journal of Broadcasting 3: 293-303.
——— (n.d.) "Stigma: social functions of the portrayal of mental illness in the mass media."
——— M. MORGAN, and N. SIGNORIELLI (forthcoming) "Programming health portrayals: what viewers see, say, and do."

GORDON, B. (1979) I'm Dancing as Fast as I Can. New York: Harper & Row.

GREEN, H. (1964) I Never Promised You a Rose Garden. New York: Holt, Rinehart & Winston.

HARRIS, T. (1969) I'm OK, You're OK: A Practical Guide to Transactional Analysis. New York: Harper & Row.

HARRISON, E. (1962) "TV show assailed by psychologists." New York Times (December 4): 53.

HELLER, J. (1961) Catch-22. New York: Simon & Schuster.

KALBFLEISCH, P. J. (1979) "The portrayal of the killer in society: a comparison study." Michigan State University. (unpublished)

KALLEN, K. (1960) "My 'lost' years." American Weekly (March 6).

KESEY, K. (1962) One Flew Over the Cuckoo's Nest. New York: Viking.

LEGMAN, G. (1948) "Statement." Neurotica 9: 3.

LESSER, S. (1959) Fiction and the Unconscious. Boston: Beacon.

MONSKY, M. (1974) Looking Out for Number One. New York: Simon & Schuster.

NUNNALLY, J. C. (1961) Public Conceptions of Mental Health. New York: Holt, Rinehart & Winston.

Office of Social Research, CBS (1976) Messages received and other perceptions of children and teenagers who viewed an episode of Shazam. New York: CBS.

PEALE, N. V. (1954) The Power of Positive Thinking. Englewood Cliffs, NJ: Prentice-Hall.

PLATH, S. (1971) The Bell Jar. New York: Harper & Row.

RAGAWAY, M. A. (1974) The World's Worst Psychiatrist Jokes. Los Angeles: Price/Stern/Sloan.

REDLICH, F. C. (1950) "The psychiatrist in caricature." American Journal of Orthopsychiatry 20: 560-571.

SCHNEIDER, I. (1977) "Images of the mind: psychiatry in the commercial film." American Journal of Psychiatry 134: 613-620.

STEADMAN, H. J. and J. J. COCOZZA (1977-1978) "Selective reporting and the public's misconceptions of the criminally insane." Public Opinion Quarterly 41: 523-533.

STELTZER, D. (1977) The Star Treatment. New York: Bobbs-Merrill.

SZASZ, T. S. (1974) The Myth of Mental Illness. New York: Harper & Row.

TORREY, E. F. (1975) The Death of Psychiatry. Baltimore: Penguin.

WALLACE, M. (1957) Interview with Tony Curtis. New York Post (October 28): 19.

WARD, M. J. (1946) The Snake Pit. New York: Random House.

WINICK, C. (1978) "Mental illness and psychiatrists in movies," pp. 45-77 in C. Winick (ed.) Deviance and Mass Media. Beverly Hills, CA: Sage.

——— (1976) "The social contexts of humor." Journal of Communication 26: 124-128.

——— (1963a) "The psychiatrist in fiction." Journal of Nervous and Mental Disease 136: 43-57.

——— (1963b) "A content analysis of orally communicated jokes." American Image 20: 271-291.

——— (1962) "Celebrities' errancy as a subject for journalism: a study of Confidential." Gazette 7: 320-324.

——— (1961) "Censor and sensibility: a content analysis of the television censor's comments." Journal of Broadcasting 5: 117-136.

——— (1959) Taste and the Censor on Television. New York: Fund for the Republic.

——— and M. WINICK (1970) The Television Experience: What Children See. Beverly Hills, CA: Sage.

10

LIFE EVENTS, SOCIAL SUPPORTS, AND MENTAL HEALTH

RONALD C. KESSLER

AUTHOR'S NOTE: Work on this chapter was supported by a grant from the National Institute of Mental Health (MH-34479).

Over the past two decades a great deal of evidence has been amassed to show that life stress is causally associated with mental illness. Nonexperimental surveys, quasi-experimental panels, case control studies, and clinical assessments of disaster victims all demonstrate that the incidence of some psychiatric disorders increases as exposure to stressful life experience increases.

Beyond this fact we know very little about the role of life stress in the occurrence of mental illness. We do not yet understand what types of stresses lead to psychiatric disorders under what conditions. Current research on the relationship between life stress and mental illness is aimed at specifying the stress-illness relationship in these ways. Progress is being made, but serious conceptual and methodological hurdles remain.

In this chapter I review one branch of this current research: surveys and case control studies of the relationship between life events and mental illness. My review has three purposes: first, to sketch out briefly the major lines of research in this area; second, to review critically major conceptual and methodological problems; and third, to offer suggestions for resolving these problems where I think I have sug-

gestions worth making. I purposely emphasize conceptual and methodological issues and devote only minimum attention to description of the
research literature. Excellent reviews of the latter can be found in Dohrenwend and Dohrenwend (1974, 1981) and Barrett (1979).

The title of this chapter mentions social support because I devote a
good deal of attention to it when I come to discuss modifying influences
of the life events-mental illness relationship. Although many modifying
forces currently are being studied, social support is the most promising of
these. Thus in the limited space I have available I have elected to discuss
this one type in detail rather than to present a less complete review of a
broader set of modifiers.

LIFE EVENTS AND MENTAL ILLNESS

The central feature of the studies I consider here is that they all contain
summary scales of exposure to life events based on life event checklists.
Checklists of this sort were originally assembled from the life events most
frequently mentioned by patients in treatment as having happened to
them in the recent past (Holmes and Rahe, 1967). More recent checklists
have added events thought to be particularly important or have dropped
events thought to be uncommon in the population under investigation.

Respondents are asked if each of the events happened to them or (in
some cases) to a loved one in the recent past. There is usually some precise
time frame stated by the interviewer (the past year or the past six months
are the most common of these). Summary scales of exposure are created
by adding up the raw number of events or weighted transformations that
take into consideration differences among the events.

As noted earlier, there is consistent evidence that summary life event
scores of this sort are significantly and positively associated with the
measures of mental illness obtained in surveys and with clinically defined
disorders in case control studies. But two basic difficulties arise in the
interpretation of these associations. First, we have to determine the
dimensions by means of which life events influence mental illness. And
second, we have to determine whether these associations are really indicative of a causal influence.

Dimensional Representation
of Life Event Scales

There are many reasons to think that life stress can cause mental illness,
but the most influential of these has been the view that illness is the result

of disequilibrium in the organism. This view, based largely on Selye's (1976) work on physiological stress diseases, led early researchers to interpret life event effects as influencing mental illness through the changes they create in the individual's life.

Not all events are equally important in bringing about change, and it was not long before life event scales took this fact into account. Holmes and Rahe (1967) did this by developing a weighting scheme based on public perception surveys about the relative amounts of "life change" associated with a great many events. This scheme allows events to be added together into a scale of the amount of life change experienced by an individual over a specified period of time.

There has been a good deal of disagreement in recent years about using life change weights. It is widely known that these weights do not meaningfully increase the association between life events and mental illness in the normal population. A simple count of events is just as adequate a predictor (Ross and Mirowsky, 1979). Therefore, some researchers have recommended that unweighted event counts be used instead of the more complicated weighted list (Lorimer et al., 1979).

There is a much more fundamental reason for disputing the use of weights. As I said, these weights are based on public perceptions about the "life change" associated with events. If this is the only characteristic of events that leads to mental illness it is obviously appropriate to use this weighting scheme. But other dimensions are known to be important as well. Several researchers have demonstrated that undesirable events are more highly related to symptom screening scale scores than are desirable events (Myers et al., 1974; Vinokur and Selzer, 1975; Mueller et al., 1977; Ross and Mirowsky, 1979). There is some evidence that anticipation, control, and long-term threat are also important dimensions (Brown and Harris, 1978; Dohrenwend and Martin, 1979; Streiner et al., 1981). Therefore, the wisdom of using a weight based only on the life change dimension is questionable.[1]

I would like to comment on two important areas of confusion about the dimensionality of life events. One involves the strategies used to discover the dimensions that underlie life event effects. The other involves strategies used to estimate the relative importance of these effects once they are conceptualized and measured.

There have been several efforts to discover the dimensions that underlie the effects of life events. Some of these have factor analyzed reports of exposure to events across a sample of responding individuals (Newcomb et al., forthcoming); others have asked people to sort events into those more or less "alike" and then analyzed the similarity matrix thus derived with multidimensional scaling (Ruch, 1977). I find neither of these approaches satisfactory. The factor analysis approach clusters events into groups that occur empirically together, but there is no reason to think that there is any relationship between this and the underlying dimensions in terms of which life events exert their influence on mental illness. Multidimensional scaling gets at the latter more directly, by studying the dimensionality of public perceptions about the ways in which different events are similar or dissimilar. This type of analysis has proved useful in research on consumer perceptions about salient differences among alternative purchase choices (Shepard et al., 1972). But there is much less reason to believe that people have insight into the dimensions of events that influence psychological functioning. A more reasonable approach would be to cluster events in terms of their relative impacts on mental illness, but this would not be entirely accurate either. Events do not occur randomly to people in the population, and the individual-level correlates of exposure are also cor-relates of responsiveness to stress (a topic discussed below). This means that event effects do not give a true picture of the dimensions in terms of which events influence mental illness (Dohrenwend, 1980; Kessler, 1980).

I doubt that any multivariate technique can be of much assistance in discovering the dimensions that are important. This means that clinical insight will have to be used for progress in this area. There is already a large case study literature on personal adaptation to different sorts of stressful experiences (Coelho et al., 1974; Coelho and Irving, 1981). Theoretical synthesis of these investigations might be a source of insight about relevant dimensions.

Now I want to consider problems of analyzing life events after relevant dimensions are found. To date, researchers have contented themselves with subgroup analyses. In this approach an overall scale of events is broken down into subscales, for instance, a subscale of undesirable events and one of desirable events. Analyses are then carried out using the two separate subscales rather than the overall scale. This is a primitive sort of weighting scheme, with events judged undesirable scored 1 on the "scale" and events judged desirable scored 0. It is possible that this captures the covariation between some dimensions and onset of mental illness. But this is almost surely not true for other dimensions, such as the predictability of the event or the extent to which the event has long-term versus short-term implications for the victim's life.

If we are going to make any progress at all on a multidimensional conception of life event effects, we have to derive detailed weights, just like those currently available for the life change dimension, for all other dimensions considered potentially important. When this is done it will be possible to study simultaneously the effect of life change, undesirability, threat, and other characteristics in a single prediction equation. And it will be possible to investigate the interactive effects among multiple dimensions. I suspect that interactions of this sort will prove to be highly significant in explaining the influence of life events on mental illness.

A few words should be said about weighting life event scales in terms of the time lag between the occurrence of the event and the onset of mental illness. Brown and Harris (1978) and Paykel (1978) have presented evidence from case control studies that onset of depression follows within a period of about six months after the occurrence of a serious life event. They discovered this by taking random samples of onset cases from clinical populations and comparing them to respondents selected randomly from the community on average exposure to stressful life events one week, two weeks, three weeks, and so on, in the past. There was very clear evidence that depressed people had significantly higher events for about six months before onset.

Making use of this finding, Surtes and Ingham (1980) have proposed using a time-based weighting scheme to construct event scales. It is too early to know how useful this will be. The situation is a good deal more complex when it comes to predicting distress in a community survey than when we are predicting onset in a case control design. In the community survey we do not have a date of onset, which means that the stability of disorder must be taken into consideration. If stability is high over a period of six months, then events experienced six months ago might predict current depression more strongly than events experienced in the past month (since events six months in the past have exposed the individual to high risk longer than events experienced in the past month). It would be easy to conclude from this that there is a six-month lag in the effects of events, when in fact a confounding of the distributed lag effects of events with the stability of disorder leads to this result. With panel data it is possible to separate these influences as long as events are accurately dated, but no work on this has been done yet. Nor is it clear that we are currently at a refined enough level of questioning to make serious work on this problem profitable.

Causal Direction

One important problem in life events research is that some events can be effects of mental illness, as well as causes. Several approaches have been used to deal with this possibility of reciprocal causation. One, suggested by Brown (1974a), is to discard from the life event index all events that might

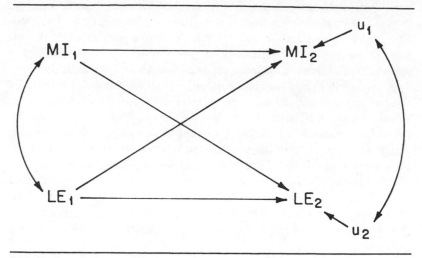

Figure 10.1

be results, rather than causes, of mental illness. This approach has an obvious limitation: It throws out most of the life events that have the greatest impact on well-being, events such as marital disruption, job loss, even physical illness (since many physical illnesses can be psychosomatic). A better approach is to devise some method to separate out the reciprocal effects between events and mental illness explicitly. This has been done in several investigations by making use of data collected over time. Here the assumption is that mental illness at time 1 can influence the events to which an individual is exposed over the interval between times 1 and 2, and that these events can influence change in mental illness between times 1 and 2 (Myers et al., 1974).

It is also possible with panel data to estimate the reciprocal effects between time 2 events and time 2 mental illness by using the time 1 measures as instrumental variables. Readers unfamiliar with this technique should refer to Kessler and Greenberg (1981: chs. 2-3) for a discussion. The basic idea can be grasped by looking at Figures 10.1 and 10.2. These present two path diagrams, each of which can be estimated from the correlations among measures of life events (LE) and mental illness (MI) at times 1 and 2. Each model is estimable only because it imposes some constraints on a completely general solution. For instance, in Figure 10.1 it is assumed that the causal paths from LE_2 to MI_2 and MI_2 to LE_2 are zero, while in Figure 10.2 it is assumed that the effects of LE_1 on MI_2 and of MI_1 on LE_2 are zero.

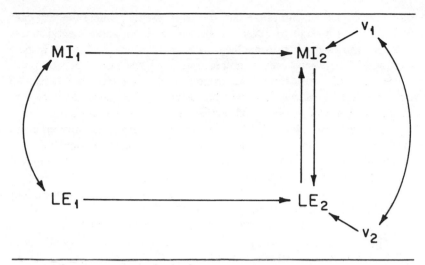

Figure 10.2

Depending on the time lag between the first and second waves, it will be more reasonable to estimate one of these models rather than the other. If the 2 waves are separated by a period of 10 years, there is little reason to think that MI_1 will influence the life events to which one is exposed shortly before time 2. It makes more sense to think that one's recent mental health influences recent events. If, on the other hand, the two waves are separated by a year or less it is probably better to assume that the reciprocal effects are lagged.

This use of instrumental variables raises another possibility: that panel data can be bypassed if one is interested in using them only as a means of separating reciprocal influences, so long as some reasonable instruments can be found in the cross section. One such instrument might be the impairment scores of siblings or other first-order relatives. There is reason to think that these will be significantly associated with the respondent's impairment because of common childhood socialization experiences and genetic makeup. But there is no reason to think that siblings' impairment will be associated with the life events to which respondents are exposed other than through the intervening link of respondents' impairment. It might, then, be more reasonable to take the money that would otherwise be invested in multiple time points interviews and obtain interviews with first-order relatives.[2]

An even more useful instrument is the subscale of life events known not to be influenced by mental illness. This subscale could be used as an instrument on the assumption that it causes "events," where the latter are defined as the overall life events scale, but does not cause mental illness other than through the intermediary of "events." This will allow reciprocal relationships between "events" and mental illness to be estimated.

I realize that this strategy seems too good to be true, but it can be conceptualized in a way that is more intuitive. The model assumes that each event (or unit on the weighted events scale) influences mental illness in the same way, with the same effect. This is an assumption made implicitly in creating any scale that adds up more than one piece of information into a larger whole. The model also assumes that despite this common pattern of influence there is a reciprocal influence of mental illness on a subset of the events in this scale. This means that we could write two structural equations:

$$MI = a_1 + b_1 LE_i + b_1 LE_j + u$$

and

$$LE_i = a_2 + b_2 MI + v,$$

where LE_i is reciprocally related to MI and LE_j is not caused by MI.

Notice that we have assumed that the effects of LE_i and LE_j on MI are the same (b_1). Since LE_j is unrelated to u, we can estimate b_1 without bias from the reduced form. And since this coefficient also is the effect of LE_i on MI, we have the latter as well. This allows us to estimate the influence of MI on LE_i (b_2). Both coefficients, in fact, can be estimated simultaneously in a maximum-likelihood approach that allows equality constraints to be imposed on some coefficients in the model (Joreskog and Sorbom, 1978).

EXPOSURE TO STRESS

In a community survey the correlation between recent events and scores on a symptom screening scale is usually no higher than .15 or .20. This result was first reported by Langner and Michael (1963: 375), who concluded that life stress is only "a moderately efficient screening device" for detecting psychiatric impairment. Even with the most recently developed scales and the most complex research designs, no more than 5 percent of the variance in symptom screening scales can be accounted for by life events in a normal population survey (Ross and Mirowsky, 1979). This has convinced those of us working with life events data that something other than exposure to events is important for understanding onset of mental illness.

Several possibilities exist: (1) It might be that stressful life experiences really do not play the important part we think they do in leading to mental illness; (2) it might be that chronic stresses are more important than events; and (3) it might be that the objective occurrence of an event is less important than the way the event is subjectively appraised and responded to.

Triggering and Formative Effects

The first of these possibilities has been argued by Brown et al. (1973) and Brown (1974b) for the case of schizophrenia. Here, they suggest, life events play no part in causing an individual to have a schizophrenic break. They have no "formative" effect. But they do help determine when it is that an individual who is constitutionally predisposed to schizophrenia will have the inevitable break. This effect on timing is referred to as a "triggering" effect.

There is debate about whether life events have formative or only triggering effects for schizophrenia (Brown et al., 1973; Dohrenwend and Egri, 1981), but it is likely that they have a formative effect for more common types of disorders, especially mood disorders (Brown and Harris, 1978). Since most research on the relationship between life events and mental illness has concentrated on these more common disorders, I limit my comments in the remainder of this review to the latter and ignore entirely the relationship between events and more serious forms of psychiatric impairment.

Chronic Stress Effects

Research on the relationship between chronic stress and mental illness is much less developed than work on the events-mental illness relationship. There are two reasons for this. First, it is easier to determine whether or not an event has occurred in the recent past than to measure objectively a chronic stress. Second, there is much less interpretive ambiguity when working with measures of life events than with chronic stress measures. If we discover, for instance, a relationship between death of a loved one and depression we will probably say that the death brought on the depression. But what of the relationship between job strain and depression? Typical indices of job strain (and other chronic stresses) consist largely of subjectively reported features of the work environment. As a consequence, we cannot distinguish (a) job conditions leading to depression from (b) chronic depression leading to distorted perceptions about job conditions or (c) reciprocal influences between undesirable job conditions, depression, and distorted perceptions. As a result, researchers have favored life event measures over chronic stress measures in their studies.

Neither of these reasons argues that life events are more important than chronic stresses in explaining the distribution of mental illness in society. They are rather methodological expedients. But there are approaches available to help overcome the limitations of chronic stress measures that lead to these expedients. For roles that are changing over time, such as traditional female roles, it is possible to investigate time trends (Kessler and McRae, 1981). For strains tied to a particular role, such as that of being a parent, it is possible to study the intrapsychic forces that influence one to adopt that role (Kessler and McRae, forthcoming). When neither of these approaches is possible, instrumental variable techniques are required. Although this approach has not yet, to my knowledge, been applied in this area of research, it is possible to do so without a great deal of difficulty. All that is required is information about objectively defined role strains as well as about subjectively experienced stresses. The objective strain measures can be used as instruments for separating the effects of stress on mental illness and mental illness on subjectively experienced stress. This is identical to the approach I presented earlier for studying reciprocal effects between life events and mental illness, and it need not be described in greater detail again.

Pearlin et al. (1981) and Brown and Harris (1978) have done the most important work to date on the relationship between chronic strains and mental illness. Pearlin and his colleagues found that feelings of chronic strain importantly mediate the relationship between life events and depression. Brown and Harris suggest an even more complex interplay between events and chronic difficulties. They argue that events can influence depression by forcing an individual to see his or her chronic situation in a new, and more negative, light. Events of this sort will often be trivial in themselves, but take on a new meaning in the context of chronic difficulties. For example, one divorced woman in the Brown and Harris study became severely depressed shortly after her daughter went away on a vacation. In her words, her daughter's temporary departure led her to "realize then for the first time that one of these days I would lose both of the children. It made me realize just how lonely I was and how I depended on their ways" (Brown and Harris, 1978: 145).

If life event effects are modified by chronic stresses of this sort, then it is little wonder that research to date has failed to find large relationships between events and the onset of mental illness. Clearly, explicit consideration of this type of interaction is necessary. But this gets us into the third of the possibilities enumerated above, that the objective occurrence of an event is less important than its meaning in the context of the individual's life.

Modification Effects

When we break down the modest correlation between events and distress in community surveys we find that not being exposed is a better predictor of not being distressed than being exposed is of being distressed. Apparently a traumatic event in one's life increases the odds of becoming psychiatrically impaired, but most people who experience such an event do not become impaired.

Langner and Michael (1963) happened upon this finding when they tried to explain the relationship between social class and impairment with their index of stressful experience. They reasoned that class differences in impairment might reflect nothing more than class differences in *exposure* to stressful experiences, so they plotted a graph in which the relationship between degree of life stress and level of impairment was shown separately for the working-class and middle-class members of their sample. They found only a very small difference in the impairment ratings of working-class and middle-class people at low levels of exposure, but as the number of events increased, so did the difference in the average impairment scores in the two groups.

Langner and Michael (1963: 396) speculated that this differential could be due to class differences in "resistance and resilience" to stress. In other words, a stressful experience might have a more damaging emotional impact on people in disadvantaged social positions.

RESPONSIVENESS TO STRESS

Work on "resistance and resilience," or what is equivalently called responsiveness or vulnerability to stress, has taken two forms. The first has looked for sociodemographic patterns of responsiveness. For example, Brown and Harris (1978), Dohrenwend (1973), Kessler (1979b), Kessler and Cleary (1980), and Turner and Noh (1981) have all shown that the relationship between life events and psychological distress is more pronounced in the lower class than in the middle class. Pearlin and Johnson (1977), Kessler (1979b), and Kessler and Essex (forthcoming) have shown that nonmarried people are more responsive to stress than married people. The documentation of these patterns tells us very little about *why* lower-class people or nonmarried people are vulnerable to the effects of stress. They do tell us, though, that differential responsiveness is important to consider. Indeed, when adjustments are made for differences in responsiveness to stress, a substantial part of the relationships of social class and marital status with symptoms of distress are explained.

The second type of work has looked at factors thought to determine responsiveness directly. A variety of these determinants have been examined: concrete aids in dealing with stress such as knowledge, political power, and money; social resources of a more general sort, such as information and assistance from friends and relatives; emotional resources available from others, such as affiliative support and intimate caring during times of need; and intrapsychic resources, such as personality characteristics that might modify the emotional effects of stress. Sources of vulnerability that can exacerbate the impact of stress have also been examined. The existence of many low-level, chronic stresses, for instance, was mentioned earlier as one feature of an individual's social environment that can exacerbate the effects of life events. Maladaptive coping styles can do the same.

Pearlin and Schooler (1978: 6) have suggested that all responses that help an individual cope with stress can be classified into three functions:

These are: (1) responses that change the situation out of which strainful experience arises; (2) responses that control the meaning of the strainful experience after it occurs but before the emergence of stress; and (3) responses that function more for the control of stress itself after it has emerged.

In this quotation the terms "strain" and "stress" are used in more precise ways than I have used them so far. This becomes necessary when talking about responsiveness to stress, for we want to distinguish the objective life events or ongoing conditions that have a potential for being problematic (strains)[3] from the subjective experience of upset that may accompany these objective conditions (stress).[4]

In their analysis of coping with chronic role strains, Pearlin and Schooler found that the first of these three responses is relatively uncommon. Responses that change the situation are frequently not possible because the individual is not aware of the source of the stress, lacks the resources to remove the problem, finds that new problems arise when the old one is removed, or finds that the problem situation is impervious to efforts to remove it.

A more common coping response is to avoid the subjective experience of stress associated with the strain by controlling its meaning. A great many strategies function in this way: selective ignoring of characteristics of the situation that might arouse feelings of threat, worry, or sadness; devaluing parts of one's life experience that are made problematic by an event; or trying to see one's situation in a better light by making positive comparisons with less fortunate people.

Some events make such drastic changes in one's life that they cannot successfully be managed entirely by controlling their meanings in this way. For events such as these a third type of response is necessary: keeping the subjective stress associated with the event within reasonable bounds. Responses of this sort can involve the control of meaning, as do the complex psychological adjustments made by people who have serious physical impairments. They can also involve objective changes in one's life situation that make the best of a bad situation.

Each of three functions can be realized through several different coping responses. It is useful to distinguish what Pearlin and Schooler call "strategies" of coping, the things people actually do to cope with stress, from the resources that make it possible to employ these concrete strategies. Resources can be social or personal. Social resources include the various characteristics of one's interpersonal environment that make it more or less easy to know how to use, and to use successfully, various strategies for dealing with stress. Personal resources can be objective in the same way as social resources, but they can also be intrapsychic and less easily detected by the observer. As Pearlin and Schooler (1978: 5) note, "personality characteristics that people draw upon to help them withstand threats posed by events and objects in their environment . . . can be formidable barriers to the stressful consequences of social strain." This is true in two senses. First, some stress responses generate psychiatric impairments by first operating on personality resources. Self-esteem loss, for example, is thought to play a crucial part in depression (Brown and Harris, 1978). Second, social resources can operate by bolstering intrapsychic resources. Kohn (1978) has argued that objective life conditions influence onset of schizophrenia in this way, by determining intellectual flexibility. This personality characteristic is thought to play a central part in responsiveness to the life experiences that might lead to a schizophrenic break. Brown and Harris (1978) have argued that some types of social support operate in this way, by bolstering feelings of self-worth in the face of self-esteem assaults.

We are only beginning to know very much about these approaches to the control of life events' effects: about the resources and strategies people use in various situations, where they fit into the overall coping process, which of them are effective in reducing responsiveness to stress, and which of them exacerbate the effects of stress. Much of our knowledge about these things comes from case studies of people coping with particular kinds of life problems. There have also been several attempts to make generalizations across disparate types of stress situations (Haan, 1977; Lazarus and Launier, 1978; Pearlin and Schooler, 1978; Benner et al., forthcoming).

It is much too difficult to summarize here the information we have about all these various ways of responding to stress. Instead, in the next section, I focus on one type of resource that is currently the subject of great interest: social support. Most of the conceptual and methodological problems I discuss in relation to that concept apply equally well to other areas of research about responsiveness to stress.

THE STRESS-BUFFERING EFFECTS
OF SOCIAL SUPPORT[5]

The notion that the absence of social ties can lead to mental illness has roots in classical sociological theory (Leighton, 1974; Kadushin, 1981). People need other people not only because of the material goods and services they provide; people need other people *inherently*. They need intimacy, affiliation, nurturance, and the opportunity to play nurturant roles (Weiss, 1969).

There is something more specific in current ideas about the influence of social supports as modifiers of the relationship between life events and mental illness. This is the belief that supportive relationships in some way *buffer* the individual from the emotional damage that can follow on the heels of life events. Evidence that social supports have a stress-buffering effect of this sort has been reviewed by Cobb (1976), Dean and Lin (1977), and House (1981), all of whom show that this effect appears consistently in both animal and human studies.

For example, Liddell (1950) conducted a series of experiments with baby goats in which physiological reactions to a noxious stimulus were monitored. When mothers of the baby goats were placed with them in the experimental chamber, stress reactions were much less pronounced than when they were left alone. This finding is similar to one reported by Cobb and Kasl (1977) and by Gore (1978) in their study of two plant closings. They found that mental health problems were associated with unemployment only among men who lacked social supports at home or in the community.

Findings like these appear consistently in the stress literature. Yet we need to know more about what it is to be "supported." It is easy to interpret the buffering effect of a plant closing as due to the supportiveness of the social environment. But what is it exactly that is reducing stress in this way? An answer requires the resolution of two problems: First, we need to conceptualize what we mean by social support and, second, we need to determine how to operationalize this conceptualization.

Defining Social Support

The concept of social support is used to help make sense of the fact that people in what seem to be "supported" social environments are in better health than their counterparts without this advantage. When we get down to specifics, though, there is little agreement among researchers about the core meaning of the term "social support." As House (1981: 15) notes in his review of this literature:

> Social support, like stress, is a concept that everyone understands in a general sense but it gives rise to many conflicting definitions and ideas when we get down to specifics. Surprisingly, the experts are sometimes vague or circular, even contradictory. Cassel (1976), for example, in one of the two major reviews of the impact of social support on stress and health, provides no explicit definition of social support. Lin, Simeone, Ensel, and Kuo (1979, p. 109) essentially define social support as support that is social.

One way to approach the problem is to examine concrete instances of problem solving and see how it is that social resources are used. Gottlieb (1978), Veroff et al. (1981), and Warren (1981) have all done this. House (1981) has reviewed some of this information and concludes that there are four major types of support: instrumental, informational, appraisal, and emotional. Instrumental support involves concrete assistance. Informational support consists of giving information that may be used by the person receiving it for self-help. Appraisal support involves information about subjective definitions of the situation that might help redefine the event in such a way that it loses its problematic character. Emotional support, finally, is the transmission of concern.

There is a sense in which emotional support is *displayed* in all the other types of more concrete support, since these latter are usually expressions of the concern one person feels for the plight of another. But these concrete displays are not necessary for emotional support to exist, nor do they exhaust its meaning. Indeed, Gottlieb (1978) found that many people who describe themselves as having been the recipients of support during a time of crisis characterize the support as purely emotional.

There are a number of finer discriminations one would surely want to make. Within emotional support, for instance, we can distinguish affiliation from intimacy. By the former we mean feeling part of a larger collectivity, and by the latter we mean feeling part of a special, confiding, dyad. As Weiss (1973) has demonstrated, these are quite separate feelings, with distinct effects on emotional well-being. Other distinctions among types of instrumental, informational, and appraisal support could also be made. These are discussed by Cobb (1976), Dean and Lin (1977), and House (1981). But for our purposes the foregoing suffices to give a flavor of the major types of support and some more subtle distinctions among subtypes.

Measuring Social Support

Given the confusion in conceptualizing social support it is not surprising that operational measures are at times "conglomerations of anything that might protect people from stress and disease" (House, 1981: 15).

In the Cobb, Kasl, and Gore study of plant closings, for instance, social support was operationalized in a scale consisting of 13 items. Of these, 6 asked respondents about the perceived supportiveness of their wives, 1 asked about the supportiveness of friends, 1 asked about relatives, 2 asked about neighbors, and the last 3 asked about the frequency of social interaction with family, friends, and relatives. This is a fairly typical measure of social support. It adds together subjective responses about emotional transactions and more objective ones about frequency of interactions summed across a variety of people, with no apparent rationale for choosing the relative weightings.

A good deal of work is currently going on to develop more conceptually clean and psychometrically sound scales of support (Procidana and Heller, 1979; Lin et al., 1981; McFarlane et al., 1981; Duncan-Jones, forthcoming). In this section I mention some of the more important issues confronting those who are working on this task.

One of these issues is whether we should measure *access* or *utilization* of support. In work done to date, the buffering hypothesis has been assessed by estimating the influence of life events separately in subsamples of people defined in terms of their social support. This requires a measure of support for people who have not experienced life events as well as for those who have. Obviously, since it makes no sense to talk about utilization among people who have not had recent life problems, this strategy requires the use of a support scale emphasizing access. This might not seem a bad strategy, especially since people who lack access obviously will not be able to utilize support. However, people who have access to supports do not always make use of them in times of need. There is evidence, in fact, that the best mental health outcomes are found among people who do not make use of the supports they have available to them (Jones, 1981). This is consistent with evidence that attachment to supportive others encourages an individual to attempt independent action as long as the support is perceived as a readily accessible source of concrete help (Bowlby, 1973; Kahn and Antonucci, 1980). When this action is successful it obviates the need for concrete support. If this conditional influence of utilization on access it to be investigated, it will be necessary to develop support scales that make a clear distinction between access and utilization.

Another issue is whether to measure *perceived* or *objective* support. Most research has used measures based on respondents' perceptions that they are supported. These may or may not be accurate. House (1981) has suggested that the people perceived to be supportive could be interviewed about their conscious support. Or some unobtrusive methods might be devised to measure in a more objective sense the extent to which support is available or used. This is probably more important for appraisal support than any of the other types, since here it is likely that support will be downplayed in the perceptions of focal respondents. Instrumental and informational support are likely to be perceived accurately. And emotional support is in a fundamental sense housed in perceptions. Therefore, research that is concerned with appraisal should bear in mind that perceptual measures could distort the real importance of this type of support.

Yet another issue in the measurement of support is whether to use measures of network structure along with questions about the content of relationships. Over the past decade a great deal of research has been done on the structural properties of social networks (Mueller, 1980). These properties influence the ease with which social support transactions of various sorts can occur (Jones, 1981). And some measures about the structure of networks have consequently crept into social support scales. At issue is whether it is appropriate to use these measures as proxy indicators of support. I think it is not. It adds more confusion than anything else.

Network structure measures can be useful in another way: as predictors of support. This is discussed by House (1981), who emphasizes the importance of learning more than we currently know about how to facilitate the development of natural supportive relationships. Even if we eventually come to understand the dynamics of support buffering effects, practical intervention will require understanding the features that help generate support. Analysis of the links between network structure and support could be a productive first step on a road to understanding.

Implicit in all of these measurement issues is the importance of disaggregating and operationally distinguishing components of support that have in the past been lumped together into heterogeneous scales. Ultimately we want to know what it is about people having other people available to them that leads to support. We want to know what types of people help most in dealing with what types of problems. This requires the separation of access from utilization, the separation of perceived from objective support, the separation of support content across actors in the support network and across the variety of problem situations people confront.

Estimating Buffering Effects[6]

There has been some confusion in the literature about how to analyze the buffering effects of support. Although it is now generally recognized that a buffering effect should be conceptualized as a statistical interaction between stress and support, interactions are occasionally not estimated (Pearlin and Schooler, 1978; Miller and Ingham, 1976) or are misinterpreted (Tennant and Bebbington, 1978).

At its simplest, the buffering model can be expressed in the following linear equation:

$$MI = a + b_1 LE + b_2 SS + b_3 LE \times SS$$

where MI is mental illness, LE is life events, SS is social support, and LE $\times$ SS is the multiplicative interaction between life events and social support. In this model, the main effect of life events (b_1) represents the impact of events on mental illness among those who *have a score of zero* on the *social support scale*. I emphasize this because b_1 does not represent the effect of life events independent of support, or the effect of life events among people at the lowest level of support. It is a parameter tied directly to the zero point on the support scale. When this zero point is meaningful, as it is for a 0, 1 coding of marital status (0 = not married, 1 = married), b_1 is meaningful. But when the zero point is an arbitrary value on a multiple-item index this coefficient is meaningless in itself.

The main effect of social support (b_2) represents the impact of support on mental illness among those who have had no life events. This effect is usually interpreted as the "inherent" importance of support for mental health once the "secondary" importance of support as a buffer is taken into consideration (Cassel, 1976; Cobb, 1976; Kaplan et al., 1977). It is worth mentioning that this is a correct interpretation only if all stressful life experiences that are buffered by support are included in the prediction equation. Otherwise the main effect will be a weighted combination of the inherent effect of support and its buffering effects for types of stress not in the equation.

The buffering effect of social support (b_3) represents the extent to which the effect of life events on mental illness changes as values of social support change. If social support is zero, then the equation is

$$MI = a + b_1 LE$$

If social support is 1, the equation is

$$MI = (a + b_2) + (b_1 + b_3)LE$$

And if social support is n, the equation is

$$MI = (a + nb_2) + (b_1 + nb_3)LE$$

We see here that b_3 represents the change in the regression of mental illness on life events as we shift our attention from a group of people with a low level of social support to a group with a higher level. This coefficient is usually negative, which means that the impact of life events on mental illness decreases as we go from people who lack social support to those who enjoy a great deal of social support.

This model can be generalized to include the type of interaction between access and utilization discussed earlier. In this model, for each type of support considered, access and utilization must be distinguished, and utilization must be measured in the context of a life event, which means that there are no "users" who have not experienced an event. In a model of this sort we want to evaluate three things: (1) the buffering effect of access; (2) the buffering effect of utilization; and (3) the possibility that nonutilization has a different implication for mental health depending on whether the individual had access to help but decided not to use it or lacked access.

If we think of life events, access, and utilization as 0, 1 variables (0 = no events, no access, no utilization; 1 = at least one event, access, utilization), this model is

$$MI = a + b_1 LE + b_2 ACCESS + b_3 UTILIZE + b_4 LE \times ACCESS + b_5 LE \times ACCESS \times UTILIZE$$

Notice that there are no interactions between events and utilization or between access and utilization, since utilization can only occur among those who have experienced an event and among those with access. This means that there are six parameters in the model, corresponding to the six nonzero cells in the three-way cross-classification of the three dichotomies.

Among those who lack access, the equation is

$$MI = a + b_1 LE$$

Among those who have access and use support, the equation is

$$MI = (a + b_2) + (b_1 + b_4)LE$$

And among those who have access but do not use support, the equation is

$$MI = (a + b_2 + b_3) + (b_1 + b_4 + b_5)LE$$

The buffering effects of b_4 and b_5 have the following interpretations. The first, b_4, is the difference in the impact of life events on mental illness between people who lack access to social supports and those who use supports. The second, b_5, is the difference in this impact between users of support and people who elect not to use support even though it is available to them.

This model can be generalized easily to a situation in which multiple types of support are being considered and to a situation in which the variables are continuous rather than dichotomous.

DISCUSSION

I began this chapter by stating that we need to know more about what types of stresses lead to psychiatric disorders under what conditions. This is a task requiring refined conceptualization, measurement, and analysis of the dimensions in terms of which stressful life experiences, psychiatric disorders, and modifying influences of the relationship between life stress and mental illness operate. These different refinements go hand in hand. It is of little use to make conceptual refinements while we work with life event and social support scales that combine multiple dimensions into unidimensional representations. And even if we manage to develop conceptually precise and psychometrically sound scales, these will not be useful unless we make use of analysis procedures more appropriate to the substantive issues than those currently in use.

My assessment is that we are lagging in the area of measurement more than in conceptualization or analysis methodology. Our conceptualizations of the dimensions important for understanding life event effects and social support effects are a good deal more highly developed than the measures of events and support currently used in research. And, as I have tried to show at various places in my review, the methods appropriate for analyzing these effects are available. It is time, then, for us to refine our operationalizations. Only then will we be able to push our knowledge of the relationship between life events and mental illness forward.

NOTES

1. I discuss only group-level weights here. There has been some work done allowing individuals to supply their own weights to each event they experience (Gersten et al., 1977). This procedure is advertised as being able to measure the idiosyncratic meanings events have for those who experience them. A problem with this procedure is that it also leads to interpretive ambiguity, since mental health problems can magnify the subjective appraisal of an event's meaning. One way around this difficulty is to use group-level weights as instrumental variables when separating the reciprocal effects between idiosyncratically weighted events and mental illness. Another is to use expert judges to classify events in terms of the likely subjective meanings they have for individuals in situations like those in which respondents are found. This latter approach was used by Brown and Harris (1978) to good effect.

2. This is not to say that panel data are not useful for other purposes. I merely want to point out that the problem of attributing causal order can be resolved as successfully in other ways. When there is substantive reason to think that the time lag of the causal influences one is concerned about is short relative to the time interval in the panel, it will be necessary to estimate reciprocal cross-sectional relationships whether panel data are available or not.

3. The term "stressor" is often used as a synonym for what I have defined here as "strain."

4. Many different indicators of subjectively experienced stress are used in the research literature. These include not only feelings that people realize they have but also physiological responses that they might not be aware of. The detection and study of these different stress responses is an endeavor that extends well beyond the consideration of mental health.

5. My thinking about the issues discussed in this section was greatly facilitated by discussions with James House and Peggy Thoits.

6. A fuller discussion of the statistical issues raised in this section can be found in Cleary and Kessler (forthcoming).

REFERENCES

BARRETT, J. [ed.] (1979) Stress and Mental Disorder. New York: Raven.

BENNER, P. E., E. ROSKIES, and R. S. LAZARUS (forthcoming) "Stress and coping under extreme conditions," in J. M. Dimsdale (ed.) The Holocaust: A Multidisciplinary Study. Washington, DC: Hemisphere.

BOWLBY, J. (1973) "Self-reliance and some conditions that promote it," pp. 23-48 in R. Gosling (ed.) Support, Innovation, and Autonomy. London: Tavistock.

BROWN, G. W. (1974a) "Meaning, measurement, and stress of life events," pp. 217-243 in B. S. Dohrenwend and B. P. Dohrenwend (eds.) Stressful Life Events: Their Nature and Effects. New York: John Wiley.

――― (1974b) "Life events and the onset of depressive and schizophrenic conditions," pp. 164-186 in E. K. Gunderson and R. Rahe (eds.) Life Stress and Illness. Springfield, IL: Charles C Thomas.

――― and T. HARRIS (1978) Social Origins of Depression: A Study of Psychiatric Disorders in Women. New York: Macmillan.

――― and J. PETO (1973) "Life events and psychiatric disorders, Part 2: nature of the causal link." Psychological Medicine 3: 159-176.

CASSEL, J. (1976) "The contribution of the social environment to host resistance." American Journal of Epidemiology 102: 107-123.

CLEARY, P. D. and R. C. KESSLER (forthcoming) "The estimation and interpretation of modifier effects." Journal of Health and Social Behavior.

COBB, S. (1976) "Social support as a moderator of life stress." Psychosomatic Medicine 38: 300-314.

――― and S. V. KASL (1977) Termination: The Consequence of Job Loss. Publication NIOSH 77-224. Washington, DC: Department of Health, Education and Welfare.

COELHO, G. V. and R. I. IRVING [eds.] (1981) Coping and Adaptation: An Annotated Bibliography and Study Guide. Washington, DC: Department of Health and Human Services, Government Printing Office.

COELHO, G. V., D. A. HAMBURG, and J. E. ADAMS [eds.] (1974) Coping and Adaptations. New York: Basic Books.

DEAN, A. and N. LIN (1977) "The stress-buffering role of social support: problems and prospects for systematic investigation." Journal of Nervous and Mental Disease 165: 403-417.

DOHRENWEND, B. P. and G. EGRI (1981) "Recent stressful life events and episodes of schizophrenia." Schizophrenia Bulletin 7: 12-23.

DOHRENWEND, B. S. (1980) "The conflict between statistical and theoretical significance (comment on Ross and Mirowsky)." Journal of Health and Social Behavior 21: 291-293.

――― (1973) "Life events as stressors: a methodological inquiry." Journal of Health and Social Behavior 14: 67-75.

――― and B. P. DOHRENWEND [eds.] (1981) Life Events and Life Stress. New York: Neale Watson.

———— [eds.] (1974) Stressful Life Events: Their Nature and Effects. New York: John Wiley.

DOHRENWEND, B. S. and J. L. MARTIN (1979) "Personal versus situational determinants of anticipation and control of the occurrence of stressful life events." American Journal of Community Psychology 7: 453-468.

DUNCAN-JONES, P. (forthcoming) "The structure of social relationships: analysis of a survey instrument, Parts I and II." Social Psychiatry.

GERSTEN, J. C., T. S. LANGER, J. G. EISENBERG, and O. SIMCHA-FAGNAN (1977) "An evaluation of the etiologic role of stressful life-change events in psychological disorders." Journal of Health and Social Behavior 18: 228-244.

GORE, S. (1978) "The effect of social support in moderating the health consequences of unemployment." Journal of Health and Social Behavior 19: 157-165.

GOTTLIEB, B. H. (1978) "The development and application of a classification scheme of informal helping behaviors." Canadian Journal of Science 10: 105-115.

HAAN, N. (1977) Coping and Defending: Processes of Self-Environment Organization. New York: Academic.

HOLMES, T. H. and R. H. RAHE (1967) "The social readjustment rating scale." Journal of Psychosomatic Research 11: 213-218.

HOUSE, J. S. (1981) Work Stress and Social Support. Reading, MA: Addison-Wesley.

JONES, B. B. (1981) "Mental health and the structure of support." Ph.D. dissertation, University of Michigan.

JORESKOG, K. G. and D. SORBOM (1978) LISREL IV: Estimation of Linear Structural Equation Systems by Maximum Likelihood Methods. Chicago: National Educational Resources.

KADUSHIN, C. (1981) "Social density and mental health." Department of Sociology, Graduate Center of the City University of New York. (unpublished)

KAHN, R. L. and T. C. ANTONUCCI (1980) "Convoys over the life course: attachment, roles and social support," pp. 154-178 in P. Baltes and O. Brim (eds.) Life-Span Development and Behavior, Vol. 3. New York: Academic.

KAPLAN, B. H., J. C. CASSEL, and S. GORE (1977) "Social support and health." Medical Care 25: 47-58.

KESSLER, R. C. (1980) "'A comment' on a comparison of life-event-weighting schemes." Journal of Health and Social Behavior 21: 293-296.

———— (1979a) "A strategy for studying differential vulnerability to the psychological consequences of stress." Journal of Health and Social Behavior 20: 100-108.

———— (1979b) "Stress, social status, and psychological distress." Journal of Health and Social Behavior 20: 259-272.

———— and P. D. CLEARY (1980) "Social class and psychological distress." American Sociological Review 45: 463-478.

KESSLER, R. C. and M. ESSEX (forthcoming) "Marital status and depression: the role of coping resources." Social Forces.

KESSLER, R. C. and D. F. GREENBERG (1981) Linear Panel Analysis. New York: Academic.

KESSLER, R. C. and J. A. McRAE, Jr. (forthcoming) "The effects of wives' employment on the mental health of married men and women." American Sociological Review.

———— (1981) "Trends in the relationship between sex and psychological distress: 1957-1976." American Sociological Review 46: 443-451.

KOHN, M. L. (1978) "Reassessment, 1977," pp. xxv-1x in M. L. Kohn, Class and Conformity: A Study in Values. Chicago: University of Chicago Press.

LANGNER, T. S. and S. T. MICHAEL (1963) "Life Stress and Mental Illness: The Midtown Manhattan Study. New York: Macmillan.

LAZARUS, R. S. and R. LAUNIER (1978) "Stress-related transactions between person and environment," pp. 287-327 in L. A. Pervin and M. Lewis (eds.) Perspectives in Interactional Psychology. New York: Plenum.

LEIGHTON, A. H. (1974) "Social disintegration and mental disorder," pp. 411-423 in G. Caplan (ed.) American Handbook of Psychiatry, Vol. II. New York: Basic Books.

LIDDELL, H. (1950) "Some specific factors that modify tolerance for environmental stress," pp. 155-171 in H. G. Wolff et al. (eds.) Life Stress and Bodily Disease. Baltimore: Williams & Wilkins.

LIN, N., A. DEAN, and W. M. ENSEL (1981) "Social support scales: a methodological note." Schizophrenia Bulletin 7: 73-89.

LIN, N., R. L. SIMEONE, W. M. ENSEL, and W. KUO (1979) "Social support, stressful life events and illness: a model and an empirical test." Journal of Health and Social Behavior 20: 108-119.

LORIMER, R. J., B. JUSTICE, G. W. McBEE, and M. WEINMAN (1979) "Weighting events in life-events research (comments on Dohrenwend et al.)." Journal of Health and Social Behavior 20: 306-307.

McFARLANE, A. H., K. A. NEALE, G. R. NORMAN, R. G. ROY, and D. L. STREINER (1981) "Methodological issues in developing a scale to measure social support." Schizophrenia Bulletin 7: 90-100.

MILLER, P. and J. INGHAM (1976) "Friends, confidants and symptoms." Social Psychiatry 11: 51-58.

MUELLER, D. P. (1980) "Social networks: a promising direction for research on the relationship of the social environment to psychiatric disorder." Social Science and Medicine 14A: 147-161.

——— D. W. EDWARDS, and R. M. YARVIS (1977) "Stressful life events and psychiatric symptomatology: change or undesirability?" Journal of Health and Social Behavior 18: 307-317.

MYERS, J. K., J. J. LINDENTHAL, M. P. PEPPER, and D. R. OSTRANDER (1974) "Social class, life events and psychiatric symptoms: a longitudinal study," pp. 191-206 in B. S. Dohrenwend and B. P. Dohrenwend (eds.) Stressful Life Events: Their Nature and Effects. New York: John Wiley.

NEWCOMB, M. D., G. J. HUBER, and P. M. BENTLER (forthcoming) "A multidimensional assessment of adolescent stress: derivation and correlates." Journal of Health and Social Behavior.

PAYKEL, E. S. (1978) "Contribution of life events to causation of psychiatric illness." Psychological Medicine 8: 245-253.

PEARLIN, L. I. and S. JOHNSON (1977) "Marital status, life-strains and depression." American Sociological Review 42: 104-115.

PEARLIN, L. I. and C. SCHOOLER (1978) "The structure of coping." Journal of Health and Social Behavior 19: 2-21.

PEARLIN, L. I., M. LIEBERMAN, E. MENAGHAN, and J. MULLAN (1981) "The stress process." Journal of Health and Social Behavior 22: 337-356.

PROCIDANA, M. E. and K. HELLER (1979) "Toward the assessment of perceived social support." Presented at the meetings of the American Psychological Association, New York.

ROSS, C. E. and J. MIROWSKY (1979) "A comparison of life-event-weighting schemes: change, undesirability, and effect-proportional indices." Journal of Health and Social Behavior 20: 166-177.

RUCH, L. O. (1977) "A multidimensional analysis of the concept of life change." Journal of Health and Social Behavior 18: 71-83.

SELYE, H. (1976) The Stress of Life. New York: McGraw-Hill.

SHEPARD, R. N., A. K. ROMNEY, and S. B. NERVOLE [eds.] (1972) Multidimensional Scaling: Theory and Applications in the Behavioral Sciences, Vol. II. Applications. New York: Seminar.

STREINER, D. L., G. R. NORMAN, A. H. McFARLANE, and R. C. ROY (1981) "Quality of life events and their relationship to strain." Schizophrenia Bulletin 7: 34-42.

SURTES, P. G. and J. G. INGHAM (1980) "Life stress and depressive outcome: application of a dissipation model to life events." Social Psychiatry 15: 21-31.

TENNANT, C. and P. BEBBINGTON (1978) "The social causation of depression: a critique of the work of Brown and his colleagues." Psychological Medicine 8: 565-575.

THOITS, P. (1981) "Conceptual, methodological, and theoretical problems in studying social support as a buffer against life stress." Department of Sociology, Princeton University. (unpublished)

TURNER, J. J. and S. NOH (1981) "Class and psychological vulnerability: the significance of social support." Presented at the meetings of the Society for the Study of Social Problems, Toronto.

VEROFF, J., E. DOUVAN, and R. KULKA (1981) Mental Health in America, 1957 to 1976. New York: Basic Books.

VINOKUR, A. and M. L. SELZER (1975) "Desirable versus undesirable life events." Journal of Personality and Social Psychology 32: 329-337.

WARREN, D. I. (1981) Helping Networks: How People Cope with Problems in the Urban Community. South Bend, IN: University of Notre Dame Press.

WEISS, R. S. (1973) "The study of loneliness," pp. 7-30 in R. S. Weiss (ed.) Loneliness: The Experience of Emotional and Social Isolation. Cambridge: MIT Press.

––– (1969) "The fund of sociability." Transaction 6: 36-39.

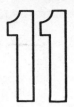

THE CURRENT STATUS OF THE LABELLING THEORY OF MENTAL ILLNESS

WALTER R. GOVE

For the past 20 years labelling theory has been the dominant theoretical perspective among sociologists who are students of deviance. This dominance is reflected in Gibbs and Erickson's (1975) review of the major developments in the sociology of deviance, Cole's (1975) citation analysis, and Sagarin and Montanino's (1976) review of texts and readers in the area of deviance. Labelling theorists proclaim their own dominance (see Spector, 1976) and it seems clear that, except in the case of crime, where conflict theory (which shares many of labelling theory's premises) has become a competing perspective, no sociological theory of deviance has emerged to compete with labelling theory. By far the most original and precise version of the labelling theory of mental illness was published by Scheff in 1966. His book still provides the most articulate statement of the labelling theory of mental illness and, for all practical purposes, labelling theorists have suggested no changes modifying Scheff's basic formulation.

In the area of mental illness the perspective that competes with labelling theorists' explanation is, of course, the one posed by psychiatrists. In 1970, I published my first attempt to evaluate labelling theory's explanation of mental illness and concluded that the evidence, while providing partial support for some of the tenets of labelling theory, overall overwhelmingly supported the psychiatric perspective (see Gove, 1970). There ensued a debate that both Immershein and Simons (1976) and Horwitz (1979) have referred to as the Gove-Scheff debate. Although it is my position that the accumulating evidence now provides overwhelming support for the psychiatric perspective, I agree with Horwitz (1979) that for most sociologists the issues seem to be no closer to resolution than when Scheff's and my original work was published. In this chapter I will (1) sketch what I see to be the basic tenets of labelling theory, (2) critically evaluate the current status of the labelling theory of mental illness, and (3) attempt to explain the persistence of the labelling theory of mental illness. Points 1 and 2 have been covered in more detail elsewhere and I will refer to these works, as well as the works of labelling theorists, so that the interested reader can get a better grasp on the issues and evidence. In what follows the reader should be very aware that I take a general antilabelling propsychiatry position and, although I present as fair a statement of the issues and evidence as I am able, my perception of some issues may slant toward that position.

A SKETCH OF LABELLING THEORY

In this section I will outline what I see as the basic thrust of labelling theory. For a more comprehensive discussion, the reader is referred to Cullen and Cullen (1978), Gove (1980), and Gibbs (1981).

One of the most fundamental distinctions made by labelling theorists is between primary deviance and secondary deviance. Regarding the two, Lemert (1967: 17) says:

> Primary deviation is assumed to arise in a wide variety of social, cultural, and psychological contexts, and at best has only marginal implication for the psychic structure of the individual; it does not lead to symbolic reorganization at the level of self-regarding attitudes and social roles. Secondary deviation is deviant behavior or social roles based upon it, which becomes a means of defense, attack or adaptation to the overt and covert problems created by the societal reaction to primary deviation.

The labelling theorists do not attach significance to an act of primary deviance except insofar as others react toward the commission of the act. To them, deviance is not a quality of an act, but instead is produced in the interaction between a person who commits an act and those who respond to it. Erikson (1962: 311) says:

> Deviance is not a property *inherent in* certain forms of behavior; it is a property *conferred upon* these forms by the audiences which directly or indirectly witness them. The critical variable in the study of deviance, then, is the social audience rather than the individual actor, since it is the audience which eventually determines whether or not any episode of behavior or any class of episodes is labelled deviant.

What concern the labelling theorists have with an individual's personal and social attributes is focused on how these attributes affect the way others respond to an act of primary deviance. Thus they are not concerned with whether a particular societal attribute is related to the likelihood that an individual will commit a deviant act, but with whether that societal attribute facilitates or impedes the individual's ability to avoid the imposition of the label of deviant.

According to this approach, the most crucial step in the development of a stable pattern of deviant behavior is usually the experience of being caught and publicly labelled deviant. Whether or not this happens to a person "depends not so much on what he does as on what other people do" (Becker 1963: 31). Erikson (1962: 311), writing about the public labelling process, states:

> The community's decision to bring deviant sanctions against the individual . . . is a sharp rite of transition at once moving him out of his normal position in society and transferring him into a distinctive deviant role. The ceremonies which accomplish this change of status, ordinarily, have three related phases. They provide a formal confrontation between the deviant suspect and representatives of his community (as in the criminal trial or psychiatric case conference); they announce some judgment about the nature of his deviancy (a verdict or diagnosis, for example), and they perform an act of social placement, assigning him a special role (like that of a prisoner or patient) which redefines his position in society.

Erikson (1962: 311) goes on to state: "An important feature of these ceremonies in our culture is that they are almost irreversible." Why might this be the case? According to the labelling theorists, the status of deviant is a master status which overrides all other statuses in determining how others will act toward a person. Once a person is stigmatized by being labelled a deviant, a self-fulfilling prophecy is initiated—others perceive and respond to the person as a deviant (Erickson, 1962; Becker, 1963). Furthermore, once persons are publicly processed as deviants, they are typically forced into a deviant group (often by being placed in an institution). As Becker (1963) notes, such groups have one thing in common—their deviance. They have a common fate, they face the same problems, and, because of this, they develop a deviant subculture. This subculture combines a perspective on the world with a set of routine activities. According to Becker (1963: 38), "membership in such a group solidifies a deviant identity" and leads to rationalization of the members' position. According to the labelling theorists, once labelling has occurred it is extremely difficult for a person to break out of the deviant status.

In summary, the labelling theorists have focused on the societal attributes of those who react and those who are reacted against in order to explain why certain persons and not others are labelled as deviant. They argue that once a person has been labelled a deviant—and particularly if that person has passed through a "degradation ceremony" (Garfinkel, 1956) and been forced to become a member of a deviant group—the person has experienced a profound and frequently irreversible socialization process. He or she has not only acquired an inferior status, but has also developed a deviant world view and the knowledge and skills that go with it. And perhaps equally important, he or she has developed a deviant self-image based upon the actions of others.

Labelling as a Dependent Variable

The traditional view is that persons are labelled deviant primarily because they either act in a deviant manner or have characteristics that mark them deviant. In contrast, according to labelling theory persons are labelled deviant primarily as a consequence of their marginal societal characteristics.

Labelling as an Independent Variable

The traditional perspective is that if someone is seriously deviant in behavior or condition, affixing a deviant label to that person and treating him or her accordingly will have certain positive consequences. The labelling theorists, however, argue that reacting to persons as if they were deviants is the major cause of deviant identities and lifestyles. It is assumed that without a societal reaction most deviant behavior would be transitory, but that if the individual is reacted to as a deviant, the deviant status will tend to become permanent.

By far the most explicit theoretical statement of how labelling theory explains mental illness is to be found in Scheff's (1966) book *Being Mentally Ill: A Sociological Theory*. As I interpret Scheff's position, he views mental illness as an ascribed status, entry into which is primarily dependent on conditions external to the individual. His formulation is, first, that virtually everyone at some time commits acts that correspond to the public stereotype of mental illness; second, that if these acts become public knowledge, the individual may, depending on various contingencies, be referred to the appropriate officials. Scheff (1966: 182, 110) argues that whether or not this will happen depends upon the marginality of the patient, the patient's lack of power, the nature of the acts of residual rule breaking, the social distance between the rule breaker and the control agents, the community tolerance level, and the availability of nondeviant roles. Third, once the person is reacted to he or she will be routinely processed as mentally ill and placed in a mental institution. Fourth, Scheff (1966: 92-93) postulates that this labelling process is the single most important determinant of a career of mental illness.

Among the factors that are crucial to understanding the labelling theory of mental illness are that its proponents see mental illness as behaviors associated with a role and that for all practical purposes mental illness *is* the enactment of the role of the mentally ill. Thus labelling theorists treat mental illness as a unitary phenomenon (a role) and not a set of phenomena such as a group of distinct disorders. In contrast, as Spitzer and Williams (Chapter 1, this volume) make clear, for psychiatry mental illness refers to a set of fairly distinct disorders that a person may have.

A second factor that is important to understand is the labelling theorists' ideological orientation, for it shapes the way data are interpreted and the theory formulated. Scheff (1975b: 12) argues that the medical model, when applied to the phenomenon of mental illness, helps reaffirm the current culture and the political status quo in our society. Thus the mentally ill, to use Becker's (1963) term, are "outsiders" whose way of behaving challenges the status quo. In the outsider's struggle with society, virtually all the major labelling theorists tend to side with the "deviant" as opposed to the "establishment." Lofland and Lofland (1969: 21) state, "Indeed, if throughout what follows I appear to be less friendly towards normals than towards some sorts of deviants, it is because I am." One may also perceive this attitude in looking at Becker's (1967) rhetorical article "Whose Side Are We On?" Finally, one should recognize that labelling theory is explicitly posed as an alternative to traditional explanations of deviance. As Scheff (1975a: 22) states, "The sensitizing function of the labelling theory of mental illness derives precisely from its attempt to contradict the major tenets of the medical model."

Old Evidence for
the Labelling Theory

As the chapters in this volume by Klerman and Morrisey make clear, in 1955 public mental hospitals contained a large number of chronic mental patients. Studies conducted of mental hospitals at this time tended to show that the hospital milieu contained a number of features that rein-forced institutionalism (Caudill, 1958; Goffman, 1961; Standon and Schwartz, 1954). Furthermore, studies such as the classic work by Hollings-head and Redlich (1958) show that persons from the middle and upper classes tended to receive preferential treatment. Existing data thus strongly suggest that through the 1950s mental hospitals contained a large number of persons who occupied the role of the chronically mentally ill. Present statistics, however, suggest that under present treatment conditions many of those persons would not chronically occupy the role of the mentally ill. This suggests that labelling theory focuses on processes that, at least in the past, had a substantial impact on large numbers of people.

The evidence from the fifties would indicate that another tenet of the labelling theory of mental illness was correct—namely, that the public was ignorant about mental illness and had a very negative image of persons identified as mentally ill. For example, the studies by Star (1961), Nun-nally (1961), and Cumming and Cumming (1957) indicated that during that era the public's information about mental illness distorted and exag-gerated the amount and type of disturbance. Nunnally (1961: 46) found that "the mentally ill are regarded with fear, distrust and dislike." In the public's conception mental illness appeared to involve unpredictable and potentially dangerous behavior. There was a halo effect: Once a person was perceived as mentally ill, he or she was not only seen as unpredictable and dangerous but also "dirty, unintelligent, insincere and worthless" (Nunnally, 1961: 233). These investigations thus indicated that the public had a negative, highly stereotyped image of mental illness and generally treated mental illness as a master status that overrode other characteristics of the individual.

Present Psychiatric Care

As Klerman and Morrisey show in their chapters, in spite of an increased admission rate the resident population of public mental hospitals has declined every year since 1955, a trend that has been brought about by a very sharp decrease in the length of hospitalization. During this time there has been a marked shift away from treatment in mental hospitals to treatment centers more closely tied to the community. The rate of inpatient hospitalizations has remained relatively constant, but there has been a marked change in the place of treatment, with more persons receiving inpatient treatment in general hospitals, community mental health centers, and, to a lesser extent, Veterans Administration (VA) hospitals. Furthermore, in all settings the length of treatment is now relatively brief. In 1975 the median length of inpatient care in public mental hospitals was 25 days; in private mental hospitals, 20 days; in community mental health centers, 13; and in VA hospitals (psychiatric admissions only), 12 days (Klerman and Schechter, 1979). According to Regier et al. (1978), in 1975 3.1 percent of the total U.S. population received treatment from mental health professionals, .5 percent received inpatient care in a nonpsychiatric setting, and 9.0 percent received treatment as outpatients from physicians. In total, 11.8 percent of the population received some form of psychiatric treatment from physicians during that year. Given the changes in the setting and the brevity of treatment, it is difficult to imagine that most mental patients are in the formal role of the mental patient for a long enough period of time to be socialized into the role of the chronically ill in the manner suggested by the labelling theorists.

As Morrisey makes clear in his chapter, the deinstitutionalization movement has not only been characterized by shifts in both time spent in institutionalized care and locale of treatment, but also by a number of changes in procedures. The reader is referred to Morrissey (Chapter 6) and Klerman (Chapter 7) for a general discussion of the deinstitutionalization movement and the continuing psychiatric revolution. One aspect of the deinstitutionalization movement that I would like to emphasize is the twofold problem of the legal processes involved in commitment and the legal rights of patients.

One of the major concerns of labelling theorists is that the civil rights of prospective patients are violated during the commitment process and subsequently when they are in the hospital. At the time Scheff (1966) was writing his book, a case could be made that such violations frequently occurred; however, because of court rulings, new laws, and changes in procedures, it is very hard to make such a case today. First of all, it should be noted that this issue deals almost entirely with committed patients and such patients are becoming increasingly rare. Virtually all committed patients are committed to public mental hospitals and, as noted above, these patients constitute only a small proportion of all patients receiving psychiatric care. Furthermore, the majority of patients admitted to public mental hospitals are voluntary admissions (Meyer, 1974).

In 1971, in Wyatt v. Stickney, the Federal District Court in Alabama held that involuntarily committed patients "unquestionably have a constitutional right to receive such individual treatment as will give each of them a realistic opportunity to be cured or to improve his or her mental condition," and this has become the accepted standard for all hospitals. In 1975, in O'Connor v. Donaldson, the U.S. Supreme Court ruled that "a state cannot constitutionally confine a nondangerous individual who is capable of surviving safely in freedom by himself or with the help of willing and responsible family members or friends" (Crane et al., 1977: 827). As a consequence of this ruling, the Connecticut Valley Hospital instituted a systematic review of all involuntary patients at the hospital. Although the review found no other patients like O'Connor, it did find a substantial number of patients who could be cared for in other institutional settings, particularly nursing homes.

The case of Nason v. Bridgewater confirmed a person's right to an individualized treatment program. A follow-up in the four hospitals against which this suit was filed showed a marked improvement in the hospitals' psychiatric treatment (Kaufman, 1979). Since these court rulings, right-to-treatment suits have become fairly common and follow-up studies in other hospitals also demonstrate a marked improvement in the care provided (Kaufman, 1979). In short, right-to-treatment suits appear to be a positive force in improving mental health care and there is some evidence that institutional psychiatrists will use them to further their own program goals (see Macht, 1978).

On April 30, 1979, in Addington v. Texas, the Supreme Court handed down a ruling that more clearly delineates the nature of the evidence required for commitment. The court ruled the evidence must be "clear and convincing." While the standard of proof is not as stringent as that required in criminal cases, in which the standard is "beyond a reasonable doubt," the ruling clearly indicates that it is almost as stringent. Moreover, at that time 39 states already had laws requiring the standard used in criminal cases (see Addington v. Texas). The Supreme Court also has imposed stringent limits on how long defendants found incompetent to stand trial can be hospitalized (Steadman, 1979).

The court rulings are complemented by changes in the law. In 1965 the laws affecting the admissions to New York state mental hospitals were reformed and updated. These reforms, characterized at the time as the most revolutionary in the country in the field of mental health in a century (see the chapter by Morrissey), encouraged the use of voluntary admission procedures and required the conversion of all possible involuntary patients to a voluntary or informal status. The legislation abolished court certification of involuntary hospitalization and established a system of initial admissions based on medical judgment (two-physician certificates) for a two-week period. A number of legal safeguards were introduced. The law established a Mental Health Information Service, which guaranteed that the patient was notified of his or her rights and was automatically provided with legal assistance for a judicial hearing to be held after two weeks in the cases where treatment was still deemed necessary and the patient had not changed to a voluntary or informal status. By 1969 only 7 percent of the patients requested court hearings, and of those who did approximately 50 percent were released. Additional legal safeguards were introduced for involuntary patients hospitalized beyond 60 days (for example, see Kumasaka et al., 1972; Morrissey, Chapter 6, this volume).

In 1967 California passed the Lanterman-Petris-Short (LPS) Act, which limited all involuntary hospitalization to 17 days and imposed very strict legal safeguards regarding both the requirements for commitment and the procedures to be used in commitment. Urmer (1978: 143) reports that "in the first two years post-LPS the average treatment duration of involuntary patients dropped from 180 days to 15 days while the average duration of voluntary patients dropped from 75 days to 23 days." The California law has received the most careful scrutiny and it has been used as a model for laws in other states (see Sata and Goldenberg, 1977; Bonovitz and Guy, 1979).

There has been no systematic published review of the present laws in the 50 states; my colleagues and I, however, have recently completed a preliminary review (Gove et al., 1982). A consideration of the laws must be viewed in light of Dixon v. Weinberger, where it was ruled that committed patients have a statutory right to treatment in the least restrictive appropriate facility and that such facilities should be created if they do not exist. In practice this has meant that in considering commitment the court must conclude that a mental hospital is the least restrictive treatment setting in which the patient can be treated, it being the case, for example, that the patient could not be effectively treated in an outpatient facility.

Our preliminary review shows that the laws have tightened considerably in recent years. All 50 states specify that the prospective patient has the right to a lawyer. The reasons for commitment are becoming considerably more narrow. In 22 states the law specifies that the patient, in addition to being severely mentally ill, *must be* a danger to himself or herself or to others. The legal terms vary, but the most common terms are "a clear and present danger" or "poses an immediate danger to self or others." In 25 states, in addition to the dangerousness question the law specifies that the patient may also be committed if he or she is gravely disabled, usually with the specification that the patient is unable to care for himself or herself in the community (even with the assistance of others). In the remaining 3 states, in addition to the patient posing a danger there is the specification that the patient may also be hospitalized if he or she poses a serious threat to property. And in 43 states the law specifies that commitment is either for a specified period of time or that a review will be held at a specific time. In most states this is a continuous process; that is, the patient may be recommitted only for a specific period of time, such as 6 months, but in a few states after the second hearing the commitment may be for an indefinite period. In the remaining 7 states the commitment period is unspecified and there is no periodic review; however, in 4 of these states the hospital must report to the court or a review board at specified intervals. And, finally, in 45 states the law specifically states that the patient may appeal a ruling that results in hospitalization. This brief review of the laws does not touch on all of the changes. For example, in Michigan all patients are notified of their rights as specified by the new mental health code and each institution has a special person designated as a rights advisor who investigates complaints (Coye and Clifford, 1978).

In summary, as the law stands at present, in the majority of the states persons can be committed to mental hospitals only if they pose a serious danger to themselves or others. And in these states laws often impose stringent standards. For example, in Pennsylvania a "clear and present danger" is limited to the determination that "within the past 30 days the person has inflicted or attempted to inflict serious bodily harm on another or on himself" (Bonovitz and Guy, 1979: 1045). This means in these states that the majority of persons whom psychiatrists would see as severely mentally ill (for example, persons who are so mentally disabled that they are unable to care for themselves) cannot be committed. As a consequence many severely mentally ill individuals receive little or no treatment and are to be found in what Lamb (1979) has referred to as "asylums in the community."

With many severely mentally ill persons in the community it is not surprising that a number of social control techniques have been developed to contain persons residing in the community who are seriously disturbed (for example, see the chapter by Morrisey). Perhaps not surprisingly, jails and prisons appear again to have become places for housing the mentally ill. There is at least one study that clearly shows that this has occurred. As noted above, Pennsylvania has implemented a law with very stringent standards for commitment. On June 10, 1977, the Philadelphia police commissioner issued a policy directive which stated in part:

Persons who, by their actions, are unruly or disorganized but do not present a danger to themselves, or any person present, may no longer be taken into custody under the provisions of the Mental Health Act of 1976. However, persons who make unreasonable noise, use obscene language, make obscene gestures, engage in fighting or threatening, in violent or tumultuous behavior, create a hazardous or physically offensive condition by any act which serves no legitimate purpose of the actor, may be charged with violating Section 5505 of the Crime Code, Disorderly Conduct [Bonovitz and Guy, 1979: 1045].

Bonovitz and Guy (1979) studied a Philadelphia prison that had a psychiatric unit to see if there appeared to be an increase in the number of mentally ill prisoners. They found that the "number of requests from prison staff rose substantially during the 6-7 months after the implementation of the act" and that this increase persisted throughout the remaining 15 months of the study (Bonovitz and Guy, 1979: 1046). Looking at patients admitted to psychiatric wards and comparing them to patients admitted before the implementation of the Mental Health Procedures Act, they found "subjects admitted to the psychiatric unit after implementation of the act were less likely to have committed a violent crime and there was a marked increase in such crimes as disorderly conduct, trespassing, and making terrorist threats" (Bonovitz and Guy, 1979: 1047). A discernible number of subjects admitted after the act had been arrested at the request of their families, while there were no family-initiated arrests in the group admitted before enactment. Furthermore, the majority of the families who had initiated arrests had attempted to persuade the subject to obtain psychiatric treatment during the two weeks before the arrest (Bonovitz and Guy, 1979: 1047).

While the prison studied by Bonovitz and Guy is just one case, with the deinstitutionalization movement the increase in the number of mentally ill in jails appears to be pervasive. For example, at the conference on Mental Health Services in Local Jails held in Baltimore on September 27-29, 1978, there was a constant refrain from the jailers present (and they constituted the majority of the participants) that (1) they now had a substantial number of mentally ill persons in jail, (2) these mentally ill inmates cause serious problems in the administration of the jail, and (3) they were unable to provide any form of effective treatment even though legally required to do so (Gove, forthcoming).[1]

Labelling Theory and Deinstitutionalization

Dietz (1977: 1356) has presented a strong case, demonstrating that not only are psychiatrists concerned about the proliferation of class action suits, but also "most psychiatrists perceive such legal actions as unjustified attacks on psychiatry by attorneys and other outsiders and they fear that the success of such actions will seriously handicap their efforts to care for patients." While Dietz sees the consequences of recent court rulings and legislation as having an overall positive effect, he also perceives the field of psychiatry as "under siege" and the practice of psychiatry as unduly hampered by legal restrictions. He argues that psychiatry is unable to provide the necessary treatment for a significant proportion of patients who are severely mentally ill because of these restrictions.

Dietz is not alone. There also appears to be a growing concern that although the deinstitutionalization movement has been largely beneficial, the legal rules and regulations have become overly stringent, so that the most appropriate care is not provided to many persons who are severely mentally ill. The general feeling is that the deinstitutionalization movement has to be reconceptualized and reorganized (Jones, 1975; Jalbolt, 1979; Scherl and Macht, 1979; Stone, 1977; Ashbaugh and Bradley, 1979). The overregulation of the deinstitutionalization movement is a consequence of the fact that the movement, initiated by psychiatrists, is now largely regulated by attorneys and legislators. This shift in control is probably obvious to most psychiatrists. What is less obvious and often not even recognized is that the view of mental illness and psychiatric practice held by the attorneys, judges, and legislators is derived from what Dietz (1977: 1356) identifies as "sociological writings." "Sociological writings" is much too broad a term, however, because the work referred to by Dietz comes from one particular perspective among sociologists studying deviant behavior, namely, *labelling theory*. That labelling theory provides the perspective on mental illness held by the judicial and legislative system is well documented (Benson, 1979; Bardach, 1972; Gordon, 1980), and is something I personally was made profoundly aware of when I testified as an expert witness for the defense in a case filed against the Commissioner on Mental Health in Georgia. In that case, the entire theoretical foundation of the plaintiffs rested on labelling theory. To illustrate the view of psychiatric institutions held by the attorneys, I would note that the two attorneys cross-examining me were visibly shocked when, in response to their question, I stated that I could conceive of conditions under which I would seek the mental hospitalization of someone close to me. (The plaintiffs won the case.) In short, labelling theory provides the rationale behind the court rulings and laws that appear to impose overly stringent requirements on the practice of institutional psychiatry.

PRESENT EMPIRICAL STATUS
OF LABELLING THEORY

I will now turn to a review of evidence bearing on the labelling theory of mental illness. This review will show that the evidence against labelling theory as a *general explanation* of mental illness is pervasive and that labelling theory's critique of the psychiatric perspective is both overstated and largely incorrect. I would remind the reader that, as noted above, labelling theory does point to some very real and important processes that in the past had an important impact. In this review I will focus, first, on the process of initial labelling and, second, on the consequences of being labelled.

The Process of Initial Labelling

(1) Labelling theorists argue that under a variety of circumstances it is relatively easy to be labelled mentally ill. However, the evidence indicates that this is not the case. In a pioneering study, Yarrow et al. (1955) investigated how wives came to define their husbands as mentally ill. The research demonstrated that wives utilized strong defenses to avoid seeing their husbands' behavior as deviant, while making every effort to interpret their husbands' behavior as normal. If that failed, they would minimize the importance of the behavior and balance it against more normal behavior. Only when a husband's behavior became impossible to deal with would the wife take action to have her husband hospitalized. Even at this time the husband was not always viewed as mentally ill. This pattern is similar to that described by numerous other investigators (Gove, 1980).

Thus the evidence indicates that, although the prospective patient is seriously disturbed, hospitalization is delayed for a considerable length of time. This does not mean that others do not treat him or her as a deviant. As Goffman (1971) and Sampson et al. (1964) make clear, due to the havoc created by the prospective patient, the family virtually has to collude against and exclude the prospective patient.

(2) A basic proposition of labelling theory is that the more social power a person has, the more likely he or she will be able to avoid (or at least delay) being channeled into a deviant role. However, the literature consistently indicates that a person who occupies a critical and thus a powerful position in the family is more likely to be hospitalized and is hospitalized more quickly than persons not in such a role, and studies of rehospitalization report similar results (Gove, 1980).

(3) A careful reading of the labelling theory of mental illness will show that its proponents are focusing exclusively on persons who have been involuntarily committed to a mental hospital. It is also clear that they assume hospitalization (and treatment) takes a prolonged period of time. The basis for this image of the location and characteristics of treatment is that labelling theorists are relying on studies conducted in the 1930s, 1940s, and early 1950s (Dietz, 1977). In short, empirical data on treat-

ment that presumably support the image that labelling theorists currently hold are dated, as a review of the statistics on treatment noted above and in the chapters by Klerman and Morrissey indicate. Given the changes in the setting and the brevity of treatment, it is difficult to imagine that most mental patients are in the formal role of the mental patient for a long enough period of time to be socialized into the role of the chronically ill in the manner suggested by the labelling theorists.

Before turning to the issue of commitment, we must briefly consider the case of voluntary patients. Regarding voluntary patients, labelling theorists make essentially two points. The first is that such patients have been strongly pressured into seeking treatment. However, a review of the literature indicates that this is only rarely the case (Gove, 1980). The second point is that hospitals routinely accept psychiatric applications for admission; but there is now a substantial body of evidence that this is not the case and that on the average a voluntary applicant has about a 50 percent chance of being admitted (Gove, 1980, forthcoming). Furthermore, as Morrissey makes clear in his chapter, with the recent tightening of procedures, some persons who could benefit from hospitalization apparently cannot get admitted.

With regard to committed patients, it might be noted that in 1972 for the United States as a whole only 41.8 percent of the admissions to public mental hospitals involved civil commitments (Meyer, 1974), and as a consequence of recent legislation and court rulings the rate has dropped substantially since then. It is interesting to note that among persons who have graduated from grade school these national data show no relationship between being committed and amount of education (Meyer, 1974), a fact that is inconsistent with an aspect of labelling theory articulated by Rushing (1978), namely, that education is related to avoiding hospitalization. It might also be noted that the recent evidence on involuntary patients clearly suggests that the treatment they receive can be effective (Gove and Fain, 1977; Sata and Goldenberg, 1977).

(4) Labelling theory does not view individuals who are mentally ill as intrinsically different from persons who are not so labelled (Scheff, 1966; Gove, 1980). Evidence that there are significant attributes of individuals labelled mentally ill would be evidence against this fundamental premise of labelling theory. There is in fact evidence that the mentally ill differ from those not so labelled in a substantial number of ways. First, there is clear evidence of a genetic component to many mental illnesses, particularly schizophrenia and the affective disorders (Allen, 1976; Fieve et al., 1974, Gershon et al., 1976; Gove, 1980, forthcoming; Rosenthal and Katz, 1968). Second, a review of the psychiatric literature shows that there is a rapidly growing body of evidence that the mentally ill tend to have a number of biological abnormalities. Third, a basic tenet of psychiatric theory is that stress is often a precipitating factor in the onset of mental

illness. The evidence on stressful life events clearly indicates that such events are strongly related to the manifestation of symptoms of mental illness as well as a variety of physical disorders (Dohrenwend and Dohrenwend, 1974; Eaton, 1978; Gove, 1980, forthcoming; Kasl et al., 1975; Kessler and Cleary, 1980; Rabkin and Struening, 1976). Thus, contrary to labelling theory, the social environment of those identified as mentally ill, by being more stressful, would appear to be significantly different from the typical environment. Fourth, also contrary to labelling theory, the evidence consistently indicates that persons labelled mentally ill are much more symptomatic than those not so labelled and that these symptoms typically are severe and disabling (Gove, 1980, forthcoming).

(5) A basic tenet of labelling theory is that, after the level of primary deviance is controlled for, the more marginal the person's societal attributes, the more likely he or she is to be channeled into a deviant role. Looking at the relationship between social class and mental illness, one finds that persons in the lower class are more likely to be treated for mental illness, particularly in mental hospitals (Hollingshead and Redlich, 1958; Meyer, 1974; Rushing, 1969). In general, this evidence is consistent with labelling theory. However, since traditional psychiatric explanations see stress as more common in the lower class, they thus also predict higher rates of mental illness there. Evidence for the psychiatric perspective is provided by the fact that most community surveys find higher rates of mental illness among the lower class (Dohrenwend et al., 1980). The evidence consistently indicates that members of the lower class tend to see only a narrow range of aggressive, antisocial behavior as creating a need for psychiatric treatment, whereas persons in the middle and upper classes perceive a much wider range of psychopathological behavior as indicating such a need (Gove, 1980; Kulka et al., 1979). As this would imply, members of the lower class are less likely than members of the upper class to identify disturbed behavior as mental illness, are more apt to delay seeking treatment, and, when treatment is finally initiated, it is frequently due to the acts of members of the general community because the patient and his or her family either did not act or acted inappropriately (Gove, 1980; Hollingshead and Redlich, 1958). The literature also consistently indicates that at the time of admission patients from the lower class typically have more serious disorders, tending to be more disorganized and violent, whereas the symptoms of the middle-class patients tend to reflect intrapsychic concerns (Gove, forthcoming, 1980).

Labelling theorists argue that the greater the individual's social or family resources, the greater the likelihood that he or she will be able to avoid hospitalization, particularly in a state mental hospital. In contrast, the psychiatric perspective suggests that family resources would play an important role in identifying the disorder promptly and initiating proper treatment and that, as a consequence of prompt actions, a severe disorder would be much less likely to develop (Gove, 1980). The data consistently show that family members are much more willing to initiate commitment proceedings than are unrelated individuals. The evidence also indicates that persons who occupy critical roles in the family tend to be hospitalized much more quickly than others. In short, the data show that a lack of social resources, such as a family, is associated with a delay in seeking psychiatric treatment (Gove, 1980).

In summary, there is a substantial amount of data which suggest that, when the degree of disorder is controlled for, hospitalization is more frequent among the upper classes and those with social resources. Not only is the labelling theory not supported, but processes are working in the direction opposite of that which the theory predicts.

THE CONSEQUENCES OF
BEING LABELLED MENTALLY ILL

The labelling theorists believe that once a person has been labelled mentally ill, and particularly if he or she has been hospitalized, it is extremely difficult for the person to break out of the deviant status. First, it is argued that the mental patient may have been misled, lied to, jailed, and testified against by those he or she trusted; and by the time the individual arrives at the hospital, he or she feels deserted, betrayed, and estranged from family and friends (Goffman, 1961; Gove, 1980). Second, the labelling theorists view the patient in the hospital as surrounded by severe restrictions and deprivations that are presented as "intended parts of his treatment, part of his need at the time, and therefore an expression of the state his self has fallen to" (Goffman, 1961: 149). Third, the events recorded in the patient's case history are almost uniformly defamatory and discrediting, they are public knowledge among the staff, and they are used to keep the patient in his or her place and to validate the patient's mental illness (Goffman, 1961; Scheff, 1966).

Institutionalism. From past experience it is clear that mental hospitals can be debilitating places where some patients come to accept the preferred role of the insane and, over time, develop skills and a world view adapted to the institutional setting. The available evidence, however, suggests that this is not a common reaction to the modern mental hospital. One of the reasons that modern mental hospitals do not routinely produce the debilitating reaction described by Goffman (1961) and others is that these investigators have viewed the hospital procedures from the perspective of the mentally healthy middle-class individuals and not from the perspective of someone who is severely disabled. This is clearly shown in Weinstein's chapter, in which he shows that patients tend to have a favorable reaction to hospitalization, to the staff, and to their treatment.

When we shift to those residual patients who have been hospitalized for a number of years, the effects of institutionalism become more discernible, with patients manifesting increasing apathy toward events outside the hospital, and a few becoming generally apathetic and withdrawn (Wing, 1962). However, contrary to what one would expect if one believed that psychiatric symptoms were primarily a response to cues in the immediate environment, prolonged hospitalization is not associated with changes in symptomatic behavior (Wing, 1962; Townsend, 1975) and individuals do not typically acquire social identity based on their social roles (Karmel, 1969) in the hospital.

Restitutive processes. The finding that there are important restitutive processes associated with being labelled mentally ill and that most mentally ill patients benefit from being patients would run directly counter to labelling theory. There are in fact a number of restitutive processes associated with hospitalization.

The most obvious restitutive processes involve treatment. Although there are a variety of types of treatment, I will limit my discussion to drug therapy and psychotherapy. As I have emphasized elsewhere (Gove, 1979), labelling theorists have virtually ignored the area of psychopharmacology. To my knowledge only Scheff (1976, 1975a, 1975b) has seriously addressed the issue, and he views chemotherapy in a highly critical light and suggests that it probably does more harm than good. However, there is by now a very extensive literature demonstrating the effectiveness of chemotherapy, which is very well reviewed by Berger (1978) and reflected in Klerman's chapter, which shows the critical role psychopharmacology has played in the psychiatric revolution that has occurred in the past 25 years. The efficacy of psychotherapy has been hotly debated (for example, see Eysenck, 1965, 1952); however, in recent years a very substantial body of evidence has developed that demonstrates that psychotherapy is effective with a number of disorders (Bergin and Garfield, 1971; Mosher and Keith, 1979; Smith and Glass, 1977). As psychiatric practitioners are aware, however, therapy is not without its costs; chemotherapy frequently produces adverse side effects (Berger, 1978), and not only is psychotherapy not always effective but there are times it can have harmful effects (Strupp et al., 1977).

Although treatment is the most obvious restitutive process associated with hospitalization, it is not the only one. An important study by Sampson et al. (1964), which looked at patients (all were married women) before, during, and after hospitalization, found that hospitalization initiated major restitutive processes that were not consciously guided by the hospital personnel. It was found that hospitalization interrupted a situation that was experienced as intolerable and, by doing so, blocked actions that threatened irremediable damage to family life. This interruption was legitimated by the act of hospitalization, which ratified the wife as ill and in need of special consideration and treatment. The ratification of illness was found to be decisive in redefining the negative implications of the havoc that occurred prior to hospitalization. As a consequence, the acts leading to commitment were not viewed as alienative, but as necessary actions that served the present and future interests of the patient and her family. Thus hospitalization redefined the mentally ill person's behavior and led to the adoption of the sick role, which had a number of beneficial effects.

The label of mental illness. As noted above, the evidence of the 1950s would indicate that one of the tenets of the labelling perspective was correct—namely, that the public was ignorant about mental illness, had a very negative image of persons identified as mentally ill, and excluded them. Since then there has been a massive education effort focused on mental illness; furthermore, the generally transitory nature of mental illness and effectiveness of treatment has become fairly visible. Nevertheless, as Rabkin (1974) shows in her review of public attitudes toward mental illness, on some issues the literature is inconsistent. In large part this is probably due to methodological problems revolving around what is meant by the term "mental illness."

In an earlier work (Gove and Fain, 1973) I speculate that one reason a substantial number of patients do not view themselves as mentally ill is that the stereotype of mental illness depicts such a severe disorder and bizarre behavior that the majority of mental patients (and those they deal with) recognize that a patient's condition does not conform to the popular conception of mental illness. Thus, although they may realize that a patient needs help, many will conclude that he or she is not mentally ill. There is now strong evidence that this is the case. As a number of recent studies indicate (Gove, forthcoming; Askenasy, 1974; Whitt et al., 1979), laypersons have very stringent criteria for labelling someone mentally ill, and they think of the mentally ill as extremely impaired. To laypersons, most people receiving psychiatric treatment, including brief hospitalizations, are suffering from "nervous breakdowns." Such persons are not perceived as mentally ill even if they are in treatment, and the evidence indicates that they experience relatively little stigma. In short, it would appear that the public stereotype of mental illness is so derogatory and bizarre that the vast majority of persons treated for mental illness do not conform to the stereotype and thus escape the label. This is especially true if the "other" is a long-term acquaintance of the ex-mental patient and/or sees the ex-patient after the more severe symptoms have been brought under control.

Most mental patients experience some stigma; however, in the vast majority of cases the stigma appears to be transitory and does not appear to pose a severe problem (Gove, 1980). Regarding stigma, the following issues appear to be well established: (1) While being labelled mentally ill appears to be stigmatizing and may produce an exclusionary reaction, being labelled an ex-mental patient does not (Olmsted and Durham, 1976); (2) persons who have had experience in dealing with the mentally ill are less rejecting than persons without such experience (Trute and Loewen, 1978); (3) family members tend not to be particularly rejecting of the mentally ill because close ties override the stigma and enable them to see positive qualities in the individual (Kreisman and Joy, 1974); (4) in general, families experience little fear, shame, anger, or guilt regarding a family member who is mentally ill, and if they do experience such feelings, they tend to be reactions to the actual behavior of the mentally ill member who creates serious problems (Gove, 1980; Kreisman and Joy, 1974); and (5) although employers are apt to express prejudice against the mentally ill, the evidence suggests that employers do not discriminate against ex-mental patients in their hiring practices (Olshansky et al., 1960; Huffine and Clausen, 1979).

Expectations and symptomatology. Labelling theorists state that the major reason a person continues to manifest a psychiatric symptom is because of the expectations of others. However, two major studies of former mental patients found that an ex-patient's manifestation of symptoms was not a consequence of the expectations of family members (Freeman and Simmons, 1963; Angrist et al., 1968). Perhaps not surprisingly, what they found was that the expectations of family members were determined by the behavior of the former patients. Similarly, a four-year prospective study of ex-mental patients found no support for the proposition that the level of a person's psychiatric symptomatology would be influenced by the expectations of his or her significant others (Ellsworth, 1980).

Maintenance therapy. Labelling theorists would argue that the longer formerly hospitalized mental patients were in a situation where they were constantly confronted with the fact that they were mentally ill, the more chronic they would become. However, with the deinstitutionalization movement it has become obvious that a substantial number of former mental patients cannot function effectively without maintenance therapy and, furthermore, when maintenance therapy is provided it is very clear that these patients benefit from it (Gove, forthcoming).

In summary, there is a large body of evidence that indicates that the two main propositions of labelling theory of mental illness are not supported. It particularly appears that (1) the vast majority of persons labelled mentally ill are seriously impaired and their impairment is the major reason for labelling, and (2) labelling is not a major factor in a chronic career of mental illness but, in fact, labelling tends to initiate processes that minimize the length and severity of a person's disorder.

THE PERSISTENCE OF LABELLING THEORY

In light of the overwhelming evidence against the labelling theory of mental illness, the question arises as to why it not only persists in an essentially unmodified form, but (apparently) remains the dominant perspective among sociologists. To answer this question we need to turn to a set of interrelated issues that underlie the assumptions of most sociologists.

Relativity versus pathology. For psychiatry, mentally ill individuals are seriously disturbed. They are not healthy but ill. In short, they have a pathological disorder. Thus, their disorder is not simply normative but instead reflects a deviation from a healthy psychological state. For sociologists deviance is almost always thought of in normative terms. Thus a deviant is someone who violates rules, and rules are seen as socially constructed and relative to a particular social system. Thus, acts that label one as deviant in a particular social system are not seen as intrinsically deviant, but only deviant with regard to that particular system. Thus deviance is system-specific, and the concept of pathology, with its connotation that something is intrinsically disordered, is seen as not applicable to human behavior. The concept of mental illness as a pathological condition violates most sociologists' understanding of the nature of social order and the human condition.

Irrationality versus rationality. Psychiatry views human behavior as having a substantial irrational component and mental illness as reflecting an irrational state. Sociologists tend not to deal with irrationality, but instead see persons (and organizations and institutions) as acting in their own best interests. While sociologists tend not to have as explicit a focus on rationality as economists or lawyers, they do have a functional model of human behavior. Thus they see persons as almost always either acting consciously in the best interests (their behavior is manifestly functional) or subconsciously in their own best interests (their behavior is latently functional). Thus when someone is put in a mental hospital, sociologists ask the question, "Who benefits?" Because they do not see the person labelled mentally ill as intrinsically deviant, that is, as having a pathological condition, they frame the question in terms of normative systems and social power. They see hospitalization as a consequence of someone violating the normative rules of powerful others, who are acting in their own best interests and who use their power to get the "offending" individual hospitalized. They also recognize that for the psychiatrist a latent function of collaborating in the hospitalization of the "offending" individual is the justification of his or her job and the institutional practices of psychiatry.

The tenuousness of the social order. Since sociologists understand reality to be socially constructed and an outcome of political maneuvering, they see social reality as essentially tenuous. Thus, as Erickson (1966) has so forcefully argued, the labelling of individuals as deviant when they act in ways that violate the existing social order has the function of reinforcing the normative structure of the established order. As Goffman (1971) notes: "Mental symptoms are specifically and pointedly offensive and they are acts by individuals which openly proclaim to others that they must have assumptions about himself which the relevant bit of social interaction can neither allow or do much about. It follows that if the 'patient' persists in his symptomatic behavior, then he must create organizational havoc and havoc in the minds of others." For Goffman these "mental symptoms" call into question the reality of the micro social system. It then becomes essential for the other actors in that micro system to reestablish order by labelling the individual as mentally ill and thereby undercutting the "patient's" assumption of reality. Laing (1969) and his associates see the social reality of our society as so askew that the "healthy" reaction is to become "mentally ill." As with Goffman, mental symptoms call into question the normative structure of the social system, but in this case it is the normative structure of society. From Laing's perspective, labelling someone who manifests "mental symptoms" mentally ill serves as an assertion of the validity of the normative structure of societal structure. Many sociologists are disenchanted with our society and, as noted above, most labelling theorists tend to take the side of the deviant. For such sociologists the arguments of Goffman and Laing have a certain intrinsic appeal, for they suggest that the social system is seriously flawed.

The elusiveness of the psychiatric perspective. For the layperson there is no way to "know" that an individual is mentally ill in the absence of the voice of authority (that of the psychiatrist). If the individual manifests mental symptoms and persists in behaving in ways inconsistent with the assumptions of the normative frame of others, social interaction breaks down, and efforts will be made to establish a new frame vis-à-vis the "deviant." At first these efforts will usually involve defining the individual as "troublesome," and attempts will be made to structure interaction so that the individual's behavior can be controlled or ignored. If the unacceptable behaviors of the "deviant" persist, some kind of help will probably be sought. These initial efforts will generally lack focus because, for the emotionally disturbed, there is no prescribed script to follow that leads to psychiatric treatment, and the problem tends to be perceived as the disturbed person operating within a normative frame unacceptable to his or her associates. Thus efforts by the individual and others will tend to be haphazard and ineffectual and will not lead to a compatible definition of the situation. It is only when the individual is admitted to psychiatric treatment and a new social definition of reality is created that he or she becomes defined as mentally ill. This, of course, provides a new, institutionally sanctioned way for perceiving and dealing with the person's behavior.

The fact that an individual is not mentally ill in terms of either symbolic conceptualization or societal roles until he or she has been labelled by a psychiatrist corresponds to one of the tenets of labelling theory. By treating the problem purely in terms of social definitions and ignoring, on theoretical grounds, the issue of the actual emotional and intellectual state of the individual, labelling theorists are able to develop a plausible argument. The fact that there are no clear scripts leading the disturbed individual to psychiatric treatment is, of course, one of the problematic aspects of the psychiatric process, and it lends credibility to the argument that psychiatrists create mental illness by labelling someone mentally ill and treating them accordingly. I would note that two psychiatrists, in reviewing an earlier version of this discussion, argued that this was not a valid point because in community studies it is possible for a clinician to identify persons who are mentally ill but who are not in treatment. It is, of course, true that clinicians appear to be able correctly to identify mental illness in persons who are not in treatment. However, as these persons do not typically identify themselves as mentally ill, and they are not typically identified by others as such, they do not occupy the role of the mentally ill and, according to labelling theory, they are not mentally ill. It is not necessary for psychiatrists to agree with the labelling theorists' conclusions, but it is important to recognize that in terms of societal definitions and societal roles these persons are *not* mentally ill (for a further discussion of this issue, see Gove and Hughes, 1981).

The psychiatrist as political agent. Psychiatrists see themselves as providing therapy for disturbed individuals; however, they also play a pivotal political role. When the issue of mental illness is raised, it is the psychiatrist who must evaluate the situation, make alliances with various participants (family members, the "patient," friends, associates, and so on), and then in an exercise of legally and socially legitimated authority decide if the patient is mentally ill, what sort of mental illness it is, and what sort of treatment, if any, should be instituted. The political role of the psychiatrist is unique, because the psychiatrist and no one else in the situation has the legally sanctioned power to define reality. Furthermore, psychiatrists, by controlling patients' symptoms (typically through the use of medications) and helping them to adjust to their situation, are acting as agents of society who help maintain the status quo, a point emphasized by labelling theorists (see Scheff, 1975a, 1975b). Psychiatrists are generally naive about the extent to which they play a political role and this naivete provides ready ammunition for labelling theorists, who are already highly critical of the psychiatric perspective.[2]

The psychiatrist as entrepreneur. According to labelling theorists, deviance is something created by society; the types of behaviors defined as deviant are viewed as relative and, within a particular society, are seen as a product of a political process. Medicine in general and psychiatry in particular are perceived as attempting to expand the domain of the medical-psychiatric model so that physicians, particularly psychiatrists, become primarily responsible for the care and treatment of a variety of forms of deviant behavior. This is particularly true in the cases of alcoholism and drug addiction, which most social scientists view as falling primarily outside the domain of psychiatry—that is, as forms of deviant behavior that do not fall under the category of mental illness. Thus even social scientists who accept the expertise of psychiatrists in the treatment of psychosis and neurosis will frequently join labelling theorists when the medical-psychiatric model is expanded to cover alcoholism and drug addiction. The expansionistic tendency of psychiatry provides support for the labelling perspective in two ways. First, it attracts critics who find themselves siding with and supporting labelling theory. Second, and perhaps more important, because psychiatry's claim to expertise in drug addiction and alcoholism is readily seen by those relatively uninformed about psychiatry as resting on a tenuous base, this claim tends to raise questions about the whole enterprise of psychiatry.

In summary, when the existence of mental illness as a "pathological" disorder is denied, which sociologists are strongly inclined to do, then it can be seen that the labelling theory of mental illness makes a great deal of "sense," for it is closely tied to many of the premises on which sociology is based. In fact, I would go so far as to guess that as long as the existence of "pathology" is denied by sociologists, the labelling theory of mental illness will always touch a sympathetic cord among sociologists. Furthermore, the affinity of sociologists for the labelling theory of mental illness is reinforced by the entrepreneurship of psychiatrists and by psychiatrists' naivete about their political role.

CONCLUSION

The labelling theory of mental illness points to some real processes, but these processes were more important in the past than they are in the present. In fact, a careful review of the evidence demonstrates that the labelling theory of mental illness is substantially invalid, especially as a general theory of mental illness. Nonetheless, labelling theory is having a substantial effect on the evolving deinstitutionalization process, and this has become particularly true as the deinstitutionalization process has come under the control of legal institutions. Furthermore, there are biases build into the social sciences, particularly sociology, that incline the discipline toward a favorable view of the labelling theory of mental illness.

NOTES

1. Like Bonovitz and Guy (1979: 1048), I find it both strange and unfortunate that the law, which protects the seriously mentally ill from involuntary hospitalization where it has been demonstrated that effective treatment is provided, allows the same mentally ill individuals to be placed in jails and prisons where treatment is either nonexistent or less effective than that available elsewhere.

2. Some psychiatrists, of course, work to change aspects of the patient's environment, which may mean changing the behavior and attitude of others and raising the patient's "consciousness," and in these cases the psychiatrist should be seen as an agent of social change. For a further discussion of the political role of the psychiatrist, see Gove and Hughes (1981).

REFERENCES

ALLEN, M. G. (1976) "Twin studies of affective illness." Archives of General Psychiatry 33: 1476-1489.

ANGRIST, S., M. LEFTON, S. DINITZ, and B. PASAMANICK (1968) Women After Treatment: A Study of Former Mental Patients and Their Normal Neighbors. New York: Appleton-Century-Crofts.

ASHBAUGH, J. W. and J. BRADLEY (1979) "Linking deinstitutionalization with hospital phase-down: the difference between success and failure." Hospital and Community Psychiatry 30: 105-110.

ASKENASY, A. R. (1974) Attitudes Toward Mental Patients: A Study Across Cultures. The Hague: Mouton.

BARDACH, E. (1972) The Skill Factor in Politics: Repealing the Mental Commitment Laws in California. Berkeley: University of California Press.

BECKER, H. S. (1967) "Whose side are we on?" Social Problems 14: 239-247.

——— (1963) Outsiders: Studies in the Sociology of Deviance. New York:

BENSON, P. R. (1979) "Labeling theory and community care of the mentally ill in California: the relationship of social theory and ideology to public policy." Presented at the annual meeting of the Southern Sociological Society, Atlanta, April.

BERGER, P. A. (1978) "Medical treatment of mental illness: pharmacotherapies revolutionize psychiatric care and present scientific and ethical challenges to society." Science 200: 974-981.

BERGIN, A. E. and S. L. GARFIELD [eds.] (1971) Handbook of Psychotherapy and Behavior Change: An Empirical Analysis. New York: John Wiley.

BONOVITZ, J. D. and E. B. GUY (1979) "Impact of restrictive civil commitment procedures on a prison psychiatric service." American Journal of Psychiatry 136: 1045-1048.

CAUDILL, W. (1958) The Psychiatric Hospital as a Small Society. Cambridge, MA: Harvard University Press.

COLE, S. (1975) "The growth of scientific knowledge theories of deviance as a case study," in L. Coser (ed.) The Idea of Social Structure: Papers in Honor of Robert K. Merton. New York: Harcourt Brace Jovanovich.

COYE, J. L. and D. CLIFFORD (1978) "A one-year report on rights violations under Michigan's new protection system." Hospital and Community Psychiatry 29: 528-533.

CRANE, L., H. ZONANA, and S. WISER (1977) "Implications of the Donaldson Decision: a model for periodic review of committed patients." Hospital and Community Psychiatry 28: 827-833.

CULLEN, F. and J. CULLEN (1978) Toward a Paradigm of Labelling Theory. Lincoln: University of Nebraska Press.

CUMMING, E. and J. CUMMING (1957) Closed Ranks: An Experiment in Mental Health Education. Cambridge: Harvard University Press.

DIETZ, P. E. (1977) "Social discrediting of psychiatry: the protasis of legal disenfranchisement." American Journal of Psychiatry 134: 1356-1360.

DOHRENWEND, B. P., B. S. DOHRENWEND, M. S. GOULD, B. LINK, R. NEUGEBAUER, and R. WUNSCH-HITZIG (1980) Mental Illness in the United States: Epidemiological Estimates. New York: Praeger.

DOHRENWEND, B. S. and B. P. DOHRENWEND [eds.] (1974) Stressful Life Events: Their Nature and Effects. New York: John Wiley.

EATON, W. W. (1978) "Life events, social supports, and psychiatric symptoms: a re-analysis of the New Haven data." Journal of Health and Social Behavior 19: 230-234.

ELLSWORTH, R. B. (1980) "Familial expectations, post-hospital adjustment and the societal reaction perspective on mental illness." (mimeo)

ERIKSON, K. T. (1966) The Wayward Puritans: A Study in the Sociology of Deviance. New York: John Wiley.

——— (1962) "Notes on the sociology of deviance." Social Problems 9: 307-314.

EYSENCK, H. J. (1965) "The effects of psychotherapy." International Journal of Psychiatry 1: 97-144.

——— (1952) "The effects of psychotherapy: an evaluation." Journal of Consulting Psychology 16: 319-324.

FIEVE, R. R., D. ROSENTHAL, and H. BRILL [eds.] (1974) Genetic Research in Psychiatry. Baltimore: Johns Hopkins University Press.

FREEMAN, H. E. and O. G. SIMMONS (1963) The Mental Patient Comes Home. New York: John Wiley.

GARFINKEL, H. (1956) "Conditions of successful degradation ceremonies." American Journal of Sociology 61: 420-424.

GERSHON, E. S., W. E. BUNNEY, Jr., J. F. LECKMAN, M. VAN EERDEWEGH, and B. A. DeBAUCHE (1976) "The inheritance of affective disorders: a review of the data and of hypotheses." Behavior Genetics 6: 227-261.

GIBBS, J. (1981) Norms, Deviance and Social Control: Conceptual Matters. New York: Elsevier North-Holland.

——— and M. ERICKSON (1975) "Major developments in the sociological study of deviance." Annual Review of Sociology 1: 21-42.

GOFFMAN, E. (1971) Relations in Public: Microstudies of the Public Order. New York: Basic Books.

——— (1961) Asylums: Essays on the Social Situation of Mental Patients and Other Inmates. Garden City, NY: Doubleday.

GORDON, R. A. (1980) "Labelling theory, mental retardation, and public policy:

Larry P. and other developments since 1974," pp. 175-225 in W. R. Gove (ed.) Labelling Deviant Behavior. Beverly Hills, CA: Sage.

GOVE, W. R. (forthcoming) "An evaluation of labelling theory's explanation of mental illness: an update of recent evidence." Deviant Behavior.

——— (1980) "Labelling and mental illness: a critique," pp. 53-99, 99-109 in W. R. Gove (ed.) Labelling Deviant Behavior. Beverly Hills, CA: Sage.

——— (1979) "The labelling versus the psychiatric explanation of mental illness: a debate that has become substantively irrelevant." Journal of Health and Social Behavior 20: 301-304.

——— (1970) "Societal reactions as an explanation of mental illness: an evaluation." American Sociological Review 35: 873-884.

——— and T. FAIN (1977) "A comparison of voluntary and committed psychiatric patients." Archives of General Psychiatry 36: 129-134.

——— (1973) "The stigma of mental hospitalization: an attempt to evaluate its consequences." Archives of General Psychiatry 28: 495-500.

GOVE, W. R. and M. HUGHES (1981) "Labelling theory and mental illness: some insights to be gained." Presented at the meeting of the Eastern Sociological Society, New York, April.

——— and M. TOVO (1982) "A review of the law regulating psychiatric hospitalization in the 50 states." Presented at the meeting of the Southern Sociological Society, Memphis, April.

HOLLINGSHEAD, A. B. and F. C. REDLICH (1958) Social Class and Mental Illness. New York: John Wiley.

HORWITZ, A. (1979) "Models, muddles and mental illness labeling." Journal of Health and Social Behavior 20: 296-300.

HUFFINE, C. L. and J. A. CLAUSEN (1979) "Madness and work: short- and long-term effects of mental illness on occupational careers." Social Forces 57: 1049-1062.

IMMERSHEIN, A. and R. SIMMONS (1976) "Rules and examples in lay and professional psychiatry: an ethnomethodological comment on the Scheff-Gove controversy." American Sociological Review 41 (June): 559-563.

JALBOLT, J. A. (1979) "Deinstitutionalization: avoiding the disasters of the past." Hospital and Community Psychiatry 30: 621-624.

JONES, M. (1975) "Community care for chronic mental patients: the need for a reassessment." Hospital and Community Psychiatry 26: 94-98.

KARMEL, M. (1969) "Total institution and self-mortification." Journal of Health and Social Behavior 10: 134-141.

KASL, S. V., S. GORE, and S. COBB (1975) "The experience of losing a job: reported changes in health, symptoms, and illness behavior." Psychosomatic Medicine 37: 106-122.

KAUFMAN, E. (1979) "The right to treatment suit as an agent of change." American Journal of Psychiatry 136: 1428-1432.

KESSLER, R. C. and P. D. CLEARY (1980) "Social class and psychological distress." American Sociological Review 45: 463-478.

KLERMAN, G. L. and G. SCHECTER (1979) "The impact of psychopharmacology on the mental health service system." Presented at the Conference on Human Behavior: A Bio-Psycho-Social Phenomenon, Nashville, April.

KREISMAN, D. and V. JOY (1974) "Family response to mental illness of relatives: a review of the literature." Schizophrenia Bulletin 10: 34-57.

KULKA, R., J. VEROFF, and E. DOUVAN (1979) "Social class and the use of professional help for personal problems: 1957 and 1976." Journal of Health and Social Behavior 20: 2-17.

KUMASAKA, Y., J. STOKES, and R. GUPTA (1972) "Criteria for involuntary hospitalization." Archives of General Psychiatry 20: 359-404.

LAING, R. D. (1969) Politics of Experience. Baltimore: Penguin.

LAMB, H. R. (1979) "The new asylums in the community." Archives of General Psychiatry 36: 129-134.

LEMERT, E. M. (1976) "Response to critics, feedback and choice," pp. 244-249 in L. Coser and D. Larson (eds.) The Uses of Controversy in Sociology. New York: Macmillan.

——— (1967) Human Deviance, Social Problems, and Social Control. Englewood Cliffs, NJ: Prentice-Hall.

LINN, L. (1968) "The mental hospital in the patient's phenomenal world." Ph.D. dissertation, University of Wisconsin.

LOFLAND, J. and L. H. LOFLAND (1969) Deviance and Identity. Englewood Cliffs, NJ: Prentice-Hall.

MACHT, L. B. (1978) "Commissioner: a special clinical executive." Psychiatric Opinion 15: 1133-1135.

MEYER, N. G. (1974) "Legal status of inpatient admissions to state and county mental hospitals, 1972." Statistical Note 105, National Institute of Mental Health.

MORRISSEY, J. (1979) "Keeping patients out: organization and policy implications of emergent state hospital deinstitutionalizing practices." Presented at the annual meeting of the Southern Sociological Society, April.

MOSHER, L. R. and S. J. KEITH (1979) "Research on the psychosocial treatment of schizophrenia: a summary report." American Journal of Psychiatry 136: 623-631.

NUNNALLY, J. C. (1961) Popular Conceptions of Mental Health, Their Development and Change. New York: Holt, Rinehart & Winston.

OLMSTED, D. W. and K. DURHAM (1976) "Stability of mental health attitudes: a semantic differential study." Journal of Health and Social Behavior 17: 35-44.

OLSHANSKY, S., S. BROB, and M. EKDAHL (1960) "Survey of employment experiences of patients discharged from three state mental hospitals during the period 1951-1953." Mental Hygiene 44: 510-521.

RABKIN, J. (1979) "Who is called mentally ill: public and professional views." Journal of Community Psychiatry 7: 253-258.

——— (1974) "Public attitudes toward mental illness: a review of the literature." Schizophrenia Bulletin 10: 9-33.

——— and E. L. STRUENING (1976) "Life events, stress and illness." Science 194: 1013-1020.

REIGER, D. A., I. D. GOLDBERG, and C. A. TAUBE (1978) "The de facto U.S. mental health services system: a public health perspective." Archives of General Psychiatry 35: 685-693.

ROSENSTEIN, M. and R. D. BASS (1979) "The characteristics of persons serviced by federally funded community mental health centers program, 1974." National Institute of Mental Health, Division of Biometry and Epidemiology.

ROSENTHAL, D. and S. S. KATZ [eds.] (1968) The Transmission of Schizophrenia: Proceedings of the Second Research Conference of the Foundation's Fund for Research in Psychiatry, Dorado, Puerto Rico, 26 June to 1 July, 1967.

RUSHING, W. A. (1978) "Status resources, societal reactions, and type of mental hospital admission." American Sociological Review 43: 521-533.

——— (1969) "Two patterns in the relationship between social class and mental hospitalization." American Sociological Review 34: 533-541.

SAGARIN, E. and F. MONTANINO (1976) "Anthologies and readers on deviance." Contemporary Sociology 5: 259-267.

SAMPSON, H., S. L. MESSINGER, and R. D. TOWNE (1964) Schizophrenic Women: Studies in Marital Crisis. New York: Atherton.
SATA, L. S. and E. E. GOLDENBERG (1977) "A study of involuntary patients in Seattle." Hospital and Community Psychiatry 28: 834-837.
SCHEFF, T. J. (1976) "Medical dominance: psychoactive drugs and mental health policy." American Behavioral Scientist 19: 299-317.
——— (1975a) "The labeling theory of mental illness," pp. 21-34 in T. Scheff (ed.) Labeling Madness. Englewood Cliffs, NJ: Prentice-Hall.
——— (1975b) "On reason and sanity: some political implications of psychiatric thought," pp. 12-20 in T. Scheff (ed.) Labeling Madness. Englewood Cliffs, NJ: Prentice-Hall.
——— (1966) Being Mentally Ill: A Sociological Theory. Chicago: Aldine.
SCHERL, D. J. and L. B. MACHT (1979) "Deinstitutionalization in the absence of consensus." Hospital and Community Psychiatry 30: 599-604.
SMITH, M. L. and G. V. GLASS (1977) "Meta-analysis of psychotherapy outcome studies." American Psychologist 32: 752-760.
SPECTOR, M. (1976) "Labelling theory in social problems: a young journalist launches a new theory." Social Problems 24 (October): 69-75.
STANDON, A. A. and M. S. SCHWARTZ (1954) The Mental Hospital. New York: Basic Books.
STAR, S. (1961) "The dilemma of mental illness," cited in the Joint Commission on Mental Illness and Health, Action for Mental Health. New York: Science Editions.
STEADMAN, H. (1979) Beating a Rap? Defendants Found Incompetent to Stand Trial. Chicago: University of Chicago Press.
STONE, A. A. (1977) "Recent mental health litigation: a critical perspective." American Journal of Psychiatry 134: 273-279.
STRUPP, H., S. HADLEY, and B. GOMES-SCHWARTZ (1977) Psychotherapy for Better or Worse: The Problem of Negative Effects. New York: Jascon J. Arnson.
TOWNSEND, J. M. (1975) "Cultural conceptions, mental disorders and social roles: a comparison of Germany and America." American Sociological Review 40: 739-752.
TRUTE, B. and A. LOEWEN (1978) "Public attitude toward the mentally ill as a function of prior personal experience." Social Psychiatry 13: 79-84.
TUCKER, C. (1974) Personal communication.
URMER, A. (1978) "An assessment of California's mental health program: implications for mental health delivery systems," pp. 137-152 in C. J. Frederick (ed.) Dangerous Behavior: A Problem in Law and Mental Health. Rockville, MD: Center for Studies of Crime and Delinquency, National Institute of Mental Health.
WHITT, H. P., R. L. MEILE, and L. A. LARSON (1979) "Illness role therapy, the labeling perspective and the social meanings of mental illness: an empirical test." Social Science and Medicine 13A: 655-666.
WING, J. K. (1962) "Institutionalism in mental hospitals." British Journal of Social and Clinical Psychology 1: 38-51.
YARROW, M. R., C. G. SCHWARTZ, H. S. MURPHY, and L. C. DEASY (1955) "The psychological meaning of mental illness in the family." Journal of Social Issues 11: 12-24.

About the Authors

WALTER R. GOVE is a Professor in the Department of Sociology and Anthropology at Vanderbilt University. He received his Ph.D. in 1968 from the University of Washington, Seattle. His present and future research activities are in the fields of density; sex, marital roles, and mental health; labelling theory; statistics and methodology; crime and deterrence; race; and mental illness. He has authored or coauthored many articles in professional journals and is an Associate Editor for *Social Science Research*. His edited volumes include *The Labelling of Deviance* (second edition, 1980) and *The Fundamental Connection Between Nature and Nurture* (1982).

RONALD C. KESSLER is an Assistant Professor in the Sociology Department at the University of Michigan. He received his Ph.D. from New York University and has worked at the New York State Psychiatric Institute and the Psychiatry Department at the University of Wisconsin. His research is concerned with the structural determinants of emotional vulnerability.

GERALD L. KLERMAN is currently Professor of Psychiatry at Harvard Medical School and Director of the Stanley Cobb Laboratories at Massachusetts General Hospital. He has previously served as Administrator of the Alcohol, Drug Abuse and Mental Health Administration, Public Service, Washington, D.C. Among the awards he has received are the Menninger Memorial Award for the American College of Physicians and the Hofheimer Prize of the American Psychiatric Assoiation.

DONALD W. LIGHT is currently Professor of Sociology and Community Medicine at the NJSOM Unit of the University of Medicine and Dentistry of New Jersey. He holds graduate degrees from the University of Chicago and Brandeis University, and since he first taught deviance at Princeton with Robert Scott he has been focusing on how professionals learn to carry out their gatekeeping and labelling functions.

JOSEPH P. MORRISSEY is a Senior Research Scientist with the Special Projects Research Unit, New York State Office of Mental Health, and an Adjunct Assistant Professor in the Department of Sociology, SUNY— Albany. He formerly held positions at Brandeis University and the National Institute of Mental Health. He is author or coauthor of numerous publications on the sociology of mental hospitalization and the delivery of mental health services, including *The Enduring Asylum* (1981) and *Interorganizational Relations: A Sourcebook of Measures for Mental Health Programs* (1982).

JANE M. MURPHY, Ph.D., is Lecturer on Anthropology in the Department of Psychiatry, Massachusetts Mental Health Center at the Harvard Medical School. Her training at Cornell University included a year of clerkship in psychiatry designed to give behavioral scientists experience in recognizing psychopathology. She has conducted several studies of psychiatric disorders among non-Western groups in Alaska, Nigeria, and South Vietnam. She currently directs a longitudinal study of psychiatric epidemiology, the Sterling County Study.

PETER SEDGWICK worked for ten years as a psychologist and educator in psychiatric fields before becoming a politics lecturer (currently at the Politics Department of Leeds University, in whose Psychiatry Department he also works as a Tutor). He is on the Council of Management of the National Schizophrenia Fellowship and is an Area Co-Ordinator for the Alzheimer's Disease Society. Apart from his writing on the politics of psychiatry, his main work is on European novelist and political commentator, Victor Serge.

ROBERT L. SPITZER is Professor of Psychiatry, Department of Psychiatry, Columbia University College of Physicians and Surgeons, and Chief of the Biometrics Research Department of the New York State Psychiatric Institute. He was Chair of the American Psychiatric Association's Task Force on Nomenclature and Statistics during the development of DSM-III.

RAYMOND M. WEINSTEIN is Associate Professor of Sociology at the University of South Carolina at Aiken. He has published articles in scholarly journals on the attitudes of mental patients, motives of illicit drug users, and characteristics of social service organizations. He is currently working on several articles concerning labelling theory and the attitudes of mental patients, and on a book that will integrate these aspects of his research

JANET B.W. WILLIAMS is Assistant Professor of Clinical Psychiatric Social Work, Department of Psychiatry, Columbia University College of Physicians and Surgeons, and a Research Scientist in the Biometrics Research Department of the New York State Psychiatric Institute. She was Text Editor of DSM-III and Coordinator of the DSM-III Field Trials.

CHARLES WINICK, Professor of Sociology at City College and the Graduate Center, City University of New York, has conducted content analyses of most of the mass media. He has previously taught at the Postgraduate Center for Mental Health in New York City, Columbia University, University of Rochester, and MIT. He is currently examining images of pathology in the mass media.